D1053163

Huntington Library Publications

SIR AUGUSTUS JOHN FOSTER, BART.
[*From the portrait at Glyde Court, County Louth. Through the courtesy of Mrs. Arthur Charles William May and Miss Phillipa Eugenie Vere Foster.*]

JEFFERSONIAN

AMERICA

Notes on the United States of America

Collected in the Years 1805-6-7 and 11-12 by

Sir Augustus John Foster, Bart.

EDITED WITH AN INTRODUCTION BY

RICHARD BEALE DAVIS

The Huntington Library

SAN MARINO : CALIFORNIA : 1954

Library of Congress Catalog Card Number: 54-8926

PRINTED IN U.S.A.
BY ANDERSON, RITCHIE & SIMON : LOS ANGELES
DESIGN BY JOSEPH SIMON

CONTENTS

ACKNOWLEDGMENTS

THE EXISTENCE of the Huntington Library version of Foster's "Notes on the United States" was first called to my attention in 1949 by Professor Lewis Leary. A few months later, while I was working with other Jeffersonian materials at the Huntington Library under a grant from that institution, I read the manuscript and felt at once that it merited publication. The Library generously provided funds through which a typescript was made.

When the editing was well under way I discovered that there were many Foster papers at the Library of Congress, including a somewhat later and more polished text of the "Notes." Mr. Douglass Adair and his staff of the *William and Mary Quarterly* were then engaged in preparing portions of the Library of Congress "Notes" for publication in that journal without knowing of the Huntington manuscript. Correspondence between us resulted in the *Quarterly*'s decision to limit its publication to a few excerpts and to assist me in preparing the whole manuscript for publication in book form. Most generously Mr. Adair lent me his microfilm and typescript. Therefore I was able to prepare a working collated text of both libraries' manuscripts even before I was able to check personally at the Library of Congress.

Director John E. Pomfret of the Henry E. Huntington Library, chairman of its Publications Committee, has made many helpful suggestions for the improvement of the edited manuscript. Messrs. Godfrey Davies and Robert G. Cleland of the Research Staff of that institution through their interest and efforts originally made the material available. Mr. Frederick B. Tolles, also of the Huntington's Research Staff, has given useful editorial advice.

The Library of Congress has hospitably provided working quarters and other facilities during two separate stays of several weeks each in Washington. The English Department of the University of Tennessee, through its Chairman, Professor John C. Hodges, has provided considerable secretarial assistance.

Since Foster's "Notes" cover all the American states of his time and mention scores of individuals European as well as American, it has been necessary to seek information from widely scattered persons and places. Among those who have been especially helpful are Irving Brant, James Thomas Flexner, Eleanor Goehring, Fiske Kimball, John L. Lievsay, Samuel Eliot Morison, Albert Rapp, and Royal E. Shanks. The staffs of the following libraries and institutions have also been most cooperative: Alderman Library, University of Virginia; Alexandria (Va.) Library; American Philosophical Society; Bibliothèque Nationale; Bodleian Library, Oxford; British Museum; Cambridge University Library; Columbia (D.C.) Historical Society; Columbia University Library; Connecticut Historical Society; Edinburgh University Library; Enoch Pratt Free Library, Baltimore; Essex Institute Library, Salem, Massachusetts; Fairfield (Conn.) Historical Society; Hall of Records, Annapolis, Maryland; Greenwich (Conn.) Library; Howard-Tilton Memorial Library, Tulane University; Lancaster County (Penna.) Historical Society; Maine Historical Society; Maryland Historical Society; University of Maryland Library; Massachusetts Historical Society; National Archives; New Jersey Historical Society; New York Historical Society; Pennsylvania Academy of Fine Arts; Historical Society of Pennsylvania; Rhode Island Historical Society; South Carolina Historical Society; Library of the Supreme Court of the United States; Virginia Historical Society; Virginia State Library; West Virginia Department of Archives and History; Yale University Library.

RICHARD BEALE DAVIS

January, 1954
University of Tennessee
Knoxville

INTRODUCTION

THIS extensive survey of the early republic came into being when a British diplomat in his mid-fifties decided that he must have his say about the America he had known as a young man. He composed his first draft between 1833 and 1835, at a period when the travel accounts of such people as Basil Hall and Mrs. Trollope were attracting a great deal of attention to America, and an equal amount of acrimonious discussion. He felt sure he could present a fairer picture than they had done.

Through twenty-odd years of useful service in Stockholm, Copenhagen, and Turin, nothing had happened to him that was as exciting as those years in the United States before the War of 1812. And fairly or unfairly, he had sometimes been held responsible as a major factor in precipitating that war. Here was an opportunity to exonerate himself and at the same time describe a stirring and dramatic scene.

As he reminded an old friend in Massachusetts, he had the materials ready at hand. In his study were dozens of notebooks and journals crammed with his first-hand observations. He knew much to praise, he would "set down naught in malice," yet he would be critical when occasion warranted.[1] He would, he believed, produce the first balanced book about America.

From such complexity, or perhaps it was simplicity of motives, Sir Augustus John Foster, Baronet, set about writing the account here printed. To understand his book, the reader should know something more about the man himself than he reveals in its pages.

Foster was born in 1780, the second son of an Irish M.P. and of Lady Elizabeth Hervey Foster, daughter of an earl who was

[1]Augustus John Foster to Josiah Quincy, Sept. 30, 1833. Edmund Quincy, *Life of Josiah Quincy of Massachusetts* (Boston, 1867), p. 487.

also a bishop.[2] His mother, one of the beautiful and alluring women of her age, was separated from her husband in the year her son was born and spent the next two decades in the household of her good friend the famous Georgiana, Duchess of Devonshire, who died in 1806. Though Augustus grew up on good terms with his father's family, he appears to have been much more intimate with the Devonshire House circle.[3] In 1809 Lady Elizabeth became the second wife of the Duke of Devonshire. Her sister was already wife of the second Earl of Liverpool, a rapidly rising political figure who became Prime Minister while Foster was in America. Though these people had always had Whig affiliations, the government which Lord Liverpool formed in 1812 and under which Foster served was liberal Tory, strongly conscious of the importance of English trade and manufacturing.

Foster was educated at Christ Church, Oxford, which he mentions more than once in his book, and at Drogheda and Weimar. A letter from Germany in 1799 from the young man to his mother mentions his familiar conversations with Goethe, Kotzebue, Wieland, Schiller, and a number of noblemen.[4] In Paris a little later he knew Napoleon and Talleyrand and dined with Madame de Staël. Before 1804 he had also visited Sweden, Constantinople, and Greece. When he was in that year appointed Secretary of Legation at Washington, he brought with him a wide experience in the polite societies of several countries and an intimate personal acquaintance with many of the great Europeans of the dawning Napoleonic era.

Foster reached America in December 1804. Unfortunately for any real sympathy he might possibly have developed for ways of life in this country, the young man was soon in the company of

[2]The principal biographical materials regarding Foster are to be found in the "Papers of Sir Augustus John Foster" in the Library of Congress, and in the articles concerned with him in the *Dictionary of National Biography*, in the *Gentleman's Magazine*, XXX, N.S. III (Sept. 1848), 317, and in Vere Foster, *Two Duchesses* (London, 1898), p. 474. Many of the letters from the LC collection are printed, often in abbreviated form, in *Two Duchesses*.

[3]Hugh Stokes, *The Devonshire House Circle* (London, 1917), pp. 180, 313, etc., and the letters to his mother in LC.

[4]Aug. 20. LC.

his chief, the Minister Anthony Merry, a thin-skinned, almost stupid man already soured on everything American.[5] Though Foster's letters to his mother indicate that he had no high opinion of Washington manners and men, he did manage to enjoy himself socially. Somewhat disappointed when he himself was not appointed to succeed Merry, he applied as early as 1806 for permission to attend the affairs of his Irish estates.[6] He actually did not return to Great Britain until 1808.

During these years, at the times Congress was not in session, he visited people he had known in Washington. The New Englanders, New Yorkers, and Pennsylvanians were cordial, and Virginians like Jefferson and Madison went out of their way to be hospitable when he journeyed southward. Despite this kindness of so many American leaders to a young minor diplomat, he left the country with a feeling of dislike, or at least of distaste, a feeling no doubt largely induced by the comparison he inevitably made, consciously and unconsciously, between American society and those brilliant social groups with which he had been familiar in the European capitals.

From 1808 to 1810 Foster was chargé d'affaires at Stockholm, where he apparently showed considerable diplomatic ability. Soon after his expulsion from Sweden by Napoleon in 1810, he was appointed Minister to the United States. His mother reminded him that the tense Anglo-American situation made this an important post.[7] At all events, he reluctantly gave up his courtship of Annabella Milbanke (who soon married Lord Byron) and sailed once more for America.

Foster succeeded Francis James Jackson, an envoy who had been distinctly *persona non grata* in the United States. Everything about Foster's appointment indicates that his government believed he was the man peculiarly suited to present to America its policy of general firmness softened by minor concessions. He

[5]Beckles Willson, *Friendly Relations, A Narrative of Britain's Ministers and Ambassadors to America (1791-1930)* (Boston, 1934), pp. 38-54. Merry had arrived in the company of the poet Thomas Moore in November 1803.

[6]Letters of 1806-1807, especially March 27, 1806. LC.

[7]*Two Duchesses*, pp. 347-48.

had a wide acquaintance and some personal popularity in this country, and his rigid instructions would allow him to settle the *Chesapeake* affair.[8] He was to make clear England's position in regard to the Orders in Council, and to remonstrate regarding the occupation of West Florida, the harboring of French privateers with British prizes, and the recent Non-Importation Act. He faced a strained and complex situation.

But the new Minister was agreeably surprised by the cordiality of his reception in Washington. He liked Americans better than he had before, and he now found "many sensible worthy men in Congress."[9] He lived in some style, giving weekly dinners to government officials and the diplomatic corps, and a great ball on the Queen's birthday.[10] He could not personally have been too much displeased when he was called an opiate designed to make certain British measures less painful.

Socially, then, life proved quite pleasant. Officially it was most harassing. Historians generally agree that if Foster's mission was to prevent war, he and it were unconsciously doomed in advance by his instructions. In accordance with them, he began on his arrival a long series of notes to the State Department. This correspondence shows that he followed his instructions precisely, used his discretion judiciously in the few rare instances when he could exercise it, and kept his government informed of the progress of events.[11] On paper he was a model diplomat.

But his weakness, for he had a weakness, lay in his inability to perceive and interpret for his home government the full implications of the events he reported so regularly and meticulously.

[8]Bernard Mayo, ed., *Instructions to the British Ministers to the United States, 1791-1812*, Vol. III of the *Annual Report* of the American Historical Association for 1936 (Washington, 1941), pp. 310ff.

[9]Foster to Elizabeth, Duchess of Devonshire, Jan. 2, 1812. LC.

[10]Foster to the Duchess of Devonshire, Jan. 2, 1812; Elizabeth Donnan, ed., *Papers of James A. Bayard, 1796-1815*, Vol. II of the *Annual Report* of the American Historical Association for 1913 (Washington, 1915), p. 189; and text below.

[11]For his reports home, see notes on text below; *The Papers Presented to Parliament in 1813* (London, [1813]); [James Madison,] *Message of the President of the United States Transmitting Copies of a Correspondence between Mr. Monroe and Mr. Foster* . . . June 11, 1812 . . . (Washington, 1812); and the *American Review*, 1811-1812, appendices.

Occasionally when perception did come, the consequent warning reached London too late to be of use. As this book affords evidence, he gave undue weight to the wrong things as basic causes of the War of 1812. He admitted later to Lord Castlereagh that he had not realized until the last moment that war was coming;[12] yet all his official reports and private papers record what might have been significant events in the eyes of a more perceptive man. In justice to him it should be noted that his government appears to have been equally obtuse in the face of the evidence actually before it.

At any rate, on June 18, 1812, war was declared on the basis of several stated grievances, among which the Orders in Council held last place. Even then the British Minister believed that if the Orders in Council were revoked, hostilities might never begin.[13] One of the lesser ironies of American history, and perhaps of Foster's personal career, was that they were repealed in part on June 17, the day before the declaration of war, but that the news took weeks to cross the Atlantic. Whether American knowledge of the action would actually have prevented war is of course a moot question.

After a brief and unsuccessful period in Parliament in defense of the government's American policy, Foster returned to diplomacy. From 1814 he spent ten years as Minister to Denmark and from 1824 the remaining sixteen years of his diplomatic career in a similar mission to the court of the King of Sardinia at Turin. Modest honors accompanied a moderate success. He was sworn a member of the Privy Council, knighted, and in 1831 created a baronet of Glyde Court, county Louth. He married a sister of the Earl of Buckinghamshire. In 1848, during a fit of temporary insanity brought on by physical illness, he committed suicide. Such was the life of an English gentleman who had known personally perhaps as many of the world's great as any man of his generation.

[12] *Papers Presented to Parliament*, p. 661.

[13] Ibid., pp. 702-706. Willson's statement (*Friendly Relations*, p. 92) that Madison assured Foster that such would be the case is not quite what Foster himself says. He clearly records that he has "the impression" from the American President and Secretary that hostilities would cease, etc., under the condition mentioned.

Though Foster was right in feeling that he had good reasons for writing a book about the United States, he could certainly never have been objective in depicting New World democracy. Politically, religiously, and socially he was a born conservative. From his first months in America he had come to believe the Federalists were England's natural allies and the Democrats her natural enemies. He may seem at first glance amazingly gullible in swallowing almost any anti-Democratic story he was told, or anything else related by a Federalist, but Foster heard what he wanted to hear.

Perhaps there were no more militantly orthodox Anglicans than the Church's Irish members in Sir Augustus' time. Grandson of an Irish bishop and a devout believer in the Established Church in a region where it retained a certain virility through its rivalry with the more numerous Catholics, Foster looked with horror on religious liberalism, especially in political leaders. Catholicism, with which he was more familiar, seemed far less dangerous. He could champion Catholic Emancipation at home and enjoy thoroughly the company of Archbishop Carroll in America, though the Irish Catholic laborer's rise to power in Pennsylvania appeared ominous in several ways.

Nurtured in aristocratic English and European society, he measured men by its standards. In America he recognized instinctively certain "gentlemen." With the farmer or artisan in his proper place he could always be at ease, as aristocrats have always been. But for the self-made man, especially in government, Foster had no use. Though he occasionally jokes about these diamonds-in-the-rough with an assumed tolerance, fundamentally his attitude is that they are dangerous to the stability of society's basic institutions.

Because his book is among other things an apologia for his own conduct as British Minister during the crucial period just before the War of 1812, Foster consciously and unconsciously presents facts as they bear out or defend his and his government's position. When the personal equation is not involved he tries to observe objectively, or at least impartially, as when he records laconically in his journal after he had met with a group of Federalists, "a dinner of malcontents." And in his sharpest criticism he is at times putting his finger on a real American weakness. Greed for land and power did exist in the United States, sometimes in shameful proportions, and many Americans, not all of them Federalists, were as sour as Foster in predicting that the weeds might yet spoil the crop.

Something should be said of his fundamental misconceptions, chief among them being his ideas on the Virginia gentry, the Pennsylvania Democrats, and the Connecticut state government. The Virginians, whose simplicity of manners sprang from their agrarian way of life and proximity to the frontier, were hardly cunning aristocrats posing as plebeians in order to gain political power. Their sense of *noblesse oblige*, their reading in contemporary French philosophy, and their economic alliance with their yeoman neighbors combined to make of them sincere deists with strong ethical convictions, consistent opponents of industrial capitalism, and natural champions of the common man. Again, though American attitudes towards slavery were already changing, the Jefferson-Madison group of Virginians, to which Foster usually refers, were fundamentally opposed to it.

The Pennsylvania Democrats, too, were hardly the motley assortment of German boors, Irish rascals, and unscrupulous city demagogues he makes them out to be. Perhaps his greatest injustice is to the Germans, the orderly, quiet, industrious Palatines who had in Foster's time just elected the first governor of their nationality. Though the Irish and Scotch-Irish may have possessed some of the unruly traits he assigns to the Germans, he refuses to see the alert minds and ardent temperaments which made of them the ideal frontiersmen who were to build the new nation in the West. And the Philadelphia Democrats included among their leaders such highly educated and distinguished republicans-by-conviction as Dr. Benjamin Rush, Dr. Michael Leib, and Joseph Clay. The fact that all these Pennsylvanians were staunch supporters of the War of 1812 was among the reasons for Foster's antipathy.

Connecticut, the social and political unit Foster admired most as genuinely "democratic," had in reality as government a tight oligarchy composed of a few distinguished families in alliance with certain Yale professors and Congregational clergymen. That these leaders feared a Calvinistic God, hated Jefferson, and admired most things British of course did much to establish them and their state in his favor.

But something should also be said of Foster's peculiar fitness for the task of writing this book and of its useful and attractive features. His detailed observations sprang from a real variety of intellectual and social interests. His careful description of the American aborigines has behind it his archaeological and anthropological observations in Asia Minor with Baron John Leslie Foster. Architecture and city planning he had studied in more than half the capitals of Europe; therefore he eyed Washington and Philadelphia's physical features with critical curiosity. In his interest in agriculture, he was a typical English landowner. Banking and manufacturing, the machinery of a local election, the state of religion, were all natural interests of a visiting public official, and his record of them is colored by his personal attitudes. His gallery of pen-portraits of the eminent and the "original" is perhaps unequalled in other American travel literature.

Foster was a natural raconteur. When he narrates he is always entertaining. When he moralizes he is less so, and occasionally, when he preaches about religion, democracy, or the need of Anglo-American understanding and cooperation, he is downright dull.

A natural kindliness appears in his intercession for the Maryland clergyman who wanted to return to Scotland. A certain prudishness is manifest in his account of the dinner in honor of the new state of Louisiana. A strong moral sense is evident everywhere, in his official relations with the American government, in his account of a commercial agent's attempt to bribe him, in his analysis of an individual like Aaron Burr. Appearance meant much to him. He enjoyed fine clothes and a smart equipage, and he saw demagogic pose or mere crudeness in those who did not.

The limitations of his background as much as of his mind are apparent when he actually pondered and failed to understand such matters as the urge of the frontier or the seeming paradox of the Democratic Virginia aristocrat.

There is much to warrant the publication of this book over a century after it was written. First, here is Jeffersonian America from the point of view of a cosmopolitan Briton who measures our society by the yardstick of his own experience. Whatever his intentions, America does not fare badly in the comparison. Second, here is an analysis of factors leading to the War of 1812 by a diplomat who helped to develop them. Even when his analysis is faulty, he supplies later historians with new materials for an understanding of the causes of that conflict. Third, here in profusion are new details of our early national habits and new anecdotes regarding our eminent and typical men, all related with sprightliness and humor spiced by an occasional bit of malice—despite disclaimers to the contrary. This book is not at all like Fanny Kemble's *Journal* (1835), which Foster thought the fairest account of America he had seen published, nor is it like Mrs. Trollope's nor John Davis' nor Basil Hall's nor any of the rest. Like so many of the persons Sir Augustus liked to describe, his book is an "original," a fresh view of our national life as it developed from the dignity of infancy to the rough-and-tumble of active childhood.

Foster's Method of Composition

In 1833, as we have pointed out, Sir Augustus began arranging his notebooks and journals in preparation for writing a book on the United States. In 1834, after he had requested from his old friend Josiah Quincy certain books which might refresh his memory on names and events, he received copies of the *American Almanac* for 1831, Obadiah Rich's *View of the United States* (London, 1833), and Theodore Dwight's *History of the Hartford Convention* (1833).[14] For five years he continued to put his materials "in order," all the while reading

[14] Quincy, *Life of Josiah Quincy*, p. 458.

the new American travel accounts as they appeared, to see what others were saying about the country.[15] In a positive way the influence of other books appears to have been very slight. Though Foster's interests sometimes seem roughly to parallel those of other travelers, one has only to read his original on-the-spot notes to see how really spontaneous and genuine those interests were.

At any rate, by 1839 he had a book-length manuscript about ready for the printer.[16] A comparison of this text (now in the Huntington Library) with the materials of a surviving 1806-1807 notebook (also in the Huntington Library), and an 1806 small diary and an 1811-1812 large journal (both in the Library of Congress) indicate that it is based almost entirely on his records, bolstered, as we have indicated, by figures and full names from some of the assembled printed sources. In many sections, as in the account of the journey to Monticello and Montpelier in 1807, Foster hardly alters the phraseology of the notes made as he traveled. His 1811-1812 journal proves that his discussion of regions he never visited is almost as valuable as what he has to say about those he did visit, for in the former case he has recorded much of what Members of Congress or the Cabinet had to say about their home territories.

Apparently the text of 1839 was somewhat revised in 1840, and the new version sent to John Gibson Lockhart for use in the *Quarterly Review*.[17] In 1841-1842, probably soon after he retired from diplomacy, Foster prepared a new fair copy in several bound books, this time a revision of the *Quarterly Review* text. Still he was not satisfied, and proceeded to delete, rephrase, and occasionally add to this manuscript, now in the Library of Congress. This is the "final" version now extant.

[15]For a list of books by English travelers in the United States before 1835, see Jane L. Mesick, *The English Traveller in America, 1785-1835* (New York, 1922), pp. 347-52.

[16]Quincy, *Life of Josiah Quincy*, p. 462.

[17]*Quarterly Review*, LXVIII (June 1841), 20-57. The article consists of selections and comments made by Lockhart.

The Library of Congress "final" version has been used as a basic text because its punctuation, sentence structure, and spelling are more nearly in accord with modern usage than are those of the Huntington Library manuscript. Passages marked through in the Library of Congress version have been restored whenever they add new material, and many passages from the Huntington version have been added in brackets for the same reason. As it stands, the printed text includes all of a discreet diplomat's first-thought indiscretions, which at this distance in time are no longer questionable from his point of view or from ours. Foster's own notes, indicated as such, have been inserted in the text, also in brackets.

The Present Text

Even in the "final" version Foster was given to five-page paragraphs, capitalization of almost all nouns, inconsistent and idiosyncratic spelling, and long, involved, confusing sentences. Since a publisher in his day would have regularized these things for the sake of clarity, we have frequently undertaken this office so much more necessary for the readers of our day. Punctuation has been altered only to break up certain lengthy and confusing sentences or to clarify phrase or clause. Foster's rather unusual comma locations have in the main been preserved, for they seem more than the other mechanics of composition to represent his way of thinking.

Foster did not number his chapters but did provide titles for all of them except XIII, XIV, and XXV. The long chapters II and XVII have been broken into sections with titles for each added by the editor.

Excerpts from one or another of Foster's texts have appeared in Lockhart's article in the *Quarterly Review* mentioned above, and recently in four selections in historical journals. The first of these, edited by Margaret B. Tinkcom, appeared in the *William and Mary Quarterly* (January 1951); a second, by Harry M. Tinkcom, in the *Pennsylvania Magazine of History and Biography* (October 1951); and two others, by Margaret Kinard, in the *William and Mary Quarterly* (April 1952) and the *Maryland*

Historical Magazine (December 1952). The present work is the first publication of the complete[18] and collated text.

The Footnotes to the Text

Biographical data, historical setting or allusions are presented in these notes, numbered in sequential order by chapters. They indicate Foster's relative accuracy or veracity and also should make his text more intelligible to the modern reader. Except where the subject is of considerable historical importance, they have been kept as brief as possible. Parallel references are indicated by asterisks.

The biographical data, unless otherwise noted, come from the most obvious source or sources, such as the *Dictionary of National Biography*, the *Dictionary of American Biography*, the *Biographie Universelle*, the *National Cyclopaedia of American Biography*, the *Encyclopaedia Britannica* (eleventh ed.), or the *Biographical Directory of Congress.* Books cited are given by full title and author in the first reference, and afterwards by a short title. Periodical titles usually appear in obvious abbreviations. The Henry E. Huntington Library and the Library of Congress are referred to respectively as HEH and LC. Foster's 1811-1812 journal is designated as "Diary," and his two drafts of the present text, with locations indicated, as "Notes."

[18]With the exception of certain repetitions, a note on the Eucharist, and two sections of Moreau's comments on the Napoleonic Wars.

JEFFERSONIAN AMERICA

CHAPTER I

Preliminary Remarks

IT HAS been the fate of the United States of America to be described by the travellers who have visited them in either very glowing terms of praise or of abuse and contempt, according to the humours of the individual writer and to the reception he may have had in proceeding thither. Many of those who traverse the country undertake to give a character of the whole of the inhabitants from the impression they may have taken of them at Philadelphia, New York, Charlestown or any other port at which they first landed, or may have passed the most of their time, when the fact is that, language excepted, there is scarcely a point of resemblance between some of the states, particularly in regard to those situated in the southward and to the eastward, which might not be found between England and Holland, Russia or Germany or most European countries. The existence of slavery in some and the horror of it in others gives rise to laws and habits diametrically opposite; while the links of the connection formed by Congress, whatever may be their effects in giving union to the country in its collisions with foreign powers, are too little felt in the ordinary concerns of life to vie in any considerable degree with the nearer and more powerful influence produced by the operations of the local government.

In times of war indeed the Ministers of the United States may obtain more extensive influence from the increased patronage which such a state of things might give them, and from their being at those moments able to appeal to the moral feelings and energies of the people. But notwithstanding such inducements might tempt them to quarrel with foreigners, there are other considerations, more powerful, which must ever give a slowness to their proceedings and incline the government to preserve peace as long as they can without exposing themselves to a total loss of credit. The President of the day, if he looks to re-election, must dread the reaction which may be produced in the feelings of the public by the chances of war. And unless we could suppose such a state of things again to exist as took place at the time when Napoleon, grasping the sceptre of the earth, forced Great Britain to lay hold, in her defence of the trident of the seas, the causes of quarrel which might be expected to exist between the Americans and other nations of the Old World must necessarily diminish, when once their limits shall have been exactly defined, and become more trifling with each successive year, while the grounds of a connection will naturally be strengthened, and the loss and injury which would accrue to either side from a rupture be more palpable as well as more serious.

Even the late war was not determined on until after the most earnest secret struggles to avoid it on the part of the American government, who were pushed into it by the faction which supported them, but not before they had endured for many years what they were pleased to call the wrongs and insults which at last occasioned their determination. Nay, after the question had passed in the House of Representatives, it was fully expected that it would be lost in the Senate. In a very important stage of the bill the majority would have been against the party inclined to war (the War-Hawks as they were called) but that the debate was purposely prolonged in order to allow time for one very idle and drunken, and another very fat Senator to arrive, who were at some feast and had been sent for in a great hurry in order that they might turn the scale.[1]

This war was certainly productive of much ill-blood between England and America, but in the opinion of the Speaker, Mr. Clay,[2] and his friends it was as necessary to America as a duel is to a young officer to prevent his being bullied and elbowed in society. Certainly our naval officers did on many occasions go

[1]In his "Diary," June 30, 1812, Foster refers to "Brent the old drunken Senator from Virginia." This was Richard Brent (1757-1814), U.S. Senator 1808-1814. Foster also instructed an aide to make Brent drunk every day ("Diary," June 15, 1812). The very fat Senator is unidentified.

[2]Henry Clay (1777-1852) had been elected Speaker of the U.S. House of Representatives on the day of his entrance into that body in 1811. He was an outspoken leader of the "War Hawks."

beyond the instructions of the Admiralty and even disregard the orders of their superiors, in order to seek opportunities for venting their spleen upon the Yankees whose naval knowledge and achievements they held in too great contempt; but the Americans have had the satisfaction of proving their courage—they have brought us to speak of them with respect. The wounds suffered by their pride have been healed and henceforth there should be no remains of rancour on either side; both indeed seem to have since become more studious to please and to avoid giving offence, the highest personage in the kingdom (at the time Prince Regent) having set the example in the attentions shown by his orders to American travellers of any distinction. Baleful as the war has been, I must confess that I think in this respect something has been gained by it; while with regard to the real interests of both countries it has been clearly proved that they are, to both, essentially dependent for their prosperity on the maintenance of peace.

There are four great divisions of the United States as to the manners and the habits of the people. The east, in which Presbyterianism prevails, and *there* are no slaves—the central states including New York, New Jersey, Pennsylvania and part of Maryland—the southern states—and the western. Some of these more or less resemble each other but the above classification allows perhaps of a distinct character being given to each division. I have not been in the west, but I conceive that little can be said of a country so lately settled and where the houses with few exceptions are built of logs, a great part of the active population being composed of refugees from society or of people who have emigrated from Europe as well as the Atlantic states in order to better their condition. Who can describe the manners or the institutions of such a motley race, some living in harmony together, others carrying the vices of civilized life into forests and morasses while calling themselves a young people? It must be all a chance what one thinks of them from travelling in any particular direction, and as to giving a description of the country it would be a mere catalogue of the names of plants and trees to be found in it or a list of the rivers which run through it.

The settlers must confide in their own good fortune or the reports of their friends in searching after convenient situations, but if they are prudent they will make their purchases at the land-office, if there be one in the district where there is land to be had, or else apply at the general office in Washington, where the best information may be obtained in regard to settlements within the territory of the United States and some clue be given to those willing to purchase which may prevent their being imposed upon.

The following remarks are placed under nearly as many heads as there are states in the Union from a conviction that in a country of so vast an extent, but of which so much the greater part is wood and water, a few general notices classed in the above manner will be found to give more satisfactory ideas in regard to most of what is worthy of observation in it than could possibly be gathered from a book of travels properly so called. I must however apologise for an apparent want of method in the arrangement of the work as well as for the scantiness of the information given on many points, having been more desirous of forming a place of deposit for various detached pieces of information that my situation in the United States enabled me to collect than of publishing a detailed account of that country and its institutions. These notes too have been gathered at two different periods, from 1804 to 1807, and afterwards in 1811 and 1812.

CHAPTER II

THE CITY and district of Washington, being the seat of the general government of the United States and nearly in the exact centre of the Union as originally limited, necessarily possesses a paramount claim to the attention of a foreigner. It owes its name and indeed its very existence to the great founder of American Independence, who, on being consulted as to the fittest situation for the capital of his country, pointed out this place, partly from its position on a great river equidistant from the northern and southern extremities of the republic and partly, no doubt, from its being in his own immediate neighbourhood—a circumstance that probably rendered him partial to the spot which, it must be confessed, has also several points of natural beauty to recommend it. The ground is elevated on both sides of the Potomac, and the views are varied as well as in many parts romantic, particularly just above the city where the river is obstructed by rocks, and at the eastern branch where there are fine woods and some delightful rides. General Washington is said, however, to have also calculated upon the infant city's becoming a great mart for the productions of the upper country, and thereby increasing very rapidly in population and wealth, but here his views have been disappointed, commerce continuing its old course through Baltimore where it meets with capital to support it, and not a single great mercantile house having as yet been established within the boundaries of the metropolis.

Washington

The Congress removed to Washington at the commencement of this century and much inconvenience was experienced by everybody on this occasion: the change from such a large and agreeable town as Philadelphia to what was then scarce any better than a mere swamp having been difficult to digest, particularly for the members of the diplomatic body. And I cannot say that they have as yet got quite reconciled to it, although great improvements have taken place, especially in its markets, it being no longer necessary to send fifty miles around to collect materials for a dinner, as was the case according to what the Marquis de Casa Yrujo told me when he first came to reside there.[1] There are however no streets in the place, and the few scattered habitations are designated by the number of buildings, six, seven, or twenty, in a group, to which they belong. Excellent snipe shooting and even partridge shooting was to be had on each side of the main avenue and even close under the wall of the Capitol, while the suburbs were well stored with woodcocks and one might take a ride of several hours within the precincts without meeting with a single individual to disturb one's meditations.

It is obvious that the amusements of social life must be very limited in such a residence and in fact from the general smallness of the houses scarce any but public functionaries and foreign envoys are so situated as to be able to give entertainments. The members of the two houses of legislature are huddled together generally two in a room. There are no clubs established and no theatres in the place except for rope dancers.

The richer and more respectable deputies have therefore for the most part been always inclined to vote for returning back again to Philadelphia or for removing to some other situation where a good sized town has already been formed. But the majority, being in a great measure composed of rough and unfashioned persons to whom it is of consequence to be in a place where they are attended to more than they would be likely to be in a large city, have hitherto successfully resisted every attempt that has been made to engage Congress to the measure. They have been always backed by the government which, as it was composed of Virginians for so many years, naturally gave a preference to Washington over every other situation.

[1]Don Carlos Martinez de Yrujo, or later the Marquis de Casa Yrujo, went to Washington as Spanish envoy in 1800 or 1801. He married a daughter of Republican Governor McKean of Pennsylvania.

Mr. Jefferson in particular used all his influence to prevent the removal, giving as a reason the danger that might ensue to the Union if a door were to be again opened to disputes among the different states on a subject so interesting as the selecting a spot for the seat of government, which might give rise to countless jarring claims and finally render Congress itinerant.[2] Nevertheless whatever might be the force of this objection at the present day, Mr. Jefferson must have well known at an earlier period that the return to Philadelphia could have been easily accomplished and without occasioning any such danger. The fact was that his power was founded on the court he paid to the Democratical party, and he could not have appeared in a great town, as he did in Washington, without attendants, when he took a ride fastening his horse's bridle himself to the shop doors (as I have once witnessed his doing, when his nail was torn off in the operation), or in yarn stockings and slippers when he received company.[3] Neither could he have had the members of the legislature so dependent upon him and the rest of the administration anywhere else for the little amusement and relief which they could obtain after public business. His house and those of the Ministers being in fact almost necessary to them unless they chose to live like bears, brutalized and stupefied as one of the Federalists who did not frequent the Great House once confessed to me that he felt from hearing nothing but politics from morning to night and from continual confinement to his senatorial duties with scarcely any relaxation whatsoever.

Mr. Jefferson knew too well what he was about. He had lived in too good society in Paris, where he was employed as Minister from the United States previously to the French Revolution and where he had been admitted to the coteries of Madame du

[2]Written evidence of Jefferson's influence in keeping the capital at Washington has not been discovered. There had been much grumbling even among Democratic Congressmen, and his admonitions were probably given to them orally.

[3]Jefferson received the Danish Minister one morning in slippers and spoke at the time of his indifference to forms. Such actions were of course the result of his desire to impress the diplomatic corps—and the people—with the simplicity of our institutions.

Deffand and Madame de Staël, not to set a value on the decencies and proprieties of life; but he was playing a game for retaining the highest offices in a state where manners are not a prevailing feature in the great mass of the society, being, except in the large towns, rather despised as a mark of effeminacy by the majority, who seem to glory in being only thought men of bold strong minds and good sound judgment.

Having mentioned Mr. Jefferson, it may be interesting to the reader to have the following description of his person as he appeared to me on my arrival in the United States in the year 1804. He was a tall man with a very red freckled face and grey neglected hair, his manners goodnatured, frank and rather friendly though he had somewhat of a cynical expression of countenance. He wore a blue coat, a thick grey-coloured hairy waistcoat with a red under-waistcoat lapped over it, green velveteen breeches with pearl buttons, yarn stockings and slippers down at the heel, his appearance being very much like that of a tall large-boned farmer. He said he washed his feet as often as he did his hands in order to keep off cold, and appeared to think himself unique in so doing. I thought him intemperate in breaking out into abuse of Judge Chase who was just then under impeachment and whom he called an insolent overbearing man,[4] advising Mr. Merry[5] to avoid making his acquaintance. In general, I am told, Mr. Jefferson did not address his conversation much to strangers who were presented to him, and when Thomas Moore was introduced at the time of Mr. Merry's first audience he said not a word, which so nettled the poet that we probably owe some angry verses to the circumstance,[6] in which he has

[4]Jefferson had reasons for resentment. Samuel P. Chase (1741-1811), Justice of the Supreme Court, had denounced from the bench the democratic tendencies of the executive branch of the government and had generally fought in "partisan fashion" all Republican policies.

[5]Anthony Merry (d. 1811?), Minister from Great Britain to the U.S., appointed in 1802. He landed at Norfolk on November 4, 1803, and arrived in Washington on November 26.

[6]Moore had heard from the Merrys the "slight" the President had put upon them, and when "Jefferson gazed down on him in silence, the little poet's distaste deepened into ineradicable dislike." Moore took his unworthy revenge by repeat-

not spared the ci-devant President and which if unminded by the father succeeded at least in giving some pains to his daughter,[7] a very amiable woman who was partly educated in a convent at Paris and is married to Mr. Thomas Mann Randolph of Virginia,[8] a cousin of the well-known John Randolph.[9] She told me she had much regretted Mr. Moore's reception had not been more flattering to him, but that from his low stature and youthful appearance her father had taken him for a boy, and as he had always professed to be of the liberal party in England he felt rather surprized at his bitter censure of a person so devoted to the cause of liberty as was the President.

The District of Columbia in which the Federal City stands is ten miles square and was ceded to the general government by the states of Maryland and Virginia. It has one other town besides Washington within its limits, viz., George Town north of the Potomac, and so very near the city as almost to serve it for a suburb. In fact if the Congress had chosen to declare this little town their capital, trusting to time for its gradual increase, they would have acted much more wisely than by settling in the swamps. As it is, I know not how they could possibly have remained so long where they are if it had not been for the resources of this place, small as it is, for the population did not consist of more than 1,200 or 1,400 inhabitants when Congress first removed into its neighbourhood. Alexandria, a town of 6,000 to 7,000 inhabitants, it is true is situated just without the limits of the district at the other extremity and to go there is an agreeable excursion by water or by land, but the situation of

---

ing many Federalist libels in his verse epistle to Thomas Hume. Howard Mumford Jones, *The Harp That Once: A Chronicle of the Life of Thomas Moore* (New York, 1937), pp. 77-79; and Thomas Moore, *Epistles, Odes, and Other Poems* (London, 1806), pp. 209-10.

[7]Martha Jefferson Randolph (1790-1836) was her father's hostess during his period as President.

[8]Thomas Mann Randolph (1768-1828) was a cousin of Jefferson as well as of John Randolph.

[9]John Randolph of Roanoke (1773-1833), mentioned several times in the "Notes," was a friend of Foster until his death.

Alexandria is far inferior in point of beauty to the other, which stands on a height and has many delightful walks and rides in its immediate neighbourhood. Within the limits of the city there is little worthy of remark as may be well supposed from what has been already said. Nevertheless two or three buildings merit notice.

The President's House was erected by an Irish mason who gave as his own the plan of the Duke of Leinster's house in Dublin.[10] This being shown to General Washington was approved of by him; and the Irishman, who had been but a journeyman under the real architect and designer of the plan, was appointed to superintend the building. He left out the upper story however and built no cellars, which President Jefferson, after experiencing great losses in wines, has been obliged to add at a depth of sixteen feet under ground. These are so cool that the thermometer stood two degrees lower in them than it did in a vacant spot in the ice-house early in July, when in the shade out of doors it was at ninety-six. The hall of the house is vast and appears magnificent, but the materials are not so, the columns which are of the Doric order being of wood. The exterior looks well from its size and regularity but the style of the architecture is by no means pure. The pilasters are Ionic but the volutes are heavy and ill executed. The shafts are too long and upon small pedestals. In other respects too there is much ill executed ornament of garlands and modules, no vacant space being left broad enough for the eye to repose on. The stone is like our Gloucestershire stone of a very good grain but it was whitewashed. The room we were shown into was ill-furnished. There were some Indian ornaments and a Hooker pipe lying on the table and two prints on the walls, an apotheosis of General Washington and the other representing him surrounded by his family. The grounds about the house are surrounded by a common wooden paling and seem never to have been touched by spade or pick-axe.

On the right was a square brick building in which were the

[10]The architect of the White House was James Hoban (1762-1831), a native of Dublin. His plans were selected as the result of a competition in 1792.

Treasury offices, and on the left the Department of Foreign Affairs where the Secretary of State [Madison] received Foreign Ministers in a very indifferent little room into which they were ushered by his clerk.

Dr. Thornton a native of Tortola, settled at Washington and chief of the Patent Office, was the original designer of the plan of the Capitol.[11] There were two wings to be connected by a portico in the centre and a dome bearing upon it,[12] but only one of these wings, that to the north, was completed in 1807 and there was very little chance then of the centre being finished for many years, the expense of labour at Washington being enormous and nothing but the shame and odium that would have attended retracting having induced Congress to persevere. In that year they had given $130,000 for the completion to Mr. Latrobe, the architect, who was obliged to take up some of the foundations that had cost $18,000, but which he rebuilt for only $4,000. Mr. Latrobe was certainly a very good architect and the Capitol as far as it was finished did him credit, particularly in the distribution of the committee rooms, corridors and passages.[13] But it is a great mistake in such a building that the construction of a hall of assembly should be unfavourable to hearing. That of the House of Representatives having been very defective in this respect, and the Senate Chamber still more so, owing to its close packed arcades supporting massive Ionic pillars and to its circular shape.[14]

The pillars of the House of Representatives were of the Corinthian order, very well executed, and they had not the

[11]Dr. William Thornton (1759-1828) was born on the little island of Jost van Dyke, in a community of the Society of Friends which centered at Tortola, in the Virgin Islands. After training and experience in Edinburgh, Aberdeen, and Philadelphia, he won the competition for the design of the Capitol in 1792-93. Foster's "Diary" shows that he came to know Dr. and Mrs. Thornton quite well.

[12]For a plate showing the wings as Thornton designed them, see I. T. Frary, *They Built the Capitol* (Richmond, Va., 1940), p. 32.

[13]Benjamin Henry Latrobe (1764-1820) had trouble with Thornton and others, but Foster's judgment of him seems correct.

[14]The shape of the old Senate room appears in an old print. Frary, *They Built the Capitol*, p. 70. Latrobe resented Jefferson's advice and interference. This alone would have predisposed Foster in Latrobe's favor.

aspect of being raised by plinths as is the case with almost all the public buildings in London except those erected by Mr. Decimus Burton[15] and some few others, notwithstanding that in the Grecian temples at Athens of the Ionic order—and particularly in the temple of the Sibyl at Tivoli, which may perhaps be called the purest specimen of the Corinthian order left by the Romans—the pillars stand upon a basement or on their own round bases and not upon plinths (a fact by the by which was disputed with me, until I referred to books by three English architects, of which one was the late Sir G. Wyatteville).[16] Plinths being an invention belonging to the lower ages of very bad taste, having been introduced probably from motives of economy when marble could not easily be had of sufficient length for the shafts of the pillars. At the school house behind St. Paul's in London and Arthur's Club in St. James Street, the columns have no plinths under them, and I think to this circumstance may be attributed much of the gracefulness and beauty of those buildings.

The Senate Chamber of the Capitol was in the north wing. Each Senator had a chair covered with red morocco leather, sat at a particular table or at a part of a semicircular table where the member had his ink, papers, and books of reference before him. Instead of attending to the debates, unless they were interesting, he generally occupied himself with reading or writing. The Vice-President who is President of the Senate sat on an elevated seat under a sort of canopy, raised several steps above the rest of the room. Without the arcades was a circular corridor with two fire-places to which the members of the House alone were admitted. Strangers of every sort were let into the gallery above but the echo was so great, it was scarce possible to hear from thence. There were two portraits, one of Louis XVI and the other of his queen, on either side of the Vice-President's

[15]Decimus Burton (1800-1881), famous English architect and landscape engineer, was known especially for his villas and country estates, but he did some façades and other work at Hyde Park.

[16]Sir Jeffrey Wyatville (1766-1840) and his uncle James were architects of distinction. Sir Jeffrey is remembered for his restorations of over a hundred buildings.

chair. Ladies were allowed to go into the gallery and by special favour into the body of the House. On the 4th March every four years the President, on his election being declared, proceeds to the Senate Chamber where before a very mixed assemblage he delivers a speech, which when done, he swears on a Bible presented by the Chief Justice to be faithful to the Constitution. There is a box for Ministers and foreign envoys and on Mr. Jefferson's second election, the latter had only notice given them that they might attend on the very morning of the day of the ceremony, after which every one by common accord went to pay him a visit of congratulation. He was then in high spirits, dressed in black and even in black silk stockings. A very mixed company came into the room, some lolling about on couches and in dirty shoes, and even Negro servants were seen helping themselves to wine at the side table. There was a collection of people in procession on the road but they seemed composed of low persons, for the most part Irish labourers, and appeared very cheerless.

Plans of the Capitol and its different parts with an elevation of the eastern front as originally projected, as also a sketch of the Hall of Representatives having been very obligingly communicated to me in the year 1808 by Mr. Latrobe are here inserted,[17] the rather because the building which did him so much credit, does I believe no longer exist, having been either wholly destroyed or much injured during the war in an expedition which no American can have regretted more than I did, at least in so far as it was attended with the burning of these edifices—a measure in my opinion never to be justified even under circumstances of the utmost provocation and which could not have been contemplated by the King's Government as likely to occur, even though the occupation of the Federal City might have formed part of the plan of the campaign as laid down for the year in

[17]The plates from Latrobe's 1807 drawings appear in *Restoration of the White House, Message to the President of the United States Transmitting the Report of the Architects* (Washington, 1903), passim. They do not survive among the Foster Papers in LC.

which it took place. [*Note*: Since writing the above I have been informed that the troops had been fired upon from several of the houses, which may in some measure serve to excuse their fury but the retaliation went too far and would no doubt have been regretted on the following day.]

Very few private gentlemen have houses in Washington. I only recollect three. Mr. Brent[18] who was the mayor in my time had one close to the river but at considerable distance from the rest of the inhabitants. Mr. Tayloe[19] who would be considered a man of large fortune in any country and who gave dinners occasionally to foreigners and Members of Congress, and Mr. Carroll[20] who had a good house on the Capitol hill but saw no company. Mr. Tayloe had a very fine place at Mount Airy in Virginia and was formerly a gentleman of the turf, having been educated at Cambridge University when it was still the custom here to send young men to England to school or college. A very worthy man, a Colonel Washington, cousin to the general, lived also in the city when I first went there but he was a martyr to the gout and I saw but little of him.[21] In the neighbourhood lived several gentlemen very hospitable, civil and obliging, particularly Mr. Key[22] formerly in the English service but latterly an eminent lawyer and Member of Congress, a man of much

[18]Robert Brent, appointed mayor by Jefferson in 1802, lived in the Notley Young house on G St., S.W., until 1809. In that year he left the old manor house and moved to a new mansion at the southeast corner of Maryland Ave. and 12th St., S.W. James D. Morgan, "Robert Brent, First Mayor of Washington City," *Records Columbia Hist. Soc.*, II (1899), 236-49.

[19]John Tayloe III (1771-1828?), Virginia aristocrat, was probably the most noted breeder of race horses in the country at this time. Thornton designed for him the famous Octagon House, finished in 1801 and occupied by Madison after the burning of the White House.

[20]Probably Daniel Carroll, who had his house, Duddington, built on the south of the Capitol site in 1790. Since this was pulled down by L'Enfant's builders, Foster may refer to another house. There were several other members of the prominent Maryland Carroll family living in the city.

[21]Possibly Colonel William Augustine Washington, who married Sally Tayloe of Mt. Airy in 1799.

[22]Philip Barton Key (1757-1815), Member of Congress 1805-1813, English educated, had homes in Washington and in nearby Montgomery Co., Maryland. He had fought on the British side in the Revolution in Florida and the West Indies.

good sense and eloquence—Mr. Calvert[23] descended from Lord Baltimore and married to a very distinguished looking Dutch lady—Mr. Ogle,[24] Mr. Lewis[25] and three or four others who were always happy to see and lodge their friends.

George Town too had a number of agreeable houses particularly Mr. Mason's, to whom belongs the ferry to the Virginian shore and a delightful island across which the road leads and where he had a pleasant country house and garden.[26]

Foreign ministers have great difficulty in getting suitably lodged at Washington. Mr. Merry was obliged to put two houses together to make one comfortable one in 1803[27] and I had to take three out of the group called the Seven Buildings for the same purpose and even then I was forced to turn the hall into a ball room for a party on the Queen's birthday.[28] The houses also are by no means adapted to such a climate, having been built by Irish or Scotch masons who make no difference in their style of architecture on account of the degree of latitude being the thirty-eighth instead of the fifty-sixth or fifty-seventh, but have erected

[23]Probably George Calvert (1768-1838), who married Rosalie Eugenia Stier, daughter of a Belgian emigré, and was the son of Benedict, natural son of Charles Calvert, fifth Lord Baltimore.

[24]Probably Governor Benjamin Ogle of Maryland (1749-1809), father-in-law of John Tayloe. Possibly Foster refers here to Ogle's son. Governor Ogle was the moving spirit of the Washington City Jockey Club during its golden age from 1801 to 1806. William Woodward, "The Thoroughbred Horse and Maryland," *Md. Hist. Mag.*, XVII (June 1922), 149.

[25]Probably Representative Joseph Lewis, Jr. (1772-1834) of Virginia, chairman of the House committee on the District of Columbia.

[26]General John Mason not only owned an estate on Analostan Island, but also a residence at 25th St. and Pennsylvania Ave.

[27]Merry's brick legation was on the south side of K St., between 26th and 27th. The houses were built by Robert Peter, Sr., of Georgetown, and were numbered in 1944 as 2618 and 2620. Charles O. Paullin, "Early British Diplomats in Washington," *Records Columbia Hist. Soc.*, XLIV-XLV (1944), 246-47.

[28]Foster's official residence occupied the northwest corner of Pennsylvania Ave. and 19th St. The houses were later used as a temporary executive mansion after the burning of Washington in 1814. A photograph made before 1902 shows a corner house with rounded door, then a 4-story, then three 3-story, then a 4½-story building. The three 3-story buildings also have half-visible basement floors. Allen C. Clark, "James Greenleaf," *Records Columbia Hist. Soc.*, V (1902), 231; Paullin, op. cit., pp. 248-49. Though the buildings still stand in 1953, the corner one has been converted into a drugstore.

habitations such as they would have built them in a small street of Edinburgh or Dublin. Very few have even the advantage of a garden notwithstanding the quantity of land that lies untenanted, the genius of speculation having divided almost the whole of the ground into lots for building which are continually expected to rise in value and are therefore left to be parched up and baked by the sun so that the whole place has a deserted dry appearance.

There are no paved streets in the city and the roads, excepting the central or Pennsylvanian Avenue, are not kept in the best repair; this however is the chief line of communication and in its whole extent it may be above four miles long from George Town Bridge to the bridge on the eastern branch of the Potomac passing by the President's House and the Capitol as well as most of the houses belonging to the inhabitants which are scattered along here and there in groups, or singly, my house being about two miles from the Capitol and No. 8 as reckoned from that point. On both sides of the Pennsylvanian Avenue are planted rows of lombardy poplars, their tops being topped off to make them branch out. They have flourished very well in this climate and grow to a great size, being as large as any I have seen in Europe but they are said to injure the soil from the great extent of their roots.

The walks in all directions where there are any bushes are enlivened by the mocking bird, of which this seems to be the favourite district for I have never seen them in such numbers elsewhere. It is a bird resembling a thrush though more beautifully shaped, continually on the move hopping from spray to spray and singing with great variety of note. Many are caught and instructed, when they sell for five or six guineas or even more according to their proficiency in imitating different tunes. They have been sent by great care with safety to Europe but it too frequently happens that they perish on the voyage, or, if embarked before their education is finished, they may learn to mimic only the creaking of boards. Of other birds there is a great variety about the city but there are none which sing so agreeably. Beyond the eastern branch is to be found the bird called here and in the Alps a pheasant, but which is in fact the Tetrasse or large heath fowl that we call black cock and that is called faisant de montagne in Savoy. The feathers of its belly are streaked like those of a hawk. It has a fan tail, a short thick beak and feathers on the legs. Plovers and lapwings are also to be seen, more especially the latter, within the city bounds, as also snipes in great numbers and in the suburbs kinds called here partridges, but which more resemble quails and when disturbed light upon trees.

The whip snake is the prettiest of the tribe that is met with here, being very beautifully striped but I have never seen above two or three though I have often met with the black snake, which is harmless, and killed adders in the woods. One of the most curious animals found in this neighbourhood is the tree frog, which is of a small size and lives on insects which he finds on the hickory and tulip branches in the day time but at night descends to enjoy the dew and the water near which it likes to dwell. Its back is covered with irregular streaks and resembles a piece of rock with blotches of white moss upon it; the insides of its hinder legs are striped with brown and yellow of a great brilliancy; its eyes are like those of other frogs as are its feet except that they have a glutinous quality that enables them to cling even to a pane of glass, which they can crawl up. They have little joints like nails at the extremities of their feet; their tongues are long and they dart them on their prey.

Great quantities of excellent wild ducks, familiarly called canvass-back ducks, from the colour of their feathers, are shot with long guns on the Potomac in the winter season. They are most delicious eating and I have frequently seen four dishes of them served up at the same time on the same table. They are said to owe their excellent flavour to a particular kind of grass seed, wild celery, found only in the Rivers Potomac and Susquehannah. The ducks to be got in the markets of Rome approach the nearest in goodness to them of any I have tasted in Europe.

In the river Tiber, or Goose Creek, shoals of perch are to be seen in the spring so thick that by shooting in among them one may get a good dish full, for as many will leap on shore from fright probably as can be killed with the shot. Plenty of sturgeon are caught at the little falls of the Potomac a short distance above George Town where the river becomes narrow and the scenery is very romantic; such abundance was there indeed of this fish that I determined to try if the roe might not be cured so as to afford caviar. My maitre d'hotel having nothing to do in the summer, I gave him a receipt out of *Chambers' Dictionary*[29] for the purpose which he so successfully followed that I had some excellent caviar for the following winter. But on its being served to the Members of Congress, the precaution of telling them to taste a little first not having been observed, they took such quantities thinking it was black raspberry jam that the stock was soon exhausted. Very few of them liked it but spit it out very unceremoniously as a thing excessively nasty. Nevertheless it had met the approbation of some of the gentlemen of the Russian legation and I trust that the manufacture of it being thus introduced into the country it may by degrees become an object of consumption and even of exportation.

The sturgeon is caught simply by letting a large hook with a line into the stream against which when he rubs himself by a sudden jerk, you haul him out of the water. There are some which weigh as much as two hundred pounds. There are rockfish also in this river, called sea bass at New York, which weigh from forty to sixty or seventy pounds. Wild turkeys are sometimes tho' rarely brought to market in George Town and are delicious, particularly the leg or black meat; they are brought from some distance up the country and weigh from fourteen even to twenty-five pounds. I weighed one which came from Chester County on the other side of the Chesapeake but it only weighed fifteen and one-half pounds, feathers included. The plumage is more burnished than that of tame turkeys, the upper feathers being quite black except at the ends which are of a bright brown colour.

[29]Ephraim Chambers, *Cyclopaedia, or an Universal Dictionary of Arts and Sciences . . . compiled from the Best Authors . . .* (London, first edition 1728).

Crawfish are to be found in great abundance in the Potomac as are also lampreys in the small streams but no one will touch either, the latter, owing to its odd appearance of having nine eyes or holes in or about the head, being thought to be poisonous, while the former from its crawling in the mud is looked upon with as much horror as a spider, so much so indeed that a Member of Congress at President Jefferson's table on being told that crawfish were thought a delicacy in Europe sneeringly said to Mr. Merry he thanked God necessity had not yet driven the Americans to eat such vermin. This gentleman like many other persons here fancied that in Europe the mass of the people must be greatly put to it to make out a dinner, and that everybody in England of the middle orders of society is obliged to have his food cut into squares and portions in order that nothing may be lost—an idea which from hearing it repeated continually during a residence of above three years in the United States at a period of unexampled ferment in the political world, at length began to make some impression upon myself when in 1807 I returned home and was pleasingly disappointed at finding the same ease and abundant hospitality existing among nearly all classes of H.M.'s subjects as I remembered before I left the country. The French alone perhaps of all European countries being obliged to ask for portions and demi-portions and even quart-de-portions at their dinners, while if there be more waste among the citizens of the United States they cannot at any rate be said to have as much variety of food, in the neighbourhood of the capital particularly, where you may look in vain for fresh meat at the single houses of farmers along the road side, or for wine or beer, and think yourself lucky if you can get some indifferent whisky to qualify the bad taste of the water. Indeed I had proof of this when Mr. Merry with whom I was making an excursion was taken suddenly ill and faint and we stopped at a log-house for assistance, but were unable to get even a glass of good water. I am well aware, however, that this would not have been the case in the well settled northern parts of the United States nor even in the hilly country to the westward where you meet with the effect invariably produced among mountainous tracts where population is thin—viz., greater simplicity of manners and a more hearty welcome as well as greater comfort.

There are a great many Negroes in and about Washington and slaves are advertised for sale frequently in George Town, most families having them for servants, nor could I find that they are often worse treated here than domestics in Europe. They are dressed as the whites are. Yet I cannot help thinking that if the Moorish or Eastern costume were given to the blacks they would not only look better and more cleanly but be less offensive, the rank smell that they carry about with them, and which is no doubt promoted by a woollen livery, being at times so intolerable that I have been obliged to take my leave at a ball or party in consequence of my utter inability to bear it. The oath of a Negro is not taken anywhere, I believe, south of the Susquehannah against a white man.

The "Wild Natives" from the West

I had some opportunity of getting acquainted with the Indians during the two periods of my residence at the Federal City, more especially during the presidency of Mr. Jefferson, who was so much attached to them from philanthropy and because they were savages as if they were his own children. He paid them infinitely more attention than he ever vouchsafed to show to a foreign minister, a circumstance which annoyed not a little Mr. Merry with whom I went on New Year's Day 1806 to make our compliments according to custom. Just as we arrived the Indians were going in and the President was bowing to them. He made a bow also to me and to Mr. Merry asking him how he did but said nothing more to us.[30] He was

[30]Mrs. Margaret B. Smith (*First Forty Years of Washington Society*, ed. G. Hunt [London, 1906], p. 400) comments concerning Foster's statement that he and Mr. Merry were given only a bow: "It really may have been so, and not only the President but the whole assembled company may have participated in this neglect, so lively was the interest and the curiosity excited by the appearance of the *Osage-Chiefs* and their attendant *squaws*. And likewise of the Tunisian Minister, Meley Meley, and his splendid and numerous suite." Merry had other similar humiliations.

dressed in a suit of black, his gala dress on those occasions when it was the custom for him to speak some little while to members of the diplomatic corps. But this time he passed on to the upper end of the room and appeared wholly taken up with his natives. Mr. Merry declared he would not stay to be treated so and we went away after remaining five minutes, Mr. Merry telling Dr. Logan, a Senator of the Democratic party, the reason which the latter was sure to repeat to the President.[31]

There were two parties of savages in Washington in the winter of 1806, the Cherokees and the Indians from the Mississippi and Missouri. The first set[32] arrived on the 12th January with Colonel Hawkins,[33] a very worthy and amiable officer, who had been for ten years resident among them, as their guardian, under the authority of Congress. He had made himself so popular with the tribe that they gave him the appellation of "the beloved man." There came but six with him of whom only three were thoroughbred, the others being sons of white men, English officers, who had had squaws for their wives during the time that Florida was in possession of the British. When I went to visit them they all rose from the ground where they had been seated in conversation, gave me their hands and touched their hats; they had the appearance of coachmen, each being dressed in a blue coat, with a red collar and gold lace round the hat. They had also pantaloons on and mocassins, and one was smoking a pipe that served

[31]George Logan (1753-1821), of a prominent Philadelphia family, had been U.S. Senator since 1801, and was an old friend of Jefferson. In 1798 he had undertaken a self-instigated trip to France to try to prevent war. The result was the "Logan Act," forbidding private citizens to undertake such ventures.

[32]These were Creeks, according to Charles William Janson (*The Stranger in America, 1793-1806*, ed. Carl S. Driver from the 1807 London ed. [New York, 1935], pp. 232, 244). The Creeks and Cherokees were apparently in Washington at the same time, for Jefferson spoke to the Creeks on November 2, 1805, and to the Cherokees on January 10, 1806.

[33]Benjamin Hawkins (1754-1818), member of a wealthy and influential Virginia family, gave up the life of a southern planter to become agent to all Indian tribes south of the Ohio. He started from the South in the autumn of 1805 with 6 of his leading Creek chiefs to visit Washington. Merrit B. Pound, *Benjamin Hawkins, Indian Agent* (Athens, Ga., 1951), pp. 186-87; and Margaret Kinard, ed., "Sir Augustus J. Foster and 'The Wild Natives of the Woods,' 1805-1807," *Wm. & Mary Quart.*, 3rd ser., IX (April 1952), 193n.

occasionally as a hatchet. They had by them some blow guns and bows—the former about seven feet long and very thin, through which they can blow with great force an arrow eighteen inches long and kill a squirrel with it. They use a reed for the purpose, hardened in the fire and sharpened at one end, the down of thistles being fastened to the other. The bow is made of the locust tree or the mulberry, and the string of deer's gut. At the distance of thirty-five yards, they can drive an arrow through a common deal board. One of the Indians told me his bow had belonged to one of a nation which dwelt an immense distance off, the Shawnees as I understood. The wood was lighter coloured than mahogany and he agreed to sell it to me for a piastre but I gave him two as it seemed really to be a very good bow, two Osage chiefs who were present having praised it much, and said that the tree of which it was made grew nowhere else but there.

Colonel Hawkins gave me some information respecting the manners and customs of the Indians. Their habitations generally consist of four connected houses of one story each and are built of clay, one for the parents and as the sons and daughters marry, each adds a side till they form a quadrangle, leaving an open space at each corner. Behind is a building with a sort of balcony in front for containing provisions of corn and other articles; there is also a separate house for strangers. They have an idea that four angels came from four different corners of the earth originally to instuct them in their duties. They believe in a God whom they style the Master of Breath and hold an annual festival in his honour, when they place two beams cross-ways to form the four cardinal points and on these they put fire till they are consumed, throwing on the first offerings of their harvest. This festival is held in August. They fast one day and take an emetic; they next they spend in jubilee and feasting. Missionaries have gone among them but the Indians complained to Colonel Hawkins that their lectures only wearied them, that they listened from politeness but could comprehend nothing from their preaching. He strongly discourages any premature attempt to introduce Christianity among them, though I should think they were fully able to understand and be interested by a short and simple story of the world from its commencement; and of the necessity of Christ's coming to show to mankind by example what sort of conduct a man should hold to make himself acceptable to his Creator. Perhaps the tale of Robinson Crusoe would be as good a book as any to put into their hands. [*Note*: It undoubtedly would interest them much more than many of the little tracts which I have seen distributed for purposes of conversion and which were stupid beyond description.]

Colonel Hawkins once demanded of the Creek nation a deputation of five of their wisest chiefs to be sent to his house to consult upon some important questions which he wished to propose to them for the purpose of ascertaining whether they believed in a God and a future state of rewards and punishments. They deliberated and came accordingly. The result was that they answered they did believe in a God who made them and governed them and that they did believe that those who behaved well would in the other world be taken under his immediate protection and be placed near him, whereas the bad would be treated like the beasts of the fields and left to themselves. They had no idea of any further punishment, and seemed to consider the sufferings from eternal fire as too great.

The men wear a flap in front with mocassins and sandals, and a few feathers on their heads. The Creeks, Cherokees, Choctaws and Chickasaws were, with the Seminoles, those who were under Colonel Hawkins' superintendence. *Mico* which answers to the word "king" in English, is the title of their chiefs who are chosen out of a family which they suppose, was first recommended to them by the Master of Breath, but the monarchy is not hereditary excepting in so far that they must elect the properest person out of this one family alone. Colonel Hawkins has employed the females a good deal in his plans of civilization. These were formerly treated like beasts of burthen but now many of them ride and meet with great respect. Thirteen, some years ago, in allusion to the thirteen United States, came on horseback in a kind of riding habit with switches in their hands to wait on the Colonel, who when they came up desired some of the men present to help them off, which however they declined as a thing beneath their dignity to do. On this Colonel Hawkins went up himself and lifted off the lady nearest him, when the rest all remained seated till their men were shamed into doing the same service for the others. He added that formerly women were obliged to leave the pathway when they met any of the men but by his example the men will now show their respect to the women and the women expect it.

The Colonel tells a good story of the ingenuity of a squaw who had married an old Indian and had also a young lover who happened to be a white man. The old fellow was so confident of his wife's virtue that none of his friends could persuade him to believe her unfaithful, however evident the proofs. At last the strongest of all began to display itself in the person of the lady, and the colour of the coming child would necessarily place it beyond dispute. In this emergency the lady who had been well acquainted, unknown to her husband, with some circumstances attending the early part of his life when he had been much among the whites and a great favourite with them, resolved to try her talents upon his credulity, pretending that she had been visited in the night by the Master of Breath of the whites and that he had revealed to her that her husband had been among the white people at a particular time and that he was a favoured red man, as also that the Master of Breath liked him for some conduct of his, which she accounted, towards the whites. The Indian owned to the facts, but was in amazement how she could have heard of them, he having never recounted them to her. Yet he was mightily pleased at being thus noticed by the Master of Breath.

She further declared that in the same visitation the Master of Breath promised that to show his partiality to the favoured red man and how he held him on a par with the white people for his good offices towards them, he, the Indian, should be blest with a child whose colour should be white. Accordingly the good squaw was delivered naturally enough of a white child and the good easy Indian, grateful for the favour and pledge of the Master of

Breath's goodness to him, went about with it in his arms to the surprize of all his friends, boasting of its white colour and of the distinction shown him. Had he suspected the truth the squaw would have run considerable risk, adultery being a grievous offence among the Indians, though before marriage ladies are under little or no restraint particularly among the Creeks and Cherokees, where a stranger on arriving though only for a day, may obtain a temporary wife, the lady simply inquiring how many he had had already, that she may ascertain her number on the list. The children all follow the destiny of the mother. There must however be some dowry given, but for this a few blankets suffice and the squaw is never the worse esteemed for having had this transitory husband. On the contrary it contributes to her reputation to have had many such before she finally settles.

The usual punishments among the Indians are shooting, cropping the ears and flogging. Stealing horses out of another dominion is punished by the second of these, stealing them in their own territory by the last.

President Jefferson told me in 1806 that it was then about six years since the American government had strictly forbidden the use of spirituous liquors to the Indians under their control and he assured me that the prohibition had already had a very sensible effect in civilizing them. He pretended and I am sure was sufficiently sanguine to believe that the Cherokees would in a very short time be civilized enough to be allowed a representative in Congress and Double-Head who was at Washington the year before seemed to be very much pleased with the idea. Since then however they have had reason bitterly to lament the loss of his friendly and protecting influence.

It was in the evening of the 28th December, 1806, that Captain Lewis who performed the journey up the Missouri and down the Columbia River to the Pacific Ocean, agreeably to the orders of Congress, arrived at Washington[34] in company with the chiefs

[34]Captain Meriwether Lewis (1774-1809), explorer famous for his part in the Lewis and Clark Expedition, 1803-1806, had left St. Louis in November 1806. He did not actually arrive in Washington until December 31.

of the Mandan nation, a Frenchman acting as interpreter, who had lived for sixteen years among that tribe, the wife of the chief, the wife of the interpreter (otherwise an Indian squaw) and three children, two of them being a boy and girl belonging to the interpreter and the third a son of the chief.[35] On the 29th they went to the theatre to see the rope dancing at which they were exceedingly delighted, though the Mandan endeavoured as much as he could to hide his laughter pulling and pinching his cheeks and chin but all in vain, while the squaws grinned and giggled during the whole of the performance, the interpreter's wife observing to her husband that certainly the dancing girls who twisted themselves into a thousand contortions must have had their bones taken out of them when they were children. When any feat very marvellous indeed was exhibited she made use of an exclamation which her husband translated as meaning "that is great effect of medicine." She supposed a spirit must be in the dancers, good or bad, to enable them to tumble about so actively.

As an interlude to the performance the savages were prevailed upon to dance. The five Osages and the Mandan chief and a Delaware Indian all squatted in a row, an arm chair having first been provided for the chief, which was said to be meant as a royal distinction towards him in order to qualify the making him exhibit before the public. Three in the centre then beat upon a drum, raising the sound by degrees until the Osage war-chief rose up and appeared to be sent forward as a scout and ran back again pretending to have discovered an enemy. Then the three leaped about like frogs in a sitting posture as if to conceal themselves as they moved behind bushes. They retired after stamping about a while when four came forward with tomahawks and swords hacking the air as if fighting in close

[35]The Mandan nation are of North Dakota. Shahaka, or the Big White, Mandan chief, refused to accompany Lewis to Washington unless his family might go along. With him went René Jessaume, the interpreter, and his family. R. G. Thwaites, ed., *Original Journals of the Lewis and Clark Expedition* (New York, 1904-1905), V, 343-45. For a portrait of Shahaka, see Kinard, ed., "Foster and 'The Wild Natives,'" opp. p. 200, plates 13 and 14.

battle. When they ran in, the war whoop, or rather a frightful yell, was uttered by all. The drum still beating, the war whoop was repeated and renewed at intervals during their manoeuvres, and I distinctly caught the same sounds uttered by them at the end of the entertainment as the Osages made on entering Washington last year and passing by the President's House. It is therefore I presume their song of joy and triumph.

They afterwards sent to know of Captain Lewis if they should dance the Calumet dance which was agreed to and the same drum continued beating when two pipes were introduced, ornamented with tassels hanging down from them made of porcupine quills. The Osage chief came forward with one and proclaiming his battles and victories in several places, ejaculated with vehemence that he was now about to smoke the pipe of peace, and retired, when the hereditary chief and another appeared naked except about the loins on which they wore a short kind of breeches and a girdle. They faced the drum and began stamping about and crossing their pipes and then squatted opposite the drummers and smoked to them. The squaws remained in the boxes each with her child in her arms.

I asked Captain Lewis if he believed that there existed cannibals among the Indians when he assured me that to his knowledge, as far as it went, there were none, that among the Indians the most unconnected with Europeans—and he was informed of it by one who lived beyond the Rocky Mountains—it was held wrong to eat of the white bear's flesh from the circumstance of that animal being known to be fond of the flesh of man. He believed that from motives of revenge such as on the event of a father being slain in battle a son would make a vow to eat of the flesh of those who killed his father but that the accomplishment of such a vow consisted merely in the roasting some part of one of their enemies and in passing the teeth through it, perhaps eating a morsel. This custom prevails among the Sawkees, Potowatemies, etc.

Among the Mandans when a man wishes to marry he leads three or four horses to the hut of the father of the lady whom he admires and ties them to the wall. If the father takes them away then the match is considered as agreed to and the young man comes to take his wife. If she has sisters, as they grow up they all become his wives as a sort of natural consequence. The chief now in Washington is a singular exception to a general custom in having but one wife. The situation of cook ranks high among the Indians. He is water-carrier to the whole camp as well as preparer of food and he executes the decrees of the council against individual offenders. The Mandans have a kind of palisadoes about their towns and it seems an understood thing among their neighbours that they are never to attempt forcing such fortifications although they should be at war with them.

It is necessary for every individual of the tribe to attach himself to some chief or party if he wish to be able to revenge affronts and injuries. When a man is murdered the friends and relations of the deceased are even encouraged by the chief to take revenge, which is summary unless the party interested be bought off.

The bows of these Indians are made of yellow wood of a very close grain; they sometimes make them of hickory, the locust and even the cedar but these they generally line with the sinews of the buffalo on the outside, fastened on by a glue extracted from elks' horns. Their arrow is made of the willow, the feathers serve as the guide to it and it goes equally true with or without a head. They shoot at squirrels and birds without heads to their arrows; but they use flint or stone when they cannot get iron for larger beasts. Thirty paces is their common shooting distance but they can aim true at forty-five. They have a smaller bow made of elk's horn. When they kill a buffalo they cut off the hump as the most delicious part and Captain Lewis thought the tongue superior to that of any other animal. The American buffaloes will intermix with cows which the Italian buffalo is said not to do.

I have now to describe another set of savages who also arrived at Washington while I was there and who were perhaps the most interesting of all, coming as they did from the Mississippi and the

Missouri.[36] They had been long expected and at length entered the city on the 22nd December, 1805. As they passed by Mr. Merry's door, I had an opportunity of seeing them in their procession and accompanied them to their lodgings. They all rode on miserable little horses with saddles and bridles like our own. The interpreters and Americans who came with them went first, and the Orator went before the rest. He was in a great coat but his left eye was surrounded by a circle of green and white paint and the rest of his face was red. He carried a tomahawk which was extremely well made, serving at the same time as a pipe, otherwise in shape like a common hatchet. It came from the Northwest Company. Next followed two, naked to the waist and painted reddish yellow, their hair shaved as far as the crown where it was ornamented with feathers and formed into a tail behind inclosed in silver. They wore blankets about their middles and mocassins and pantaloons of deer's skin. They carried instruments in their hands made of hollow gourds with something to rattle in them, singing or rather bawling all the while as loud as they could. Their ears were pierced in two places which were much widened by the weight of the ear-rings suspended from them. Others of the savages wore quantities of feathers hanging from their hair behind and the rattles of the rattle-snake at the end of some of them. There was one very handsome young man with black hair and on his forehead was a broad streak of light green paint, highly rouged cheeks and green ears.[37] He could not have been more than sixteen or seventeen years old and wore a crest of red feathers on his head. When arrived at the house prepared for them he sat down on a chair and smoked his

[36]The Osages. Lewis and Clark persuaded their chiefs to send a deputation to Washington (Janson, p. 230). Janson states that they arrived in October 1805, but his date is probably too early. The report of their presence in Washington appears in the *National Intelligencer* of December 27, 1805, and of their visit to Congress in the issue of December 30.

[37]On December 27, 1805, Foster wrote (*Two Duchesses*, pp. 257ff.) to his mother that he had "formed an acquaintance with a young man of the Sac nation who is very good looking, about 17, and who is the son to a very principal chief of that country." He described to her also the sitting for the portrait (see below), and observed that the youth's name, Wa-Pawni-ha, meant White Hare.

hatchet-pipe with great apparent indifference and the paint really looked well upon him.

There were in all twenty-one of which from the Osages there came five; the others were Panis, Sacs, Sioux, Missouris and Mississippis.[38] The Panis are from 500 leagues beyond St. Louis, which is 1,200 miles from hence. These 1,200 miles they performed in sixty days of which eighteen were days of rest. All except the Panis use the musket though they employ the bow for wild animals. In general they are tall stout men, and in physiognomy something like Germans; their hair is not of a very dark colour when not painted. The Indians were put in a house opposite to where the Cherokees lodged, and those, who are dressed like Europeans and are really half civilized, were very much pleased at the arrival of the Louisianians, one of them observing to Colonel Hawkins that he now more than ever felt the obligation he and his nation owed to the United States for the favour done them. The Cherokees are at war with the Osages, and one of them observed that he now viewed them with very different sensations from those he felt on seeing them a few months since.

I had a conversation with Melli Melli, the Tunisian Ambassador, on the subject of these Indians and he argued that they must have originally come across the sea from Yemen, Arabia, and that they cannot be a native American race; for, he observed, Shem, Ham and Japhet were the only great fathers of all generations and they each of them had a portion of the world to people, and if one of the three had come here there would be millions of inhabitants in the country as there were in Africa, Asia and Europe. But this was not the case. They were thinly scattered over the land and therefore they could only be descendants of people who some few hundred years ago might have

[38]After the Louisiana Purchase, the Pawnees lived near St. Louis. The Sacs, or Sauks, were one of the Algonquin tribes in Michigan. There were many types of Sioux; here Foster probably refers to the Dakotas. The Missouris were a tribe of one group of the Siouan family, and the Mississippis may have been the Missisaugas, an Algonquin tribe, subtribe of the Chippewas who lived on the north shore of Lake Huron.

emigrated from Asia, the nearest part of which he conceived to be Yemen. He had had a conference with both Cherokees and Louisianians and had asked them several questions. Among the rest he inquired of the Cherokees which prophet they believed in—Moses, Jesus Christ or Mahomed—and they answered, neither. On which he observed that this was singular as he had never known a man not a follower of one of the three before. Then he asked what they worshipped. "The Great Spirit," they replied. "But who is your interpreter with him?" he anxiously rejoined. "No one, we manage that business ourselves," was the answer. He puzzled them, however, by asking what the Great Spirit was and he evidently seemed to pity their ignorance.

The Indians from Louisiana wear no eyebrows tho' they preserve their eyelashes, nor do they wear hair except on the crown of their heads which forms the scalp and in a line down from it behind which they bind in a metal case and ornament it with feathers. Colonel Hawkins said that the greatest humiliation for them would be for this hair to be cut off. The Cherokees however who are here wear eyebrows and even let their beards grow a little and dress very much like us except that they are fond of a good deal of ornament. Double-Head their chief wears powder and has a laced coat and a sword by his side. He is called Double-Head by his countrymen from his being supposed to have as much sense as two, in their opinion. He has been since killed, I heard, in a duel fought on horseback.[39] When I went for the first time among the Louisianians two of the Osages were in the room engaged in a game played with reeds; one put five together and the other took up four and making a short address to each placed them in opposite directions. They seemed much interested, and I am told that some of them play at cards, having been taught by the Canadians. Others took tobacco which they

[39] Apparently Double-Head was slain by another chief by order of his own tribe for signing a secret treaty with the whites on October 25, 1825, at Tellico, Tennessee, and thus gaining certain secret privileges and rewards. R. G. Thwaites, ed., *Early Western Travels 1748-1846* (Cleveland, 1904-1907), XI, 247; XIII, 181-82; James Mooney, "Myths of the Cherokees," *Nineteenth Ann. Rep., 1897-1898,* Pt. I, *Bur. Am. Ethnology*, pp. 75-76, 85, 384.

mixed with some pounded bark of a tree and smoked out of their tomahawks.

The Sacs being at war with the Osages dined in a separate room and I found one of them making his toilette. He laid on the red powder with a small lath on his cheek and nose, taking care not to colour the end of his nose which remained yellow and was pierced for a ring. He powdered with his own hands his hair and the case behind, and with the same rouge, keeping all the while the looking-glass before his face. His ears were painted with a verdigris green and his under-lip red. The young Sac had on the following day changed the design of his painting and instead of the whole but the half of his forehead was now left green and he had an undulating stream of verdigris down the left cheek with a cross on the right. He caught hold of my gloves and said, "buckskin gloves," on which I tried them on him and finding them fit I made signs that he would oblige me by keeping them which he did and bowed to me. I saw him on the 25th December again in church, and tapping him on the shoulder shook hands with him and he seemed very glad to see me. He had the gloves on. He listened to the music with great attention and bent forward to look at the choir. They all sat however when everybody else rose and several went away apparently very tired. I saw no expression of surprise on their countenances at anything, but one of the party had evidently a considerable struggle with himself to suppress a smile.

They wear shoes of skin so closely fitted that they appear to walk barefooted and they turn their toes inwards, as it is said, in order to take up less room, in the narrow pathways of their woods. Their teeth are short as if they had been ground down; their hands and feet very small; the forehead and occiput in general broad, the colour of the skin not so deep as that of an Arabian. The young [Yakai?] Sac chief wore his hair down on the forehead which indicates the age of a youth as at sixteen. They train the ears, the sign of manhood piercing them in two places, and at eighteen or nineteen they shave to the crown, the mark of reception among the warriors.

Wa Pawni Ha the young Sac chief was to have come to me on the 26th December to have his portrait taken by Boudon a Genevesi miniature painter, but he had had some vexation from the older Indians or perhaps, as I afterwards suspected, some difficulties were thrown in his way from jealousy of me on the part of the Americans who thought I must have some political views in my paying attention to their savages.[40] He cried a good deal and was vexed he could not visit me. To-day however after some trouble I got him to come in company with a young man of the Chipewa nation who live near Lake Superior and who is here to be educated. This Chipewa could speak French but very little and English not at all; he was dressed however like a Frank and had a high forehead with luxuriant brown hair; he is but seventeen years old. Wa Pawni Ha and he came in a carriage and leaned back with as much ease as if they had been used to it all their lives.

When I called on him in the morning he was not painted but he kept the carriage at least two hours until he had finished his toilette. I left the choice of colours to himself, and he appeared with a green forehead, rouged cheeks and two crosses one on each cheek, with green ears, a great coat and a blue collar, and a loose blanket by way of mantle. When he came in he shook hands with me and sat down in an arm-chair. He seemed very shy and embarrassed at first, but by degrees and by leaving him alone he soon became at his ease and smiled and talked a good deal. He drank a glass of Madeira with great pleasure and ate grapes, raisins and cakes, but with most pleasure of the oranges which as well as the European grapes, were quite new to him. Wa Pawni Ha said he had three brothers and one sister, his father was killed in their present war with the Osages and his mother is likewise dead. I showed him a map of the United

[40]Foster apparently refers to Bourdon, a French refugee who flourished about 1810 in Pittsburgh, Pennsylvania. Theodore Bolton, *Early American Portrait Painters in Miniature* (New York, 1921), p. 16. Apparently Bourdon did complete the portrait eventually. Reproductions of a remarkable gallery of St. Memin portraits of Indians once owned by Foster appear in Kinard, ed., "Foster and 'The Wild Natives,'" pp. 200ff.

States and he pointed out his river, which is the Moin,[41] and told me the names of several other rivers marked down on the map, the Metché Sepé, the Missouri and the Arkansas. As the map only gave the United States, and several of the rivers flowing into them were not laid down entirely, he confessed himself at a loss with regard to them. I showed him my terrier dog and a Newfoundland dog, but he expressed no surprize at them, saying that there were dogs like them in his own country. The Chipewa was very much struck when I told him that wine was made of the juice of the grape he was eating. His name is John Riley and he is the son of a Flemish man and an Indian woman. He is come here to learn English and to be educated.

Wa Pawni Ha at last, after sitting for two hours, yawned and I took him upstairs to show him the house. He was surprized at seeing a mocking bird in a cage and always expressed his surprize by a laugh in which he particularly indulged himself on seeing a little hand organ that he had listened to for a time with great attention [on seeing the lid]* opened and the work moving within it. He appeared less embarrassed when Mrs. Merry was gone and he was alone with Riley and me. I took him then to my room and gave him a military plume. A view I had of Lago Maggiore he was very much pleased with and pointed to a vessel on the lake with delight, and cried out "Wig Wam" when he saw the drawing of a church. But at the caricatures he laughed immoderately, observing that John Bull had very short legs,[42] and Lord Salisbury's figure in that of "The King and Gulliver"[43] tickled both their fancies excessively. They both at once seized the joke. I had a book of caricatures made of cards and the noses

*Marked out in LC version of the "Notes."

[41]Or Des Moines, in modern Iowa.

[42]Satirical prints were a regular institution in England by the time of George III. There were a number of popular John Bull caricatures, such as "John Bull taking a Luncheon," "John Bull Transformed," "John Bull in Bonnet Rouge." Thomas Wright, *Caricature History of the Georges* (London, [1868]), passim.

[43]A reference to a caricature by James Gillray, "The King of Brobdingnag and Gulliver," which appeared on February 10, 1804. It depicts Bonaparte, princesses, the Queen, George III, and Lord Salisbury. Lord Salisbury has straight shapeless legs, a characteristic of Gillray's work. Wright, *Caricature History*, p. 596.

composed with the corners of the diamonds amused them greatly.

Wa Pawni Ha expressed no surprize at my gun nor did he ask a single question about anything from the time he entered the house, which perhaps is a greater proof of the effect of artificial education than could be met with in the most polished country in Europe. I showed him my uniform and sword which he appeared pleased to handle and I asked him for a lock of his hair which he allowed me to cut which is nearly as fine as mine. I made a mistake which amused him very much. The Chipewa told me that *Nioush* was the Sac word for "ma femme," and I thinking that he said only "femme" frequently pointed out the ugly figures of women in the caricatures calling them *Nioush* which diverted him a good deal.[44] His hands were singularly formed for I had on a pair of extremely tight gloves which I took off to try on him; the palms were too wide for him, tho' too tight for me and yet at the knuckles they were so tight for him that he could not get his fingers into the glove.

On the 31st December, 1805, Wa Pawni Ha came to me again and he and a companion whom he brought with him ate of oranges and raisins in great quantity and were particularly delighted with the former. Mashenac (the name of his companion) put up the seeds very carefully with the intention of sowing them in the ground when he goes home. His taste was fine enough to discriminate egg in the composition of a soft biscuit that I gave him to eat. Mashenac had very long hair as well as Wa Pawni Ha and it was even finer and more curling—indeed he made a very good crop. The walnut and Mississippi nut they immediately recognized. The latter they call *Cassibocano*.[45] It is of a long oval form and not so hard as the hard hickory nut.

On the 30th some of the Indians who were ever ready to be persuaded that it was an honour for them to appear on the stage of the miserable little rope-dancing theatre, the only one there

[44]The Sac Indian word for "my wife" is ned-ōs′, and perhaps in earlier times was ne'ōs′. The editor is indebted to Dr. John P. Harrington of the Bureau of American Ethnology for this information.

[45]Cassibocano, cassibogano, or Mississippi nut certainly means the pecan.

is in Washington, exhibited a dance of their own and music and fireworks were provided for them.[46] I could not go as Melli Melli the Tunisian Ambassador dined at Mr. Merry's and I had to sit next to him being the only one that could speak Italian of the company present. There was a party too in the evening. I understood, however, the subject of the Indian dance to be this: a chief begins an harangue, asks his friends, "Have I not killed so many of such a nation and scalped so many of another?" The others agree by acclamation and then in a mass they dance together in the grotesque style, leaping and jumping about. The haranguer, on this occasion, it seems, exerted himself too much. He burst a blood vessel, which helped, as I understood, by a good dose of strong liquor, brought on an apoplectic fit of which he died in the night.[47]

I called on Melli Melli in the morning and went with him in his carriage to the Indians' house where we found the Secretary of War, General Dearborn.[48] He had come to express his sorrow at the event and to hope that there would arise no injury from it to the friendship subsisting between the two nations. Three or four of the chiefs there made short discourses, each in his turn and the purport, as appeared from the interpreter's explanation, seemed to be the same of all, that God was God, it was His work and it belonged to Him to name the day of every man, when he should go, that they were not, on account of having lost one of their brothers, prejudiced against their Fathers (as they call the Americans) but that they came to hear their counsels and expected to be consoled by them and hoped they would not think the worse of them for weeping. The Secretary

[46]The *National Intelligencer* of December 27, 1805, announced in a theater advertisement that a party of savages of the Missouri nation would present a "Grand Indian Dance" as an additional feature (to concert and fireworks). Janson is more cynical than Foster regarding their motives in providing entertainment. He states that "they stipulated with the managers to be paid half the net proceeds, with a supply of rum during the entertainment." *Stranger in America*, pp. 234-35, 244n.

[47]Janson (p. 235) simply says, "... his death was imputed to excess of drinking, and his great exercise during the preceding evening."

[48]Henry Dearborn (1751-1829), a native of New Hampshire, served through eight years in Jefferson's cabinet.

told them in reply, that he thought it did them credit that they did feel and were (as he called it) solemnized on the occasion. It was an Osage chief who died and one of the most considerable in his nation. The chiefs who spoke used a great deal of action and emphasis and pointed frequently to the heavens. The body was put into a wooden coffin and carried in a hackney carriage to the city burying ground, all the Indians following in procession. There were then three volleys fired over the grave by a dozen of the marines, the Indians attending with great gravity but without uttering a word.

While we were at their lodgings Melli Melli frequently observed to his secretary that the language must be Tartarian and that they looked like Tartars. The Choctaws, Colonel Hawkins said, hang their dead in the air, keeping off the birds until the bodies become dried, when they pick off the flesh and store the bones in a common charnel house. The Creeks bury theirs under their houses, each man directly beneath the very mat on which he slept. He told me a horrid story of a Seminole man and woman who after doing every thing to preserve their child during an illness that it had, on its dying gave it a grave from pure affection in their own stomachs, eating the flesh between them and carrying the bones home, for it was at a distance from their habitation that its death took place.

Wa Pawni Ha has got dark hazel eyes, short blunt teeth, the upper lip a little pressed upwards, straight nose and very fat cheeks. It was now near four years he said since he began to hunt with the men, being then about twelve years old. The Osages are divided into two tribes, the great and the little Osages; they are very friendly to one another and make common cause, tho' living in different villages, and when the little Osages happen to have a child among them that promises to be tall, they occasionally swap it for one, if there be one among the great Osages, that appears dwarfish.

All the nations which the Indians who came as deputies to Washington in 1805 belong to, are said to be anthropophagi; tho' not sufficiently so I believe to be called cannibals. Mr.

Barron[49] told me that he had been present at the tormenting of prisoners among the Sacs, that they were burnt with cedar wood, their fingers having been first smoked, that is each finger having been placed in the bowl of a pipe full of burning tobacco and smoked until it cracked, at the same time that red hot irons with sharp points were driven thro' different parts of the body, particularly the most sensitive to pain. When a man has lost his son in battle or a son his father, the father or the son makes a vow that he will be revenged by eating of the enemies who have killed him. Accordingly after the first battle a prisoner is reserved for the table, cut in pieces and cooked up for those who have to satiate their revenge. If any of these be too young to have followed the army, men's meat, as it is called, is brought home, dried, and given to the child. This I am sorry to say was the case with my friend Wa Pawni Ha whose father was killed by the Osages and who was obliged by the customs of his tribe to partake of this species of revenge, tho' he assured me he had only put a bit in his mouth and not swallowed it. The said species of revenge, however, is not unknown even to Christians; at Naples, during the [series?] of [revolutions?] men and even women having been seen eating of the hearts and drinking the blood of their fellow creatures from the mere impulse of hatred and revenge.[50]

A party of Chickasaws arrived on the 12th January, 1806, some of whom were from the territory bordering on the possessions of the Spaniards.[51] They had travelled most of them barefooted, and when I went to see them were furnishing themselves with shoes. Their feet were remarkable from the extreme thickness of the instep which rises almost immediately from the toes. Many of them wore cocked hats and one had on the Spanish uniform, green, faced with white. They had very much the appearance

[49]This was probably Joseph Barron, interpreter for Governor William Henry Harrison at Vincennes, Indiana, 1809-1810, and later at Detroit.

[50]Foster could be referring to the Sicilian-Neapolitan revolutions of the 17th century, or the French-Royalist-Republican revolutions between 1799 and 1820.

[51]Very likely a part of the group Foster refers to above on this date as "Cherokees," a delegation probably including representatives of several tribes.

of gypsies, exactly their colour and their lank black hair. One boy in particular had very black eyes. One of them held in his hands a bow which he had taken from an individual of a nation that lived he said at an immense distance called, as I understood, the Shawnie. . . .*[52] I was very near seeing a treaty struck up on the spot among these savages, for the two Osage chiefs had been introduced to and sat down among them, when the Chickasaw chiefs who till then knew nothing of the nation of the Osages took the opportunity of explaining by sign (there being no interpreter) that they wished to eat together with them, shook their hands and asked for Calumets or the pipe of peace. Unfortunately however the head chief was out walking, and the treaty was put off till his return.

Last year one of the Osages, then in Washington for the first time, was taken to see the frigates and gun boats in the Eastern Branch, where the Captain of the Port made every show he could in order to astound him, but all in vain. He was even taken to the gun boat in which the cannon is discharged by pulling a string and without letting him know what was to happen, the string was put into his hand and he was told to pull it. He did so and altho' the sudden sound, one might have supposed, would have startled him, he did not move a muscle. Had these savages arrived a few weeks sooner, the same experiment that was tried by King Pyrrhus upon Fabricius might have been repeated upon them for there was an elephant in George Town.[53] There cannot be a doubt, however, after what has been stated, that they would have stood this proof, and it may at once be admitted that savage nature has in this respect a superiority over that of civilized man. Fabricius' intrepidity was held to be almost a miracle at Rome,

*Here follows a statement concerning his buying of the bow for "one dollar," the same details he gave above.

[52]Presumably the Shawnee, who were originally in South Carolina, Tennessee, Pennsylvania, and Ohio. They were still living at no great distance in Foster's time, though some of them were in Missouri.

[53]Pyrrhus, King of Epirus, tried to bribe the Roman general, Gaius Luscinus Fabricius, when the latter was sent to treat concerning prisoners. Finally Pyrrhus tried intimidation, drawing aside a curtain and confronting Fabricius with a huge elephant, which began to roar. The Roman merely smiled.

and as such has been handed down to us—but what wonder [or honor?] does an Indian keeping his countenance during the thunder of artillery, heard by him for the first time, excite among his countrymen when every man of them could be a Fabricius?

The principal part of the Indians were taken on a tour to Philadelphia in order that they might be properly impressed with a conviction of the power and population of the United States. But Wa Pawni Ha and his two companions of the Sakai race were left behind and they came to make me a visit in a hackney coach, desiring to see the gentleman who had had the picture done. We shook hands and Wa Pawni Ha seemed really glad to see me again as I had not been to his quarters for some time for fear of the jealousy of the government being thereby augmented. His paint was now all off, as he had been in bad health, and he was of a complete olive colour. His earrings were also off, and he wore a round hat with the feather in it that I had given him and which he had kept very clean. After they had eaten a few cakes of which they seemed to be very fond, I took them upstairs to my room and made the young chief sit down with a pencil in his hand and after some little time he drew two uncouth figures one of which he said represented a Sakai chieftain and the other an Osage, the former with a sword in his hand, and the other on his knees. Aw Paoussa and Chaaskahac were the names of the other two. Aw Paoussa's teeth were ground as if by a file but otherwise they seemed good tho' very dirty; yet these Indians could pass a couple of hours at their toilette having their hair cut and pulled on the crown and forepart, and painting their cheeks differently every time they dressed.

The whole of them left Washington in April 1806, in five stage coaches. They were to be carried in them as far as Pittsburgh, and thence to proceed by water. Six of the number who originally set out to come to the city died, of whom the Ricara or Big-bellied Indian was one. He died at Washington and some days before his death declared that he expected his fate, that he should have wished to expire among his friends at home, but it could not be helped and he requested his pipe and tomahawk might be buried with him. He had been interpreter at a congress from thirteen different tribes on the Missouri and he explained himself by signs, which mode of communication he is said to have carried to great perfection. He could draw a map of his country and expressed a lake called the Buffalo Lake by drawing the head of a buffalo in the centre of it. His tribe is the only one of those who visited Washington the present year that live upon beef, to which of course is to be attributed their superior fatness as it is notorious that no animals which live only upon game or fish ever become fat.

The Osage chief would never sit when he saw a lady without a chair. They were particularly observant not to commit the slightest impropriety and their manners were perhaps more gentlemanlike than those of the greater part of their civilized superiors, for the very natural reason, they were anxious not to offend. At table, tho' unused to knives and forks and other articles of luxury, they could never be detected in handling them improperly, always waiting to see what their American neighbours did with each instrument before they would put out their hands to take one like it. At the theatre when there was a performance on the tight rope I have kept my eyes on five of them with a squaw during the whole time it lasted and seen them make the most violent efforts to contain their laughter pinching their cheeks and pulling down their muscles, till at length nature got the better and they burst out on seeing the part of a drunken man played by a droll Italian who kept spilling his brandy as he danced, on the head of a boy. The squaw who sat by her husband with whom she talked in a whisper had been the first to give way. She had pretty features, a pale yellowish hue, bunches of ear-rings and her hair divided in the middle, a red line running right across from the back part to the forehead–tho' no paint was on the face.[54]

I have now done with the Indians, one of the groups of people

[54]Foster apparently refers back to one of the Mandan squaws, known for their lightness of complexion and beauty of feature. The portrait of a "Mandan Queen" owned by Foster appears in Kinard, ed., "Foster and 'The Wild Natives,'" plates 11 and 12, after p. 200.

occasionally to be met with in the Federal City, and I have been more inclined to dwell upon their visit because they perhaps are the last solemn deputation from the unfortunate aborigines of the country which may be ever seen there, owing to the rapid diminution of their numbers and the change in the disposition of the American government towards them.

When Jefferson retired, his paternal fondness for the wild natives of the woods and the affectionate regard felt for him by his friend and immediate successor, Madison, still held a shield of protection over the Indians, but their interests and their feelings have ever since been becoming less and less an object of respect and they had lately to do with a President, Mr. Jackson, not only unfavourable but as it is said even hostile towards them. They appear to be as a nightmare upon the cupidity of land-jobbers and some of the state governments actually tyrannise over the poor creatures and buy or suffer their lands to be bought for whiskey, when they unfeelingly provoke a quarrel or force them out of their forests and gradually push them beyond the Mississippi, alleging that it is great waste to let so much land as their hunting requires lie fallow. South Carolina and Georgia have, I fear, much to reproach themselves with on this score and I have been assured, tho' I hardly believe it, that where land has been bought by individuals on condition of entering on possession only after the death of the parties selling, agents have been base enough to hasten the period by the temptation of strong liquors. Yet is this wild and noble-minded race less thought of and less pitied by the philanthropists of Europe than the Negro whose lot it is found so difficult to improve in consequence of his own national defects and whose obstinate propensity to sell his countrymen at home, with his too often vindictive and treacherous disposition abroad, might render him a much less interesting object. But the poor Indian whose pride forbids him to complain is left to the mercy of backwoodsmen and the base underhand tricks of unfeeling speculation.

It was not so formerly, and Mr. Madison related to me that he was present at the peace made with the Five Nations when

Lafayette took with him to Paris a young Indian boy whom he had instructed in dancing, fencing and everything that was thought necessary to form what was called a gentleman's education.[55] The boy profited wonderfully and became perfectly fashionable in every sense of the word. He stayed some years at Paris and then sailed for New York where he distinguished himself as a complete petit maître. However at last he set out for his own nation and Mr. Madison who had seen him in his emerging from the savage state, as well as in his zenith of fashion in New York, having been curious enough to enquire into his further history was informed that a fortnight after his return to his tribe he had cast off his whole French wardrobe and its appurtenances and resumed his former habits, becoming to all appearance an Indian hunter that had never stirred out of his native forest.

While still on this topic I must in justice to one part of the Union mention that whatever reproaches may be made to other state governments in regard to their treatment of the Indians, the state of Connecticut scarcely deserves to be included in it, there being still, notwithstanding the highly cultivated and civilized condition of that district, or at least there having been till very lately, altho' one of the oldest-settled parts of the continent, two remnants of tribes in existence within its boundaries.[56] It is true they were in a miserable state and one in particular had been reduced to nine males and a female, but they were attended to and had guardians to look after their interests and prevent any unfair advantage being taken of them. The ten resided at Chustown[57] near New-haven which is inhabited and surrounded by as charitable and humane as well as religious a population as can be

[55]Lafayette and Madison attended a treaty at Fort Schuyler, New York, in 1784. Here Lafayette met Peter Otsiquette (Ouekchekaeta), an Oneida half-breed, who later went to France and lived with Lafayette for three years, astonishing everyone with his knowledge of French, English, and music. After his return to America, however, he "reverted to barbarism, became a hard drinker, and died within a few years." Louis Gottschalk, *Lafayette between the American and the French Revolution* (Chicago, 1950), pp. 102, 405, 433-34.

[56]These were perhaps the Pequots and Mohegans. Actually, 4 groups survived as late as 1850, and these were really amalgamations from many former tribes.

[57]A section of the present town of Seymour, Connecticut, was once known as Chusetown after Chuce or Chuse, last sachem of the Derby Indians.

found and who would have done anything to give the savages habits of industry. The men all decamped however one morning leaving the woman sole heiress to their lands and the only reason that they assigned for marching off was their inability to bear any longer the eternal noise of some saw-mill which had recently been erected in their immediate neighbourhood. The land lay uncultivated and the woman lived by net-making at which she worked two days in the week, rambling about the other five, true Indianlike as they always were and ever will be, as was observed by one of the millers who had seen but too clearly that the unfortunate natives were discouraged and oppressed at the sight of their own deficiencies instead of being excited to exertion by the example of the Americans.

Had the Pelasgi, Picts and Scots or other aborigines of Europe been cast in the same mould what an insuperable bar there would have been to the refinement of mankind unless indeed we are to suppose that they, as well as the Lethragons[58] and Cyclops, were once as the Indians now are and were exterminated by the Asiatics or Egyptians as these are likely to be by the Europeans. But we excuse in the early history of mankind what we are less ready to forgive in its present state, and certainly it is to be lamented that no steady plan of introducing by degrees some sort of civilization among the natives by means of early education has as yet been adopted. It is beginning at the wrong end to take full grown men from the woods and push them forward into the broad blaze of civilization. It is like presenting the sun to one recovered from blindness. But the young might be schooled and the old be persuaded to allow of it, and by degrees cultivation of roots at least or the care of the cattle as in the Creeks' country might be introduced among them.

Such charity and humanity would not suit however the purposes of land-jobbers and these are not a mere fraction of society in the United States but nearly a whole race. Had Lafayette acted with judgment he would have got his countrymen to

[58]The Lethragons, or Laestrygones, a mythical race of giants and cannibals visited by Odysseus.

establish a school for young Indians at Paris and followed up the plan systematically, when perhaps by this time a nation might have been raising their hands in gratitude for his care. But he who never was good for anything but destroying did not know how to use his influence the right way or the single experiment he made was too discouraging to be repeated.

The Tunisian Ambassador whom I have mentioned as having shown so much curiosity about the Indians was Sidi Suleyman Melli Melli. He came to the Federal City in the autumn of the year 1805 having been sent by the Bey of Tunis partly, as I have heard, to ascertain what sort of country America was, if really such a nation as the United States existed, and to claim of them, if they did, indemnization for the capture of the Tunisian vessels that had been taken by American cruisers for attempting to violate the blockade of the port of Tripoli, with which state the Federal Government was then at war.[59] He was a man of high rank, above fifty years old and had been twice employed on a diplomatic mission to Naples. He wore a vest embroidered in gold and a white turban with a red skull cap.

Diplomats and Democrats

He came in the *Congress* frigate and brought two horses out for the President, one a beautiful black, and also a bay mare for Mr. Madison as well as some other articles for presents, which were all received but directed to be sold for the state, as the Constitution forbids men in office from accepting presents. During his stay on board the frigate, the officers amused themselves with imposing on his credulity, telling him strange stories of floating islands, of trees of monstrous size overshadowing the waters, of krakens and sea serpents and flying fish, and they assured me that he believed every tale except that of the fish which he said he could not credit. Anything else he thought

[59]A detailed and hostile description of this gentleman and a revelation of his "real" reasons for coming to America appears in Janson, *Stranger in America*, pp. 225ff. Janson gives his full name as Sadi Suliman Mala Manni. According to Janson (p. 244n) the Tunisian arrived on November 30, 1805, with 2 black domestics and 2 Turkish secretaries.

possible, but that fish should fly about like birds was more than he could swallow. He was however no fool though he may have played the part of one sometimes, and when the Government ordered everything to be provided for him at the inn, he requested they would rather let him have the amount assigned for the purpose, to provide himself what he wanted, on pretext that he was not served in the true Turkish style. The Treasury having assented to this, his secretary received the money in bank notes. But Melli Melli again made a request, that as he had never been used to paper money it might be given him in gold. On this being done, it was discovered that he regularly sent the gold to be exchanged at Baltimore where it was bought at a premium from its great demand for exportation, this being a time when eagles as well as guineas (paper money serving well enough for home purposes) still continued to be sold as merchandise, to supply the want of gold in France and other countries where the precious metals alone inspired confidence as mediums of exchange.

He also succeeded in the object of his mission, for tho' the United States denied the claim made upon them and maintained the vessels to be lawful prizes they could not resist the appeal to their humanity which he put forward in a most lamentable tone of voice, saying that he knew well if he succeeded in his embassy all the praise would be given to Allah, but that if he failed he alone would be blamed and probably his head be cut off. Accordingly the ships were ordered to be released, the officers being I believe indemnified for the loss of their prize money.

I once dined with Melli Melli at the inn where he lived. His cook unfortunately had followed the example of most foreign servants and run away from him, so we had no Turkish or African dishes, but instead of them there was some tolerably good plain cookery. The soup too was of the true Neapolitan genus of excellent maccaroni. It was his last provision of it and he enjoyed it, for not content with two large soup plates full to which I had helped him he sent for the tureen and finished all that remained. He drank no wine but he had some of three different sorts on the table. After dinner he retired for a while to smoke but came back again and was very entertaining, giving us an account of his domestic concerns and of the state of Tunis. He said the pashalic is hereditary and if the Sultan be at war, Tunis must send eight ships to his assistance. In time of peace she sends him presents of horses and ostriches and receives from Constantinople in return vessels or provisions. Melli Melli told me he had married a girl of fifteen and that he had built himself a house in the country in his own village at about six hours' ride from Tunis eight years ago which cost him $130,000. He was a Turk by birth and a soldier by profession, tho' latterly more of a diplomat. The Bey had given him the post of banker for Mecca and Medina as a reward for his services. Melli Melli travelled by land from Washington to Boston whence he sailed for Africa in May 1806.

Being obliged to write in a desultory manner of this city that is like no other in the world, from its consisting of groups of individuals as well as of houses and not possessing a single street or even a single shop, I may as well place here, what I have to say of the diplomatic corps to which Melli Melli belonged. They were but ill off when I first arrived, which was in 1804, about four years from the time when Congress took up its residence, or rather squatted, upon this waste, being put to it to get even ordinary provisions and having to send as far as Baltimore for the commonest articles of luxury. But what was more intolerable was the treatment they received at this raw and rude court which exasperated them in their turn and led to perpetual jarring and quarrelling. For it was far different to what they had a right to expect considering the respectability that had surrounded General Washington and the elder Adams, but particularly the former, whose example considering his known good sense and the great services he had performed might have been expected to serve as a rule to his successors, if not as far as regarded the hoops and full dresses introduced into his drawing rooms, in imitation of the Court of St. James, at least in as far as depended upon gentlemanly bearing and that outward decorum that should be found in the social assemblies of the first magistrate of a great and cultivated nation. Mr. Jefferson too being a Virginian, and, consequently, born an aristocrat, having besides lived in the best society in Paris and long enough to see it give place to a disgusting democracy, might have been expected to have gone rather into the opposite extreme. But excessive vanity and speculative doctrines on imaginary perfection, together with the love of popularity, and paradox, as also of running counter, since he could not run parallel, to Washington, were his weaknesses, and to indulge them, he flattered the low passions of a mere newspaper-taught rabble, and seemed pleased to mortify men of rank and station, foreign or domestic, unless they paid him servile court, or chimed in with his ideas on general philanthropy.

Of the foreigners the most obnoxious to him was the Spanish envoy the Marquis de Casa Yrujo. What gave rise originally to his dislike of this Minister I do not remember, but no sooner had he come down to Washington in the winter of 1805 than he received a letter from the Secretary of State, to say that his absence would be pleasing to the President, that his recall had been asked for at Madrid, and that his arrival was dissatisfactory. The Marquis however refused to go and complained in a circular note to the different missions of the infraction of his diplomatic privileges. He likewise addressed two notes to the Secretary of State, in one declaring that he received no orders but from his own sovereign and in the other reasoning upon the causes which might have led to so singular a communication, one of which was a charge against him of having bribed the editor of the *Commercial Register*,[60] a paper published at Philadelphia, an affair a year and a half old. The Government however took no measure for following up their intimation and the Marquis after a stay of several days, went back to Philadelphia. But soon afterwards Mr. Adams brought a bill into the Senate for enabling the Presidents to send away a foreign minister in case of disrespectful conduct on the part of the latter.

M. de Casa Yrujo's successor was not on any better terms with the Government, which positively declined answering any

[60]The *Political Register*, edited by Major William Jackson (1759-1828).

of his letters.[61] But this was in 1812 when they were thinking of a war with us, and wished to include Spain in it, for the sake of making her compensate any losses they might suffer from Great Britain. On this occasion they were manifestly acting in a discreditable way, a state officer of high rank, civil as well as military, being well known to have been engaged at the time in exciting an insurrection in Amelia Island by way of producing underhand a pretext for his marching into Florida as it were to prevent the disorder from extending to the United States,[62] and this, while every remonstrance made by M. de Onis on the subject was returned unopened. So that I, as British Minister, had to act on the part of Spain, then our ally, and wrote two notes which I got a friendly Member to call for in Congress and which after a considerable delay, being at length printed, made the Government so ashamed of the whole proceeding that they felt obliged to answer me, however irregular my interference when the general was disavowed.[63] I possess a letter of thanks for this service which was sent to me by order of the Spanish Cortes. The British legation were on better terms at Washington than that of Spain altho' in fact, at that skeleton city "Quisque suos patimur manes."[64] The President's popularity was unfortunately connected with his manners as well as with his acts and he and his party seemed sometimes to be on the look-out how best to humble us and run counter to all our received notions of propriety and etiquette.

[61]Señor Valentino de Foronda followed de Yrujo in 1808-1809 and was succeeded in 1810 by the Chevalier Luis de Onís. For Onís' troubles after 1815, see French E. Chadwick, *The Relations of the United States and Spain* (New York, 1909), pp. 121ff. For those of 1812, see Philips C. Brooks, *Diplomacy and the Borderlands: the Adams-Onís Treaty of 1819* (Berkeley, 1939), pp. 20-25, 29, 56.

[62]In 1810 Don Vicente Folch, Governor of West Florida, offered to surrender or surrendered West Florida. Foster refers here to George Mathews (1739-1812), Revolutionary soldier, congressman, and brigadier-general, who led the "insurgents" at Fernandina on Amelia Island and was disavowed by the American government.

[63]For a summary of the American government's replies to Foster, see [Robert Walsh, Jr., ed.,] *American Review*, IV (July 1812), Appendix, pp. 11-12.

[64]Virgil, *Aeneid*, VI, 743. Loeb transl.: "Each of us suffers his own spirit" [*i.e.*, *manes* = attending genius or spirit, precise meaning uncertain].

I have already mentioned how he took care to show his preference of the Indian deputies on New Year's Day by giving us only a bow while with them he entered into a long conversation. I have now to speak of his change in the established rules of politeness or even hospitality as practised all over the globe, on the occasion of a first entertainment given to a foreign envoy to whom even savages would naturally endeavour, on his reception as a stranger, to make his entertainment agreeable. But I conclude Mr. Jefferson and Mr. Madison were too much of the gentleman not to feel ashamed of what they were doing, and consequently did it awkwardly, as people must do who affect bad manners for a particular object. The circumstance I allude to was the sudden alteration in the etiquette heretofore practised by General Washington and Mr. Adams on dinner being announced, which was introduced by Mr. Jefferson. Mr. and Mrs. Merry were so thoroughly unaware of their intention that they had not had time to think of what they should do on the occasion and Mr. Jefferson had not requested anyone present to look to the strangers. So when he took to dinner the lady next him, Mr. Madison followed his example, and the Senators and Members of the House of Representatives walked off with their respective dames, leaving the astonished Merry, who was of the old school, having passed a great part of his life at Madrid, gazing after them, till at last he made common cause with his better half offering her his arm with a formal air, and giving a hint to one of the servants to send for his carriage he took her to table and sat by her, the half ashamed and half awkward President not even attempting an excuse. This same scene was for consistency's sake repeated nearly in the same manner at the house of the Secretary of State.

Ever afterwards Mr. Merry refused their invitations tho' messages were sent to beg he would dine with the President as Mr. Merry, putting aside his quality of British Minister, which he could not well do without, as he thought, sanctioning in some sort their previous treatment of the representative of Great Britain, so long as no apology was offered for the past. So he never met His Excellency any more at table since the President, unlike our social monarchs of the North, keeps his state, neither he nor his wife accepting of invitations.[65] Mr. Dawson,[66] a Virginian Member of Congress was employed in carrying the above messages to Mr. Merry, and notwithstanding the latter had declared that he would reply to any invitation through the Secretary of State, the President was so anxious to blot out a circumstance which did not tell very well that he actually wrote to invite him some weeks afterwards. Mr. Merry, as he said he would, answered thro' Mr. Madison, that however it might grieve him personally that any occurrence should prevent his seeing as much of the President and of the chief officers of the American Government as he could wish, yet he dared not comply with what might compromise the dignity of his situation and be disapproved of by his Government.

Many persons may think, seeing the desire of the President to be on friendly terms, that Mr. Merry should have met him halfway but then it must be observed that no attempt whatever had been made to excuse the incivility already received and had the English Minister accepted another invitation without some sort of understanding on the subject, he might have had to submit to a constant repetition of the same scene, however modified. At any rate, he would have fallen in with the then prevailing humour of the American Government to show contempt of European usages and forms and to gain popularity by trampling upon them and those who favoured their continuance in the United States.

This change of manners too it must be remarked was quite new, the first person upon whom it was tried having been Mr.

[65]Some historians go so far as to say that Jefferson's rudeness to Merry in a great measure hastened and did much to provoke the War of 1812, a statement for which there seems no foundation in fact. Jefferson himself best defends his own action, as necessitated by democratic principle, in a letter of January 23, 1804. "Jefferson to William Short on Mr. and Mrs. Merry," *Am. Hist. Rev.*, XXXIII (July 1928), 832-35. See also William E. Curtis, *The True Thomas Jefferson* (Philadelphia and London, 1901), pp. 201-205, and Adams, History, II, 366-78.

[66]John Dawson (1762-1814), Member of Congress 1797-1814.

Pederson[67] the Danish chargé d'affaires who, on his coming to Washington soon after the transfer of the government into these marshes, to pay his respects to the President on his election, was received by him in his slippers. There was some contradiction likewise between the doctrines and the practice of the new government in respect to forms, for while such perfect nonchalance was affected in the highest quarter all the heads of department claimed the first visit from the foreign minister. Yet in Sir Robert Liston's time[68] the rules observed towards him and Lady Liston consisted in receiving the first visit from every lady except the wives of the President and Vice-President, in her being conducted by the President to his table and sitting by his side, Sir Robert being placed at table next to the lady on the other side of the President. But now while these latter distinctions were to be laid aside the Secretaries of the Navy and Treasury claimed the right of first visit, and in such a desolate spot as Washington there was no choice but to submit unless one was to live quite in solitude especially during the recess.

Another mortification Mr. Merry had to submit to was the suppression of the privilege of a chair in the Senate on the right of the Vice-President, which had hitherto been enjoyed by foreign ministers, the question having been debated in the Senate and carried against him by a large majority. I am inclined to believe the object of these changes was to induce European courts to send out *ambassadors* and men of high rank by treating *envoys* so ill, for they occasionally complained of the position of the diplomatic agents not being sufficiently high in their own countries. Mr. Madison took an opportunity of telling Mr. Merry that an ambassador would be treated with every distinction, but that an envoy could not expect any more favour in society than a private person. They had a particular fancy too to have a peer of the realm sent out to them and were much disappointed when

[67]Peder Pederson, Foster's frequent dinner and traveling companion, actually was consul and acting chargé d'affaires 1803-1805, consul general and chargé d'affaires 1805-1814, minister resident 1815-1830. "Diary."

[68]Sir Robert Liston (1742-1836) was in Washington as Minister Plenipotentiary from 1796 until the Peace of Amiens (March, 1802).

Lord Selkirk and Lord William Bentinck declined the honour.[69]

The above questions of etiquette it is true were but of little real importance. Nevertheless they occupied the thoughts of the Republicans a great deal more than they need have done, and were consequently a source of considerable annoyance at the time to the mission, because some of the most vulgar of the Democratic party took their cue from the style adopted at the Great House. In one way or other, either by remarking on her dress or diamonds or treading on her gown, they wearied Mrs. Merry to such a degree that I have sometimes seen her on coming home burst into tears at having to live at such a place, particularly on seeing the affected impoliteness of those who should have known better, but who, being ratters from the Federal party seeking favour and place, made use of her assemblies in order to render their boorish humours, as well as their concurrence with the systematic manners of Mr. Jefferson, more conspicuous. Among these was one of a stern, sour and Republican countenance who had been used to the best society but who purposely came to the parties in dirty boots, disordered hair and quite the reverse of what he knew to be the fashion in European capitals.

This was certainly difficult for a lady to digest but I must be just and add that I found among the Democrats many highly respectable and worthy persons and even among the lowest in station of the Members of Congress several droll, original but unoffending characters. Such was the tavern keeper who committed an act of great impropriety in my house when I gave a ball for the Queen's birthday.[70] When the drawing rooms being

[69]Thomas Douglas, fifth Earl of Selkirk (1771-1820) had been active in the colonization of Canada. Lord William Cavendish Bentinck (1774-1839) was later governor-general of India.

[70]According to Foster's "Diary," and the "Notes" below, this was William Anderson (1762-1829) of Chester, Pennsylvania, Member of Congress from 1808, a distinguished Revolutionary soldier. The ball for the Queen's birthday, at which this incident occurred, was held on January 20, 1812. No references to the episode have been located in the Washington *National Intelligencer* or the *Universal Gazette*. The third District of Columbia paper, the *Spirit of Seventy-Six*, does not survive in issues for this period.

left empty on the company going to supper, he thought poor fellow that he was alone and unobserved, but two stray Federal Members who were rambling about espied his attitude and the joke was too good to be lost so they had it in all the papers and all over the states in prose and verse ringing the changes on "the Extinction of the British Fire." My poor guest wrote me an humble letter saying he would rather burst another time. I most graciously answered and hoped to have gained his vote for peace by my soothing, but the graceless dog voted all the same for war and proved how hard it is by any good words to sever a party man from the mass of his political friends.

Another original was a Philadelphian butcher[71] who used to frank his linen, there having been once no limit to the privilege, and send it to be washed at home. The weight however as some of the Federalists assured me, was not so tremendous as might be supposed for the post-bag, since he was known to change his shirt only once a week. I visited him at his stall at Philadelphia and insisted on his giving me a feast on his beef, to which he agreed. I, profiting by a general invitation, went to his home on the banks of the Delaware where I really did get a luncheon of as fine beef as I ever tasted and had only one regret which was that my honest host happened to be absent. I found him afterwards again at his stall, shook his hands and thanked him very cordially and I believe he had afterwards the good sense to leave his prejudices, and War-Hawks, and give his vote for peaceable measures. It was told of him that at the President's table, observing a leg of mutton of a miserably lean description he could not help forgetting the legislator for a few moments, expressing the feelings of his profession and exclaiming that at his stall no such leg of mutton should ever have found a place. I also heard that being one day invited with several Members of Congress to dine at the President's, he took his son the young butcher with him, who was a great country lout, and on going up to the President, told him he had heard one of his guests had been taken ill and

[71]Possibly James Sloan (d. Nov. 1811), Member of Congress from New Jersey, 1803-1809. For identification of him as a butcher, see p. 270 below.

could not come and therefore he had brought his son with him who was very anxious to see him and would not be in the way as there was, he knew, a spare plate.

Another eccentric Member from the south, a printer and publisher, wrote as an answer to an invitation from the President, "I won't dine with you because you won't dine with me." Then there was a tavern keeper from the north who when elected sheriff in his own county used to hang criminals himself to save a dollar and make his son drive the cart.[72] Yet was he by no means an ill-meaning or uncivil person, tho' not particularly agreeable. Of Irish Members of Congress there were no less than ten, and their voices, I am sorry to say, were in general against their mother country; but with few exceptions they had not much weight and were almost all from the newly settled states.[73] I asked them to dinner occasionally but was obliged to sort them with a particular set to avoid duels, though twice I was very near having one originate at my table and should but for the assistance of an excellent Virginian, Mr. Brackenbridge, who is since dead.[74] One of the Irish used to ask me for news from *Bounos Eares* and tell me of the *volumnious* reports of the Secretary at War. We were however always on good terms and they had not forgotten how to relish a glass of good wine.

As to the higher Democrats I was on the best terms with many of them and they were in point of fact, and in habits, much more aristocratic than perhaps any of the Federal party. Some indeed had quitted or were about to quit the camp for the reason that they did not and could not approve the vulgarity real or affected of the men in power, and their consequent sympathy with the Jacobin or republican upstarts of France. Of these, one, Mr. Randolph, was particularly distinguished by pride of birth, being

[72]This tavern keeper and the southern printer are unidentified.

[73]These included John Smilie, Matthew Lyon, John Rhea, and Stephen Ormsby, all Irish born. Foster was probably thinking also of men like James Sullivan, Samuel Taggart, Samuel M'Kee, William M'Coy, Alexander M'Kim, and Patrick Magruder, no one of whom was actually born in Ireland.

[74]James Breckinridge (1763-1833), a Member of Congress 1809-1817, was a leader of the Federalist party in Virginia.

a descendant of a respectable old English family, the Blands of Kippax Park, and a native Virginian princess. He was as honourable and gentlemanlike a person as could be and one whose slaves were by all accounts so much attached to him that they would not hear of being made free.

But I must return to the diplomatic corps, of which the Russian legation seemed to be on the best terms with the Americans. For, strange to say, they have always had a leaning of affection to the most absolute of all governments and have been publicly as well as individually assiduous in counting the good graces of the autocrat, notwithstanding any quarrels they may be exposed to have as neighbours and rival claimants on the coasts of the Pacific Ocean. One of their envoys[75] to my certain knowledge presented his letters of credence to the Emperor on his knee, when His Imperial Majesty, who himself told the story to my informant, confounded at the sudden act, most graciously hastened to raise him and to disclaim such signs of adoration.

With regard to the French mission, it was impossible for Bonaparte to show greater indifference for the good opinion of the American people than he did by sending to them as his representative General Turreau, the man who deluged La Vendée with blood, and who wrote to the Convention that he should not leave a bush in that country that was not republican.[76] His looks, tho' with handsome features, were ferocious, and he quite frightened the little Secretary of State with his large mustachios, red complexion and fiery eyes, whenever he had any serious complaint to make to him. His fury, however, was once changed to smiles, for he sometimes loved a joke, when in the midst of a warm dispute, the door was quietly opened, a head thrust in, and Dixon, the barber, announced that he was come to shave and dress the Secretary.

Turreau had been in jail for his cruelties committed under the

[75]Foster again refers here to John Randolph, later American Minister to Russia. In a letter to Josiah Quincy, July 10, 1839, Foster relates the story as from a reliable informant. Quincy, *Life of Josiah Quincy*, p. 463.

[76]Baron Louis-Marie Turreau De Garambourville (1756-1816), lieutenant-general under Napoleon, arrived as Minister November 23, 1804, and was recalled in 1810. Sérurier succeeded him in 1811.

atrocious orders of Robespierre and his colleagues and he only escaped by the assistance of the gaoler's daughter whom he promised to marry, and did marry, in gratitude for the service. It was, however, a sad match for her, and although she followed him to the United States, he took care to tell everybody that he was more anxious for the arrival of the ship that carried his wines. He often beat her and had a private secretary who played on the violincello while she was crying, to prevent her screams from being heard, till at last they became so loud and frequent that Dr. Thornton, the magistrate, attended by a posse comitatus, thought himself called upon to violate the sacredness of diplomatic privilege, and, forcing open the door, obliged this Bluebeard to let out his wife and even to subscribe a paper by which he consented to give her an allowance, which, nevertheless was never paid, though he restored to her what jewels she possessed, and never dared to protest, officially, at least, against so great an infraction of the immunities and rights of a foreign envoy. The poor woman afterwards was reduced to great straits, and even we, of the English legation, were called upon to subscribe to give charitable assistance to the wife of Napoleon's minister. While such were the ungentlemanly novelties introduced by Bonaparte into diplomatic society that Turreau had to send as an excuse, but a little while previously, to Mr. Tayloe, who had invited him to dinner, that he was ordered by his Instructions not to meet the British envoy anywhere, unless it should be at the President's house; and he had just learned that Mr. Tayloe (as I afterwards discovered, for his own amusement) had invited Merry after he had made sure of Turreau.

Turreau was succeeded by Mr. Serrurier,[77] nephew to the general of that name. The Russian minister was Count Pahlen, who left the country however about the period of my arrival.[78]

[77]Louis Barbé Charles Sérurier (1775-1860).

[78]Count Frederick Petrovitch Pahlen (1780-1863) was appointed Minister to the U. S. in 1809 about the same time Jefferson appointed William Short as Minister to Russia. When Short's nomination was rejected, Pahlen was already on his way. A Russian chargé d'affaires arrived in June 1809, and Pahlen was transferred in 1812 to the court of Brazil.

Portugal had a chargé d'affaires, but who resided altogether at Philadelphia. No other European government had any representative in my time.

Travelers and Adventurers

Many foreigners or Americans of distinction occasionally visited Washington during the sessions of Congress and gave an interest to society, which was always in some degree like that of a bathing place, being almost entirely composed of strangers to the spot, scattered about in single houses here and there. Of those whom I became acquainted with, were General Miranda,[79] Moreau,[80] Madame Jerome Bonaparte,[81] Joel Barlow,[82] Count Andreani,[83] General Pinckney,[84] Mr. Fulton,[85] Joe Allen Smith,[86] Mr. Correa,[87] etc., etc.

[79]Francisco Miranda (1754?-1816), the South American "Liberator," reached Washington December 6, 1805, and sailed from New York for Santo Domingo (Jacmel) in February 1806.

[80]Jean Victor Marie Moreau (1763-1813), perhaps the greatest general of the French Republic except Napoleon, had been brought to trial by Napoleon because of his sincere republicanism, condemned, and his sentence commuted to banishment. He was a friend of Foster's mother, Lady Elizabeth Foster, later Duchess of Devonshire.

[81]Elizabeth Patterson Bonaparte (1785-1879), Baltimore belle and heiress, had married Napoleon's younger brother. Her son's legitimacy was finally recognized by Napoleon, but his right to succession was disallowed. Foster often mentioned her in letters to his mother, and the "Diary" shows that he visited her frequently in Washington. He wrote his mother that "she has a good figure."

[82]Joel Barlow (1754-1812), American poet and liberal, was appointed Minister to the Court of St. Cloud from September 1811.

[83]Mentioned in Foster's letters and "Diary" as a fairly frequent dinner companion, Count Andreani "of Milan" told amusing stories.

[84]Charles Cotesworth Pinckney (1746-1825), soldier, statesman, and diplomat, was a Federalist of the conservative states-rights group.

[85]Robert Fulton (1765-1815), during Foster's years in America, was busy demonstrating his steamboat and organizing his steamboat lines.

[86]Joseph Allen Smith was a South Carolinian who had first informed Jefferson from Paris (March 22, 1801, received August) that Napoleon might possibly be willing to dispose of Louisiana to the U.S. Letter in LC, MSS Div.

[87]The Abbé Joseph Corrêa da Serra (1750-1823), distinguished Portuguese botanist and historian, had fled his native country because of his liberal views. After many years in London and Paris, he came to the U.S. in 1812. In 1816 he was appointed Portuguese Minister in this country.

Miranda was a very sunburnt, dark featured man, whose life seemed to have been employed in smuggling or fighting for freedom, or exciting the Spanish Americans to revolt. He had imbibed free sentiments in his youth at Gibraltar and was persecuted by the Inquisition and sent to Cuba, where he was dismissed from an employment he had got in the customs on account of his contraband practices, having been while acting as secretary to the captain general in secret association with Mr. Allwood, a British merchant. It was subsequently discovered by means of the seizure of some correspondence on board a Spanish prize that he had undertaken to revolutionize Mexico of which he was a native, in favour of France, as also that the French Government had given in to his plans although they were at the time in alliance with Spain. He was then proscribed and a price set on his head, when he fled to Paris, where he got employment and became known as a Revolutionary general. But finding the Parisians more revolutionary than suited his purposes he fled away again and went to Russia where he was presented to the Empress Catherine at Kiow at the same time with Beau Dillon.[88] He came to Washington in November 1805 and sailed on a clandestine expedition which he had assurance enough to say was favoured by Mr. Jefferson, for the port of Jacmel in January 1806.

General Moreau, with his family, arrived in Philadelphia from Cadiz in August 1805, and after passing a short time at that city, they established themselves at Morrisville which he got leave from the state government to hold as his own, having bought the property, consisting of a house and about twenty-five acres, of Mr. Siemen[89] for $10,000. He could not however prevail upon the Pennsylvanian legislature to allow of his adding afterwards to his purchase although he wished very much to do so and had applied for the permission. Had he asked for and obtained

[88]Probably Sir John Dillon, bart., who traveled widely in Spain and the Empire, residing for some time in Vienna and receiving a title from the Emperor Joseph II.

[89]Siemen, otherwise unidentified, appears to have been an occasional dinner companion of Foster in Philadelphia. "Diary," Sept. 21, 1811.

naturalization as a citizen, there would of course have been no difficulty.

The General made a visit to Washington in April 1812 and called on both French and English Ministers, as he gave out that he intended to do, but I, as an old acquaintance,[90] had been beforehand with him and visited him at the inn. He called on me afterwards while we were still at wine and sat down with us. He said that the American Government had been very civil to him and granted what he wanted, which was permission during the embargo to get a vessel for his wife who was going to the Baths of Barrège. General Wilkinson[91] the American commander in chief happened to be of our party and immediately got Moreau upon military details of discipline, even before he had time to drink off his first glass of wine. The conversation however soon became more general and he talked of Bonaparte, who he asserted had never been within the shot of a pistol in battle and tho' he allowed him courage of the head, he denied his being possessed of intrepidity. We spoke of Arcole and Lodi. . . .*

When we went up for coffee he took me aside and asked a passport for his aide-de-camp Rapatel[92] who, he told me in confidence, was going into the Russian service, which I granted on consulting about it with Count Pahlen who was still in Philadelphia. I also gave him a passport for Madame Moreau.

General Wilkinson who had been all this while waiting impatiently for an opportunity to put in a word, in his eagerness to profit by the experience of so great a commander, now came bustling up and again began asking questions of Moreau on all sorts of military subjects even the most commonplace, about dis-

*Here follow five pages of comment on Napoleon, French generals, and Moreau's opinion of strategy in the Napoleonic wars. None of it seems especially significant or relevant.

---

[90]In a letter of April(?) 1800(?) from Paris, Foster mentions being presented to Talleyrand when Moreau was present. He speaks of Moreau in several letters. Foster, *Two Duchesses*, passim.

[91]James Wilkinson (1757-1825), governor of Louisiana from 1805.

[92]Colonel Rapatel was with Moreau for many years. *Mémoires du Général Bon Dé Marbot* (Paris, [1891]), III, 275.

cipling and provisioning, etc., etc., but poor Moreau who could stand it no longer begged he would put his queries on paper and he would answer them, and took up his hat and went away. When Bayard a Senator and a very worthy man,[93] tho' ponderous and rather prolix but who could speak for hours with great good sense, railed at Lavater and his science, for he looked hard at the General, he said, but could find nothing remarkable or expressive in his countenance. And it is true that we might have said of Moreau as of Agricola, "Bonum virum facile crederes magnum libenter."[94]

Moreau talked to me aside of the United States and described them as a "Geant sans os ni nerfs," said he did not think they were "assez fous" to go to war with us, tho' he had been positively assured they meant to fight both us and the French.

Madame Moreau was a thorough royalist and an excellent woman, but one of the most incessant talkers I ever met with.[95] The Philadelphians were very angry with her for dancing and playing music as well as cards on a Sunday. She certainly danced to perfection and no doubt did not at once recollect that she was in a country where dancing on the Sabbath is almost looked on as a crime. Neither she nor her husband liked much the manners of the Americans, particularly their boasting qualities, and he told me with some complacency of his answer to a lady, who asked him, if he had ever seen as fine a bridge in France as that over the Schuylkill, "Oui Madame, mais nous les faisons en pierre pour qu'ils durent plus long temps." He told me Talleyrand had said of America that he could not bear it because it was a country where a man would sell his favourite dog, a saying, like many others of Talleyrand's, which was probably composed and put forth as a "mot" for the great world, rather than a well grounded

[93]James A. Bayard (1767-1815), Federalist Senator from Delaware, was an intimate friend of Foster.

[94]Foster's "Diary" states that the quotation is from Tacitus. It appears in Tacitus, *Agricola*, 44, 6. Loeb transl.: "You can easily credit him with goodness, and be glad to think him great."

[95]Born Mlle. Hullot, she was a Creole of Josephine's circle, an ambitious woman who is said to have completely dominated her husband.

reflection and which certainly cannot be applicable to the long settled districts, where people are fond of country sports.

Among the chief grievances of Moreau while he was in America was the passion for questioning him which he had to endure, from almost all his acquaintance. At last however he found a companion free from this defect who was as fond of fishing as he was himself, lived at Morrisville and who could speak no French. A gentleman asked him how he could like to be so constantly in society of a man whom he could not understand and who could not understand him. "For that very reason," Moreau replied, "I like him, and I am happy to have at last found a man who will not bother me with questions."

This anecdote brings to my mind the story of Brooke Watson, who lost his leg in bathing.[96] He was riding in one of the states and had put up his horse and gone into a coffee room to eat his dinner, when he was assailed with questions on all sides. At last just as dinner was served and he had seized his knife and fork, a person who had already been rather troublesome, spying his wooden leg, inquired how he had lost his leg. Brooke out of temper sharply said, "You have asked me, sir, very many questions, and I have answered you as well and as civilly as I could. I am now going to eat and I will answer this one more, if you will give me your word of honour it shall be the last." The gentleman did so. "Then, sir, it was bit off." Brooke Watson having had an encounter with a shark, but he would not give the questioner the satisfaction to know that and left him burning with curiosity and wondering how and where the accident had occurred.

Next to Moreau the most interesting person that visited the United States in my time was Bolivar, who arrived at Washington in the winter of 1811, but of whom I could see very little owing to our being in alliance with Spain and to the circumstance of his being engaged in plans for throwing off the Spanish yoke.[97]

[96]Sir Brook Watson (1735-1807) had his leg taken off by a shark at Havana and this encounter is the subject of one of Copley's most famous paintings. He served under Wolfe and Monckton and in 1796 was Lord Mayor of London.

[97]Simon Bolivar (1783-1830), liberator of the Spanish colonies in America.

There came two others with him from Caracas, Orea and Revenga.[98] But he, tho' not by any means good looking, was the most distinguished in appearance of the three. He had very dark features and was possessed of good natural eloquence. I met him at other people's houses, but could not invite him to mine. His object was to try to obtain some assistance from the United States for the insurgents, knowing how cordially the American Minister hated Spain.

Jerome Bonaparte was at Washington in 1804 or 1805 and had just married, after having been the object of much dispute among some of the young ladies of Baltimore, who seemed determined not to let him escape as a bachelor. The moment he arrived, he had to defend his heart against some very warm attacks. A young lady whom he met on a visit, having invited him to a ball, to be given at a house where he was not acquainted, and moreover with unsophisticated simplicity having proposed to go with him there in his own carriage, he took or was supposed to have taken on the way some slight liberties which afterwards being talked of and exaggerated necessitated an explanation, tho' some ladies would have it that his only fault was in not having proposed. However that may have been, three challenges were sent to him, one of them from an Irish gentleman who insisted on instant satisfaction or an apology. Jerome very sensibly observed that a duel would not settle anything about a lady's reputation, and that he was perfectly ready to affirm he had not meant to offend her. The whole was a mistake, he said, that had arisen from his own corrupt European education and the simplicity of American female manners, alleging that at Paris a young lady who would go alone with a gentleman in his carriage will very rarely complain of the latter's attempting to embrace her, but in America it was otherwise he now saw and he owned the superiority of transatlantic virtue which could admit of such close contact between young people without causing the least alarm.

The above passage which was of greater length for the *Q.*

[98]Telésforo de Orea and José R. Revenga. Foster talked to them at Dr. Thornton's on November 2, 1811. "Diary."

Review[99] has been altered* from its having led to some misapprehension both as to the fact itself related and as to the state of the fashionable world at Baltimore, where it is well known that female education and manners in general were and are most exemplary. We know more indeed of Baltimore than of any other town in the United States, so many Europeans, particularly English, having married Maryland belles who are an ornament to society. The lady in question, it will, I think, be admitted in America as well as here, acted with considerable imprudency as well as indecorum, but such a story is no more to affect the general character of her countrywomen for delicacy and tact than any strange conduct of an individual Englishwoman should be thought characteristic of the rest of the fair sex in this country.

I saw M. Jerome at Washington at a party at Mrs. Smith's, wife of the then Secretary of the Navy, and thought him a well mannered young man.[100] His brother Napoleon did not at all approve of his marrying Miss Patterson, and not content with declaring the act null and void according to the laws of France, endeavoured as much as he could to invalidate it in the United States.[101] For which purpose he wished to induce her to take another husband, no less a person than General Turreau, his Minister Plenipotentiary who used all his eloquence to persuade her, proposing it as an affaire de convenance and urging that it was a shame she should vegetate in such a country, whereas at Paris she would shine in the first circles and he would be created a Baron of the Empire. A condition nevertheless was added, viz., that her son

*Here Foster has marked through a long passage on American parents who go to bed and leave their daughter with her lover, etc. He puts the passage below in place of it.

---

[99]A reference to the selections from Foster's "Notes," edited by J. G. Lockhart and published in the *Quarterly Review*, LXVIII (June 1841), 30ff.

[100]In a letter to his mother of February 15, 1805, Foster stated that he saw Jerome the night before. Robert Smith (1757-1842), Secretary of the Navy and later Secretary of State, was the brother of the more able General Samuel Smith (1752-1839), who married an aunt of Elizabeth Patterson Bonaparte.

[101]Most of the information concerning the Bonapartes Foster received from Madame Jerome herself rather than from society rumor or gossip. "Diary."

should be separated from her. Madame Jerome however as was very generally reported would not hear of his proposals, and no wonder if she rejected them with indignation, both as coming from such a man, whose conduct to his later wife was supposed to have occasioned her death and out of consideration for what she owed to her own character, as well as to the interests of her child. The most singular part of Napoleon's conduct in this affair was his apparent disposition, while he was annulling the marriage of his brother with an American lady, to take advantage of his own family connection by blood with her son; for soon afterwards, tho' this humour lasted but for a short period, an officer of the rank of colonel, a M. Toussard was appointed guardian to the infant, and there were, as I have been assured, regular drawing rooms at his brother's residence at Philadelphia. On these occasions the Colonel would receive visitors in the anteroom, and present both ladies and gentlemen, the boy being styled Prince, and his mother doing the honours. She then thought no doubt, that Bonaparte would relent, and, as I have heard, expected to be created Duchess of Oldenburgh.

It is not improbable too that he might have entertained some such vague intention at that time of making use of the boy in his Spanish intrigues, from seeing him, as it were, made to his hand on the American continent. Or, as he was then in the zenith of his glory and intoxicated with the prospect of destroying all opposition to his power in the Old World, may he not, in conformity with his well known exclamation "cette vieille Europe m'ennuye," have conceived some gigantic plan for North America that along with other visionary projects he was never allowed to ripen and that it would now appear too ridiculous to mention, but which there might have been political gamblers enough to second even in the United States, where there are, at all times, plenty of young adventurers ready to set law at defiance and to invade their neighbour's rights careless of the consequences. What is certain is that I have been assured the populace applauded most vociferously upon an occasion when Madame Bonaparte appeared for the first time at the theatre of Philadelphia with her child upon her lap, and let anyone who may fancy such a conjecture as too extravagant to be probable turn to the first volume of the "Memoires de Napoleon," under the title of "Melanges Historiques" "dictes au Comte de Montholow," page 192, where he will find the following passage: "Que ne pouvoit il pas entreprendre avec une armee de 25 a 30,000 Noirs sur la Jamaique, de Canada, *sur les Etats Unis* sur les Colonies Espagnoles?"[102] This in allusion to his policy in regard to St. Domingo at a time when he could have had no cause of quarrel with America. What a key it gives us to his ambition! What a vista of wars and expected conquests! Had he continued to be the favourite of Fortune what would have been now our fate, let those answer who glory in a conqueror.

Fulton, to whom America and Great Britain are so indebted for the practical use of steam navigation now employed almost over the whole world, was at the Federal City proposing steam frigates and catamarans to the Government while I was there. I met him occasionally, tho' I own I felt some repugnance to be intimate with a man who was going from coast to coast, offering engines of destruction, of a diabolical kind, indiscriminately to all parties.

Monsieur Correa de Serra, an old Portuguese gentleman who had just escaped from the clutches of Napoleon, having been forced to live at Paris for some years, was an interesting addition to our society and full of anecdote of the state of tyranny in France. He dined with me in company with Chief Justice Marshall and Judge Washington,[103] both eminent and very amiable men, who came every year with five other judges to open the Supreme Court, which was a great resource, for men at least, against the dullness of the place.

[102] *Memoires pour Servir a l'Histoire de France Sous Napoleon, Ecrits à Sainte Hélene, par Les Generaux qui ont partagé sa Captivité et Publiés sur les Manuscrits Entierement Corrigés de la Main de Napoleon. Mélanges Historiques . . .*, 8 vols. (London and Paris). Foster's reference is actually to Vol. VI of the complete set, the last 3 volumes being *Mélanges.*

[103] Bushrod Washington (1762-1829), son of George Washington's brother Augustine, was an Associate Justice of the U. S. Supreme Court from 1798.

I also met with General Pinckney who told me that he had been a school fellow of Doctor Jackson, Dean of Christ-church, and that on the latter's taking orders, he was to have had a living at Charlestown, the Parish of St. Michael's, with 400 a year which was in the gift of the Pinckney's, in South Carolina.[104] But his father declined it, and Doctor Markham[105] got him to be sub-preceptor to his pupil the Prince of Wales.

General Pinckney told me the Dean was much liked at school and college, and was an excellent scholar and that 200 a year was a good allowance for a gentleman commoner in those days. In 1798 he and Major General Hamilton[106] were of the Council of War under Washington. He said that the latter would take out his watch every day without fail for a month, and showing it up to them when they separated in the morning, warn them that in whatever company they might be in the evening, they must remember to be off to the Council rooms precisely at seven.

General Pinckney was a Knight of Cincinnati, of which an eagle suspended from a blue ribbon at the button hole is the badge, and he was to be present at a great meeting of the order in the autumn of 1811.[107] The principal object of the institution he told me was to provide for the families of soldiers who had fought the War of Independence. It was meant to be hereditary in the eldest son.

Governeur Morris,[108] who was American Minister at Paris in Robespierre's time, David Parish, Ouvrard's English agent or partner in his Spanish Dollar speculation,[109] Joe Allen Smith, who

[104]Cyril Jackson (1746-1819) became Dean in 1783 and soon became famous. He and Pinckney had been together at Christ Church in 1764.

[105]William Markham (1719-1807), later Archbishop of York, in 1771 was appointed preceptor to the young Prince of Wales and to Prince Frederick, Bishop of Osnaburg.

[106]Alexander Hamilton (1757-1804).

[107]Foster's "Diary" shows his great interest in the Society of the Cincinnati, the organization of former Revolutionary army officers. Apparently he hoped it might lead to the establishment of some sort of caste system, if not nobility, in the U.S.

[108]Gouverneur Morris (1752-1816).

[109]David Parish came to America in 1805 as agent of Hope & Co. to direct one of the gigantic financial operations which marked the Napoleonic wars. Ouvrard was a French financier.

had passed many years at St. Petersburg, General Eaton who took his title of General from having fought in the service of the Pasha of Tripoli,[110] Count Andreani of Milan and many other persons more or less interesting passed before our eyes, almost as in a dioramic review. For they stayed generally but a little time at the capital unless they had business to detain them, but I shall be thought to have digressed too much upon individuals in describing the Federal City, tho' I conceive the less apology to be necessary on that account, as in fact, there is little else at this capital to speak of but the strangers who frequent it, or the animals to be found about it, woodcocks, snipes, partridges and snakes. There were however a set of harpies very abundant in my time, of whom I must say something, namely, swindlers and adventurers.

First and foremost among these must be named, Count Edward Crillon (as he called himself) a pretended son of the Duke de Crillon who commanded at the Siege of Gibraltar and whom he described as having left property in Spain, Majorca and Chile, from which latter place he had received $10,000 for several years, till lately when this revenue ceased and for the purpose of looking after it, he, Count Edward, was going to South America.[111] He sailed from Ryde in England for Boston and came out in the same ship with Mr. Henry, who believed, or pretended to believe, the story, and as far as lay in him confirmed it.[112] [*Note*: Mr. Henry was the gentleman employed by the Governor of Can-

[110]William Eaton (1764-1811), born in Connecticut, fought in 1805 in Tripoli to reinstate Hamet Karamanli, the exiled Pasha. Louis B. Wright and Julia H. Macleod, *The First Americans in North Africa; William Eaton's Struggle for a Vigorous Policy Against the Barbary Pirates, 1799-1805* (Princeton, 1945).

[111]Crillon was much in favor at the White House in January and February 1812. He left Washington with dispatches from Monroe to Barlow and from Sérurier to Bassano. Sérurier reported the hatred of the British Minister for Crillon. Apparently Foster never knew positively what was revealed much later, that Crillon was an agent of Napoleon's secret police. For accounts of Crillon's career in Washington, see Henry Adams, "Count Edward de Crillon," *Am. Hist. Rev.*, I (Oct. 1895), 51ff.

[112]John Henry was Sir James Craig's secret agent in Boston in 1809. He returned to America in 1812 with Crillon, as stated. For Foster and Henry, see E. A. Cruikshank, *The Political Adventures of John Henry, the Record of an International Imbroglio* (Toronto, 1936), pp. 76-187.

ada, Sir James Craig, to correspond with him from Boston and who came to Washington with the correspondence which he sold to Congress for $30,000, although it proved nothing but the fact of his having been so employed and was too insignificant to compromise anybody but Sir James and Mr. Henry himself who betrayed it.] Crillon represented himself as having escaped with Romana from Denmark, and as having served against General Sebastiani[113] in the Isla de Leon, where he was wounded and got permission to go to the baths. He went afterwards to Corfu and Hungary, Russia and Sweden, and spoke with great familiarity of Governors Ipsilanti,[114] Armfeld[115] and others, but he said he lost the passport, with which he had travelled in quality of a merchant, at Fredericshald in Norway. He stated himself to have lived during nine months in England where he pretended to have been introduced to Lord Lauderdale, the Duke of York and even the King, then Prince Regent.

Altho' he had come to Boston without a passport, or a recommendation of any kind, this was no impediment to his schemes, the Democratic governor having been completely dazzled by his pretended rank, and not only invited him to his own house, but having given him a letter for the President, to whom he presented it in the month of January 1812, when he was immediately asked to a dinner to which I and several other persons were invited to meet him. He was rather short in person with very thick legs and I thought that I had never beheld such a vulgar-looking bully, being at once persuaded from his personal appearance that he was an impostor. For tho' the Spanish grandees, generally speaking, were very cramped in person as well as mind by the effects of the miserably effeminate and domestic life that they have now been trained to by a succession, during centuries, of

[113]Count François Bastien Sébastiani (1772-1851), Marshal of France.

[114]Alexander Ypsilanti (1725-1805) or more probably his son Constantine (d. 1816), appointed by the Sultan hospodar of Moldavia after a pardon following his attempt to liberate Greece.

[115]Gustave Maurice, Baron Armfeldt (1757-1814), was commander in chief of Swedish forces in Pomerania, 1805-1807. He was a personal friend of Foster and his mother.

suspicious and jealous ministers or sovereigns, there still is an air of nobility and a gentlemanlike appearance about them which this fellow had not. Having in a very marked and awkward manner pushed himself into the first place at table, next Mrs. Madison, he immediately commenced talking in a vain vaunting way of his noble acquaintances or connections and of his family estates in Chile as well as Spain. When, therefore, he came to dine with me, for as he had been taken to my house by Mr. Brent a Senator of Virginia, I invited him as a compliment to the introductor, I took care to have a large map of Chile on the table and taking my cue from his questions of the day before as to the best mode of getting to that province, I spread it out asking him to show whereabouts his property lay. I observed that he seemed embarrassed, and he put his finger down, at random, into the middle of where there seemed to be a desert, not a single name of a town being apparent in that part of the map. Tho,' on my lamenting over his ill luck to have land in such a barren district, he pretended to have made a mistake and looking again asserted that his family property lay near the bay and town of Concepcion.

I had no doubt after this of Crillon being an impostor and I questioned Mr. Brent as to what letters he might have brought for persons in the United States, and how he in particular had become acquainted with him, till I perceived that the Senator, who was apt to be in his cups, knew nothing at all about him beyond what he had been told by Crillon himself. Next day, however, he told the Count of my questions and the latter sent me a note to complain of my having expressed suspicions in regard to him while I was receiving him hospitably. And as in fact I had no proofs of his being an adventurer, I merely replied that I certainly had no right to suspect him and that Mr. Brent had done wrong in telling him what I had asked merely for the sake of information, while I regretted that he had brought no letter from England for me or any of H.M.'s consuls.[116]

[116]The French Minister, Sérurier, wrote to the Duke de Bassano on February 18, 1812, that Foster had received a very harsh and insulting letter from Crillon and that Foster's moderate answer had made the British Minister ridiculous in all eyes. Adams, "Crillon," pp. 62-64.

The next thing I heard of him was his adventure at the mess where he dined with Madame Bonaparte, the Vice-President and other lodgers in a house in which he went to reside and paid three times as much as anybody else for his rooms as a proof of his rank and wealth. He was showing off at table and produced a portrait of a well known baron whom he asserted to be his brother, when a young Dutchman[117] who had lately escaped from Holland and was present and who agreed with me that Crillon was an impostor could contain himself no longer but maintained that the Baron could be no relation of his and that Crillon himself must be an impostor if he said so. This produced a scene. The ladies made off; the gentlemen rose and Crillon appeared for a moment to be confounded. He recovered himself however in the evening and went to Mrs. Madison's drawing room with a star on and there snapping his fingers in the Dutchman's face he challenged him, repeating his challenge the same evening in writing. The Dutchman came to consult me what was to be done. He was ready to fight him but of course if the fellow was a swindler he could gain no credit by it, so I advised him merely to insist upon knowing whether there was anyone in the country to whom Crillon had letters and who would answer for his being the person he stated himself to be, when of course having insulted him he must give him satisfaction. This he did and the other was at once nonplussed. People avoided his society, his fellow lodgers said they would leave the house if he continued at their mess and the owner of the house was forced to request him to withdraw. He then came to beg protection from my secretary, from the American officers and at last found a colonel who was good enough to take up his cause and to maintain that he was as he represented himself to be, a grandee of Spain and that anyone who maintained the contrary must fight with him, the colonel.

At the same time there appeared a kind of mysterious connection between Crillon and the French Minister. He now dined with the latter every day and the Dutchman was even threatened

[117]Foster refers to Willingk, "a Dutch gentleman," and later mentions that he was "of Amsterdam" and had been 4 years in London. "Diary," Feb. 6 and 12, 1812.

with the displeasure of the Emperor Napoleon to be exercised against his family in Holland if he and the fellow subject of his Imperial Majesty did not make up matters. On this the Dutchman came again to me for advice which I declined to give as he was to be the best judge of the force of the argument used by the imperial envoy. It altered the case certainly as the latter seemed by his interference to acknowledge the rank of Crillon, however extraordinary that might appear, and the Dutchman therefore decided on yielding so far as to admit that he had made assertions concerning Crillon without sufficient proof and should not persevere in them.

On this the Count triumphantly cast his eyes about in search of some one on whom to wreak his vengeance. There happened to be in the same house with him a gentleman of fortune who had rather taken the lead in refusing to dine with him when considered as an adventurer, and whom he guessed at bottom not a little afraid of his cut-throat appearance. Him he singled out, and at a public ball in George Town reproaching him with his conduct and calling him a shoeblack he spit upon him. Crillon had then got not only a star, but a ribband of the Spanish order of St. Charles so that the scene was observed by all present, and became very ridiculous by the mode in which the victim received the affront, turning his eyes up, and pretending not to have observed the injurious act. He came, however, the next day to me and though he did not speak of that which he had affected not to see, yet as the word "shoeblack" had struck in his ears and had been commented on by his friends, he thought, he said, that he was called on to demand an explanation or satisfaction. He brought me a letter he had written upon the subject, in which he reasoned upon the term, admitted that he had cleaned his own shoes, occasionally, in travelling, but asserted that this could not authorize anybody to call him a shoeblack, and that he thought an apology was due.

Being ready to burst with laughter I excused myself from giving any opinion on so delicate a matter and finally saying, "Perhaps after all I had better burn the letter," he went away [and I heard no more of his challenge.]* though the same night he alarmed the whole boarding house by firing off a pistol at the door of his room, having as it appeared dreamt that his formidable lodger was bursting in to do him some bodily harm, in the apprehension of his doing which he had gone to bed with loaded pistols by his side.[118] The ladies were all roused up by the unusual noise and there was tremendous confusion and subsequently great laughter at the adventure.

The close connection of De Crillon with the French envoy who had the pleasure of this swindler's company at dinner almost every day became now generally known and a matter of surprize all over Washington. The fact, however, is that whether the minister knew his real character or not, he was most probably his dupe and made by him to believe that Henry was solely influenced by his advice and would withhold or disclose the correspondence of Sir James Craig[119] with the discontented New Englanders which he had brought with him according as he should advise him to do, and Napoleon's money to the amount of $4,000 was lavished upon him as upon one who could let off a mine that should produce instant war between the United States and Great Britain. I have no doubt from some advances which he made that he had designed to raise money also from me by pretending that it was in his power to prevent Henry's communication, tho' as Ministers at home had so recently declined to stop Henry's mouth when he threatened a disclosure and as there is no safety in negotiating with such fellows, I should certainly not have felt authorized to advance any money for the occasion. As it was, Crillon not only drew upon the French but also upon Henry who having

*The section in brackets appears in the earlier HEH version of Foster's "Notes." He wrote it out but then marked it through in the LC version.

---

[118]In the "Diary" (Feb. 6, 1812) Foster refers to this gentleman as Mr. D——y. The "Diary" is here, however, somewhat confusing.

[119]Sir James Henry Craig (1748-1812) had been in correspondence primarily with John Henry. Professor Samuel E. Morison, who has worked particularly with the John Henry affair, has found (letter to the editor, July 1, 1952) no evidence of New Englanders' corresponding with Craig or Henry, with the exception of a young Bostonian named Carey, of no consequence.

sold his secret to Congress for $30,000 or $40,000 was said to have been fool enough to give nearly one half to Crillon in exchange for bills which the latter gave him on bankers in Paris, but which were afterwards said to have been protested. I can scarcely however believe this to have been in reality the case and am rather inclined to suppose that Henry pretended to have been duped, as he must have found out something suspicious in his travelling companion during their long voyage together or else have been a great noodle which he did not appear to be. It was much more likely that they had an understanding in regard to their different parts and agreed to divide the profits between them, of what they could get from selling the documents to Congress or to the French or to all of us, and that Crillon was the one put most forward as having the least character to lose.

However this may be, the Count, soon after he had pocketed his money, marched off and only just in time, as letters were received on the 25th May from the real Duke of Crillon disclaiming all connection with this man and denouncing him as a swindler, which we not long afterwards ascertained to be the fact, his real name being Soubiron. He was a native of Bordeaux and brought up to be a Benedictine monk, but became a soldier during the Revolution, and had been an officer in a French regiment in Spain from which, as I learnt from Moreau, he was expelled for peculation and other mal-practices, when he went to Paris where he became notorious as head of a gambling house. What confirms me too in the belief of a complicity existing between him and Henry is that I remember the latter, while still at Washington, talked of having been persuaded by Crillon to lay out some of his money in buying an estate in the south of France and I have since heard that they were both living there a few years ago and not far from each other. I was much struck in regard to this affair at seeing that Mr. Madison's paper, in which he himself was known to insert articles of his own writing, viz., the *National Intelligencer*, under date of the 21st March, 1806, actually quoted this very Crillon in confirmation of Henry's statement and gives his examination before a committee of Congress of this impostor as if it were the testimony of a credible witness, although it was then known that there was not an individual in the United States who would answer for his being a gentleman while he impudently repeated to the committee that he was a descendant from the "brave Crillon."

Henry's disclosure took place on the 9th March, and although some of the Federalists complained we were always doing things imprudent and ruinous to our friends, and Mr. Tayloe and others were already offering to purchase my horses, furniture, etc., while Mr. Poletica observed that we had received a check.[120] Mr. Madison, on the contrary expressed to me his hopes that the occurrence might on the whole rather have a beneficial effect upon the negotiations; and Mr. Bayard assured me that the public had been so abused with lies and reports of every kind, that even these papers would make very little impression generally, and be considered in most places as an invention, like the stories which began at this time to be put about of our having employed Indians to scalp and massacre the Americans on the Canada frontier, which I was enabled by documents, sent to me at my desire from Canada through London, most triumphantly to contradict.[121] Henry's discovery, too, though it proved sufficiently that Sir James Craig, like many other governors in remote possessions of the Crown, had been too much of what the French call a "faiseur," thinking he should deal in keeping up a correspondence

[120]In his "Diary" Foster records (March 11, 1812), "Politica whispered nous avons reçu un échec." Pierre de Poletica, or Politica, appears to have been Russian chargé d'affaires from April 1811, on the departure of Count Pahlen.

[121]The documents assembled by Americans concerning British-Indian atrocities appear in *Papers Presented to Parliament in 1813*, pp. 643ff. All that Foster offered in reply in this volume (p. 427) were earlier statements from home, and denials. Foster's "documents" from Canada are included in [James Madison,] *Message from the President*, pp. 6-10. It was in reply to these that Monroe (in a letter of June 10, 1812) enclosed copies of letters received over a 5-year period concerning Indian depredations from over the border, incited by the British. Foster's "triumphant" reply seems weak and unconvincing. By implication he appears to say that the Governor could not be responsible for individuals (*Papers Presented*, p. 658), and that much of Monroe's material was mere rumor. Recent investigation would seem to indicate, however weak these documents may be, that Foster and the British were right in their vindication of themselves *in this period*, though decades earlier the atrocity accusations had more bases in fact.

with the discontented among his neighbours, and in imitating the system of espionage so much in favour at the courts of Louis XV and XVI and with most European governments of the last century, as well indeed as with the Americans themselves in regard to Florida, yet had by no means compromised the British Cabinet.

In point of fact I do not think that the American Government, or at least all the members of it, were such dupes as to believe that we were seriously plotting to dissolve the Union, as an event that would be advantageous to the interests of Great Britain. For in the first place, I do not suppose such an unprincipled and immoral project could have been entertained, while we were at peace with America, by His Majesty's Ministers, and in the next place I am prepared to maintain that even on the score of the interests, commercial or political, of Great Britain, no sound statesman could have wished success to it. For what would have been the result and consequence? Would it not have been the raising into existence a most powerful naval rival in our own immediate neighbourhood on the line of frontier of our continental colonies and whose traders were already in possession of some of the chief markets in our sugar islands? The population all white, energetic, peculiarly active and enterprizing, the country too, not, as in the south, thinly inhabited by a mixed race of cultivators, having different interests, but full of flourishing towns and villages as well as admirable ports and harbours; where were to be found gentlemen of talents and education bound together by a common interest and similar religion, rather inclined to be gratified by the possession of office and distinctions and who were much more likely to draw advantages from England than England was to extract any from them in carrying on such manoeuvres.

On the other hand the Union, under one flag, of all the states, their varied interests, with the checks and balances these produce, operate effectually to keep down warlike propensities. Louisiana, South Carolina and other neighbouring states sell us their cotton, Virginia and Maryland as well as Pennsylvania their flour and tobacco, and this their most profitable trade would be interrupted by intestine squabbles. It is true we have also great commercial intercourse with New York and Boston but this is not of a nature so indispensable as the other and is more in the hands of foreigners, whereas the interests of the south are in a great measure dependent on our manufacturers and, in spite of the democratical doctrines of the Jeffersonian band of politicians, will ever continue to present, and very naturally, a great obstacle to the views of men in power in the United States who might be led away by ambition and the love of war.

I do not mean, however, by such observations to accuse the New Englanders of ill-weaved ambition in their opposition to their government and in their correspondence whatever it might have been with Sir James Craig.[122] They were, no doubt, heartily sick of the humiliation to which Jefferson's measures had subjected the country, his partiality to the French and the embargoes as well as suicidal Non-Importation Acts, with which he had overwhelmed their trade. Thinking there would be no end to such a state of things, while they saw with fear and despondency the prodigious strides of Bonaparte towards the dominion of the world at a time that he was only kept in check by the naval supremacy of Great Britain, no wonder if they began to look about them and to doubt whether it might not be preferable to break off from the rotten part and form a vigorous state of their own. And had they done so it would have been the effect of circumstances or of despair at the ruinous conduct of the Democratic party, but not of reckless ambition. Nevertheless, the consequences of such a step, however desirable in the first instance and for a brief period they might have seemed to shortsighted politicians of either country, would, I am confident, have been at this moment deeply to be deplored both by Great Britain and the United States, but by no inhabitants of the latter so much as those

[122]Cf. Theodore Dwight, *History of the Hartford Convention, with a Review of the Policy of the United States Government which Led to the War of 1812* (New York, 1833), pp. 77-80, 206-210, for a bitterly anti-Jeffersonian defense of these New Englanders. This book Foster almost surely had before him as he wrote his "Notes," for Josiah Quincy wrote to Foster on March 7, 1834, that he was sending a copy for use in preparing the manuscript. Quincy, *Life of Josiah Quincy*, p. 458.

in the southern states where the whole coast—void as it is, with very few exceptions, of even good roadsteads—would inevitably have fallen under that worst of tyrannies, a jealous manufacturing, commercial and naval republic, after perhaps a long struggle that might retard, but could not in the nature of things be expected wholly to prevent their ultimate fate.

Henry's disclosures were in fact very insignificant, and the Federalists generally took fire at a passage in the President's Message in which was found the term "disaffected."[123] They even carried their resentment so far as to refuse to dine with him, and they absented themselves from Mrs. Madison's parties for several weeks.

While upon this subject, I will venture to predict that if ever the American Union is to be broken up in times of peace, the first crack will take place in the west, [or south]* for there is to be found the greatest degree of immorality and recklessness. The states beyond the Alleganies are notoriously full of gamblers, speculators and adventurers of all sorts, with scarcely any check from a religious establishment, far removed, moreover, from the censure of Europe or even of the Atlantic cities of America, and having already been twice the theatre of civil war or treasonable practices, viz., at the close of the last century, when General Washington was sent with 10,000 men to put down the revolt,[124] and, secondly, when Colonel Burr, the Vice-President of the United States, endeavoured to raise the standard of rebellion.[125] New Orleans would of necessity become the capital of their division, should it be erected into a kingdom or separate state. In

*Material in brackets appears in earlier HEH version.

[123]Madison's "Message" to Congress of March 9, 1812, with which he sent Henry's papers, charged the British government with employing a secret agent "in fomenting disaffection to the constituted authorities of the nation, and in intrigues with the disaffected for the purpose of bringing about resistance to the laws, and eventually, in concert with a British force, of destroying the Union and forming the eastern part thereof into a political connection with Great Britain."

[124]A reference to the Whiskey Rebellion of 1794 in Pennsylvania.

[125]Aaron Burr's abortive conspiracy of 1805-1806 to seize Spanish territory in the Southwest.

such case New York would, no doubt, make common cause with New England while the middle and southern states would become the prey of one or both.

Mr. Jefferson, however, was of a different opinion. His suspicions turned eastward and he had great prejudices in regard to commerce. He more than once told me that he wished the United States had never possessed a ship. He would, he said, have laid the American ports open to all the world, let foreign nations dispute, if they liked it, which should supply at the cheapest rate the richest agricultural market in the universe, and been satisfied in seeing his countrymen solely occupied with, and really enjoying, the rural employments of a golden age. To this feeling on his part may be in a degree attributed the facility with which he adopted or recommended, while Madison was said to steer by the long tiller of Monticello, measures of commercial hostility to one or both belligerents in preference to open war with either, while he saw no need of trade unless it came begging to be admitted at the door, tho' he was nearly single in his views in this respect, and of course obliged to yield to circumstance. To his credit, however, be it said, whatever were his prejudices and however strong against Great Britain, his theories were all in favour of profiting by the position of America for the purpose of rendering her an example to the world of the advantages of a really free trade, instead of imitating all the old systems of European governments, their restrictions protecting duties and complicated regulations for forcing the manufacturing industry of nations from natural into artificial channels. Such makeshifts being, in his opinion, unworthy of a young people and wholly unnecessary as a means of giving employment where such immeasurable tracts of rich soil were still under wood and unprofitable from want of tillage. [I met with a North Carolina Member of pretty much the same opinion, but who even went so far as to say he thought it would be no great misfortune if New York were destroyed, though of course such expressions are not to be taken literally.]*

*Material in brackets was crossed out in the HEH version and did not appear in the later LC version.

I have now to notice in a cursory manner some three adventurers who figured at Washington contemporaneously with Crillon or Soubiron, as well as Sir James Craig's secretary, and who perhaps were connected with the former. One was M. Desseyronnet,[126] a great rascal who brought a letter of recommendation from Don Luis de Onis, the Spanish Minister, and who, when closeted with me offered his services to go to Spain and assassinate the French general before Cadiz or attempt the life of Bonaparte or do any other desperate act I might choose to put him on. By way of gaining greater credit, he disclosed to me that he had rendered considerable service to the allied cause at Lisbon, in getting hold of some important papers on board a merchant ship, to the captain of which he had given a sleepy potion, when, he added with great sang froid, "Il en mourut," and, seeing me look grave, "Que voulez vous, j'en fus faché." On which I was seized with such horror of the fellow that I only thought of getting rid of him. So promising to let him hear further from me if I had any commission for him thro' M. de Onis, I rose and bowed him out of the room as fast as I could.

Two others[127] came soon after to tell me that they dined frequently with the French Minister and to offer to break open his bureau, and to bring me his dispatches. These fellows altho' strongly suspected of being impostors were very generally admitted into society, having been introduced by an elderly lady of great family connection, the highest indeed in the states, to whom if one of them did not get married it was his own fault. But he would have perhaps had to produce some title deeds in that case and this is a result which such impostors generally seek to avoid.

I have since had reason to believe that one or two of these fellows were purposely set on to try to entrap me in some manner to give them my confidence, as happened to Mr. Drake,[128]

[126]Unidentified.

[127]Their names were Graffe and Ballastero. "Diary," May 20 and 24, 1812.

[128]Drake was an English agent at Munich implicated in Cadoudal's conspiracy to assassinate Napoleon in 1804.

and that they formed a part of a band employed by the French Government for such purposes.

We had at the same time an English swindler, in the shape of a clergyman, a Mr. Audaine from the West Indies who came to me in his parson's dress, and in whose favour I made exception to a general rule of not inviting travellers, unless they were introduced by letter or by someone who served to identify the individual. The reverend gentleman, however, owed to his dress and to the circumstances of his having been allowed to preach at a church in George Town, his getting an invitation to dinner. When on sitting down to table, he with great gravity, said grace, a form which, as we were by no means used to it in that part of the world, took us quite unawares, being already seated. There was a large party present, and John Randolph then Member of Congress, who was next me, being shocked at his own inadvertency, whispered a reproach in my ear, for my not having apprized him of the clergyman's intention. I excused myself, from not having been in the habit of hearing grace of late and in the evening I placed the parson at cards with Randolph. After which to my horror, the latter came up, and again whispering and laughing told me, "Your clergyman cheats, he cheated me at whist." I afterwards discovered that, tho' he was in fact a clergyman, he was a noted swindler, and had stolen a carriage and horses from a gentleman at New York. He has since, I have heard, got into the King's Bench Prison where he probably remains if he be still alive.

There were several other adventurers of the same kind, but too insignificant to mention, and Washington City never was so full before of strangers. Officers too were pouring in to seek employment in case of war, and the boarding houses were all full. At one of them on Capitol Hill sixteen Members were lodged, two of whom had each a chamber to himself, but for the rest, they lay two in a room, even the Senators, that is to say those of New England principally. For the southern gentlemen take up a large space, and are usually great aristocrats in their domestic habits, if not in their politics. But if the New Englanders be more economical in general, they are not of the dirty set, and I must say to the credit of our English blood that these are, if not altogether, at least for the most part, to be found among the descendants of Dutch and Germans. I was shown one of the former from the state, not the city of New York, who like Mr. Butcher changed his shirts but once a week, which from his frowzy appearance, I could readily believe. When the southrons, too, were filthy it was from affectation, in general, and to appear democratical, but not often from taste as was the case with some of the others. Mr. Jefferson, although from his love of nature and simplicity he obliged his grandson, young Randolph, to come to tea and fruit of an evening with naked legs and feet, took care to order him to have them well washed.[129] The youth's skin was very white when I saw him thus enter the room at Monticello.

Washington City was, I think, in spite of its inconveniences and its desolate appearance, the most agreeable town to reside in for any length of time of all those which I have seen in the United States. There is a great deal of occupation and of interest connected with the public affairs while Congress is sitting, which is the case generally during half the year, and it is satisfactory for anyone that wishes to collect information, to meet more with so many of the principal people of the country, who are deputies from all parts of it. Besides the President and the Ministers are generally very hospitable and agreeable persons, some of them having even been in Europe, while the corps diplomatique are a great resource and would alone suffice to place society on a good footing.

Social Diversions

Most of the Members of the Congress, it is true, keep to their lodgings, but still there are a sufficient number of them who are sociable or whose families come to the city for a season, and

[129] Foster's small notebook-journal of 1806-1807, Huntington Library, contains his original entry of this incident. Foster began a tour of Virginia on August 17, 1807.

there is no want of handsome ladies for the balls, especially at George Town. Indeed I never saw prettier girls anywhere. As there are but few of them however, in proportion to the great number of men who frequent the places of amusement of the Federal City, it is one of the most marrying places of the whole continent, a truth which was beginning to be found out. It was the cause of vast numbers flocking there all round from the four points of the compass. Unfortunately, however, maugre the March of Intellect so much vaunted in the present century, the literary education of these ladies is far from being worthy of the Age of Knowledge, and conversation is apt to flag, tho' a seat by the ladies is always much coveted. Dancing and music nevertheless served to eke out the time, but one got to be soon heartily sick of hearing the same song everywhere even when it was "Just like love is yonder rose." No matter how this was sung, the words alone–were the men traps. The belle of the evening was declared to be just like both, and people looked round as if the listener was expected to become on the instance very tender and to propose, and sometimes such an insult does in reality take place after a very short acquaintance. Both parties when betrothed, use a *great deal* of billing and cooing, eat out of the same plate, drink out of the same glass and show off their love to the whole company.

Between these young ladies, who are generally not only good looking but good tempered and, if not well informed, capable of becoming so, and the ladies of a certain time of life or rather of the "Seconda Gioventu," there is usually a wide gap in society, young married women being but seldom seen in the world. As they approach, however, to middle age they are apt to become romantic, those in particular who live in the country and have read novels, fancying all manner of heroic things and returning to the capital determined to have an adventure before they again retire or on doing some wondrous act which shall make them be talked of in after times. I have myself in vain reasoned with a very beautiful lady to try to persuade her not to cut off a head of hair, one of the finest I ever saw, of an auburn colour, which she used to take the greatest pains to curl and keep in order, and had been evidently proud of, but it was all useless. She found out one day that it was a vanity and vanity was sin, and off she cut it and put it into the hands of her astonished and despairing husband. Others I have known to contract an aversion to water and as a substitute cover their faces and bosoms with hair powder in order to render the skin smooth and delicate. This was peculiarly the case with some Virginian damsels who came to the balls at Washington, and who, in consequence, were hardly less intolerable than Negroes. There were but few cases, however, of this. I must confess, tho,' as regards the use of the powder, they were not so uncommon, and at my balls I thought it advisable to put on the tables of the toilette room not only rouge but hair powder, as well as white and blue powders which had some customers.

In going to assemblies one had sometimes to drive three or four miles within the city bounds and very often at great risk of an overturn, or of being what was termed "stalled" or stuck in the mud when one can neither go backwards or forwards and either loses one's shoes or one's patience. Especially was this true when the dance was at the Navy Yard, a remote part of the city where Commodore Tingey commanded, an old English lieutenant, who made one forget his having left the service of his country in the jollity and good humour with which he received his guests.[130] I generally had to give dinners three or four times a week although I cannot say that I was well paid, my appointments having amounted to but little more than one half of what they afterwards were, and no plate having been allowed me. But it was necessary to keep a good house, and this was not too often, considering how few persons there were at that time who entertained at Washington, and how important it was, when party spirit ran so high and questions of peace or war were debating almost every day, to keep a constant and friendly connection with as many Members of Congress and public men as

[130]Thomas Tingey (1750-1829), Captain U.S. Navy, was commandant at the Washington Navy Yard. He had spent his youth as an officer in the British Navy.

possible. And there was then no other envoy who thought it necessary to reside at the seat of government but the French Minister, with whom I could have no intercourse even at third persons' houses in consequence of his Instructions not permitting it, Count Pahlen, the Russian Minister having gone away soon after my arrival, and M. de Onis, as I before stated, having quarrelled with the Government and been obliged to request me to act for him in the Florida business.

I had great trouble in arranging my parties so as to avoid giving occasion for quarrels, especially as there were several hot-headed Irishmen in Congress who would have desired no better sport than to shoot at Randolph or any other leading member of the opposition. Tho' as ill luck would have it, the latter walked in one day while we were at wine and found me surrounded with some of his bitterest foes. It was too late to retreat, besides that he was too proud, if he could, to have done so. I placed him by me, and endeavoured to guide and direct the conversation far away from subjects relating to the United States, but it was nearly all in vain. A Kentucky Irishman,[131] who had just owned to me that in his time, no Irishman was thought much of who had not stood fire and killed or maimed his man, took up the question of eloquence in the Irish House of Commons which I had introduced, and turned it into an attack upon Randolph's peculiar style. The latter fortunately was so engaged in talk with another that he did not hear him, and besides held him too cheap to think his conversation worth attending to. But a friend of his, Mr. Breckenridge, a very worthy person, since dead, told me after dinner that it was much as he could do to keep his anger, and that if it had not been at my table and from respect to me he would have taken up his words and had a fight with him.

The men of Boston and Connecticut were great favourites of mine, being, altho' generally not country gentlemen and not so sociable as the southrons, most upright worthy and friendly

[131]Stephen Ormsby (1759-1844), Irish-born, had earlier been a judge, but in 1811-1817 was a Member of Congress. "Diary," May 6, 1812.

persons. Of the most distinguished were Mr. Quincy of Boston[132] (since head of the University of Cambridge near Boston, the oldest establishment of the kind I believe in the United States), General Hunter of Rhode Island,[133] Mr. Pitkin, Mr. Hillhouse who was said to have the blood of an Indian chief in his veins, Mr. Talmadge said to be connected with the English family of Talmark, and Mr. Tracy who died at Washington during my first visit.[134] There was also Bayard of Delaware with whom I was intimate and who was afterwards employed in the negotiation for peace, besides many others from all quarters, who would suffice to redeem the character of public men in America, if it were necessary to defend them against the aspersions of so many travellers who go about putting questions or contracting bile among persons nearly as exotic as themselves in districts to which they can have no attachment and which have only become cultivated within the last twenty or thirty years.

Cards were a great resource of an evening, and gaming was all the fashion, at Brag especially, for the men who frequented society were chiefly from Virginia and the western states and were very fond of this most gambling of all games as being one of countenance as well as cards. Loo was the innocent diversion of the ladies who, when they were looed, pronounced the word in a very mincing manner.

Attending the Debates was a resource of a morning but when the note of war became louder and louder it was difficult for me to be present and even my secretary Mr. Baker was frequently

[132]Josiah Quincy (1772-1864), later President of Harvard, was a Member of Congress 1805-1813. Undoubtedly, says S. E. Morison (*The Life and Letters of Harrison Gray Otis Federalist, 1765-1848* [Boston, 1913], II, 33-35), Quincy was "one of the Federalists who advised the British minister that his country maintain the anti-neutral system, in order to force war on the United States, when Republican inconsistency would return the Federalists to power."

[133]William Hunter (1774-1849), U.S. Senator 1811-1821, though a Federalist was never a violent partisan.

[134]Timothy Pitkin (1766-1847), James Hillhouse (1754-1832), Benjamin Tallmadge (1754-1835), Uriah Tracy (1755-1807) were all Federalist Representatives and/or Senators from Connecticut.

spoken at.[135] For many months it was impossible to guess how matters would end and the most contradictory opinions were given to me by persons the most likely to be well informed, but I became seriously alarmed when one of the wavering Senators,[136] who had been hitherto supposed to be against war, asked me for some information in regard to the situation of our ships and squadrons, and let fall some expressions from which I was led to conjecture that there was a question of pouncing upon the West India return convoy by way of at once rendering hostilities popular. Congress, however, having subsequently passed an embargo act, for near three months I employed the time in writing home and recommending to Admiral Sawyer[137] to collect his ships and as much as possible to avoid sending cruisers singly along the coast, knowing, as I did, that the American captains had orders to court rather than avoid a combat. The fact was that the President was very loath to come to a rupture with us, and yet was being pushed to it by his party as a condition of his re-election. He would have been happy to have the measure forced upon him, in a manner, by some bloody action at sea which would have roused up the passions of the people, while the prize money to be got from the capture of a fleet of merchantmen would have tended to conciliate the navy and all the men of enterprize throughout the country.

Coming of the War of 1812

Admiral Sawyer acted upon my suggestion and I had the satisfaction of seeing that no handle for exciting the popular feelings was given to the War-Hawks by our captains, who usually kept hovering along the shores during the embargo, nor until the war was declared in June. And that this was no small object may be inferred from the great difficulty which

[135]Anthony St. John Baker, later consul general and chargé d'affaires. In Robert Walsh's *American Review*, IV (July 1812), 71n, it is noted that "Mr. Baker, secretary of the British legation, was, while seated under the galleries of the house of representatives, pointed out by Mr. Wright, and vociferously stigmatized as a spy."

[136]Unidentified in the "Diary."

[137]Herbert Sawyer (d. 1833) was in 1812 Vice-Admiral of the Blue.

the enemies of England had, to the very last, in working up the Congress to a degree of rancour sufficient to allow of the measure of war being carried. There was indeed so little probability of it at the end of the month of March that Mr. Milnor,[138] one of the Members for Philadelphia, told me that he was quite at a loss what to tell his constituents on the subject. Mr. Alston,[139] a Democratic deputy of N. Carolina, said he would much prefer an embargo. While Mr. Clay, the Speaker, was so indignant at the French having burnt two American ships, the *Asia* and another, on the high seas, that he protested he should be for declaring war against France as well as England. He always talked to me of war as of a duel between two nations which, when over, would probably leave them both better friends than they had ever before been. Mr. Livingstone,[140] a Member from New York State, on the other hand, gave me only thirty days to get ready my baggage, but then he had made similar predictions so often that he became like Cassandra and inspired no one with faith in his prophecies, tho' at last they unfortunately turned out but too true.

At this moment, however, even Bayard one of the Senators of most reputation for sound judgment and strong reasoning and with whom I was on most intimate terms, said he could not conceive what I could report home, he being puzzled, though having the experience of many years of stormy life spent in Congress, to form a correct notion of what was likely to be the ultimate decision of the majority, nobody in fact being able to guess what would be the effect of putting the final question, upon others and, perhaps, not even upon himself. Varnum[141] of New York was for war if it should last twenty years, he added,

[138]James Milnor (1773-1844), Member of Congress from Pennsylvania, 1811-1813, was a Federalist.

[139]Willis Alston (d. 1837) was a Member of Congress from North Carolina, 1799-1815.

[140]Presumably Robert LeRoy Livingston, Member of Congress from New York, 1809-1813.

[141]Joseph Bradley Varnum (1750/1-1821), was in 1811-1817 U. S. Senator from Massachusetts, not New York.

because he had persuaded himself that England was jealous of the commerce of America. But Smith,[142] his colleague, complained bitterly of being pushed on by trading towns which would, after all, desert the agriculturists. Meanwhile Dearborn the late Minister for War, who had come to Washington on an invitation from the President and a promise of being made commander-in-chief, was hesitating whether he should not prefer his place of Collector of the Customs as being more substantial, while Members of Congress in the interest of the administration were talking louder and louder of the injustices of the French, and a gentleman of George Town who was well acquainted with numerous individual Members, assured me there were nineteen Senators decidedly opposed to declaring war against England. Just then, however, a report was circulated that Mr. Perceval[143] had joked about a letter from the Secretary of War Mr. Eustis[144] asking a grant for blankets, and this sarcasm true or false did some harm. Joel Barlow, too, the American envoy at Paris had written much to soften the irritation caused by Napoleon's language and issuing of licences. Bonaparte had talked to him in a flattering manner, praised his poems and told him to address himself to the Duke de Bassano[145] who would give him a satisfactory reply on the subject of his complaints.

Mrs. Barlow was fond of Paris, and although the decrees were still in full vigour for seizing all neutral ships bound to England, and for burning British goods wherever found, the envoy of the United States was cajoled and made to believe the system would be abandoned. That Mr. Madison, however, was yet far from having resolved on recommending hostilities with us may be inferred from his conversation with me on the 3d April,

[142]Probably New York Democrat John Smith (ca. 1752-1816), U. S. Senator 1804-1813.

[143]Spencer Perceval (1762-1812), Chancellor of the Exchequer 1807, Prime Minister 1809-1812.

[144]William Eustis (1753-1825) of Massachusetts had in 1800 defeated Josiah Quincy in a race for Congress. He was Secretary of War 1807-1813.

[145]Hugues Bernard Maret, Duke of Bassano (1763-1839), was appointed Napoleon's Secretary of State in April 1811.

when after observing that the United States had sufficient grounds for war, whatever expediency might prompt, he asked me what Members were most influential in the upper house of Parliament and whether it would not be advisable for us rather to call on America to be our ally in opposing the overwhelming power of France, than to be trying to defend our Orders in Council on the plea of necessity. He gave me, however, no positive encouragement to think that he would be for such an alliance tho' he appeared to wish that it should be suggested as possible and, he added, "Embargo is not war. Eighteen valuable ships have been captured; it is necessary to prevent a repetition of such injustice, and one embargo may be inoculated upon another," making me understand that they would wait to hear further from us.

And that same morning the Embargo Bill for sixty days was carried in the House of Representatives and afterwards extended to ninety days by amendment in the Senate. The measure was intended to be kept a secret, that the United States ships of war might have time to stop the sailing of several flour ships then in the river, but the fact was almost immediately known at Alexandria, and the editor of the newspaper of that town who published it was summoned before the House of Representatives to answer for his conduct.[146] He, however, resolutely refused to reply to any questions on the subject. At length Mr. Smilie,[147] an Irish Member from Pennsylvania, and a Democrat, owned himself the culprit, saying that he had inadvertently spoken of it at Alexandria. The printer, nevertheless, was voted guilty of contumacy, but after a time the House entered into a sort of compromise with him. It was agreed, in his hearing, he being in the gallery, that if he would say he was ready to answer any questions which might be put to him, they would let him go

[146]Nathaniel Rounsavell, editor of the *Alexandria Herald*, appeared before the House of Representatives on Monday, April 6, 1812. He refused to divulge the names of the gentlemen from whom he had gleaned his information. He said that he had "overheard" them.

[147]John Smilie (1741-1812) was a Republican Member of Congress 1793-1795 and 1799-1812.

away without putting any. In this manner, he being again brought up, said he was ready to answer and was dismissed.

There were many other circumstances which served to convince me that the American Cabinet had no idea of declaring war at that time. Several Members, friends of the Government and others came to me and endeavoured to find out whether I considered the embargo as a war measure and appeared anxious to impress upon me that it was not meant as such. The favourite expression of the President in regard to it was "that it enabled Congress to keep their policy in their own hands." I was assured too that its duration would have been limited to sixty days but for the taunts of the Federal Members who loudly declared that the Government would not dare take such a step. I was waited on, too, by persons who seemed expressly sent to tell me that there would be a motion for taking off the Non-Importation Act. I was asked what effect that would have in England and if it would not be pleasing to our Government as a step towards conciliation. I replied that it would in all probability be so considered, tho' I could not but look upon it as one that would be more advantageous to the United States than to Great Britain, while the measure of the embargo would have but a bad appearance. A Senator of Maryland,[148] of the Democratic party in the Senate, was particularly anxious that I should soften my reports of the Embargo Act, appearing prodigiously alarmed at its probable consequences and dwelling upon the intention of repealing the Non-Importation Act as most conciliatory. The idea entertained of the great firmness of our Cabinet, and, no doubt, a strong aversion in many to become the allies of Napoleon, was working favorably for us. Mr. Madison himself observed to me that Mr. Perceval appeared to be as fixed in his place as in his purposes.

The most resolute were the South Carolina Members, particularly the younger deputies from that state who seemed to have great influence and were very cool and decided upon the

[148]The HEH "Notes" read "Senator Smith of Maryland." This was Samuel Smith (1752-1839), U.S. Senator 1804-1815 and 1822-1827.

propriety of going to war in order to protect the commerce of the country, while they affected to despise the merchants as men who would suffer any degree of wrong in their search after gain. The Speaker too was very warlike, but the old leaders of the Democratic party, Smilie and Anderson, were on the other hand become much more moderate, and Edwin Gray,[149] a Virginian deputy said he was just come up from Norfolk, where not a man was in favour of war. Two others of the same party, Newbolt and Condit from Jersey,[150] gave a similar account of public feeling in that state, and said that it was the general expectation that hostilities would be put off to a distant day. It was quite distracting to hear the different opinions and sentiments of these people, among whom Colonel Porter[151] after being for war, then against it, then for it and anew against it, set out at last for the frontiers of Canada with a commission for supplying the troops. The young Carolina Members,[152] meanwhile, and the Speaker were constantly urging on the President and there was at intervals a noisy repetition of the war cry. It was even reported to be in agitation to send me my passports. The question of impressment was again brought forward, and Mr. Wright of Maryland[153] introduced a bill about it into the House of Representatives.

In the midst of all this talk and bustle two events happened, a death and a marriage, which gave us some respite from politics, the former being that of the Vice-President of the Senate, the Honourable George Clinton,[154] a respectable old man, who was much regretted and more especially because it was feared he would have for successor his nephew, De Witt Clinton, who

[149]Gray (b. 1743) was a Member of Congress 1799-1813.

[150]Thomas Newbold (1760-1823) was a Member of Congress 1807-1813. John Condict, or Condit, was Senator from New Jersey in 1812 and Lewis Condit was a Representative from the same state.

[151]Peter Buell Porter (1773-1844), later a brigadier and major-general, was a leader of the War Hawks in Congress until he declined renomination in 1812.

[152]Such as John C. Calhoun (1782-1850), Member of Congress, 1811-1817.

[153]Robert Wright (1752-1826), Jeffersonian U. S. Senator 1802-1806, and Member House of Representatives 1810-1817 and 1821-1823.

[154]Vice-President of the U. S. and presiding officer of the Senate, Clinton died on April 20, 1812.

was, as it afterwards appeared, unreasonably dreaded as well as hated by the Federalist leaders.[155] I put off a large dinner party of which one was to have been Dr. Carrol,[156] the Archbishop of Baltimore, on this occasion, and sent my carriage with four horses to the funeral. I found I had done perfectly right, Mr. Reid of Massachusetts[157] and several other Members having told me that it was considered so, that people were glad to see it and it was a proper respect. In order, however, to avoid questions of etiquette no notification of the event had been made to the diplomatic corps, and no place was assigned to them, tho' there was a procession announced in the *National Intelligencer* newspaper, and minute guns were fired over the grave. The President himself, however, had received no notice of the event, tho' he attended, but there was a drawing room held at his house two days after, which was not approved of even by some of the Ministers.

The wedding was that of Mr. Horsey,[158] Senator from Delaware, a Federalist, and a general favourite, who married Miss Lee[159] a very pleasing young lady of George Town. It was the custom of the place to call the next day on the bride when a cold collation with punch and wine was served up. I accordingly went there in state, and found great numbers of Members of Congress who brought reports of an adjournment being to be voted, tho' others came declaring that it was out of the question and prophesying war, while Mr. Ringold,[160] a Democrat of the Vir-

[155]DeWitt Clinton (1769-1828), said to have been before "always in harmony with the Virginia leadership in Congress," in 1812 attracted both parties. In that year the Republicans of New York and the Federalists from eleven states united in supporting Clinton (then Lieutenant-Governor of his state) for the presidency. In the election he secured 89 votes and Madison 128.

[156]John Carroll (1735-1815), first Roman Catholic bishop of the U. S. and first Archbishop of Baltimore. Carroll, who as a young man had served as tutor in British noble families, must have had many acquaintances in common with Foster.

[157]Probably William Reed (1776-1837), Member of Congress from Massachusetts, 1811-1815.

[158]Outerbridge Horsey (1777-1842), U.S. Senator 1819-1821. According to Foster's "Diary" for April 17, 1812, the marriage took place on April 16.

[159]Eliza, daughter of Thomas S. Lee. *National Intelligencer* and abstract report of marriage in *Nat. Geneal. Soc. Quart.*, XXVII (Sept. 1939), 77.

[160]Samuel Ringgold (1770-1829), Member of Congress from Maryland, 1810-1815, belonged to a distinguished Maryland family.

ginian school was laughed at as having had a project of a declaration of war so long in his pocket that it was at length worn out. It now was in agitation to vote a message to the President recommending that merchant ships should be allowed to arm on the embargo ceasing. There were, however, so many projects talked of, that one knew not what to credit and the President was so undecided that he could not be brought to give an opinion either way in regard to the adjournment. Parties too were so even that a motion made to allow no pay to the Members in case of a recess, was lost by only four votes, the division having been fifty-five to sixty-two. Yet as Members are allowed pay for travelling, by the Constitution, such a resolution might have passed without much affecting their privileges. A bill, at the same time, for creating two additional major generals and four brigadier generals was thrown out by a majority of one.

Many of the Democratic Members complained at this time of Mr. Madison's allowing himself to be governed by young Carolina lawyers who were noisy and imperious. Mr. Clay, however, had also much influence as being a man of great weight in the western states, as well as from his station and talents. He assured me that in ten days after the return of the *Hornet* sloop-of-war, if she should bring no accounts of justice having been done by France to the United States, and of money being paid or promised to be paid for the spoliations committed by French cruisers upon the American trade, war would be declared against the French as well as the English. I believe he was sincere in his desire to bring about such a result for he always held this same language, was of an enterprizing spirit and ever ready to trust to chance for the success or failure of any measure, just as he was to stake his money at the game of Brag. Mr. Crawford[161] also who was a man of considerable influence, declared that if when the *Hornet* arrived no satisfaction should have been brought by her for the American goods seized under the Rambouillet De-

[161]William Harris Crawford (1772-1834), later Minister to France, Secretary of War, Secretary of the Treasury, and candidate for the presidency, was U.S. Senator from Georgia 1807-1813.

cree,[162] he would be for war with France. Pope,[163] the Senator from Kentucky, hitherto a decided supporter of the Government came forward with a resolution, which, as General Smith informed me, made the Senators stare at one another. It began "Whereas the perfidy of the French Government," and ended with proposing to take off all the restrictions upon trade with Great Britain. His colleague George Washington Campbell,[164] however, highly disapproved of the proceeding and the resolution was thrown out. But it showed the anti-English party not to be so united as they had been, and if the modification of our Orders in Council, or a conditional repeal of them, as was proposed some months later, could at this time have been known at Washington as determined on by our Cabinet, in all probability peace would have been preserved and perhaps we might even have had the United States with us against Napoleon. As it was, I did not quite expect war to take place, nor should we have it, I firmly believe, but for the approaching presidential election. Perceval's firmness made many hesitate and a letter of a Mr. Gray, an old American gentleman living in London, was shown about[165] in which that Minister was stated to have said, in answer

[162]The Rambouillet Decree had been issued by Napoleon on March 23, 1810. Under it American vessels and cargoes worth upwards of $8,000,000 were seized. It was actually French retaliation for the American Non-Intercourse Act of March 1, 1809.

[163]John Pope (1770-1845), born in Virginia, was U.S. Senator 1807-1813. He and John Quincy Adams married sisters.

[164]George Washington Campbell (1769-1848), Scottish-born graduate of Princeton, was elected Senator from Tennessee in 1811 on a platform advocating war with Great Britain.

[165]Harrison Gray Otis, Member of Congress 1797-1801, and a U.S. Senator 1817-1822, party manager for the Federalists, had several times in 1811 and 1812 written to his Loyalist uncle in London, Harrison Gray, concerning the American situation. An important letter of January 1812 was printed in the London *Evening Star*, and a copy sent to Prime Minister Perceval. Perceval's reply assured Mr. Gray that the Orders in Council were "not grounded on *extravagant and fancied punctilio* but that whether wisely or not, it is deemed by those who advise it to be of absolutely essential and indispensable necessity to the hopes of maintaining the independence and security of the British Empire." This letter of February 22 is quoted in full, and the whole matter discussed, in Morison, *Life and Letters of Harrison Gray Otis*, II, 36-40.

to some observations of Mr. Otis of Boston,[166] communicated to him, that the Orders in Council were more than a question of mere punctilio, as he had supposed them to be, and that the system would not be changed.

In the midst of the warlike preparations going on there were frequent calms, and I was advised to call for a list of impressed American seamen with a view to their being inquired after and set at liberty, which I did do. A Democratic Senator wanted me also to ask why an American Minister was not sent to London,[167] and the President himself seemed to have become more favourably disposed. Mr. Giles,[168] his great supporter, went to his estate complaining that everything was in the hands of young Carolina men just fresh from college. It was confidently reported that the ill humour of Congress would evaporate or only lead to the issuing of letters of marque and arming merchantmen when they might protect themselves. Mr. Pinkney[169] was against war and the Cabinet were divided. The *Hornet*, too, was arrived from Cherburgh[170] and brought no decisive answer from the French Government, nor any favourable news whatever, on which Mr. Anderson of Kentucky[171] openly preached an union of interests between England and the United States and gave out that Mr. Jefferson's opinions were much changed owing to Bonaparte's

[166]Foster's "Diary," May 10, 1812, indicates that he called on "Old Otis" on that date and talked of the letter his son Harrison Gray Otis had written to the Prime Minister. The father was Samuel Allyne Otis (1740-1814), Secretary of the U.S. Senate 1789-1814.

[167]On May 19, 1812, Foster himself urged Senator Pope of Kentucky "to suggest sending another envoy to London and establishing complete impartiality in the treatment of England and France by the United States." "Diary."

[168]William Branch Giles (1762-1830), Senator from Virginia, 1804-1816.

[169]Presumably Foster refers to the Marylander William Pinkney (1764-1822) rather than to one of the South Carolina Pinckneys, though he does not distinguish between the spellings of the two names. Foster received news of Pinkney's feeling from Mr. Key, a Marylander ("Diary," May 23, 1812). Pinkney had just returned in 1811 from his mission in England.

[170]The *Hornet* arrived on May 19, 1812, 22 days from Cherbourg.

[171]No Anderson represented Kentucky in Congress in the 1804-1812 period, but Joseph Anderson (1757-1837) was Senator from Tennessee, 1797-1815.

conduct. On the other hand Mr. Worthington,[172] a Senator of great weight, talked of the point of honour. He had been impressed himself and considered the question of impressment as the main point. He would rather, he told me, live on a crust than be degraded. He appeared very much embarrassed what to do, and seemed a very worthy communicative person. Mr. Clay, however, did not act up to his declaration and though the *Hornet* was come from Cherburgh and had brought nothing, the *Wasp*, another sloop-of-war he said was to be waited for.

In the meantime a manifesto was laid down before the House of Representatives by the Secretary of State, setting forth the grievances of America and her complaints against Great Britain, and a communication that I had been ordered to make stating our determination to keep on the Orders in Council until the French decrees should be effectually repealed was sent in along with it. A caucus was held at which above eighty Members of Congress agreed to support Mr. Madison for the presidency, a measure so unconstitutional that the Government paper had enough to do in defending it against the cry of shame set up by the Federal party, and numerous Republicans loudly expressed their disapprobation. It was, however, a sine qua non that the President should at length use his whole influence to promote a declaration of war. Accordingly the bill for that purpose which was introduced on the 2d of June was actually passed on the 5th, after four days of warm debate, by a majority of seventy-nine to forty-nine. In the Senate nevertheless it was still confidently expected that the bill would be thrown out or, at least, converted into an act for granting letters of marque and reprisals against both France and England. Meanwhile I had occasioned some delay by the wording of my notes[173] which gave time for the arrival of a Senator who was for peace.[174] So nearly were both parties

172Thomas W. Worthington (1773-1827), first Senator from Ohio, served 1803-1807 and 1810-1814.

173Foster's long note of May 30, 1812, Monroe's request for clarification of June 3, Foster's reply of June 3, and Monroe's further note of June 4, are printed in the *American Review of History and Politics*, IV (Oct. 1812), Appendix, pp. 45-49.

174This may have been Bayard of Delaware but was probably Hunter of Rhode Island. "Diary," June 2 and 6, 1812.

matched that a direct proposal to the above effect was only lost by two votes, there having been only seventeen against it and fifteen for it.

It was on this occasion the drunken Senator alluded to in a former page was very reluctantly brought up to vote. They were sixteen to sixteen on another occasion, and various were the tergiversations of individual Members some of whom had property in France, and among whom were to be found Mr. Condit, Mr. Anderson, the two Mr. Smiths and Mr. Varnum. Mr. Worthington and Mr. Pope voted against the measure. Nevertheless at last the Democrats prevailed and on the 17th June the bill was actually passed by nineteen to thirteen. Two or three also saw it was vain to oppose it longer, having preferred to swell the majority. On the following day it was carried back to the House of Representatives and on the 19th was signed by the President.

I went in the evening, as if nothing extraordinary had happened, to Mrs. Madison's drawing room where I found them all shaking hands with one another, but the President was white as a sheet and very naturally felt all the responsibility he would incur. He was, too, believed by many to have been much disappointed at the Senate's decision. A day or two afterwards, as I affected to know nothing of the Declaration, I received an invitation to call on Mr. Monroe when he put it into my hands with many expressions of regret and of hope that matters would soon be again arranged, which I believe for his part he very sincerely desired. He also intimated to me that Mr. Madison would be glad if I would call upon him which I immediately did; he assured me that he would use his best endeavours to prevent any serious collision and appeared to wish to impress me with an idea that the war would be but nominal. As this, however, might have been said with the view of putting us off our guard, tho' I replied in the same spirit, I did not the less advise our officers by sea and land to take every possible precaution, and while I remained within the United States I was happy enough not to hear of any engagement between their ships and our cruisers. I arranged for my secretary, Mr. Baker, being allowed to stay with the archives of the mission in quality of agent under the commission for settling the *Chesapeake* affair, trusting to the honour of a people having British blood in their veins for the safety of the deposit. Having got a license for a British brig of war sent by the governor of Nova Scotia to take me to Halifax, I set off for New York on the 25th June, passing through Baltimore and Philadelphia. I had been advised to take the back road thro' Frederick Town and Lancaster on account of the bad disposition of the Baltimore populace who, a short time previously, had stormed the house of the editor of the *Federalist*, a newspaper published by Mr. Wagner, formerly Under-Secretary of State, but then opposed to the Government.

Innumerable applications were made to me to grant licences to ships sailing to Spain and Portugal with flour from those two towns, but which I was under the necessity of refusing, though Mr. Sampayo the agent had at this time a large contract for supplying our troops in the Peninsula. Many of his cargoes had already sailed under my authorization but his was a government concern. Bills on His Majesty's Treasury had been sent to my keeping for the purchase of provisions for the army to the amount of £400,000 and had I granted licenses to others I should only have exposed their ships to capture. Yet such was the blindness of the traders to all consequences that I knew of ships having sailed for Portugal notwithstanding my remonstrances on the folly of the enterprize and my refusal to give the license required. In their eagerness the owners even insinuated to me that I might have £2000 to £3000 for a signature.

I won't suppose what one of my colleagues then in the United States would have done under similar circumstances but I am confidently told that his protection to illicit trade has been the realization to his family of very great wealth as that of his predecessor had been to him.[175] They both had for their only excuse that they were ill paid by their government and were obliged to have recourse to such means to enable them to maintain spies and

[175]Foster's unprincipled colleague is unidentified.

gain intelligence, which they certainly did obtain from time to time, of a very important nature. Tho' had they possessed a rich and liberal government, they might have done equal service to their country without blame incurring.

War was, as stated above, declared against us on the 19th June and on the 23d appeared in the *National Intelligencer* the news of Mr. Perceval's assassination.[176] I was in hopes that this event, however disastrous, might have had a favourable influence upon our relations with the American Government. I urged a suspension of hostilities in order to give time for hearing of its effect on the disposition of our Cabinet, which, I was persuaded, would become favourable to an amicable arrangement. What happened, however, on Mr. Pitt's death, happened again now. At that time Mr. Nicolson's motion for prohibiting the importation of British goods, which had previously passed by eighty to thirty-five was again passed by ninety-five, when the timid thought they might venture with safety to show their teeth.[177] Upon this occasion as our Councils appeared likely to become weaker the American Cabinet felt stronger, and had a disposition to bully. They now insisted on the impressment question as the main point at issue and declared that a modification or even a repeal of the Orders in Council would not suffice without a final settlement of the questions of impressment and blockade; and, as the Congress were separating, the Government declared they had no power during the recess to do more than listen to our proposals.

This being the case, I saw plainly that there could be no use, and might be loss of dignity, in my knocking at their doors any longer or even waiting at Halifax for a favourable turn in their dispositions. I am aware some at home were of opinion that I

[176]Spencer Perceval, Prime Minister 1809-1812, was shot by a madman named Bellingham on May 11, 1812. War was declared on June 18, though the Proclamation was not issued until June 19.

[177]Resolutions regarding a Non-Importation Act were passed on February 10, 1806. The Bill was passed 93 to 32 on March 26, 1806, after a recommitting motion failed. On March 17 a vote to change Nicholson's resolution into a bill had passed 87 to 35. Foster's figures here are difficult to read, and he *may* be nearer the actual figures than seems apparent.

might as well have waited on in Nova Scotia until I should have been joined by Admiral Warren and we might then have both tried our hands at renewing the negotiation.[178] But on my seeing the King, then Prince Regent, in London, His Majesty did me the honour fully to approve of my conduct and personally to assure me that he thought I had done right in coming home and with this approval of His Majesty I was perfectly satisfied.

It is a curious circumstance that in the first draft of the bill for declaring war against us the name of Ireland was omitted and it was sent back to the Senate for the necessary alteration to be made in it on this account.

I omitted to mention that I had the satisfaction during these debates of bringing to a conclusion the long pending apology relative to the affair of the *Chesapeake* which had been refused when proffered by Mr. Jackson[179] and afterwards by Sir George Rose.[180] The facility which Mr. Madison showed in suffering this grating question to be at length set at rest, on terms honourable to both parties, strengthened the presumption that, however obliged to bend to party feeling, the President, as an individual, was not quite so desirous of keeping up grievances against us as had been represented. The men impressed by Admiral Berkeley[181] and the indemnity agreed to be given to the families of the killed and wounded were not, however, received until after the declaration of war owing to the distance between Washington and Halifax. The convention was nevertheless by my desire most scrupulously fulfilled and as if we were still at peace.

[178]Sir John B. Warren (1753-1822), a full admiral by 1810, actually had authority to cease hostilities. Foster received letters in Halifax informing him of Warren's expedition and commission. HEH version, "Notes."

[179]Francis James Jackson (1770-1814) preceded Foster as British Minister in Washington.

[180]Sir George Henry Rose (1771-1855) was sent in 1807 as envoy extraordinary to Washington to settle the *Chesapeake* affair. Foster's "Diary," November 12, 1812, records the final settlement of the affair, years after Rose's visit.

[181]One of the reparations Rose offered was the recall of Admiral Berkeley, the chief offender.

Having now mentioned in a cursory manner the chief discussions which I was a witness to in the Federal City, and which, as they ended in war, were too important to be passed over unnoticed, I recur to what I have to add in regards to the place itself and the life which we led there.

Backwoods Metropolis and Prejudiced Europeans

It was a sad defect for a capital city that there was no public garden whatever in it, tho' this might so easily have been managed within the palings which surround the presidential house, along the river, or indeed, anywhere within the boundaries at no other cost, in the first instance, than the trouble of cutting through the woods, and, afterwards, of planting. [*Note*: Since this was written I have been told that there is a garden attached to the President's House and that the public buildings which have replaced those damaged by the fire was a great improvement.] And what trees there are for a garden indigenous to the spot! The poppinae, gum wood, Bride of China, from ten to twelve varieties of oak, the liquidambar, sassafras, laurus and numerous kinds of magnolia, and tulip trees with lofty stems, fluted in appearance like pillars, and others too many to detail. No city in the world could have a finer pleasure ground, but never was so magnificent a design for a capital so wretchedly and shabbily executed. Though ten miles square of territory had been ceded for the purpose by the states of Maryland and Virginia, instead of using the land for cultivation until it should be wanted for building purposes, or for the advancement of the city by measuring out lots conditionally to persons willing to banish themselves to so miserable and resourceless a spot, the managers continued to make that a job which ought to have been a favour, and the price of the lots soon reached a most extravagant height. Among other instances the following is extracted from a *Washington Advertiser*[182] of, I believe, the year 1800.

[182]Unlocated in the LC file of *The National Intelligencer and Washington Advertiser*, founded in 1800.

The basis of the Sorterie Institution is upwards of 1200 lots in the city, measuring twenty-five feet by 120, and lying principally between George Town and the President's Square, between that Square and the Capitol, and adjacent to the Navy Yard, a long line of above three miles, these at different prices from $60 to $140, amount to $250,000 and this sum is divided into 4000 shares of $60 each.

Thus before a settler could raise the first stone of his habitation in this discouraging waste, he had to pay from £14 to £20. Afterwards the speculators raised the price to five or six times that amount according to the site of the ground offered for building. Meanwhile the different sorteries and proprietors drawing different ways and miles asunder, single, thin, miserable brick houses were erected with no attention to the nature of the climate or to convenience on the part of the masons, who were either Scotch or Irish, the latter being in swarms at the city. While innumerable stories were bandied about of bad air and bad water being to be found in this or that direction, with a view to injure one another's interests. They were enough to frighten, and did in fact frighten away settlers, bringing in their place speculators. Anything like ornament, or even common gardening was out of the question, tho' this land is in many places excellent, and it was found by Mr. Aiken[183] of the War Department that a gentleman who possessed some ground near Mr. Tayloe's had raised thirty bushels of Indian corn to an acre, the usual crop in Maryland on tolerably good land being twenty bushels. While at the Navy Yard Colonel Wharton,[184] who had been permitted to inclose some eight or ten acres of ground set apart for streets and who went shares with his sergeant, raised 4½ tons of clover to the acre. And he deserved the indulgence, having built the barracks exclusive of materials at but $500 expence to the Government.

We were indebted to George Town for one amusement for which there was no room in the city or its neighbourhood, namely horseracing. At the end of October there was generally

[183]Unidentified.

[184]Lt. Colonel Franklin Wharton was commandant of the U.S. Marine Corps from 1804 until his death in 1818.

some good running on the heights behind that town, at which Mr. Willis[185] of Virginia, Mr. Lloyd[186] and General Ridgely[187] of Baltimore brought very capital horses. The four mile heat I have seen run in 8:4 minutes, the three mile heat in 6:1 minutes. On the third day General Ridgely's horse Post Boy won the cup, worth fifty guineas, but as the United States had no standard for plate, the silver was very far from pure. The two mile heat was run in 3:54 minutes and afterwards in 3:50 minutes. This was in 1806 and the races were as good but more fashionably attended in 1811.

There were also agricultural meetings on the same ground in the month of May and I met Mr. Monroe [*Note*: Mr. Secretary of State for Foreign Affairs] returning with a waistcoat he had purchased of domestic manufacture, and which he had in his pocket. There were Merino sheep which weighed 130 lbs. each. Tolerable cottons were to be had and other stuffs and Mr. Rush[188] insisted on it they would soon be able to surpass us in manufactures altogether, a supposition which I often heard advanced and made it a point to bow to, wishing them joy of it and hoping they would in consequence be more richer and better able to trade with us on a great scale. Two English clothiers[189] were there and wanted me to take them to the President's but the necessity of waiting beforehand to the Secretary of State, to ask a day and hour and then proposing silk stockings and a cocked hat, rid me of their demand. [There was no need however of my intervention for the purpose.]* Anybody might

*Foster's marginal insert, LC version.

[185] One of the prominent Willis family, probably Colonel Lewis Willis. Many of them lived in nearby Fredericksburg.

[186] Edward Lloyd, IV (1779-1834), governor of Maryland 1809-1811, Member of Congress 1806-1809, owned a great house at Annapolis built by Justice Samuel Chase.

[187] Charles C. Ridgely (1762-1829), owner of the mansion of Hampton, was the second master of the estate and nephew of the builder. He also was a governor of Maryland (1815-1818).

[188] Richard Rush (1780-1859), attorney-general of Pennsylvania in 1811, was appointed Comptroller of the U.S. Treasury in 1812.

[189] In the "Diary," May 20, 1812, Foster names the two clothiers as "Mr. Nevins of Ireland and Mr. Garsed of Leeds."

introduce at the President's where every blackguard might go, and at one time the dirtier the better received, tho' I believe Mr. Monroe and particularly Mrs. Monroe introduced a much greater degree of decorum in this respect.

Church service can certainly never be called an amusement, but from the variety of persons who were allowed to preach in the House of Representatives there undoubtedly was some alloy of curiosity in the motives which led one to go there to hear it. For tho' the regular chaplain is a Presbyterian, a Methodist, a minister of the Church of England, or a Quaker, and sometimes even a woman took the Speaker's chair, I do not think there was much devotion among the majority, tho' the New Englanders generally speaking are very religious, but with many exceptions I cannot say as much for the Marylanders and still less for the Virginians. And even in Philadelphia was to be found a Member of Congress, at the same time a proprietor of the Bank of Pennsylvania, who, having occasion one day to draw for money wrote down with nonchalance "pay to Jesus Christ on order."[190] He was one of a society in Philadelphia which endeavoured to establish an atheistical paper. A gentleman of the District too, a Mr. Brent,[191] but not of the family of the Mayor, told me he meant to bring up his children in no particular religion but to leave it to them when they became twenty-one years old to make their election. I should be curious to know how they turned out. I was informed nevertheless by a very respectable divine, Bishop White of Philadelphia,[192] that the Church of England has increased its flock in a greater proportion than any of the other churches, and as when I first visited the United States, in 1804, there were but four Protestant bishops in the country, and in 1812 there were already ten—of

[190]Joseph Clay (1769-1811), Member of Congress 1803-1808, a close friend of Benjamin Rush. Foster mentions Clay as the drawer of the check several times in these "Notes" and in a letter to his mother. Foster, *Two Duchesses*, p. 244n.

[191]Probably William Brent, clerk of the Circuit Court, or Daniel Brent, chief clerk of the State Department.

[192]William White (1748-1836), first Protestant Episcopal bishop of the diocese of Pennsylvania, was long chaplain of Congress.

whom two belonged to New England, one to Pennsylvania and one to Virginia—he would seem to have been borne out by the fact. Bishop Carrol the only Roman Catholic bishop, who at the same period had as he told me himself but 150 clergymen under him in all America, was afterwards created an archbishop, and no doubt the Roman Catholic Church might then also be called flourishing, for as population doubled rapidly in many parts of this continent they must all increase and the only difference would be in the relative degree of augmentation in each at a given period.

Although the city of Washington including George Town did not contain above seven thousand inhabitants there was a great deal of driving out, and I must say I think that there was no want of hospitality on the part of the natives, and particularly of those of the town. Mr. Key, a distinguished lawyer and a Member from Maryland, who lived in the neighbourhood, and who had once been in our military service, made me pass a very agreeable day with him. And General Mason, Mr. Lee,[193] Mr. Brent, Beverly,[194] Mr. Threlkeld,[195] all good old English names, feasted us in their turn, or had occasionally pleasant evening parties. Compared with the society of many an English provincial town, I confess I thought they were seen to much advantage. I would not, of course, compare the life we led at the American capital with the mode of spending time in any of the great European cities where amusements are so varied and manners are much more refined, but making allowance for its size and strange position I cannot be so severe in describing it as some travellers have been.

Nor do I think those travellers justified in hazarding such prej-

[193]Richard Bland Lee (1761-1827), brother of "Light-Horse Harry" and an ardent Federalist, was judge of the orphans' court of Washington County, and lived in Alexandria.

[194]Robert Beverly of Essex County, Virginia, bought the Oaks (later Dumbarton Oaks) in 1805. He married Jane, a sister of John Tayloe of the Octagon House. Grace Dunlop Ecker, *A Portrait of Old George Town* (Richmond, 1951), p. 302.

[195]John Threlkeld, former mayor of Georgetown, is frequently mentioned in the "Diary."

udiced descriptions as they pour forth about America and the Americans without having resided at the capital. What would be said of an American who should go to the British dominions to write about them and their inhabitants and should take up his residence, for the purpose, at Connamara or Innishowen? And then, picking up stories of White Boys or Peep-o-Day Boys,[196] should set them down as characteristic of the whole population? Yet would he be more justified in doing so, considering that Connamara as well as Innishowen have been peopled or settled for years, than are the English, who go to live in Kentucky or Tennessee, which have been settled but within the last thirty or so years and are consequently composed, for the greater part, of natives or the children of natives of Great Britain, Germany, Ireland, or the Atlantic states, justified in giving vent to abuse against the whole nation founded on the wild conduct of a vagrant set of colonists? Neither are the manners of New York or even of Philadelphia, or, at least, of those of the inhabitants of these cities who generally come into contact with foreigners, fairly to be taken as specimens of the native society, when it is considered how large a proportion of the leading commercial firms belonged to Europeans and often to factors of British merchants who, as they became rich, bought houses and villas and lived away with great expence for a few years till perhaps they became bankrupt and were succeeded by others equally adventurous.

Anybody who has long resided at Philadelphia, especially, must remember how often such houses changed owners, and how difficult it was, unless well recommended, for a traveller to get intimate with the real ancient families and descendants of William Penn's companion, the "wellborn" as they are styled, the Chews, Moylans, [Rawles, Peters, Hopkinsons, Binneys, Cadwalladers]*

*Names appearing in brackets are present only in the HEH version.

[196]"White Boys" were members of a secret agrarian association formed in Ireland in 1761. They wore shirts over their other clothing to distinguish each other at night. "Peep of Day Boys" were a Protestant organization in the North of Ireland (ca. 1784-1795) whose members visited the houses of their Roman Catholic opponents at daybreak in search of arms.

Ingersolls; and at New York the Livingstones, Clintons, Van Courtlands, and Van Rensselaers. Besides it was notorious that many respectable inhabitants were become rather shy and suspicious of prying and questioning authors, from having seen so many shallow books put forth, of which the writers appear more on the lookout for anecdotes such as are to be found in a Newgate Calendar, than for real information about the country they were visiting.

[Such authors too were thought to write only for money or to gratify their spleen, having perhaps come out on some foolish speculation, and been disappointed, for they generally find it more easy and profitable to pander to the prejudices of their countrymen than to give them exact intelligence. Besides they too often make no allowance for the peculiar situation of a particular district, whereas it is observable that American gentlemen themselves are as ready as they can be to blame where blame is due and to allow that many parts of the back country especially are the resort of numerous rascals and blackguards. They rejoice in what they think a good story and generalize and apply to a whole people some vile characteristic of a judge or a general treasured up by them at Lexington or Cincinnati or some such place. I confess I cannot understand the sense or taste of patriotism of such individuals. The great majority of the Americans are of our own blood and I have always met among those of the old breed and of old settled districts, for I cannot quite call Americans the sons of European emigrants, no more than I would in general call the sons of Frenchmen, Englishmen. Among the real Americans then, I repeat, I have always found that attachment which one might expect to find in them for the country of their ancestors and I really believe from my own experience and from that of many English gentlemen of rank and good breeding who have visited them, that they are ever ready to show it where it is due and where they know that it will be taken as it is meant. And I think them perfectly right when they show themselves cold and forbidding to the mass of travellers who come among them. Tho' I am sure they will find their account in any attentions which they shall bestow upon noblemen or gentlemen, men of the world, as it is generally found that such persons are much more candid and fair in judging them and making allowances for their situation, allowing for differences in particular districts and avoiding generalities, than are the various land-jobbers or bookmakers, who set out with democracy in their mouths and return with the spleen in their hearts, which they afterwards turn to account in order to pay the expence of their voyage.]*

A traveller for information and not a mere bookmaker should pass one season at least at the Federal City, to get acquainted with the Ministers and Members of Congress and afterwards visit as many of them as he can at their several houses, which would be flattering to them and at the same time offer the best means to himself of obtaining correct ideas with regard to the whole country. If he find not reason to be pleased wherever he goes, he will at least find that some of them may be compared for good order, cleanliness, sensible institutions and cultivation, as well as civilization, with some of the very best districts of his own country and are much superior to most provinces on the continent of Europe. [But remarks such as these will not sell nor gratify the light and the flippant who only look for easy reading and something satirical.]**

Good stories there are in abundance and I see no reason not to tell them from regard to the national susceptibility. There are as many to be found in our own papers every year and all America will not be supposed inculpated because of Anderson's act of impropriety in my drawing room chimney, no more than all England is because of Jack Fuller's tirade against the Speaker,[197] or gouging bethought an amusement of high life in the United States, any more than burking would be considered so in Great

*This paragraph was deleted in the LC version after having been "written in."

**Material in brackets is found only in the HEH version.

---

[197]The unseemly conduct of John Fuller, M. P. for Sussex, took place during the examination of Lord Chatham by the Commons over the Scheldt expedition. *Diary and Correspondence of Charles Abbot, Lord Colchester* ([London,] 1861), II, 237n.

Britain.[198] It is quite absurd to carry blame and ridicule so far as some late travellers have done, however they may be excused from the individual losses and disappointments that they met with. Such people are not fair judges any more than Brissot[199] and Liancourt[200] or Lafayette who had motives for praising the States just as extravagantly as the others abused them. Lafayette more especially, whose vanity was so flattered by the notice which Washington bestowed upon him at a time of life when all things appeared delightful, that his whole afterthought seems to have been an effort to imitate that general and, no matter how unlike the countries, or what the cost in blood and money, to preach for the introduction of the American Constitution everywhere. Brissot's book is notoriously an Utopia and there are perhaps just as many praisers of the country as blamers. Winterbotham's book has led many English astray.[201] I met one unhappy pair Mr. and Mrs. Lemon who bitterly lamented having been induced by it to sell a comfortable farm in Kent to go to settle in Alexandria. What grieved them most was the immorality of the Virginian populace, generally speaking, as well as the danger there was to their own children of being infected by the impiety of those of their neighbours, and they entreated me earnestly to procure for them a passage home in the monthly packet boat which sailed from New York. I applied in their favour to the agent, and they went in the steerage in which alone he could dispose of any berths gratis.

But why will people go so rashly to work? And is it to be

[198] *To burke*, "to kill secretly by suffocation or strangulation, or in order to sell the victim's body for dissection," as did William Burke, a notorious British criminal. British travelers in the United States, such as Thomas Ashe, delighted in describing gouging matches wherein fighters tried to squeeze out each other's eyes.

[199] Jacques Pierre Brissot de Warville, *Nouveau Voyage dans les Etats-Unis de l'Amerique* (Paris, 1791; English version, 1792). He visited the U.S. in 1788 in connection with the abolition movement.

[200] François Alexandre Frédéric la Rochefoucald-Liancourt, duc de, *Travels through the United States of America . . . in the Years 1795, 1796, and 1797 . . .* (London, 1799); *Des Prisons de Philadelphie* (Philadelphia, 1796). Liancourt was a social reformer.

[201] Thomas William Winterbotham, *An Historical, Geographical and Philosophical View of the American United States . . .* (London, 1795; New York, 1796). Winterbotham saw the U. S. as a commonwealth of small nations.

believed that any new settlers coming with real or supposed knowledge, and a disposition to be bitter critics of everything round them, would be at all better received in a remote English county, or even in any part of Europe? People must have rare good temper and make great allowances, as well as be very discreet, not to excite hatred, envy, and malice in any country town where they may go to fix their residence. Yet these grumblers who leave the friends of their youth on purposes of speculation expect to be better received, almost, by perfect strangers or rival settlers. As for Mrs. Trollope's book, her stories might for the most part suit just as well manners nearer home as they do those of Tennessee. The exclamation, "Oh! my," for one, being certainly to be heard in the country towns of old England and perhaps the girls she heard use it in America were children of English parents.[202]

But it is now time I should diverge a little from the capital of the United States, reserving to myself to revert to the subject hereafter in case I should have left anything interesting unnoticed.

Excursions: Mount Vernon and Dumfries

My first excursion was, as might be conjectured, to visit Mount Vernon to which I had been invited by the worthy Judge, nephew of General Washington. On my way, however, I had to fulfil a previous engagement in calling at the house of another nephew of the General, Mr. Lewis, who was said to be the most like him in countenance and manners of all his descendants, and who was also connected with Mrs. Washington's family, having married her daughter by her first husband Mr. Custis.[203] I rode there with Mr. Thomas Law, an

[202]The *N.E.D.* quotes Mrs. Frances Trollope's *Widow Married*, xi, "What a bonnet!—my!" The ejaculation appears in the 3 vol. ed., (London, 1840) I, 279, as the mental remark of a young girl. Mrs. Trollope's *Domestic Manners of the Americans*, 2 vols. (London, 1832), contains examples of "My! (I, 159) and "But oh! my dear Madame," (I, 266) as samples of Allegheny mountain conversation, but the expression as Foster seems to emphasize it has not been located.

[203]Lawrence Lewis (1769-1839) married Eleanor Custis, granddaughter of Martha Washington. He inherited the 2,000-acre estate, Woodlawn, from George Washington.

eccentric brother of the late Lord Ellenborough, and who had property near Washington.[204] Mr. Lewis' house lay ten miles from the Federal City to the south of Alexandria, and was, like most chateaus in Virginia, and particularly that of his brother-in-law, Mr. Custis, in a very unfinished state, wanting a centre.[205] It was in the middle of woods through which the road lies for a great part of the distance, though in the neighbourhood there is more of open cleared country than in any other district about Washington in which I had been.

But one must not imagine in hearing of these woods, that they contain fine, venerable old trees. The soil, in the first place, is very poor and the stems are tall and thin for want of air. We found the family at tea with two nice little children but all seemed more or less affected by the almost general influence of the climate on teeth, altho' I have observed in some families every individual to have beautiful teeth as if it were an affair of the blood, not of the climate. We took tea with them and went to bed at nine o'clock. The next morning we breakfasted at eight and afterwards rode out to shoot snipes and larks, the latter being of a much larger size than ours, yellow on the breast and flying near the ground. We also shot some blue birds which have red breasts and azure blue feathers on the wings, and black birds which sing with rather a squeaking voice, being like our starling and nearly as numerous, though larger. The robin too we met with but it flies here like a jay and is twice the size of an English robin redbreast. It was the spring of the year and the willow alone was in leaf, but from the variety of the trees and plants and the varied shape of the country I can conceive that the scenery must be very pretty later in the season. The fences were of hurdles to keep out pigs. The American thorn will not grow close enough and the

[204]Thomas Law (1759-1834), son of an Anglican bishop, came to America in 1793 with a fortune of $250,000. He invested much of this in Washington city lots.

[205]Arlington, now the site of the National Cemetery, was bought in 1778 in a tract of 1,100 acres by John Parke Custis, Martha Washington's son. Construction on the great house was begun in 1802 by John's son George Washington Parke Custis but was not completed until 1817. G. W. P. Custis was a strong Federalist. It will be noted that Foster does not have the Washington-Custis relationships quite straight.

cedar hedge though pretty is not strong enough for the purpose. We dined at about three o'clock but our game had been all stewed instead of roasted and of course, the snipes were not eatable.

On the next day we rode to Mt. Vernon which is about 2½ miles further on. The approach to it is through a wood and up hill, and the house is the only one that I had yet seen which resembles a chateau. It is covered with white plaster and stands on the brow of a steep bank that overhangs the Potomac, of which there is a fine extensive prospect from the lawn. There is only one good room in the house and that was unfurnished, for all the furniture that had belonged to General Washington had either been left in legacies or sold. He possessed 10,000 acres of land of which he bequeathed after the death of Mrs. Washington 4,000 to his nephew the Judge, 2,000 to Mr. Lewis, 2,000 to his cousin Colonel Washington's family[206] and 2,000 acres went I believe to pay his debts and small charges. The land in general is very bad, but bad land in Virginia has of late been wonderfully improved by the use of plaster of Paris, or gypsum, which was brought from the Bay of Fundy for little more than the cost of the carriage. This plaster is reduced to powder when it is scattered over the earth or grass, or mixed with oats, wheat, etc., and I was assured by Mr. Lewis that a farmer who formerly could maintain but five cows upon a field, can now, with the assistance of this manure, maintain thirty cows on the same land.

Mount Vernon did not seem to be very well kept up, but the 4,000 acres which formed the Judge's portion do not, in all probability, produce more than £1,000 a year net income and the salary of a judge gave him, I believe, but about £700 a year more.

The thermometer stood at 93½ degrees in the summer and in the shade when I was on a second visit at this place with Mr. Merry, and yet I did not suffer from the heat as much as might be expected. We then found the Judge and his wife with a niece there in the house and a French music master. The bedrooms were

[206]George Fayette Washington and Lawrence (or Charles) Augustine Washington, sons of Colonel George Augustine Washington, son of George Washington's youngest brother Charles. They inherited a property of 2,077 acres.

miserably small and of course dreadfully hot, tho' the portico being to the south east, sitting under it was pleasant of an evening. The grounds close to the house were tolerably well kept, and had some rare plants in them besides those common to the country such as the poppinae or honey locust that sometimes has most formidable thorns, but very pretty leaves and even sweet little flowers; the greenwood, a little shrub with extremely green twigs; and the tree called the Bride of China.

In the entrance hall I saw a print of the destruction of the Bastille with one of its keys suspended over it, which had been sent to General Washington by Lafayette. Judge Washington was very anxious to introduce white men farmers upon his estate, and keeping but about 300 or 400 acres in his own hands, to receive rent for the remainder, but several persons who came to examine the land declared they could make nothing of it and did not like to tie themselves down for a period of ten years. He told us of an European who took a piece of ground to rent of a Virginian some years ago, and who ploughed deep enough to raise up black earth. When the Virginian quarrelled with him, because, as he said, the land would be entirely spoiled in that way, the tenant however insisted that he had a right to plough as he pleased, and moreover that he, the landlord, knew nothing at all about the matter, for that his was the true method and would enrich instead of impoverishing the soil. And in fact the same land which had previously produced but five bushels of wheat was made by him to yield twenty.

Mr. Merry's horses were put into Judge Washington's stables while we remained but the oats and the hay were much too fresh and had to be procured by his coachman which was in fact less embarrassing. Perhaps it would be everywhere more agreeable if it were the practice to send a visitor's horses and grooms to a neighbouring public house, being a less burthensome arrangement for one's friends especially where fortunes are as moderate as they generally are in the United States.

Liquor was measured out for our servants but the Negroes disposed of it and the former were obliged to buy some at a neighbouring public house. There were about thirty Negroes belonging to the establishment at Mount Vernon, and an old mulatto servant[207] who had served General Washington during the war in all his campaigns, and who inquired of me very earnestly after Lord Cornwallis.

It is from hence about twenty miles to George Town and twelve to Alexandria where there was a very good inn kept by Gadsby[208] an Englishman who sunk a great deal of money on the speculation which he told me he wished he could get back again, as his business did not prosper, and in general there was no recovering debts from Virginians.

As a great favour, and after repeated entreaties, we got a small private room and some beef steaks here, the only good steaks I had had since I landed. But the ordinary was ready and we were expected to dine at the common table, at which were regular boarders who paid $300 a year for breakfast, dinner and supper.

On the occasion of this above mentioned excursion which calls General Washington so much to one's memory, I may as well here relate the little I have to say of that illustrious person, of whom, to his honour it may be said, there are perhaps fewer anecdotes to tell than there are of any other great man that ever existed. He seems to have been a plain, sensible, gentlemanlike person and a brave as well as a clear headed officer, of a good English family. Tho' having the right English feelings of a British subject, when he was roused to take a part in the quarrel between the mother country and her colonies, after well weighing his duty to both, and the reasons for or against either side of the question, being persuaded that the former was in the wrong, he took at once his determination: to abide by the latter, and having entered and engaged himself in their service to stick to whatever might be their ultimate decision.

Such was exactly the part which any military man of a calm

[207]Probably the famous William Lee, freed by Washington's will and paid an annuity by the estate until his death in 1810.

[208]John Gadsby bought the City Tavern in 1794. John Davis, the English traveler, said that Gadsby kept the best house of entertainment in America. An inventory of 1802 shows 10 buildings, including stables, kitchens, and laundry.

unimpassioned mind, owner of property in the colonies concerned, might have been expected to adopt. For it is now, I believe, pretty generally admitted that the Grenville administration, which first mooted the subject of taxing the colonies, went on a wrong principle, and were no more justified in drawing a revenue without representation from so populous and integral a part of the monarchy as the American provinces had become, than they would have been in drawing one under similar circumstances from Yorkshire. Though I have heard Mr. Jefferson and his successor, Mr. Madison, express a belief that the timely concession of a few seats in the upper as well as the lower house of Parliament, by virtue of which representation and taxation should go hand in hand, would have set at rest the whole question. The late Lord Liverpool's opinion even went further, for I have heard him say he was convinced that if Mr. Grenville had not hesitated, and invited discussion by putting forth a pamphlet to pave the way for taxation, but had quietly let the duties, once they were authorized by Parliament, be levied as a thing of course, there would in all probability have been very little stir made about them. But reasoning with Englishmen naturally leads to contradiction, and contradiction to grumbling, which easily opens the door to anger as well as ambition. And all the colonies were driven to make a common cause by lengthened discussions and communications with one another which might not have been the case but for such delay, North Carolina having, for one, refused her sanction to the rebellion until some time after all the others had come to an agreement.

Such indeed was the force of habit, of common laws or common origin, involving almost every shade of the aristocratic as well as democratic element that it required all the rashness of the Grenville administration to break through those delicate ties which bound the colonies to the mother country and which a Sir James McIntosh[209] might represent as pervading our institutions

[209]Sir James Mackintosh (1765-1832), Scottish publicist, was the liberal who replied in *Vindicae Gallicae* to Burke's *Reflections on the French Revolution.* He lectured at Lincoln's Inn on the law of nature and nations.

from their earliest times, producing harmony between all classes as well as preventing any exact line of demarcation from being visible between them. But by such perseverance in treating them as if they were our subjects instead of our fellow subjects, by imitating the Athenians rather than the Romans, keeping them in dependence instead of sharing with them the honours and offices of the realm, we had nothing to work upon in order to counteract the effect produced by taxation, and we awakened ambitions which had to seek for gratification under a different sky from ours, where rebellion found an echo in self interest and where the gentry were too few to counterbalance the disaffection of the towns. And it may be added that it is painful to see so little done, even now after such dear bought experience, towards blending the interests and feelings of our remaining colonial fellow subjects with our own, and in sharing with them the honours or even the military services of the state. Yet the latter as I have heard was strongly recommended some years ago by a minister high in the councils of King George IV and might yet easily be accomplished by holding out inducements to enter into regiments habitually quartered in Great Britain to the sons of colonial land holders, by which means connections would be formed and an intercourse kept up that would be beneficial to both. And let anyone who doubts this recollect the excellent effect produced in tranquillizing Ireland by Lord Sidmouth's[210] wise measure of interchanging the Irish and English militias, to which we owe many a neat shop in Irish country towns and a much more friendly feeling to the English people generally than ever before existed in the sister island.

The *Life of Washington* by Marshall is but a repetition of what we knew before, and I have been assured that the Judge, his nephew, had kept back some of the most important papers,[211] as

[210]Henry Addington (1757-1844) first Viscount Sidmouth, held many offices, including the Home Secretaryship 1812-1821. He was at other times Prime Minister and Lord President of the Council.

[211]Judge Washington, literary executor of his uncle, had chosen the biographer and had supervised Marshall's *Life*, which was published in 5 volumes, 1804-1807. Marshall later spent 15 years revising and verifying the text.

the General was known to have taken notes on all events which passed under his knowledge, more especially during the negotiations for peace in 1780-1. Mr. Gallatin told me he once met him when he (Gallatin) was quite a young man, in the back country,[212] and that he thought him heavy and rather stupid. He was in a small room questioning some hunters about roads and distances. He seemed to take down every answer very leisurely and was sometimes several minutes in drawing a conclusion. But Mr. Gallatin admitted that he had changed his opinion of him as he grew older. He then told me a story of a black slave who said he was once saved from a caning by the General's looking at the cane before he raised it and recollecting that it was the cane given him by Dr. Franklin. He was very punctual, divided his occupations by minutes, and was not a little provoked when he did not meet the same punctuality in others. And this was the case with Stewart, the portrait painter,[213] who loved his bed dearly, and who told me that Washington having once fixed an hour to sit to him, and, when he arrived, not having found that the room was in order, flew into a passion and gave a great scolding to the servant, which Stewart overheard as he came upstairs. But on his entering the room, he found the General quite calm as if nothing had happened.

Mr. Gallatin thought the only instance of defective judgment in him was his fixing the site of the capital of the United States where it is. He considered him as a man who had naturally strong passions but who had attained complete mastery over them, and he seems to have had fewer weaknesses than most people. His name was long a tower of strength to the Federal party because, although it was principally through his means that the Revolution was accomplished, he was not a revolutionary man, but a lover of order and decorum. Mr. Senator Giles, a leading Democratic aristocrat, used to say that he would always talk of France

[212]Albert Gallatin (1761-1849), Swiss-born Secretary of the Treasury, 1801-1813, had landed in America in 1780.

[213]Gilbert Stuart (1755-1828) painted Washington several times. The General is said to have been the only sitter in whose presence the painter was ever embarrassed.

when the others talked of Washington, as if the bloody, dirty, dishevelled French Jacobin was in his opinion a fitting pendant to the portrait engraved on the hearts of his countrymen by Washington's noble countenance and manly dignified figure.

I have been assured, on good authority, that Washington after he had thrown away the scabbard, repeatedly declared that if the colonies should have the worst of the conflict, he was determined to quit them forever, and assembling as many as would follow, go and establish an independent state in the west, on the river Mississippi or Missouri. Our generals, however, saved him the trouble, having been too cautious and too fond of their beds, and thereby having over and over again lost opportunities for crushing at one blow the whole American force in which there was great discouragement at one time as well as great desertion. Vide *Memoires du Duc de Lauzun*[214] who may be cited as an impartial authority.

Of a man so passionless, or so master of his passions, there can be but few weaknesses to dwell on. He seems to have never been a slave to female charms, and as we have seen, hardly ever burst into anger, was very regular, cool and sensible. An excellent man, in short, in his private as well as public character, but too faultless to be thought great by those who love excitement, keep their admiration for the scourges of mankind, and would imitate if they could those heroes in the eyes of all gamblers—a Bonaparte, or a Caesar. And such, I fear, are too many even of his countrymen, to whom it is a disgrace that, up to this day, no public monument has been raised over their greatest citizen. The Congress, it is true, did once demand of his widow the body of the General, and Mrs. Washington had consented, but there arose a debate about the dollars necessary to pay for its conveyance and for placing it in the Capitol. A dissolution of Congress mean-

[214]Editions of *Memoires de m. le duc de Lauzun*, by Armand Louis de G. Biron, Duc de Lauzun (1747-1793) appeared in 1821 and several times thereafter. Lauzun, who fought with Washington in America, observed that "throughout the course of this war, the English seemed to be stricken with blindness; they invariably did what ought not to be done, and refused to seize the most obvious and most golden opportunity." *Memoirs of the Duc de Lauzun*, trans. C. K. Scott Moncrieff (New York, 1928), p. 200.

while took place, a new set of Representatives let the question drop, and the body was left to remain where it still is, in a leaden coffin, inclosed within a wooden case and upon a heap of similar boxes in a large vault, under a hillock planted with cedars, and I believe not even within the vicinity of a church or any consecrated ground.

Washington does not appear to have been ambitious of retaining power, but the excessive praise that has been bestowed upon him, by some French authors, for his moderation in this respect, is only a proof of their ignorance of the nature of public feeling in America, at the time when he was either Commander in Chief or President, and of the slender ties which held together the different states. For as matters were, with all his claims to the gratitude and veneration of his countrymen, he had great difficulty in preserving his popularity, which had been much diminished long before he closed his career, and might perhaps have been wholly eclipsed had he stood a third election for the presidential chair. This, however, he (being in easy circumstances, if not wealthy, and desirous of repose) wisely declined for his own interest as well as from public feeling. But his example, which has hitherto been followed by his successors, of laying down all pretensions to office after eight years' service in the highest situation of the state, is anything but favourable to stability of measures in the government of the United States. It tends to the ruin of individuals, who, after having risen to the rank of sovereigns, find themselves, while still in the full vigour of life, reduced to the necessity of re-entering the world as private persons, without fortune perhaps, as without employment, and may have, some day, if we may judge from human nature, and from history, the most disastrous consequences.

On the 30th March I left Washington with Mr. Tayloe to go to the Dumfries elections about thirty miles off.[215]

In crossing the ferry of the Potomac (the bridge not having been then built) I was struck with the situation of George Town

[215]Dumfries in Prince William County, Virginia, 29 miles south of Washington, was once a flourishing commercial center and port.

which stands remarkably well on the side of a hill, and, if the houses were white, would look still better. The road for the first seven miles is, [as] at all ferries, execrable and the woods are composed of small-sized trees. From Alexandria we proceeded fifteen miles before we got to Colchester on the Ocquaquahn, a miserable little village of about twenty wooden houses.[216] The road was so bad from the deep ruts in it that I was more fatigued in a curricle than I should have been on horseback. In the middle of one of the woods we passed a wooden house which I was surprized to hear was a house of rendezvous, as it is called, where women receive the carters, riders, stage coachmen, etc., who pass by. The country here and there appeared open but the soil was poor and wet, and full of stumps of trees which in three or four years will rot away of themselves. We dined at Colchester where the inn keeper complained of the hardness of the times which, he said, were never so hard before in Virginia. The dinner was not very eatable and the wine was abominable.

From the Ocquaquahn we drove on to Mr. Tayloe's iron works[217] through a very pretty little dell, with a stream running through it, and high abrupt sides covered with wood, and stopped at his house where we found his manager and one of his captains, for he builds ships as well as makes pig-iron, and sells flour or horses. The vessel preparing at this time was to be of 150 tons burthen, was building in a wood close to the river, and would cost, when completed about $7,000, about £1,500. Dumfries is three miles further on and consisted of about two hundred wooden houses, in one long street or road and two little lanes. It was at this time full of the horses of freeholders coming to vote.

The election of a Member of Congress is carried on in this state at three different times and places. Three counties form a District. In the present instance, Prince William County, Fairfax and Loudon were the three. Each sends two members to the state legislature, which has its sittings at Richmond on the James River,

[216]Colchester, laid out in 1753, has shrunk since Foster's time to two old buildings and a few modern houses.

[217]The Neabsco Iron Foundry on Neabsco Creek (founded 1734).

and the three together return one Member to Congress. To save trouble the votes are taken for both assemblies at the same time, on the first Monday in April at Colchester, on the next at Loudon and on the third the matter is decided. To entitle a man to vote, he must be possessed of fifty acres, or of twenty-five acres with a house twelve foot square, or have a lease for lives or by deed. Of the 33,000 who send a Member to Congress two-fifths are Negroes, though they are not allowed to vote in their own persons.

The intervals of the three periods and the having the election at different places makes it more convenient to the voters and less subject to disorders than ours are, and as the court house is small in which the poll is held, a number could not well assemble sufficiently great to cause confusion.

The members both of the Senate and of the House of Representatives in Virginia receive three dollars a day when on duty, the value of which may be judged of from knowing that seven dollars per week is the price of good boarding and lodging at Richmond. The number of representatives sent to the general Congress by this state is twenty-two.

Among the three or four hundred persons who came to vote at Dumfries, I remarked some with a strong peculiarity of countenance which seems to belong to the mass of the Virginians. The eyeball appeared to me to be larger and more drawn under the eyelid than is observable among their neighbours in the north, and gives them the appearance of being blear eyed. The nose too has a greater breadth of bridge and is thicker, nor have I ever observed so great an interval as they exhibit between the nose and mouth. Their countenances too are not very animated, and there is a heavy dulness in the eyes. Of the two candidates for Congress, whose canvass I attended, one was Mr. Lewis,[218] a gentlemanlike good humoured person as I ever met with, and the other a Democrat who stood up with his waistcoat wide open and his shirt hanging out and deliberately began to comb his hair with a dirty horn comb he had just taken out of his coat pocket. There was a circular seat on which he and Mr. Lewis, the other candi-

[218] Joseph Lewis, Jr., Member of Congress 1803-1817.

date, and their friends sat, and below them the operation of polling was carried on very quietly and Lewis obtained the majority. Kemp, one of the Members chosen for the county, was an Irishman who came over to be editor of a newspaper in 1789,[219] and is, perhaps, one of the many adventurers who live in the United States by following the trade of exciting hatred against their own country, to justify their having abandoned it, and who are allowed to dispose of the votes and fortunes of the less active Democrats of the United States. I say "perhaps," advisedly because I knew nothing of Mr. Kemp personally, but his having been an editor and come from Ireland for the purpose looked suspicious, the quickest way to make a fortune by editing newspapers in America being to fill the pages with disparaging articles about Europe and especially Great Britain, while flattering the native propensity to consider the social system of the United States as far superior. The predecessor of Mr. Kemp was a schoolmaster who was paid £1 per quarter by his scholars.

The country about Dumfries is varied and pretty, but the creek has retired about the distance of a mile from the town since the place was first settled and this will no doubt injure its prosperity.

Mr. Tayloe had about 1,000 Negroes on all his estates of which he had some even in Kentucky and his lands being so scattered he had an overseer to each large farm, over whom was the manager of that particular estate, and over the whole there was a superintendent.

The wages of his white men cost him nearly £1,000 per annum in Virginia currency which is about a third less than it would be in sterling money—£30 currency being but £20 sterling. The slaves and even free men are familiarly talked of as having been raised in such or such a county, and the black man who ferried us over the Ocquaquahn said that "he came off Hodges' Estate," was sold last year to such a one and bought by his present pro-

[219] James Kempe represented Prince William County in the Virginia House of Delegates during the sessions of 1805-1806, 1806-1807. His weekly *Republican Journal* (published at Dumfries) began in 1795 and appears to have suspended operations in 1796.

prietor. The dress for all the Negroes belonging to Mr. Tayloe costs also nearly £1,000. The men and women appeared to take equal shares of work, but he treats them with great indulgence and they seemed to like him. Labourers among the free blacks were to be hired at 2s. 6d. currency per day. But the fisheries, when I visited Dumfries, were taking away all the labourers, as their managers could afford to give $15 or $20 per month.

On our return we went along the Potomac for a good way on horseback. The banks are not very high but they interlock each other occasionally and appear to advantage. A truly romantic part of the river, however, is to be seen about the Great Falls, at the distance of nearly fifteen miles from Washington, up the river, and a considerable way above the Little Falls near George Town. The country thereabouts is in parts very open and cultivated, much more so than I had expected to find it anywhere in these latitudes. There is also a great appearance of good timber in the woods, tho' no very large trees are to be seen, and there are a vast many springs and streams to be met with and plenty of wild honeysuckle as well as dogwood, the white flowers of which give a cheerful gay appearance to the scene. The Potomac rushes over a sheet of craggy dark rocks and these rocks appear as if they had been hurled down together in huge masses. One of them has been hewn through to the depth of near sixty feet to make a dock, and it appears a stupendous work. The river is split into several channels and on the banks of each, which are very steep, grow a vast luxuriancy of shrubs and small plants. It is, however, a great drawback to the beauty of the forests in these parts that their tops, in general, should be so level, there being nothing to break through their even appearance and prevent fancying them to be mere bushes at a distance. This defect arises from a practice the people have of always cutting down the tallest and largest trees.

There is, nevertheless, a great deal of boldness and beauty in the scenery. In the autumn all these rocks are generally covered by the freshes (alias the floods) and mills, houses, trees, etc., are sometimes hurried down with the torrent. The locks and canal extend about a mile and had been open but two years when I visited the place in 1805, having been a consequence of General Washington's plans for the foundation of a capital.[220] The long boats which use the canal will carry one hundred and fifty barrels of flour occasionally, but when the water is scanty they will carry only seventy-five. Twenty thousand barrels were sent down the stream in the fall of 1804, and Mr. Jefferson then told me that there must be another canal cut through the rocks, as the trade had already exceeded the ordinary means of conveyance. There was a wretched wooden house at the place with stables attached to it, by way of an inn.

In reference to the currency of this state, I may here add that during the Revolutionary War, and before the great depreciation of the paper money had taken place, a merchant, as I was told by Mr. Jefferson, who had purchased tobacco in Virginia and taken it to Europe where he exchanged it for dry goods, found the latter sell for so many more pound notes than he had given for the tobacco that he fancied himself to have made an immense profit. Therefore he immediately laid his money out again in a second speculation of the same sort, ascribing to anything but its real cause the rise in the price of tobacco. And as the still increasing depreciation made his second venture appear even more advantageous than the first had been, it was not until after a third trial that he found out his error, when he made what haste he could to get rid of his notes as they were rapidly sinking in value. He held himself fortunate in being able to exchange them for one-half the sum with which he had originally set out on his purchase. A hogshead of tobacco in ordinary times is worth about sixty dollars or about twelve guineas. It is opened by an iron wedge, previous to exportation, in three places, in order to be inspected, which is a process necessary for the purpose of keeping up the credit of the staple produce of the state. Virginia being allowed to grow the best tobacco for making snuff, whereas that of Maryland is acknowledged preferable for smoking.

[220]The Old Potomac Canal carried $10,000,000 worth of goods before being superseded by the more ambitious Chesapeake and Ohio Canal in 1825.

CHAPTER III

VIRGINIA is the part of the United States with which I first became acquainted, having landed at Norfolk in 1804 on the 4th December, after a passage in the American merchant ship, the *Thomas Wilson*, of between six and seven weeks. It was a stormy season and the waves were like mountains, for though they only are computed to be about twenty feet high in the roughest gales they appear by comparison, or rather, from there being no object with which to compare them, of boundless length and to have deep ravines between them. The wind carried us sometimes ten or eleven miles an hour, and the ship was over the Gulf Stream when the captain imagined we were still four hundred miles distant from it. Yet while passing this stream the thermometer rose from fifty-four to seventy degrees in the course of the morning, but this change was attributed to an alteration of the wind from north to south which had taken place, though it was no doubt owing to the exhalation of the water which felt warm to the hand. Long before we saw land we could smell the pines and the dogs on board were snuffing the air with delight. A frigate was lying at the entrance of the Chesapeake for Jerome Bonaparte, but it was too well watched by our cruisers to allow of his venturing on board. The pilot boats of the Chesapeake are remarkably swift sailing vessels. They have no shrouds but the sails are made to run up and down on circular reeds. Each vessel may cost about $11,000. My secretary whom I sent on board one from Lynhaven to Norfolk and who came back in a storm gave me a sad account of the state of discipline on board, every individual sailor wanting to command, and the steersman hollowing out in accents of despair, "Sons of Liberty, boys, for the love of Jesus, hawl down the mainsail."

Virginia

The coast, in approaching Norfolk, is very uninteresting on both sides. The entrance of the Chesapeake Bay is about seven miles wide, though it becomes gradually wider after passing the two capes, Henry and Charles, the main waters lying to the right in a straight direction while a smaller bay opens on the left. Into this flow the James and Elizabeth Rivers, on the latter of which stands Norfolk, on a neck of land large at the point. The face of the country would seem not to have suffered much alteration since Sir Walter Raleigh first visited it, one immense forest appearing to cover it of which the trees are generally of the fir tribe, and not of a very fine species, while here and there you may spy out a wooden or even a brick house.

To an eye long accustomed to nothing but the vast waste of the Atlantic, Norfolk appears an animated and a busy town. Numbers of ships are generally at anchor in the port, some belonging to the town, others to Richmond and to different places on the River James, of which the traders have their rendezvous here, two hundred ships being said to muster at Norfolk which are concerned in the tobacco trade alone. And there is a great variety of water scenery and points of land, with much wood growing in the environs, the place, on the whole, tho' low and monotonous, is rather prettily situated. In summer, or rather in the spring I have no doubt that the landscapes in the neighbourhood may be still more interesting than at the season when I landed. From the extreme verge of Great Britain to the Chesapeake the distance is reckoned at between eleven and twelve hundred leagues which has been performed in nineteen days. This, however, is not to be compared with the passages from New York from whence, an American captain assured me that he had reached England in fifteen days. And Captain Hotham of the *Revolutionaire* frigate carried money to the value of £200,000, in 1805, in sixteen days from New York to Plymouth.[1]

On the first day of my landing in America I dined at the Exchange Tavern at Norfolk with my fellow passengers.[2] We were shown into a large room in which were several people playing at

[1]Sir Henry Hotham (1777-1833), later vice-admiral, was appointed to the *Revolutionnaire* in 1803 or 1804, and was on the coast of North America in this ship in 1804-1805.

[2]The Exchange Tavern, or Exchange Coffee House, was located on Main St. next to the Post Office.

backgammon while waiting for dinner. We were waited on by Negroes, the race of which is hideous in these parts, a prominent chin and crushed nose being their most remarkable features, whereas the black slaves of Constantinople showed great variety of countenance and some of the females, with beautiful figures, had really pretty faces. But here there seems little variety and they are disgusting to look at, tho' when very young some of the girls have rather elegant shapes. I was much struck with the frank familiarity of the Norfolk people who shake one another's hands most heartily, men and women whenever they meet. Even in my case, though a stranger, the hat was never touched to me, but my hand was seized hold of in the street, and again the same cordial salutation was repeated by way of welcome on my entering a gentleman's house. In some respects, too, manners seem to have acquired as high a polish as in the best European circles for after the first salutation and when seated round the fire, you may get up, take your hat and gloves, and walk away without risk of being bothered with questions as to where you are going, "what's your hurry," as they say more northwards, or being pressed to stay in an embarrassing manner. In short, all is done without ceremony. And at table you are not, as sometimes will happen in English country towns, disagreeably urged to eat more than you like, but you are left at liberty to make use of your own will as much as possible, either as to breakfasting, going or coming to dinners and suppers, and you are always welcome. They drink either punch or toddy, which is made of whiskey or brandy and water, before dinner and as the Turks offer coffee, so these people offer drams at each visit. I lived at a most hospitable house, that of our consul, Colonel Hamilton,[3] and I dined at two other gentlemen's houses in the town. The dinners consisted generally of but one course, and they sit after dinner, as in England. Cigars and singing are frequent accompaniments after dinner and Madeira is almost the only wine that is drunk.

[3]Colonel John W. Hamilton was appointed consul December 18, 1789. "Notes from Foreign Consuls to the United States," I (1789-1826), MSS., Foreign Representatives, Dept. of State, National Archives.

Norfolk is pretty much like an English town though the houses are irregularly built. I went with Colonel Hamilton about twelve miles across the country to the point which is near the entrance of the Chesapeake.[4] The road was pretty good but lay through a wood nearly the whole distance, cleared pieces of ground or wooden houses being to be seen only here and there and at considerable intervals. The holly trees with their bright green leaves and red berries were quite beautiful, though almost smothered among the pines. There were also some small cedar trees and tulip trees, and some oaks, but by no means fine specimens, to be seen, and these are covered with a species of moss that hangs like hair from the branches, of a whitish colour in winter but in summer, green. Colonel Hamilton told me that during his long residence in America, clearing the woods has not visibly increased in this neighbourhood, and yet land under timber bears a higher price than land that has been worked, the latter being worn out. The chief produce of the cultivated part of the country is Indian corn.

The mode of conveyance by land from Norfolk to the capital of the United States was, I was informed, very bad and the roads were said to be detestable. One may, however, with the assistance of a good breeze, get up to Baltimore easily in two days, which I did, sending my heavy baggage up the River Potomac.

The great breadth of the Chesapeake Bay is about opposite the mouth of this river, where it is nearly thirty miles from shore to shore while opposite the Patuxent it is already diminished to twelve or eighteen miles. The land is extremely flat on either side and it is only occasionally that a few houses of wood or brick are to be seen in the pine forests. Patuxent Bay is very deep and safe and ships of any size may securely enter and anchor in it. There are, however, not above twenty-five houses in the place, scattered up and down, one of which was a gin shop. Dippers and wild ducks were to be seen in vast multitudes on the water, and flocks of wild geese were flying over our heads.

[4]The point was probably Willoughby Spit, opposite Old Point Comfort at the entrance to Hampton Roads.

The party whom I met with in the packet were not of a very polished description [consisting for the most part of French settlers and captains of merchant vessels].* They were not numerous, however, as good fortune would have it, being only five, tho' in general they have room for ten or twelve and one cannot avoid in some degree associating with them. And seeing them spit and smoke, and when detained by foul wind they are constantly at the gin shop, where they drink, dance and sing and put themselves out of their way for nobody. Indeed they seemed very jolly fellows and during the four days we were detained they went frolicking to farmers' houses where great hospitality prevails. A fiddle is usually sent for and they get up a hop.

The northwest wind is terrific in Chesapeake Bay and comes on so suddenly at times as to shiver all the sails before you are aware of its approach. It generally comes on with such violence after a southerly wind and with a clouded sky, which was the case when we ventured out from Patuxent harbour much against the captain's better judgment. In eight hours, however, we were carried to Baltimore, but just as we were landed the northwester did come and with such violence that we blest our good stars we were not under its influence, while we rejoiced that we had got the better of the captain's scruples.

The whole length of the Chesapeake from Cape Charles to the northernmost point is about two hundred miles, and it is seven miles broad in the narrowest part of the channel. Baltimore lies beyond the Bay on a small river up which large ships cannot sail.

Maryland and Virginia share in the honour of producing the finest hams in the United States, and at Washington in my time the small end of a ham was familiarly called Maryland, while the larger part took the name of the greater state, a distinction which the latter merited as well from its size as because of the great annual slaughter that is made at Norfolk, and in its neighbourhood, of well fatted pigs.

*Material in brackets is from the HEH version.

I have now to advert to a short tour which I made inland. I left Washington early in the month of August,[5] which, though about the hottest season in the year and not likely to be rendered cooler, to the imagination at least, by the idea of proceeding from latitude 38.53 to latitude 37.40, yet I found a very agreeable time for travelling. About Ocquaquahn through which I had again to pass there is some very romantic and rocky scenery, but the road from George Town as far as Stevensburg in Culpepper County is on the whole a dreary ride. Alexandria, indeed, as I before observed, is a well built flourishing little town, of about seven thousand inhabitants, and possessed of shipping to the amount of 11,861 tons. It has a small but tolerably good theatre and when I happened to visit it Mr. Jefferson, a native of America, was acting the part of a provincial country fellow with a good deal of humour, though he appeared to be far too vulgar for high comedy or tragedy. Mrs. Woodham, who was a very prettily made woman, made an excellent peasant girl. But Mrs. Melmoth, who was monstrously fat, was the only individual who seemed to feel her part in tragedy, the rest being mere ranters or whiners.[6]

I dined on the way to Ocquaquahn at Mr. Lewis,' where we did not sit down to table until five instead of three, the usual

[5]Foster began this excursion on August 17, 1807. His letter to his mother from Monticello of August 27, 1807 (Foster Letter Book III, LC) and his notebook journal of 1806-1807, HEH.

[6]Joseph Jefferson the elder (1778-1832) appears, despite Foster, to have been born in England. Mrs. Woodham was a luminary of the 1808 season in New York. George C. D. Odell, *Annals of the New York Stage* (New York, 1927-), II, 307. Mrs. Charlotte Melmoth (1749-1823) arrived in America in her maturity in 1793. T. Allston Brown, *History of the American Stage . . . Biographical Sketches . . . 1733 to 1870* (New York, 1870), pp. 243, 402. All three were members of the cast that played at the Alexandria Theatre July 25-September 22, 1807. It is probable that Foster saw the performance of August 19, consisting of the play "School for Friends." John Bernard the actor agreed with Foster concerning Mrs. Melmoth, once a beauty: "her misfortune in later years, was to expand to a size that no tragedy and black velvet had power to subdue. In the matrons, of course it was not so much noticed; but on her performing the *Grecian Daughter*, in which she made her *début*, at her cry to save her father, 'Tyrant, strike here!—here you will find blood enough,' a laugh was the result, that almost ruined the play." John Bernard, *Retrospections of America 1797-1811*, ed. Mrs. Bayle Bernard et al (New York, 1887), p. 266.

dinner hour of the family, owing to the preparations thought necessary to be made for my modest stomach, which can at all times be satisfied with the plainest fare. But who has the courage to stick to their offer of potluck as long as there is an unlucky old cock or hen in the farmyard to furnish fowl, however tough, for a second course? I went to sleep at a tolerable inn kept by a man of the name of Shuman, from whence it is ten miles distant to Dumfries, a miserable town of wooden houses, many of them decayed and tumbling down, its situation being notoriously unhealthy, upon a creek that has shrunk in size very considerably and had left marshy ground all about it, a circumstance not uncommon in these primeval forests so soon as the hatchet has made way for the sun's rays to act upon streams which for ages had been protected by the shade of trees. At Dumfries I quitted the main road[7] that leads to the southern states and took some port wine with me against the ague, which is a thing the more necessary to do, as you rarely meet in the interior of the country with anything to drink but whiskey, brandy or rum. It is twelve miles of uninteresting and almost uninhabited forest from Dumfries to Lansdown's, a wretched log-house on a lofty hill. That was kept by an old couple of whom the wife was a dirty talkative creature who contrived to empty one of my bottles of port, and then treated me to a song in a squeaking voice which she declared vociferously to be as good as when sixteen summers old. I dined there and amused myself with seeing some hornets feeding on flies. So eager were they for their prey that the old woman had almost tamed them by sticking the flies on pins and holding

[7]Foster's itinerary is very much like one of three Jefferson suggested to other acquaintances who were journeying from Washington to Monticello. For example, in a letter of August 26, 1805 (LC), Jefferson gave General Henry Dearborn a choice of three routes, though he did not recommend one of them, that by way of Fredericksburg. For the other two he gave locations of taverns from Georgetown Ferry straight to Monticello, with the number of miles between, and a rating of *good*, *so-so*, and *bad* for the stopping places he listed. Because Foster wished to travel by way of Dumfries, he did not get on the first of Jefferson's preferred routes until he reached Elk-run Church. Of the places Foster mentions, it is interesting to note that Jefferson ranked Elk-run Church, Herring's, Stevensburg, and Downey's [sic] as *so-so*, and Gordon's as *good*. It seems probable that Jefferson recommended this route to the young diplomat.

them up when the hornet would plunge on the flies' heads and carry them off, eat them and come again for more.

After dinner I went on to sleep at Elk-run Church[8] thirteen miles further, by an almost equally uninteresting road. The tavern was mean-looking and the fare equally so. However I got a bed-room to myself, and as for eating, if a man cannot live on fried chicken and fried ham he must starve on this road, and in lower Virginia, generally speaking, for he is sure to get nothing else. And if he cannot stomach whiskey and marsh water he will be equally ill off for drink. Having been obliged to walk about for an hour until some jovial fellows who had taken possession of the only eating room had sung all their songs and taken their leave, I went to see the church belonging to the place which is—as well as that at Alexandria, and another at Ocquaquahn—in a very ruinous state, the roof having fallen in and the floor broken down in every direction.

It had remained so the people told me ever since the War of the Revolution, serving now but as a building place for birds, and a local mark of the downfall of the Anglican Church in this district of the state of Virginia. The people about Elk-run do not indeed profess to be of any religious sect, or, at least of any that they know of, as a man told me whom I met in my walk. It is not that they despise religion, he added, but the state legislature having resumed the glebes and withdrawn the regular provision of the Episcopal Church, no person can be found who will take the chance of gaining his livelihood by collections from the piously inclined, so that the Church is falling into decay nearly everywhere for want of funds. And I was assured that the far greater number of individuals who are to be met with in Virginia having no religion at all, were formerly Episcopalians that have not yet joined the Baptists or the Methodists who are daily increasing the number of their proselytes. The private conduct of the clergy here and in Maryland before the Revolution was, generally speaking, it must be owned, not calculated

[8]Elk-run lies in eastern Fauquier County.

to ensure respect to them individually or continuance in their functions after the States had become independent.

All agree in describing those established in Virginia in particular as a set of as debauched fellows as any under the sun—commonly Scotch Presbyterians who turned Episcopalians, and contrived to get consecrated by the Bishop of London for the purpose of coming out here and getting into livings, where they did as they pleased and passed their time without any control or shame whatever, in the most careless voluptuousness. The Virginian gentlemen of the present day are, for the most part, free-thinkers, and one, who possesses great property, told me that he should not send his son to Princeton College in New Jersey, because the young men were there obliged to attend divine service on Sundays, whereas he did not choose his sons to be biased by the doctrines of any single sect or to be preached to on the subject until they should be of an age to choose a religion for themselves—though I did not perceive that he took sufficient steps to have the youths instructed and prepared so as to give them a chance of being able to make the choice with reflection and judgment. The lower classes are, on the other hand, very eager in attending Methodist and Baptist preachers, who contrive to get a very good livelihood by the theatrical appearance of their meetings and the other allurements including facilities of rendezvous which they suffer the initiated to mix up with their religious exercises, while the passions of the zealous are excited to a degree that appears almost incredible. Individuals allow themselves, as I have myself been witness, to suppose that they are possessed of the Devil and that these preachers really have power to relieve them.

From Elk-run Church it is a long stage of sixteen miles to Herring's Tavern, and after the first ten miles the Rappahannock is to be crossed, to the banks of which river you arrive, if you take the longest road (as was my case) over a frightful stony pass, called most appropriately "the Devil's Race." The Rappahannock is very rapid and very rocky, and as some very heavy rain had lately fallen my little carriage was very near floating and all but overturned among the rocks. The freshes which had taken place on the 11th and 12th of August were the most sudden known during thirty years, the water having in one day and night increased in depth eight inches, and the average quantity in a common year being but two inches per month. Three bridges had been carried away and one gentleman[9] had lost to the value of $5,000. All along the road the people were in a state of consternation and still dreading more rain. The rivers had risen sixteen feet higher than they had done to the knowledge of any of the inhabitants for the last thirty years. The trees were actually loaded with wheat hanging from the branches and with tobacco leaves which were carried along by the deluge. One woman was obliged to take refuge in the garret of her house as far as a hundred yards from the River Rapidan, and to row out of the window in a canoe. The road was broken up, and so gullied that I was frequently obliged to leave it, and go into the corn fields and the swamps to find a safer way for my gig. Several persons said they calculated that it would take two years to repair the damage done to the paling alone.

From Herring's to Stevensburg, a little village of about forty houses, is four miles.[10] The situation of it is lofty and commands an extensive view all round. From Stevensburg it is twelve miles to the ford of the Rapidan, which I crossed.[11] There is another ford lower down, but you avoid a hilly road by taking the upper ford. In going along the road I perceived evident marks of the mischief done, mills destroyed, miles of paling washed away and the road so bad, that, though I left Stevensburg at

[9]In the 1806-1807 notebook and in the HEH version of the "Notes," Foster identifies the "gentleman" as "Mr. Ellicot of Ochaquaun." Presumably this is the Quaker Ellicott in whose family John Davis lived as tutor for several months. John Davis, *Travels of Four Years and a Half in the United States of America During 1798, 1799, 1800, 1801, and 1802* ... (London, 1803), pp. 224-309.

[10]Stevensburg, a small village still, lies seven miles east of Culpepper on Virginia Highway 3.

[11]The ford on the Rapidan River in the section in which Foster traveled, according to the Bishop Madison map of Virginia, 1818 (rev. 1807 ed.), is Raccoon Ford. It contained in 1835 only 8 dwellings and 80 people. Joseph Martin, *A New and Comprehensive Gazetteer of Virginia* ... (Charlottesville, 1835), p. 159.

two o'clock, I found myself almost benighted at the ford, and still five miles remained between me and the tavern where I was to sleep. Fortunately, however, Mr. Downie, a Scotchman who had been settled upon the Rapidan for twenty years and at whose house I stopped to apply for information respecting the road—not without hopes of being asked to pass the night there—invited me in, and after a good deal of hesitation caused by the litter his house was in from the effects of the flood, when I was taking my hat up in despair, took pity on me and offered a bed. With the assistance of grog and good spirits I got over the danger of sleeping in a damp room which he and his wife had just deserted on account of the unwholesome air.

Mr. Downie in the morning made me acquainted with a drink which, he said, the Virginians were in the habit of taking before breakfast, but which he, perhaps, had imported himself from Scotland, called a Mint Julap, compounded of brandy, sugar, mint leaves and water. A drink, he observed, not known in London where a friend of his, who had asked for some early in the morning at a merchant's where he lodged, so puzzled the servant, who conceived the gentleman to want jalap savoured with mint, that he brought him a dose from the apothecary's smothered in leaves and sprigs of mint, which the other took off in part at least before he was aware of the mistake till it made him sputter and swear and hollow out for some pure spirit to wash it all away. Our breakfast was coffee with fried chicken and ham but no game, and it is an extraordinary circumstance that I never met with a single dish of game during the month that I remained on this tour in Virginia on any table whether public or private. Which as the woods are full of game and this was the season for shooting it, I can only attribute to a want of skill on the part of the inhabitants in shooting birds flying, or else perhaps to their not liking it, for it has been often observed that labourers and hard working people do not like wild fowl in European countries where it is plentiful, and even venison is notoriously scouted at servants' tables as I have witnessed myself in Denmark where I had it in abundance.

Mr. Downie, when I visited him was about fifty years old, and his wife not much younger, and they had a grownup son, their only child. They lived in a district of very rich soil, had a good house, a fine orchard and beautiful upland possessions behind them. Yet such was their love of change and bettering themselves that they were determined on leaving their nice farm here, selling it and moving into Tennessee or Mississippi Territory where they could buy land cheap, and although they had before them the hardship and labour attending upon cutting down woods and living in a log house while preparing space and materials for a new residence. Thus it would seem, and indeed this Scotchman owned it, that the struggle to be comfortable and rich has more charms for these transatlantic settlers than the actual attainment of their object, and Mr. Downie seriously talked of feeling miserable until he could be at his up-hill work again. The object of his long pursuit having been attained, his mind, which had no resources in itself, religious or literary, was fast sinking into alternate torpor and restlessness. His seeking for a fresh occupation with his hatchet was as much an act of positive despair as is that of a drowning man when he grasps at a rope or a tree.

Beyond Downie's the country is pretty open and the "eternelle Forêt" that Volney speaks of[12] is not so much in view, while there is a more equal variety of wood, pasture, corn fields and tobacco plantation. It is fifteen miles to Mr. Madison's, thro' Orange Court House, which is called the County Town and is a little village of about a dozen houses, not above three miles from his country seat by the horse road, although by the carriage road it is a distance of five miles.

The Secretary of State (afterwards President) was a man of good family and had a considerable estate for this country. His father was Bishop of Virginia.[13] No man had a higher reputation

[12]Constantin François Chasseboeuf, Comte de Volney (1757-1820) traveled in the U.S. in 1795 and in 1803 published *Tableau du climat et du sol des Etats-Unis.*

[13]A common error made then and later. Bishop James Madison (1749-1812), president of the College of William and Mary, was a cousin of the national President.

among his acquaintance for probity and good honourable feeling, while he was allowed on all sides to be a gentleman in his manners as well as a man of public virtue. His house stands upon the Southwest Mountains, as they are called—a range of hills parallel to the Blue Ridge, and about twenty miles removed from it. The house has a fine view of the Ridge and of a well wooded plain that lies in front of it from whence the ascent is so gradual that the house scarcely appears to be upon an elevation. There is a portico to it of the plainest and most massive order of architecture, but which Palladio gives as a specimen of the Tuscan. Mr. Madison himself superintended the building[14] which he had executed by the hands of common workmen to whom he prescribed the proportions to be observed. It is of brick which requires and is intended to be plastered. It occupies about a third part of the length of the house, being forty-seven feet wide, and together with its pediments it is as high as the house, viz., forty feet. There are four columns to this portico, of common bricks diminishing from a third, and having bases as well as plinths. And I mention it as being a specimen of very plain and, except that I object to plinths, of good and massive Doric, which was executed by a proprietor without the assistance of an architect and of very ordinary materials. But he had cases made for the shape of the pillars, of wood, and filled them up with the mortar and bricks according to measure.

Mr. Madison has about ten or twelve hundred acres of land at this place which is called Montpellier, and as, from his situation in the republic, he was obliged to be often absent from home, he was under the necessity of trusting to his overseer a great deal. The latter had £60 Virginia currency or £48 sterling per annum, and was furnished with lodging and everything he or his family could want. Mr. Madison assured me that after providing for this overseer, clothing his Negroes, and deducting

[14]The center of Montpelier was built by the President's father, Colonel James Madison. The portico was added in 1793 at Thomas Jefferson's suggestion. Later 1-story wings and other alterations were made under the supervision of Dr. William Thornton.

the expences for repairs, the profits which he derived from the estate did not exceed the overseer's pay. He had, however, another estate of two thousand acres, not far distant from this one, which is more valuable though the income from it is very fluctuating.[15] Tobacco and Indian corn are the principal produce of his lands. He had a third estate not far removed from the other two. The expence of a Negro he estimated at twenty-five or thirty dollars a year according to the situation, and you can only calculate, on an average, upon half the number of slaves being fit for service at any given time.

Great depredations are committed, and continue to be committed, unknown to the owners, in the vast extent of their forests, when they remain for a long while absent from their houses in the country. Tan yards being established in the smallest villages the owners of which employ people to go about barking the trees where they are least likely to be detected, and Mr. Madison assured me that for several years an overseer on a neighbouring property had been in the habit of breaking off the branches and tops of his pine trees in order to make lampblack (the smoke of burnt pines collected on canvas being the process employed) which he sold at a considerable profit.

There were wild turkeys in great numbers in the woods about Mr. Madison's place and I very much regretted not having brought my fowling piece as the Secretary of State had none to lend me. Mr. Macon, his brother-in-law, lived but three miles off on an estate very prettily situated,[16] and there were several other families scattered about in the neighbourhood. The Negro habitations are separate from the dwelling house both here and all over Virginia, and they form a kind of village as each Negro family would like, if they were allowed it, to live in a house by

[15]A search of the Orange County records fails to reveal any second Madison estate of this size. The county deeds do indicate several smaller tracts, of 200 or 300 acres. Apparently Foster misunderstood his host, who may have meant that his other estates added up to another 2,000 acres.

[16]Thomas Macon owned a fine estate, Somerset, with a mansion house erected in 1803. W. W. Scott, *A History of Orange County, Virginia* (Richmond, 1907), p. 212.

themselves. When at a distance from any town it is necessary they should be able to do all kind of handiwork; and, accordingly, at Montpellier I found a forge, a turner's shop, a carpenter, and wheelwright. All articles too that were wanted for farming or the use of the house were made on the spot, and I saw a very well constructed waggon that had just been completed. The slaves, however, are unwilling to make their own clothes, and during the Revolutionary War, it was very difficult to get them to spin or to card wool. Yet the cloth they did make was superior to the coarser English cloth because they threw the wool of best quality into the stuff in which the English use the worst. The Negro women too preferred by a great deal working in the fields to spinning and sewing. They appeared to me to be a happy thoughtless race of people when under a kind master as was the Secretary of State.

There are some very fine woods about Montpellier, but no pleasure grounds, though Mr. Madison talks of some day laying out space for an English park, which he might render very beautiful from the easy graceful descent of his hills into the plains below.[17] The ladies, however, whom I have known in Virginia, like those of Italy generally speaking, scarcely even venture out of their houses to walk or to enjoy beautiful scenery. A high situation from whence they can have an extensive prospect is their delight and in fact the heat is too great in these latitudes to allow of such English tastes to exist in the same degree at least as in the mother country. A pleasure ground, too, to be kept in order, would in fact be very expensive, and all hands are absolutely wanted for the plantation. Great estates, and consequently great wealth were, it is true, in former days by no means uncommon in Virginia, and I have heard of a Mr. Carter who possessed eighty thousand acres, but the abolition of entails has nearly

[17]Foster would perhaps have been pleased to know that Madison later made a large formal garden, at least, in the natural amphitheater behind the house, from plans made by General Lafayette while visiting the Madisons in 1824. Descending terraces, box-bordered paths, and geometrical flower beds were kept neatly groomed by a French gardener.

ruined them all.[18] Many hard cases occurred after the act of Congress was passed for the purpose in 1776, among which I was told by Mr. Randolph of one that was in fact a great act of injustice on the part of Colonel Van,[19] who, having received an estate entailed in 1775, took advantage of the act of the following year, and left it away from his sisters to his widow who married again and left the rightful heiresses penniless. At the present day estates are very much subdivided and I believe that even so late as the commencement of the century nobody could be pointed out as possessed of twenty-five thousand acres.

On descending from Mr. Madison's I measured a chestnut tree that was eighteen feet in circumference and I saw several most beautiful umbrella magnolias of which the fruit makes an agreeable bitter that mixed in wine is considered a wholesome draft in hot weather.

It is a very delightful ride of twenty-eight miles from Montpellier to the late President Mr. Jefferson's seat at Monticello, the road lying at the foot of the Southwest Ridge. There was a good tavern too by the way where I got a comfortable bed,[20] the innkeeper being a Major Gordon who was also a farmer; and I passed a very pretty wooden house with a portico belonging to a Mr. Walker[21] at about halfway, as well as several other settlements—as farm houses on a large scale are called in these parts—on either side of the road. This is rather a populous district, besides that it is the great high road to New Orleans, to which

[18]Foster apparently refers to Robert Carter of Nomini Hall (1728-1804), who inherited over 70,000 acres from the estate of his grandfather, Robert "King" Carter. The latter held altogether some 333,000 acres. Louis Morton, *Robert Carter of Nomini Hall, A Virginia Tobacco Planter of the Eighteenth Century* (Williamsburg, 1941).

[19]Unidentified.

[20]Gordon Inn, built by Nathaniel Gordon in 1787, stood on the main highway in the town of Gordonsville until the 1940's.

[21]Dr. Thomas Walker, friend and guardian of Jefferson and famous land speculator in the West, had built the original house at Castle Hill. It was probably occupied in Foster's time by John Walker (1744-1809), U.S. Senator and member of Washington's staff, and son of the above. The house now is really two structures back to back, one of brick (ca. 1840) with a portico, the other frame (ca. 1764), 1½ stories in height.

the mail was carried in twenty days from Washington, and that it also leads to the different springs beyond the Blue Ridge, where there is a considerable resort of company in the hot season.

President Jefferson, when he withdrew, which he was in the habit of doing every month of August, to Monticello, for two months, in order to avoid the bad air of the city of Washington, had a daily mail sent to him on horseback from Fredericksburg by Mr. Madison's house. And there was a regular weekly stage coach which passed within two miles of his place and crossed the Blue Ridge at the Rock-fish Gap, so that living among these forests was far from being insulated from all intercourse with the great world. There was a disagreeable ford to cross at the North River near Monticello which lamed one of my horses just as I was preparing to ascend. The mountain itself is separated from the range on either side and lies between two gaps. The ascent is very winding, about a mile in length and very well shaded until within about two hundred yards from the house which is built on a level platform that was formed by the President's father who cut down the top of the mount to the extent of about two acres.

The house has two porticoes of the Doric order, though one of them was not quite completed, and the pediment had in the meanwhile to be supported on the stems of four tulip trees, which are really, when well grown, as beautiful as the fluted shafts of Corinthian pillars. They front north and south. On the ground floor were four sitting rooms, two bed rooms and the library, which contained several thousand volumes classed according to subject and language. It was divided into three compartments, in one of which the President had his bed placed in a doorway. And in a recess at the foot of the bed was a horse with forty-eight projecting hands on which hung his coats and waistcoats and which he could turn round with a long stick, a knick-knack that Jefferson was fond of showing with many other little mechanical inventions. Another was a sulky upon four wheels with the spring in the centre, a very rough sort of carriage but which he preferred to any other as having been made by an

Irish mechanic at Monticello under his own superintendence and to praise which was a sure way to prejudice him in your favour.

He had also got an odometer, made by a Mr. Clark, a man of good natural turn for mechanics, which was fastened upon the axle-tree of the sulky and would tell the number of miles gone over by the wheels.[22] This, however, seemed a really useful invention and Mr. Clark, who had been in the habit of using it for twenty years, declared that it answered perfectly well. It was contained in a box and looked like a mariner's compass. A blade of iron, hooked at one end, projected from the box upon the box of the wheel, and the hooked part being moved upwards with the rotatory motion, each time this occurred, the blades of iron gave an impulse to an interior small wheel which again moved another that communicated with a hand like the hand of a dial, when this pointed to the number of miles marked, which altogether only amounted to ten. Every ten miles the machine striking like a clock, after which it goes its round again until a second ten miles are completed and so on in succession. Such an invention may easily be conceived to be of great use in a country like America where it would often be difficult in any other mode to ascertain the distances one travels over with any accuracy.

In Mr. Jefferson's library there was a picture representing a battle, painted by one of the Big-bellied tribe of Indians, who live upon the Missouri, on a buffalo hide, very grotesque, as may be supposed, but extremely interesting.[23] It represents several Indians in single combat, with tomahawks or spears and shields, fighting on horseback. Where a white man was intended to be represented he is painted with the accompaniments of a gun and

[22]For a discussion of Jefferson and Clarke's odometer, see Edwin T. Martin, *Thomas Jefferson, Scientist* (New York, 1952), pp. 91-93.

[23]George Ticknor in 1815 saw the picture in the hall of Monticello representing "a bloody battle," but he does not mention this picture in the library. George S. Hillard, et al, *The Life, Letters, and Journals of George Ticknor* (Boston, 1876), I, 34. For a description of the interior of Monticello in 1825, see Francis H. Heller, ed., "Monticello and the University of Virginia, 1825: a German Prince's Travel Notes," *Papers of the Albemarle County* [*Va.*] *Hist. Soc.*, VII (1946-1947), 34.

cocked hat. The whole is rudely sketched, and the men seem sliding off instead of sitting on their horses. There is another painting of the same kind in the hall of the house but this latter is not as well executed as the first. There is also a map of a part of the Missouri, together with a couple of stone idols in a sitting posture.

Among the most interesting of the President's books was one which had been published in the year 1776[24] by the Archbishop of Toledo, but was afterwards suppressed by order of the Spanish government before many copies of it could have got into circulation. It had been, however, printed at Mexico, and contained prints representing the habiliments of war and peace of the Mexicans, and the great temple at Mexico, besides Cortes' letters and many curious details relative to the conquest by the Spaniards, and to Indian customs. Heriot's collection of voyages among the Indians in three folio volumes was also lying on the table.[25] Heriot was a servant of Sir Walter Raleigh, and Captain Lewis,[26] previously to my looking into this book, had given me an account of many usages as existing at the present day, which are described by Heriot as then peculiar to the Indians whom he visited, those described by Lewis being settled on the banks of the Missouri. If the library had been thrown open to his guests,[27] the President's country house would have been as agreeable a place to stay at as any I know, but it was there he sat and wrote and he did not like of course to be disturbed by visitors who in this part of the world are rather disposed to be indiscreet.

The family breakfast hour was eight o'clock. After breakfast

[24]Foster's date may be 1770. At any rate, he refers to *Historia de Nueva-España por su Esclarecido Conquistador Hernan Cortes, aumentada con otros Documentos, y Notas, por el Ilustrissimo Señor Don Francisco Antonio Lorenzana, Arzobispo de Mexico* . . . , Con las Licencias Necesarias En Mexico en la Imprenta del Superior Gobierno . . . , Ano de 1770.

[25]The Theodor de Bry edition of Thomas Harriot's *Briefe and true report of the new found land of Virginia*. . . , Parts I, II, and III (Frankfurt, 1590, 1591, 1592, etc.).

[26]Captain Meriwether Lewis.

[27]The library was thrown open to George Ticknor in 1815. Hilliard et al, *Life, Letters, and Journals of Ticknor*, I, 35-36.

Mrs. Randolph and her amiable daughters as well as the other female relations of the house set about cleaning the tea things and washing the alabaster lamp, which I took to be designed as a catch for popularity. After this operation the President retired to his books, his daughter to give lessons to her children, her husband to his farm, and the guests were left to amuse themselves as they pleased till four o'clock, walking, riding or shooting. The President took his daily ride at one o'clock to look at his farm and mill, at four dinner was served up and in the evening we walked on a wooden terrace or strolled into the wood, Mr. Jefferson playing with his grandchildren till dusk when tea was brought in, and afterward wine and fruit of which the peaches were excellent. At nine o'clock our host withdrew and everybody else as they pleased. Mr. Randolph's son, a youth of sixteen, who was at school at the village of Milton close by, generally came in the evening.[28] He was a fine young lad, and, according to what I was told was a general custom in Virginia among boys, he walked into the drawing room, without shoes or stockings, tho' very neatly dressed in other respects. I had, however, reason to doubt afterwards that the practice was so general and I believe it was a mere whim of his grandfather, who in the very first conversation I had with him expressed his wonder that feet were not as often washed as hands and would I dare say, if he could have ventured it without ridicule, have been for a still greater degree of nakedness, so fond was he of leaving nature as unconfined as possible in all her works.

The President was considered a very bad farmer. He had some excellent red land, however, about Monticello and a profitable estate in the county of Bedford about ninety miles from thence,[29] but his estates suffered prodigiously from the tendency of the soil to gully, which cannot well be prevented on hilly

[28]Thomas Jefferson Randolph (1792-1875), Jefferson's favorite grandson and literary executor. Apparently he attended the academy conducted close by under Jefferson's patronage by the eccentric but able James Ogilvie (1775-1820). R. B. Davis, "James Ogilvie, an Early American Teacher of Rhetoric," *Quart. Jour. Speech*, XXVIII (Oct. 1942), 289-97.

[29]Poplar Forest, to which Jefferson retired for a short period each year.

ground, and is very much promoted by the culture of Indian corn. The slightest track opens the way for a gully, and that of a plough-share dragged negligently through a field may be the commencement of a chasm in which houses afterwards might be buried. One side of the hill on which Monticello stands has been so disfigured in this way that they have been obliged to scatter Scotch Broom seed over it, which at last succeeded in, at least, hiding the cavities.[30] Tobacco is the most profitable produce of the soil, and next to it, Indian corn of which I have been told that some land belonging to Mr. Garnet,[31] on the Rappahannock, will yield forty-eight bushels to the acre.

Mr. Jefferson told me that in the year 1791 there were about 292,500 slaves in Virginia, the whole number of the inhabitants of the state being at that time but 747,500. And of those 292,500, nearly 200,000 were to be found in the forty-four counties along the Chesapeake Bay with the great rivers which fall into it, while the free persons in those counties amounted to but 198,000. About the same period there were but 700,000 slaves in the whole of the United States, of which number above 630,000 were living in the states south of the Delaware. The price of a slave on an average was about $400, and the President said he thought that they increased in population more rapidly than the whites.

Their oaths were valid against one another but not against a white man; neither was the oath of a free Negro allowed to be valid against white people. Free Negroes associated and intermarried with slaves, but the slaves of a proprietor who was master of 500 or 600 of them considered themselves as vastly superior to those of a man who owned but two or three. Mr. Jefferson told me of a Negro named Bannister, who died in the year 1806, at Baltimore, being a perfect black, the son of an African, and who had acquired considerable knowledge in mathematics so

[30]The Scotch Broom still covers part of the hillside at Monticello.

[31]Presumably James Mercer Garnett (1770-1843), son of Muscoe Garnett and a Member of Congress for two terms from 1805. The Garnett estate was Elmwood, on the Rappahannock. James Mercer Garnett was a leader in agrarian reform, a founder of the Virginia Agricultural Society, and first president of the United States Agricultural Society.

as to be able to solve very difficult problems. He annually published an almanac but the President asserted that in other respects he appeared to little advantage, particularly in his letters, he having received several from him which were very childish and trivial.[32] He told me, also, that the Negroes have, in general, so little foresight that though they receive blankets very thankfully from their masters on the commencement of winter and use them to keep off the cold, yet when the warm weather returns they will frequently cast them off, without a thought as to what may become of them, wherever they may happen to be at the time, and then not seldom lose them in the woods or the fields from mere carelessness.

Jefferson's opinions in regard to the mental qualities of the Negro race were certainly not favourable for he considered them to be as far inferior to the rest of mankind as the mule is to the horse, and as made to carry burthens, while he augured but little good as likely to result from their emancipation, observing that it was an English hobby, and that the English are apt to ride their hobbies to death, and while riding them will hardly suffer any contradiction, scouting anybody that opposes them, and he quoted Law's South Sea scheme,[33] the tea tax on America and appeared to think that we should only render the Negroes' fate more miserable by our perseverance in endeavouring to abolish the trade.

That the black race is, however, as susceptible of refined civilization, and as capable to the full of profiting by the advantages of education as any other of any shade whatever, must be admitted, in contradiction to Mr. Jefferson's prejudices, by any person who has had the honour to be acquainted with

[32]Benjamin Banneker (1731-1806) produced several almanacs, the first in 1792. Henry E. Baker, "Benjamin Banneker, the Negro Mathematician and Astronomer," *Jour. Negro Hist.*, III (April 1918), 99-118; Martha E. Tyson, "Thomas Jefferson's Thoughts on the Negro," *Jour. Negro Hist.*, III (Jan. 1918), 55-89.

[33]John Law (1671-1729), Scottish economist and eccentric financial genius, was the originator of the "Mississippi scheme" and the "Compagnie des Indes," both in France. He expected to pay the French national debt and yet make enormous profits. The scheme begun in 1716 was ended by a panic in 1720.

the daughters of Christophe, who was Supreme Sovereign or Emperor of Hayti during eight or nine years, and who spared no kind of expence in getting good European masters for his children.[34] The early and melancholy fate of his sons prevented us from forming a judgment as to what they might have become in consequence of such care, but his daughters are well known at several European courts and by many individuals of the best European society, especially at the Tuscan and Sardinian capitals, where in spite of their colour and their rank which made it difficult for them to mix familiarly in the great world, they were sufficiently seen nevertheless to let it be apparent that their wit and understandings as well as their accomplishments were of the very highest order.

Christophe, himself, too, though he had dangerous passions, had also great qualities, and I happened to meet with an American who knew him at St. Kitts while still in service and afterwards as a monarch. During the former visit the American had lent him a sum of money, but was shy of going near him when he heard afterwards that he had become the master of a nation. Christophe, however, having been informed of his arrival, sent to him, reproached him for his backwardness in coming to see him, and not only repaid what he had lent him with interest, but loaded him with presents and lodged him at his palace while he remained on the island.

I must admit that I was by no means edified by the accounts I heard of the pleasures of having property in the state of Virginia. The laws are so badly executed and it seems so impracticable even for a man of large possessions to keep off thieves, from his farm yard and his gardens. At many respectable houses where I have stopped to dine I have been surprized at so seldom meeting with fruit or even with eggs, and the greater number of small farmers whom I knew anything of admitted that they

[34]Henri Christophe (1767-1820), Negro king of Haiti 1812-1820, evidently interested Foster as early as 1805. Foster, *Two Duchesses*, p. 250. Foster later became acquainted with Christophe's daughters in Turin and other places on the Continent. Foster Letter Books and Diaries, 1824ff., LC; *Two Duchesses*.

live chiefly upon salted pork and dried fish tho' at times you get chickens.

Land about Monticello, and in the neighbourhood of Charlesville* in Albemarle County, was to be had, as I was told, for less than five dollars the acre, even with a house upon it. The soil is red, and the red-bud tree, that grows upon it abundantly, is reckoned to be a sure sign of its fruitfulness.

The Virginia hogshead, as I was informed, will usually contain from 1,200 lbs to 2,000 lbs. weight of tobacco, while that of Maryland will hold but 200 lbs. to 900 lbs. weight. The former contains the best leaf for making snuff, but the leaf of Maryland is the best for smoking and is known, from its colour, under the name of Kitefoot. The Maryland hogshead is worth $60 or $70, the other from $100 to $120, or, at 4½ to the £1 sterling, about £25. Tobacco does not exhaust the soil much. It is the culture of Indian corn that is most injurious to it, from its letting in the sun to burn up the ground and preparing the land for gullying.

The order of cultivation is, generally speaking, to plant tobacco for three years, then Indian corn and wheat alternately, and but few cultivators give their land rest during seven or eight years. The lands on the sides of rivers and in bottoms will bear for a much longer time as the rains wash away and carry into them the soil of the uplands, but those uplands are soon exhausted, and then becoming covered with briars and weeds, are unfitted for any kind of use during a long succession of years (at the least seven) unless aided by manure. Entirely new virgin land in this state, if from the first laid under wheat, would, I was assured, give forty or even fifty bushels to the acre, tho', in the usual average, they yield but six or seven, or eight, or fifteen according to their quality and treatment.

Of tobacco 3,500 lbs. weight are as much as can be raised upon an acre of very good land. It is sown in February, planted out in May and cut in October. A barrel of flour should, as determined by law, contain 196 lbs. weight, and the flour, if

*I.e., Charlottesville, but spelled thus in both MSS.

properly taken care of, should keep for eighteen months. Hard flinty stones put into the barrel are a great preservative of it, and in weighing the flour, the weight of the stones is allowed for. If meal be found mixed up with the flour, the barrel is condemned by law, though the practice is to return it, or to rate it as of inferior quality.

The Alexandrian Biscuit of Jamieson, a Scotch baker, is the finest kind of biscuit that is made, and flour exported from Alexandria was considered as the best on the American continent. It was in 1807 selling at $6¼ per barrel for bills at sixty days, sight, or $6 ready money, though it varies very frequently in value, so much so as to have been often at $10 or even $12 per barrel in the same place and at one and the same time, according to the sudden demand for it. But it is considered as being very low when it sells for but five dollars, and in order to be at all profitable to the merchant it should sell in Europe for three dollars more. He will just not lose if the price be forty-two shillings.

Mr. Tayloe might, I believe, be considered as the richest man in Virginia in 1806-7, being said to have then had $60,000 or above £12,000 per annum arising from 15,000 acres of land belonging to him in different parts of this state and of Maryland, in which latter he possessed 3,000 acres at a place called Nangemoi[35] which his father purchased for £500 and for which Mr. J. Campbell,[36] a Member of Congress, told me he should be glad to give him, now, $20,000. He was supposed to lay out every year $33,000 in purchasing land. He had a fine house at Mount Airy where he had 8,000 acres, and a house at Washington City, and had to purchase nothing but clothes for himself and family, wines furniture or other luxuries, which were however not very costly, though it must be owned that he lived, as to outward appearance, in the best style of any of the Americans not in office. President Jefferson's wines were in general very indifferent though he had a great variety of them, including some native

[35]Or Nanjemoy.

[36]John Campbell (1705-1828), was a Federalist Member of Congress 1801-1811.

juice of the grape from the Ohio, and some Nebioule from Piedmont. But he told me he had often had the bad luck to have his barrels tapped and water mixed with the wine, and sometimes even salt water. His principles of general philanthropy, however, made him indifferent to such matters, being ever ready to excuse all offences not political, though with regard to these he was violent and vindictive.

He was happy enough to have his daughters both married in Virginia, one to Mr. Thomas Mann Randolph, a gentleman of property and who claimed to descend on the mother's side from the Indian queen, Pocahontas, as his cousin John Randolph claimed to be descended from her by the father's side. The other daughter was married to Mr. Eppes.[37] Both gentlemen were Members of Congress and both were planters, as indeed more than two-thirds of the deputies are who represent this aristocratic state, which has taken the lead of all the states in preaching ultra democratical principles and in governing the Union by means of its gentleman Jacobins, who were not to be had in such numbers nor of such abilities from any other part of the continent. Mr. Jefferson was in frequent correspondence with Madame de Staël and when I visited him he had just received *Corinne* from her,[38] with a letter in which, he observed, she had written strong things in little space. She told him that there was now but one man in Europe, that she was not allowed by him to live in Paris, but at a small distance from it, and that every day there came to visit her Volney, Dupont,[39] several conservative Senators and others who were still warm republicans though they kissed the rod.

He, Jefferson, speculated on what would be the fate of France

[37]John Wayles Eppes (1773-1823).

[38]Jefferson replied to Madame de Staël's letter from Paris of April 24, 1807, on July 16 of that year. See *Writings*, eds., Lipscomb and Bergh, XI, 281-83. Her "duel with Napoleon" began as early as 1804. *Corinne*, her most famous novel, was published in 1807. In December 1807, Foster wrote his mother from Washington that the President had lent him *Corinne*. Later (December 23) he wrote that it was delightful. Foster Letter Books, LC.

[39]Pierre Samuel du Pont de Nemours (1739-1817), French liberal and longtime friend of Jefferson, established his family in America before his death.

in the event of Bonaparte's death and said he was of opinion they would agree to be under any monarch rather than hazard another revolution of a Jacobinical description. In speaking of Talleyrand[40] he told me that he had always, while in the United States, affected to be ignorant of the English language, but that when walking one day with General Dearborn, he forgot himself and came out with a question in English about some indifferent matter, and at Paris, after his return from America, though he conversed with General Armstrong,[41] the American envoy, in English to Mr. Fox and other British persons, he pretended not to know it. Mr. Jefferson had been in the south of France and said those meridional provinces would have made a fine flourishing state, on which I observed how near they were to being rendered a separate country by the Revolution, and he added he wished they had been so separated, for that if France, like North America, had been divided into small states they would not have troubled their neighbours so much.

Mr. Jefferson in speaking of the Brazils, surprized me by his ideas regarding that country, as he maintained that the United States would have to supply it with provisions, and that it had never been able to supply Portugal. Tho' when I observed that there was great variety of soil in it fit for anything, he admitted the fact, and said that he was convinced they might even make wine in some of the provinces. I ventured to ask if he intended to open diplomatic relations with the Court of Rio Janeiro but he told me he expected they would announce themselves, as in general it was the custom for strangers to make the first visit tho' it was true the contrary custom was that which prevailed in the United States.

Mr. Jefferson was famous for his holding to any opinion that he had taken up, no matter whose, with great obstinacy. Mr.

[40]Charles Maurice de Talleyrand-Périgord (1754-1834), French diplomat and statesman, lived in exile in the U.S. 1793-1795, always uneasy and discontented with his surroundings.

[41]John Armstrong (1758-1843), later brigadier-general and Secretary of War, was in 1806 special envoy in Paris.

Clarke,[42] the first delegate from New Orleans, before it was received as a state, told me that having been one evening invited to go to see him and converse about that country, he remained for three hours, during which the President, on several points on which he had been falsely informed, would, tho' set right by Clarke, constantly recur to his own sentiment founded on such false reports. His aim would seem to be to try to get Clarke to commit himself so as to be able to bring him by hook or crook into his own theory, getting at the real fact appearing with him to be quite of inferior importance.

I thought Mr. Jefferson more of a statesman and man of the world than Mr. Madison, who was rather too much the disputatious pleader. Yet the latter, however, was better informed, and, moreover, was a social, jovial and good-humoured companion full of anecdote and sometimes matter of a loose description relating to old times, but oftener of a political and historical interest. During the time when Congress sat at Philadelphia he fell in love with Mrs. Todd, who presided at the boarding house where he lived, and married her.[43] She must have been a very handsome woman and tho' an uncultivated mind and fond of gossiping, was so perfectly good-tempered and good-humoured that she rendered her husband's house as far as depended on her agreeable to all parties.

Mr. Madison was a little man, with small features rather wizened when I saw him, but occasionally lit up with a good-natured smile. He wore a black coat, stockings with shoes buckled, and had his hair powdered, with a tail. Jefferson on the other hand was, as before stated, very tall and bony and affected to despise dress. In conversation too he was visionary and loved to dream, eyes open, or, as the Germans say, "zu schwärmen," and it must be owned that America is the paradise for "Schwärmers," futurity there offering a wide frame for all that the imagination can put

[42]Daniel Clark (1766-1813), elected delegate from the New Orleans Territory in 1806, hated Jefferson's friend Claiborne and fought a duel with the latter.

[43]Dorothy Payne Todd (1772-1849), a charming widow, was married to James Madison in 1794.

into it. If he lived, however, on illusions and mystic philanthropical plans for the benefit of mankind in the country, or in his bed, he was not the less awake or active in taking measures to ensure the triumph of himself and his party at the capital of the Union, and I doubt if General Washington himself would so certainly have been elected for the third time to the presidential chair as he would have been, had he chosen to be put into nomination for it. But he preferred being consistent and to follow in this respect the example of his great predecessor, while he had enough of independence of mind and love for even trifling occupations to enable him to bear the change with composure.

It must, however, have been a painful necessity that induced him to sell his library, though, no doubt, it was prudentially done for the interests of his children, and patriotically sold to his country. Yet still there was I fear, also, the potent argument of poverty, and it was another great slur upon the character of Congress that they did not vote him the money and refuse to accept the books, at least until after his death.[44] Such men as Washington and Jefferson, and their contemporaries in the highest stations of their country, having had peculiar claims to its most generous consideration, particularly when we consider what the nature of sacrifices which they made in order to establish the republic consisted of, and that such sacrifices never can possibly be equalled by any of their successors. The founders of American independence having been well-born *Britons*, which the statesmen of the present day in the United States are not, their characters, their love of liberty and acquirements having all been attained under

[44]Foster is perhaps mistaken in surmising that Jefferson sold his library to Congress purely from necessity. Some other commentators have concluded as Foster does, but Jefferson's letters to Samuel H. Smith and to President Madison (September 21, 24, 1814), put it on another basis. Deeply distressed at the loss of the national library when the British burned Washington, Jefferson offered to sell Congress his library, at Congress' own price, to replace the lost volumes. He emphasized that he had always intended that it should go to Congress at his death, but that the few years remaining to him and the present urgent necessity caused him to proffer it now. Foster would have been on surer critical ground had he attacked Congress for the niggardly sum of $23,950 paid, estimated to have been about half its auction value, at a time when Congress knew of Jefferson's straitened, even desperate, circumstances.

British institutions, and the decision which they took to renounce their allegiance in giving birth to a new state, rather than submit to an unjust demand, having been of a nature that never can be paralleled.

I therefore say that Congress was more especially bound to have respected such claims, and I shall ever look upon it as a proof of degeneracy in the race of men succeeding to that of the founders of American independence that the great Washington was for years, and is, I believe, still left unburied, otherwise than as we bury a dog, from considerations of a wretched economy; that Jefferson was forced to sell his library in his old age to enable him to live; and that Monroe was almost left to starve, having had but a paltry pittance voted to him after he, like others, had spent his patrimony in keeping up the respectability of the offices of Secretary of State and of American President.[45] America is fond of being called a young nation but youth is seldom stingy and we have yet to learn what are the beneficial effects which may be produced by referring all things to penurious motives and rigid maxims of economy, nothing being allowed out of respect for great characters and public services.

Already have they reaped some of the evil consequences of such a system, corruption among their civil officers having fearfully increased since the front ranks have been thinned of those whose boyhood had imbibed its character from English principles as well as English education, and whose gentlemanly examples still served to influence and keep in a straight course the age they lived in. From the date of the French Revolution in 1789, which was also the date of the new American Constitution, to the declaration of war by the United States in 1812, seven judges had been, though I believe unjustly, impeached,[46] a Vice-

[45]Monroe was ruined by holding office. In 1826 Congress authorized payment to him of $30,000, and after his death appropriated a small sum to purchase his papers from his heirs.

[46]Foster must have been thinking of state as well as federal judges, for only two of the latter, John Pickering (in 1803) of the District Court of New Hampshire and Samuel Chase (in 1804) of the Supreme Court, were impeached (and only one of these successfully) in Foster's time.

President was convicted of conspiring to overturn the government,[47] three Senators were said to have been implicated in the plot,[48] a District Attorney had to fly from New York to New Orleans on being convicted of peculation, carrying off $50,000 of public property in his pockets.[49] A son of a Secretary of the Treasury had to fly from Philadelphia on being proved guilty of swindling,[50] a Secretary of State, as may be seen in the French envoy Fauchet's intercepted and published dispatches, was guilty of having been bribed by the French;[51] and many other instances might be added sufficient to show the bad policy, as well as bad economy, of meanness in a state, while even the object itself, if it be that of courting popularity, becomes no longer attainable when there is no longer anything on which to economize—generous salaries to public ministers on the part of the state being just as necessary to popular orators in the display of their eloquence as the existence of game laws is to poachers, the total extinction or insufficiency of either becoming the ruin of the one as well as of the other's daily occupation.

[The term *Popular* or *People*, however, is nowhere so much abused as in speaking or writing about the inhabitants of the United States. In Ireland we all know how it swells in the mouth

[47]Presumably he refers to Aaron Burr, though Burr was not convicted in the famous Richmond trial in 1807.

[48]Senator Jonathan Dayton of New Jersey and Senator John Smith of Ohio were presented to the grand jury at Richmond for treason but escaped indictment. The third Senator may have been General John Adair of Kentucky, who was arrested by Wilkinson in New Orleans, sent to Baltimore, but released for lack of evidence.

[49]Apparently Foster refers to Edward Livingston (1764-1836) the only New York district attorney who went to New Orleans (actually 1803-1804). He was involved in a case concerning one of his agents who absconded with funds, and he himself assumed the responsibility. Personally he was not guilty of peculation.

[50]Unidentified.

[51]This refers to Edmund Randolph (1753-1813), George Washington's second Secretary of State and earlier Attorney General, who was ruined by Federalist secretaries in the cabinet when the latter brought charges based on alleged treasonable proposals incorporated into the dispatches of Joseph Fauchet, the French envoy, in 1794. Irving Brant ("Edmund Randolph, Not Guilty," *Wm. & Mary Quart.*, 3rd ser., VIII [April 1950], 179-98) offers convincing evidence that Randolph was an innocent statesman ruined by unscrupulous Federalist machinations.

of an agitator and it becomes six or seven or eight or nine millions according as he means to thunder out his alarms. In the United States it is also a lever without shape or limits. But if you ask for its real import, off go instantaneously a full fourth of its numbers, and of the remainder how vain it is to speak as of a mass homogeneous. It is indeed in every country a difficult thing to decide who and where the *People* are, and it is not seldom that the term is made to apply to a minimum of the real population, its constituents. For an instance of this take a village, or small borough rather, nominally, we will say, of 5,000 inhabitants. Among these of course are to be deducted (as far as politics are concerned) with few exceptions three fifths for women and children. There remain 2,000, and this undoubtedly is a large allowance. Of these however we must again deduct for old men and "invalids" (the sick and blind and deaf) say three tenths. There remain 700 of these, the poor, the busy and the lazy. If we take half we shall be hardly wrong. Then comes the differences of party and we will give 200 to the one prevailing, but of these how many are taxed with acting from interest or passion? Thus the result may be that the 5,000 are in fact led by little above 100 individuals, who, very possibly, follow the cry of some four or five, or two or three, that have objects of their own.

This is the state of the world it will be said, and it can lead to but little mischief in thickly peopled lands where shark meets shark and interests keep interests in check. But apply it to America and the good people are often to be found represented by men not natives even of the soil—noisy blustering Germans or Irishmen who live by agitation, and [who,] from their European knowledge and tactics, possession of the press and so forth, have an immense influence over all the wild unruly young adventurers of the western woods especially the Democrats of the slave districts, who are of rather a rakish turn, and all those who are readers of nothing but newspapers or party pamphlets. Such a people are like tinder ever ready for blazing up, tho' the outlet, or as the Italians call it "il sfogo," open to their excesses thro' the woods after Indians or wild beasts, serves and will long serve as a diversion to their humour. But the day will come when we shall see of what this people can be capable and if the New Englander of the sound old stock will stick to the rotten portion or let it drop. In the meantime let us not confound our ideas with a word that should be void as having no further meaning than as a general expression to signify all the inhabitants as regard numbers, and not as regards manners or interests or least of all morals and the social ties. All that is good in them they have from their European ancestors and most of what is evil from their present social position, tho' Mr. Cowper in his contradictory statements says they have degenerated within the last thirty years,[52] but certainly the good predominates, else would they long ago have yielded to the same passions which render liberty, etc., precarious in the states of Spanish origin.

Their religion too, which to so large a portion is founded on reason as well as faith, will render [her?] sort of legislation more easy and the power of resistance to invasion more compact in this division than it can be to the South.]*

At Monticello I was present at some of the national sports and games, of which there are more in Virginia than in any other state that I have visited. Horse racing is carried very far and gives rise to a good deal of gambling. Cock-fighting is on the decline, but still exists here and there. Quoits and nine-pins are much in fashion. And as to festivities they are, especially the barbecues, most numerously attended on the Atlantic side of the Blue Ridge. A barbecue originally was a meeting in the woods to partake of a pig roasted whole. A pit was dug in the ground, fire

*Preceding three paragraphs in brackets appear only in HEH version.

---

[52]Foster apparently refers to James Fenimore Cooper (1789-1851), the novelist who published in 1828 his *Notions of the Americans* (written in Europe), defending his homeland against the accounts of English travelers in America. Later, on his return to the U.S. with a new and relatively objective insight into the weaknesses of his beloved country, and in irritation at attacks upon him personally and his motives, he wrote several books sharply critical of American manners and institutions. E.g., *A Letter to his Countrymen* (1834), *The Monikins* (1835), and *The American Democrat* (1838).

placed in it, and a large pig supported on four stakes was put over the fire. There is always a dance afterwards, and I was told that at some places these meetings are exceedingly numerous, even the better sort of people attending them. Barbecues are now oftener held at a tavern and are very frequent during summer. People think nothing of going ten or twelve miles to one.

On the other side of the Blue Ridge, which is near 4,000 feet above the level of the sea, and which I crossed at Rock-fish Gap[53] by a stony winding road, the people differ very much in their habits and manners from the Virginians of the plain. They even affect to give themselves and the others distinguishing epithets which, though now nicknames, may in time become national denominations. They call themselves Cohees tho' from their accent in many places one should guess them to be Highlanders. And their neighbours they call the Old Virginians or the Tuckahoe People, both being terms which are probably derived from the names of extinct Indian tribes.[54] However that may be, I was certainly struck with the more active healthy appearance of the Cohees and were I to become a settler in this part of the world I should, I think, prefer their district to that of the Tuckahoes, tho' there is a great deal to say upon the advantages of being located near a great town and though the American mountaineer is after all but a rough unfashioned kind of being.

From Monticello I proceeded to the Natural Bridge, and rode through beautiful woods which were full of wild turkeys that I in vain endeavoured to put up, they so much preferred running and were so very swift of foot. The Natural Bridge is in a delightful part of the country and well worth seeing. It is between forty and fifty feet wide at the bottom and double that at the top, serving for a passage over a river that is nearly 250 feet beneath it. From thence I turned back to the Federal City, taking

[53]Rock-fish Gap lies on U.S. Highway 250, between Charlottesville and Waynesboro. The actual altitude at the Gap is 1,900 feet.

[54]A "Cohee" was an inhabitant of western Virginia or Pennsylvania, and a "Tuckahoe" (originally an Indian name for certain vegetables) was by 1817 an inhabitant of Virginia east of the mountains.

Madison's Cave in my way,[55] which extends for near 300 feet into the ground and in which there are large stalactites of all sorts of shapes, one of them being strikingly like the figure of General Washington, so much so indeed as to be called by the people thereabouts Washington's Statue. Wherever I passed on my return I found the trees absolutely loaded with wild pigeons and I shot in among them with pistols, having no gun with me.

In passing thro' Alexandria I visited the nursery garden of Peter Billy,[56] a Frenchman, who had established himself about eight years previously on a piece of common land near the town and in three years produced out of it a very good garden where he cultivated not only fruits and vegetables, but rare American plants. He would ramble about the country and whatever interesting wild flower or shrub he might discover, take it to his garden and try to domesticate it. He had a good many of the pretty plant called Kalmia augustifolia. I inquired after the wild grape but he assured me that he never could get it to change its acrid taste for one more agreeable, though the white Burgundy vine of which he had several plants succeeded very well. He showed me some caterpillars which are described as more destructive to wheat than even locusts. They are, in appearance, not much different from the common caterpillar, only a little darker, and they spread themselves in myriads among the green corn fields, ripping down the stalks and devouring them as well as the ears of corn very rapidly. This Frenchman who was a mild, placid man, seemed to have succeeded in his emigration to the

[55] Jefferson locates and describes Madison's Cave in *Notes on the State of Virginia* (1785), under Query V, "Cascades and Caverns," locating it "on the north side of the Blue Ridge, near the intersection of the Rockingham and Augusta line with the south fork of the southern river of the Shenandoah." It is on the same hill, according to Dr. J. W. Wayland of Harrisonburg, Virginia, as Weyer's Cave (now known as Grand Caverns), about ¼ or ½ mile from the latter. Foster evidently visited it on Jefferson's recommendation. By 1831 Weyer's Cave had become the main attraction, though the traveler might dig for fossils in the "old cave." William M. E. Rachal, ed., "Richard Harlan's 'Tour of the Caves in Virginia' in 1831, Including Observations about Charlottesville and Albemarle County," *Papers Albemarle County* [*Va.*] *Hist. Soc.*, VII (1946-1947), 42-44.

[56] Unlocated.

United States to his heart's content. But not so Perkins, an English gardener in the same place, who complained that nothing would succeed there, and that a man carrying out with him $10,000 would be ruined. He paid, he told me, £5 Virginia currency per acre, and for land in the vicinity of London he would only have to pay, he asserted, three guineas per acre. Perkins was from Essex, a tall stout looking man, but he and his whole family were scarcely ever without fever.

I have here ended what I had to say respecting Virginia. It was the leading state in the Union during all the time of my residence in America and had furnished four, if not five, of the seven chief magistrates who have hitherto been elected to preside over the United States, a circumstance which it no doubt owed in a great measure, to the mixed character of its gentry, while they still remained a British colony and for a long time afterwards, even indeed to the present day, in some degree. I mean their uniting, more than any other state, the advantages in respect of wealth and education which they enjoy to the impunity with which they can profess an unbounded love of liberty and of democracy in consequence of the mass of the people, who in other countries might become mobs, being there nearly altogether composed of their own Negro slaves whose numbers are taken into the account of the votes given but who form no social check upon their masters' political conduct. At the same time it must be observed that the state itself is one of the largest dimensions, having twenty-four representatives in Congress and consequently had a fair claim to the distinction of being called a leading state. Property, however, has been much divided in Virginia since the War of Independence, by virtue of the state laws. And I doubt if many men of large estates are now to be found within it. The new generation too of gentlemen produced since the peace appeared to me rather inferior, in manners at least, to their elders or predecessors.

There were still several descendants from English noble families scattered thro' Virginia when I visited it, among whom Lord Fairfax who called himself Ferdinando Fairfax under which name he left me his card;[57] Sir Paton Skipwith;[58] the Randolphs who say they are descended from the Blands of Kippax Park;[59] and others. But many of the old houses were ruined by their hospitality, having been used to see their fathers keep open house themselves, giving dinner to fifteen or twenty guests with fifteen or sixteen horses in the stables every day, and that after the entails had been put an end to, no wonder if the purses were found too short for such a jovial life. The number of noble families was still greater formerly, though individuals who had claims to titles seldom brought them forward, as in the case of Mr. Paton who was, I was assured, the real heir to the baronetcy which he allowed to fall upon Sir Yelverton Paton, an English branch of the family.[60]

John Randolph was as great a genealogist as could be found in the mother country and like others of his countrymen, fond of claiming kindred with our old families. On the conclusion of the treaty of peace he went to visit Kippax Park, the seat of his ancestors, but I suppose he did not make himself known there, for he was afraid of being shown about as a lion, and even refused to let me introduce him at Devonshire House. He was very chary too of the credit of the English nobility and imposed silence upon me in regard to an adventure which he had had at Eaton Hall[61] which he did not think would tell well, tho' probably the inconvenience he was put to might be attributable to illiberality on the part of the steward rather than to the orders of his master. He had gone to see Lord Grosvenor's

[57]Thomas Fairfax, *de jure* Lord Fairfax of Cameron (1762-1846), never established his claim to the peerage, though his father's claim had been allowed in 1800. Evidently he assumed the name Ferdinando from his ancestor, Ferdinando, second Baron Fairfax of Cameron in the peerage of Scotland (1584-1648).

[58]Sir Peyton Skipwith (1740-1805) inherited Prestwould in Mecklenburg County, Virginia, from his father Sir William in 1740. R. A. Lancaster, *Historic Virginia Houses and Churches* (Philadelphia, 1915), p. 443.

[59]In Yorkshire.

[60]This Virginia Peyton was correct in his claim. Sir Yelverton Peyton assumed the baronetcy but the Virginia family were rightful heirs to the title after 1720.

[61]Robert, Earl Grosvenor (1767-1845), in 1803 began to rebuild Eaton Hall, his ancestral home, on a very extensive scale.

newly built house from Chester but was refused admittance, as he found out from the postillion, because he had come in a post-chaise belonging to opposite politics. On which, being determined to carry his point, he turned back, went to the other inn, took a chaise from thence and was at once let in.

He went soon after this period as Minister to St. Petersburgh which gave him the advantage of two years' pay, or about £4,000, of which he stood in need. For he told me in confidence that things were no longer as they had been with him on the Roanoke, when I was at Washington. Randolph, however, remained but a very short time in Russia the climate of which country disagreed with him.[62] He returned to London and not very long afterwards to America where he died at Philadelphia in 1833, disputing to the last moment, with that punctiliousness which had ever distinguished him, as to the proper pronunciation of a word. For he twice corrected the clergyman who attended him and who very affectedly in reading a prayer pronounced the word omnipotent omni*po*tent.[63] He died possessed of 318 slaves whom he was used, when at his country seat, to wake up every morning to the sound of the horn. These 318 slaves were valued at $350 or about from £60 to £70 each.[64] He was I was assured looked upon by them as a very kind master and could never bear to sell one of them. The eloquence of Randolph was distinguished by imagery and impetuosity with a ready flow of language, but in argument he was neither close nor powerful, and his influence arose more from the number and attachment

[62]Randolph was appointed Minister to Russia as of May 1830, and arrived in St. Petersburg about the last of August of that year. He stayed in Russia only a few weeks.

[63]For another account of this scene, see Hugh A. Garland, *The Life of John Randolph of Roanoke* (New York, 1850), II, 372. Garland states that it was the physician, Dr. Parish, who read "omni*po*tence" from a newspaper account headed "Cherokee." Foster mentions his version also in a letter to Josiah Quincy of September 30, 1833. Quincy, *Life of Josiah Quincy*, pp. 456-57.

[64]Foster got his information concerning Randolph's estate from a clipping from the *Globe*, July 1833, which is affixed in his "Diary" below his entries of May 30-31, 1812.

of his personal friends than from his debating talents.[65] He could not bear a blackguard or anything shabby, always wore a dagger, and was ever ready for a duel saying that he would shoot an impertinent fellow just as he would a mad dog. He was very particular as to his dress and regularly had his boots from Hoby[66] even before he had ever crossed the Atlantic. Randolph was tall and very thin and pale, had a little nose and sharp black eyes, with a voice of a boy. He really looked like a descendant of some Indian chief.

[65]For a somewhat divergent contemporary opinion and more extended analysis of Randolph's powers as an orator, see Francis W. Gilmer, "Sketches of American Orators," in *Sketches, Essays, and Translations* (Baltimore, 1828), pp. 18-22.

[66]George Hoby, bootmaker, conducted a shop at 48 St. James Street, London. *Post Office Annual Directory for 1812*. For indication that "Hoby's white-topped boots" were well known, see Washington Irving, *Salmagundi*, June 27, 1807, "From My Elbow-Chair."

CHAPTER IV

WITH THE states situated to the south of Virginia I am not personally acquainted excepting a small portion of North Carolina, but from what I gathered at Washington among the representatives of that state I conclude that in regard to the manners of the people and the cultivation of the land it differs little from Virginia.

North Carolina

Raleigh, a new place, was the seat of government, and there were thirteen representatives from North Carolina in Congress. A very large district sixty miles broad, extending from the Atlantic and within this state formerly belonged, and indeed ought to belong, to Lord Carteret's heirs,[1] but Mr. Key,[2] a Member of Congress, and an eminent lawyer, who was retained in their interest, assured me that the judges and juries purposely evaded giving any decision in the case, letting it be understood that from the magnitude of the property claimed the state itself as well as the many individuals were interested in opposing the claim to make it safe for any court of justice to settle it, as all admitted it ought, in justice and equity, to be decided, viz., in favour of the foreigner.[3]

[1]Sir George Carteret (1610-1680) had been one of the eight to whom Charles II granted the country of the Carolinas by the charters of 1663 and 1665. His descendant, Lord Carteret (later Lord Granville), under the Parliamentary Act of 1729, refused to sell his claims to the province but in 1744 gave up his claim in return for a strip of land in North Carolina lying between lat. 35° 34′ and the Virginia line (36° 30′). E. M. Coulter, "The Granville District," *James Sprunt Hist. Pub.*, XIII (1913), No. 1, pp. 33-56.

[2]Evidently Philip Barton Key, but Coulter ("Granville District," p. 56) gives Francis S. Key as their counsel.

[3]Coulter ("Granville District") does not mention the state courts' evasion, but does suggest (p. 56) that had the case ever reached the U.S. Supreme Court it would have been decided in favor of the heirs, for Chief Justice Marshall had already expressed an opinion that "the Treaty of Paris prohibited a state from invalidating English titles."

For sixty or seventy miles from the sea coast North Carolina is a dead level, but the back country is hilly. Cotton plants, notwithstanding that the stalk dies with the frost, are found to answer and are yearly planted in parts of this state. Charleston is the market for the southern counties, as Petersburg in Virginia is the market of those to the north, for the North Carolinians themselves have but one tolerable harbour, that of Cape Fear. One of their most valuable articles of export is pitch and the timber from the pitch pines. The forests are delightful to look at from the variety of creepers and evergreens which abound in them, especially a kind of mistletoe which grows on the tops of the trees, the root of it running under the bark, and becoming, as it were, incorporated with the wood.

The inhabitants of the hills, as was the case in the back part of Virginia, are, for the most part, descended from emigrants from the north of Ireland, speak with a Scotch accent, and are generally of the Church of Scotland, and are a very industrious, orderly people. North Carolina appeared to me, from what I heard, to be less generally known and less visited than any of the states, and for that very reason, perhaps, the old settlers have preserved their original manners and habits better than their neighbours have done in other parts of the continent.

The country was not permanently settled before the early part of the last century and even then remained under the government of South Carolina until about 1730. There is an extensive swamp, near Norfolk, that belongs to this state, which has the repulsive name of "Dismal" attached to it. It is nevertheless not an unwholesome district owing to the cedars and cypress trees which grow in it and give a mahogany colour to the waters rendering them very wholesome and strengthening. I went to see this swamp at the risk of losing my passage in the frigate which took home Sir G. Rose, and which was raising her anchor as I returned to go on board. There was but little justification, however, to compensate for such risk except in a long ride and the satisfaction of being able to brag of having seen the Dismal

Swamp, which is the scene of one of Moore's prettiest ballads.[4]

In this state and in Virginia the judges are paid but $1,500 each per annum—about £335—and one of them, of the Democratic, which is the ruling, party, not long ago declared from the bench that he would suffer no books published in England to be cited in court on any case, when a lawyer present asked if he would not permit the common law to be expounded, if necessary. On which he said, "Oh, yes, certainly, the common law is what I principally go by." "Then sir," enjoined the other, "I only want to read to you the common law."

[4] "A Ballad: The Lake of the Dismal Swamp," by Thomas Moore, begins

> They made her a grave, too cold and damp
> For a soul so warm and true;
> And she's gone to the Lake of the Dismal Swamp
> Where all night long, by a firefly lamp
> She paddles her white canoe.

CHAPTER V

SOUTH CAROLINA sent eight representatives to Congress. Its seat of government was Columbia situated in north latitude about the 34th degree. The most considerable town in the state, however, was Charlestown. But the air of that city is much too unhealthy during a great part of the year to allow of its being resorted to at all seasons and therefore, for the same satisfactory reason as is common to Georgia, and even to North Carolina, the hilly district was preferred for the residence of the government.

South Carolina

Mr. Hamilton[1] a South Carolina man was Secretary of the Navy during a part of the time that I passed at Washington, and he told me that he was owner of a vineyard on Smith's Island, one of the numerous group of islands between which and the shore of the continent there is an excellent inland navigation. He made two hogsheads of wine there every year, but I could not discover that he thought it good enough to present a sample to any of his Washington friends.

In the summer season, he assured me, the only habitable places in the neighbourhood of Charlestown were pine barrens, because vegetation is there almost entirely over-head, the moisture proceeding from any plant being fatal of a morning or an evening. Even the pine barrens are only healthy in their natural state; as soon as ever a garden is attempted to be formed, the owner finds that his atmosphere has changed. Sullivan's Island enjoys the reputation of being so healthy that even strangers can live on it with impunity.[2]

The Sea Island cotton is the best quality of cotton, but it will not grow above sixty miles from the shore. The upland or black-

[1]Paul Hamilton (1762-1816), governor of South Carolina 1804-1806, was Secretary of the Navy 1809-1813.

[2]Cf. Lawrence F. Brewster, *Summer Migrations and Resorts of South Carolina Low-Country Planters* (Durham, N.C., 1947).

seed cotton is much coarser, and it is this which a machine that was invented by Whitney of Connecticut has been able to clean, being too rough an instrument for the Sea Island cotton.[3] The cotton of the Brazils, as I was informed by Mr. Gallatin, is accounted even superior in quality to that of South Carolina.

There was a population of about 180,000 blacks to 230,000 whites in South Carolina in 1811-12, and $300 was the common average price for each. Nevertheless for a good Negro $500 is frequently given. Planters were considered fortunate who could raise fifteen in twenty, many dying young of pleurisy from the effects of being sent to work at a too early hour in the morning.

After the 10th June it is mortal to a planter to remain in the country near his rice grounds, and all who can retire to the city, from whence if they go even for a single day to visit the plantation, it is with imminent risk of life.

Beds in this and the neighbouring states are commonly made of a soft moss that hangs on trees and is suspended like hair from them in winter.

The great road from Washington to Charlestown lies through an almost unvarying wood of pine trees in a flat and uninteresting country, a few slovenly plantations or farms, the stumps of trees appearing scattered through them, being hardly to be said to vary the scene. In the marshy bottoms, however, the senses are regaled with the perfume of the jessamine and many other beautiful flowering shrubs, as well as the warbling of mocking-birds.

South Carolina of all the states of the Union is that which contains the wealthiest landed proprietors. General Hampton[4] was said to have an income of from 25 to £30,000 per annum, Major Butler[5] nearly as much, and there are the families of the

[3]The up-country cotton was green-seed cotton, the Sea Island cotton was black-seed and long-staple.

[4]Wade Hampton (1754-1835), first of the three famous Wade Hamptons, was a captain in the Revolution and a brigadier-general in the War of 1812.

[5]Major Pierce Butler (1744-1822), Senator from South Carolina 1789-1896, 1802-1806, was one of the great landowners of the state.

Pinckneys and Rutledges, Smiths and Middletons who have all large property, many of the individuals belonging to each having been educated in Europe. Admiral Graves had an estate of £3,000 per year in right of his wife.[6] The gentlemen of South Carolina visit the northern states, Ballstown Springs, or other places famed for their mineral waters, in the unhealthy season, and in the winter return to Charlestown, which is then one of the gayest towns on the continent. The racing, too, which takes place in the spring is said to be very good and I have heard that the four mile heat has been run there in 7 minutes 32 seconds.

Notwithstanding the number, however, of wealthy proprietors in South Carolina, and consequently, of persons much interested in the continuance of peace, this district furnished some of the most violent War-Hawks, as they were called, in the Congress, which can only be accounted for by the consideration that these rich proprietors have very little influence generally with the elective body, from their dependents being almost all Negroes, who, though their population be taken into the account in affixing the number of representatives due to the state, have themselves no right of voting, in consequence of which the secondary white inhabitants possess nearly the whole political influence of the district. Among them briefless lawyers and soi-disant doctors ambitious or envious of their more prosperous neighbours, having everything to gain and little to lose by commotion, too often take the lead. Most probably this state will ever be ready from this circumstance to take up arms with or without cause, merely for the sake of gratifying young fellows of eloquence or ambition as well as lacking preferment who tho' perhaps few in number may carry all before them for want of a sufficient check in the highest as well as lowest orders of the state.

Whitney's patent machine for cleaning cotton was brought to South Carolina and the patent right secured to him by the

[6]British Admiral Richard Graves married Louisa Carolina, daughter of Sir John Colleton, fourth bart. She inherited all her father's property, including Fairlawn Barony.

state legislature.[7] Several Georgians, however, who, without going to the expence of purchasing a frame from the patentee, conceived that they might construct a similar machine set about it and were prosecuted by Whitney. Nevertheless out of twenty suits which he had instituted not one was determined.[8] Mr. Day of New Haven,[9] a friend of his, assured me as a positive fact that the sheriffs were pledged, on being named to their office, to impanel only such jurymen as would be unfavourable to the claim. Let us put this example of state injustice and that of North Carolina in regard to Lord Carteret's heirs along side of the respect paid by Parliament to the Duke of Athol's absurd rights in the Isle of Man[10] and to the Butlerage of the Ormond family in Ireland,[11] and then draw a conclusion as to which form of government is most favourable to the principles of equity and honourable conduct.

Cotton should sell for twenty cents the pound in South Carolina to be profitable.

The sorrel tree is to be found in this state and in the Floridas as well as in Georgia. It is so called from the pleasant acid juice yielded by the leaves which the inhabitants are fond of chewing in the summer season. There was, I remember, a very fine sorrel

[7]Eli Whitney (1765-1825) received patent for his cotton gin in 1794. He fought infringements until his claims were validated in 1807. South Carolina in 1802 agreed to pay him $50,000 for rights to the gin, much more than any other state did.

[8]Not strictly true. Cf. Jeanette Mirsky and Allan Nevins, *The World of Eli Whitney* (New York, 1952), pp. 163-76.

[9]Jeremiah Day (1773-1867), from 1803 professor of mathematics at Yale, in 1817 succeeded Dwight as president.

[10]The Murray family, Dukes of Atholl, inherited rights in the Isle of Man from the Stanleys in 1736, but in 1764 Baroness Strange succeeded and her husband, John Murray, became Lord of Man. The Atholl regime ended in 1765, when by a "Revesting Act" the sovereign and manorial rights and the customs, revenues, and certain other perquisites were purchased.

[11]As their name suggests, the Butlers originally received it when King John made an ancestor hereditary butler to the lord of Ireland. "Butlerage" was a right enabling the holder to buy provisions for the royal household at a valuation, even without consent of the owner. Naturally it might produce great revenues to the holder. All butlerage ceased to be levied in 1809.

tree to be seen in Mr. Bartram's garden near Philadelphia.[12] It was about eighty feet high and the seed grew downwards in the shape of a lily of the valley.

Of fish belonging to the South Carolina market the drum is one of the very best; the rock-fish is also a great treat and the roe of it is pickled like the roe of a sturgeon.

[12]William Bartram (1739-1823) maintained the botanical garden of his father after the death of his brother John in 1812 (the father died in 1777). Located at 54th St. and Eastwick Ave., the garden is still open to the public.

CHAPTER VI

GEORGIA sends but four representatives to Congress. I have fewer notes on this than almost on any other state in the Union. It was colonized as late as 1732 and at the expence of the British Crown. The soil is like that of South Carolina, and I have heard that the climate suits even the tea plant.

The capital is at Louisville.

Creek and Choctaw Indians inhabit parts of this state and are amongst the most numerous, as well as civilized, of the aboriginal tribes of the continent.

Georgia

Indian claims to land have, however, been extinguished on a large scale in these parts, and the district acquired for purposes of speculation, well known under the name of the Yazoo Territory, gave rise to an important discussion as to whether the individual state or the United States were entitled to dispose of it, a question that was modified by the claims of a third party, viz., those persons already in actual possession who had either squatted, or had settled down on the land by virtue of a right to do so that they had long ago purchased of the state legislature.[1]

In Georgia, at the time I visited the United States, was situated the extreme southern boundary of the republic, viz., St. Mary's Inlet, from which to Washington the distance by the post road is 774 miles, from whence to Passamaquoddy, the northern limit, in the district of Maine, the distance is 908 miles. The

[1] The Yazoo Territory, making up most of the state of Mississippi and more than half the present state of Alabama, was granted by a Georgia legislature in 1795 to four land companies. The following year a new legislature rescinded the contracts as fraudulently made. In the meantime the U. S. Senate, investigating Georgia's right to the territory, proclaimed the state's claim invalid. The matter was settled by ceding the territory to the U.S. for $1,250,000 and the extinguishment of all Indian claims to land within the state of Georgia. After further litigation and negotiation the Creeks left Georgia for the West. The Cherokees also were finally ejected, though the U.S. Supreme Court in 1832 had decided that they were a distinct community and not subject to Georgia's laws. American magazines and newspapers for twenty or thirty years contain articles on "the Cherokee question."

whole extent of coast amounted to 1,682 miles, while the distance from the Federal City to Washington, the seat of government in the Mississippi Territory, was estimated at 1,300 miles, thus making nearly a square of the American territory.

Its length by the addition of East Florida has since attained to 2,082 miles, while no doubt the breadth contemporaneously added to the United States will, at least, have kept pace with the longitude, for the few scruples or fears which retarded the occupation of the Floridas will no doubt have no existence as respects the poor unprotected Indians of the west.

So great is the dread of their black slaves entertained by proprietors of land in this and the neighbouring states, that they are never permitted to sleep under the same roof with their masters, and to every farm is annexed a log-house for them to live in separate from the family.

CHAPTER VII

THIS STATE has been added to the Union since our last war began with America, and I am not accurately acquainted with the mode in which it was finally acquired. What I know is, that the manoeuvres and tricks set on foot by the governor of Georgia in order to excite an insurrection within the province at Amelia Island in 1811 with the view, but very little disguised, of creating a pretext for an offer of the sovereignty being made by the local authorities to the United States, and the jesuitical avowal of the United States Government being ready, in such a manner, to receive it. This is contained in Mr. Monroe's official reply[1] to my remonstrance published in the *National Intelligencer* of Nov. 9th, 1811, and of which I have inserted a copy in the Appendix,[2] [and] exhibits a moral feature in the Federal Government almost as worthy of Machiavelli's contemporaries as any which distinguished Bonaparte in his treatment of the mother country Spain.

East Florida

As to West Florida, it was laid hold of by act of Congress, or, at least, so much of it as lies east of the Rio Perdido, while still garrisoned by Spanish troops, and though it was claimed as being a part of Louisiana.[3] Yet was this plea subsequently disproved by

[1]For a summary of "replies made to Mr. Foster on his protest against the occupation of West Florida by U.S. troops," see the *American Review*, IV (July 1811), Appendix, pp. 11-12.

[2]Foster did not leave a recognizable appendix to either of the surviving versions of his "Notes."

[3]The U.S., with President Madison's approval, had by October 1810 occupied West Florida as far east as the Pearl River. On January 3, 1811, Madison's message to Congress included the suggestion that a resolution be passed to the effect that the U.S. would see with disquietude the neighboring territory pass from Spain to any other foreign power (this followed Folch's offer of the territory). Within two weeks Congress granted the President's request: the American government would accept temporary possession of East Florida and West Florida beyond the Perdido for "protection" of the region. Claiborne had supposedly taken possession up to the Perdido. The U.S. "might" redeliver territory east of

the Anglican inhabitants themselves who protested against their being incorporated with the New Orleans Territory, requesting to be added to the state of Mississippi. But to East Florida there was not even the shadow of a claim on the part of the Americans, and I should recommend a perusal of Mr. Monroe's said note dated November 2, 1811, in reply to mine of September 5th[4] (for he took time to compose it) to any doctrinaire who may be inclined to talk of the public justice and virtues of a democratic form of government. The attempt having been made too with a view to bully the Spaniards, at a time when Spain was nobly contending for existence as an independent state, struggling against the mortal foe of all liberty and while the American ministers would not even open a letter from the Spanish envoy, Don Luis de Onis,[5] for it was this circumstance that led to my interference. But I plainly perceived that I should never receive an answer unless I made a noise about the matter, and the previous reply I got was due to the cry of shame which, through Senator Bayard and others of my friends in Congress, I at length caused to be set up in regard to it. The plan of robbery was in consequence adjourned, or at least, not consummated under my eyes, and I received the thanks of the Cortes for the service in a letter from Don Luis written by order of his government, of which letter a copy is also to be found in the Appendix.

East Florida adds four hundred miles in length of coast to the territory of the United States. The live oak trees furnish the finest timber in this district as well as in Georgia, and they bear great abundance of eatable acorns from which sweet oil may be extracted. The magnolia laurus is also a great ornament to the woods, and grows to be one hundred feet high, perfectly straight

---

the Perdido to its lawful sovereign. Isaac J. Cox, *The West Florida Controversy* (Baltimore, 1918), pp. 523-24; George Dangerfield, *The Era of Good Feelings* New York, 1952), p. 127.

[4]For these notes, see the *American Review*, IV (July 1811), Appendix 11-12.

[5]Foster was a social intimate of Onís (1762-1827). "Diary," 1811, passim. Onís was not officially recognized, because of the U.S. neutral policy, until 1815, though he had arrived in this country in 1809.

like a pillar with a profusion of beautiful large fragrant flowers at the extremities of the branches. East Florida also produces good oranges and lemons, particularly about St. Augustine, which is the principal town of the state and contained in 1812 about five thousand inhabitants. I was told of a colony of Greeks and Minorcans having existed for some years in the neighbourhood of this town, who came there originally as indented servants.[6] But having been very harshly treated by their masters, the English governor at that time broke the indentures, and they were set to cultivate the orange and the vine.[7] The Greeks were said to have come from about Smyrna, and were subsequently much dispersed, some of them having gone to sea again in the hopes of getting back to their own country. Those who remained, as well as the Minorcans, wore the collar of their shirts doubled down over their shoulders and jackets of their old costume and they spoke lingua franca.

The whole population of East Florida in the year 1811 was supposed not to exceed 30,000, and Mr. Estrada[8] the Spanish governor of St. Augustine had not above 300 men to form the garrison. M. Folck[9] commanded at Pensacola, and M. Maxent at Mobile, when these territories were annexed by virtue of an act of Congress to the state of Mississippi.

Amelia Island which is fertile and capable of becoming a very valuable possession lies opposite the mouth of St. Mary's River. But Pensacola is more important perhaps as a harbour being capable of containing a fleet of ships drawing twenty-one feet of water. Port St. Josephs will admit ships drawing seventeen feet but the worms all along this coast will eat thro' an ordinary ship's bottom in the space of two months.

The rattlesnake is still to be met with in this as well as the

[6]Actually Greeks, Minorcans, and Italians, in the Scottish physician Turnbull's settlement at New Smyrna, 60 miles south of St. Augustine, founded in 1768.

[7]Governor Patrick Tonyn gave many releases from these indentures, ca. 1778, though Dr. Turnbull always claimed the people were not badly treated.

[8]Juan José Estrada, then governor of East Florida.

[9]Don Vincente, or Vicente, Folch, the Spanish governor, at first offered to surrender West Florida to the U.S. and then changed his mind. "Diary."

neighbouring states in considerable numbers, although becoming every year more and more scarce especially in Virginia and the long settled parts of the continent. It is an animal that delights to dwell among rocks and old trees which are not too distant from water and the chief cause of the great diminution of these noxious reptiles is the great increase of hogs everywhere as the land becomes generally more cultivated. Pigs being very fond of feeding upon snakes, and as they roam about in the woods they have of course many opportunities of gratifying their palates upon rattlesnakes while their own fat and tough skins defend them from the poison.

Catesby in his work upon South Carolina[10] enumerates eighteen or nineteen different sorts of snakes whereof he calls four vipers and the rest he classes as serpents. The differences he observed in these two descriptions are, that the viper is viviparous, whereas the serpent produces eggs. Besides vipers have longer fangs which are in the centre of the mouth and open at the points through which they distil or rather squirt out their poison, while their other teeth are like those of serpents. The differences externally, consist in the slender neck, the broad flat head, more ample jaws, and rougher scales of the vipers, besides the rest of the body is short and thick. They also move more slowly and raise up their heads and necks when enraged, and have a fierce savage appearance, whereas the serpents have small heads, longer bodies, and polished scales. They are besides active and bland to the eye. The tongues of all snakes, vipers, or serpents are forked. They use them to seize insects, and they thrust them out and shake them when provoked. The rattlesnake is considered as the largest and fiercest of the viper species. The greatest ever seen by Catesby weighed from eight to nine lbs. and was nearly eight feet long. It had crawled slowly into Colonel Blake's house in Carolina, where he then was, striking terror into the dogs and the poultry. They are, however, torpid and slow and unless provoked, will not bite; though when they do bite, should they

[10]Mark Catesby (ca. 1679-1749), *The Natural History of Carolina, Florida, and the Bahama Islands*..., 2 vols., (large folio, London, 1736-1743), II, 41-60 (plates).

have seized on a large vein or artery, it is all over with the person bitten. The Indians know very well when the wound is mortal, and give up every attempt at a cure at once as vain. Catesby declares that he had seen a person die of such a bite in less than two minutes. The poison is concealed under the fang, and Mr. Matlock of Lancaster,[11] who has examined many rattlesnakes, assured me that they do not unite their jaws in striking, but, letting the under jaw drop, inflict the wound with the upper teeth thro' which, at the moment of striking, by compression of a muscle, they instill the venom and squirt it through a hollow channel with great and sudden force.

The head of this formidable reptile is of a brown colour and the eyes are red. The cure of a slight wound from the bite of a rattlesnake, can, it is said, be effected by the application of snake root and by the rattles themselves concocted, though suction is considered the most sure remedy, if immediately had recourse to. The rattles, when pounded, are believed to be of use in procuring easy deliverance to women in labour. In the engravings which accompany Catesby's work, there is a snake represented having twenty-four rattles,[12] but he denies that the age of the animal is shown by the numbers of its rattles, for he observes that the smaller snakes have very often more joints in their tails than have those which are larger.

[11]Timothy Matlack (d. April 14, 1829), Quaker by birth, held many moderately important state and national offices. He was a member of the American Philosophical Society and a director of the Bank of North America (1781). His later years he spent in Lancaster as clerk of the State Senate and Master of the Rolls. Irked by Quaker restraints, he loved cock fighting, horse racing, and convivial company.

[12]Shown in plate opposite p. 41 in Catesby, *Natural History of Carolina*, II.

CHAPTER VIII

NATCHEZ was the seat of government of this state while it still went under the denomination of a Territory, but since the greater part of West Florida has been annexed to it I conclude that either Pensacola or a new town called Washington will have had the preference. It is perhaps the most unhealthy country in the Union, being generally speaking, low and flat, full of swamps, cane grounds and rice plantations. The Choctaws and Creeks are unfortunately for themselves numerous in these parts, as their numbers only render them more obnoxious to the insatiable speculations of the Americans and, from giving them more confidence in their own strength, occasion disputes which to them are always fatal, ending in treaties that by degrees must drive them to absolute despair.

Mississippi

Mr. Key of Maryland, who has made the tour of this state, told me, in speaking of alligators, that he once saw one twenty-two feet long on the River Ibberville, and forty of these animals were visible at the same time, being distant from each other about fifteen to twenty feet, their heads rising out of the water. He never knew an instance, however, of one of them attacking a man, though he saw a female alligator which had eggs, and was provoked by a hook being thrown into her mouth, run after a person, but only for a short distance.

CHAPTER IX

THE STATE of Louisiana was received into the Union during the period of my residence at the Federal City, in the year 1812. The President addressed a letter to the Senate and the House of Representatives transmitting the proceedings of the convention assembled in the Territory of Orleans in pursuance of an act of Congress authorizing them to form a constitution, and the constitution having been laid before Congress and approved of, was without delay sanctioned at the desire of M. Poydras,[1] the president of the convention, who had written to represent the necessity of no time being lost about it. Afterwards there was a great dinner given by the representatives of the new state to celebrate the event, and the corps diplomatique were invited to it.

Louisiana

The invitations were sent round by the deputies from New Orleans, who were as well as I can recollect, M. Fromentin and Mr. Magruder,[2] to a quorum of Senators and Representatives and to the Ministers. The toasts given were "The President," "The Republic one and indivisible," by M. Fromentin, and "our youngest sister, Louisiana," by the Speaker, Mr. Clay. The landlord of the hotel was sitting in a corner, drawing corks, and Mr. Senator Wright, a strange sort of original, sang us some indecent songs and gave us toasts of a similar description. I sat between the Speaker and Mr. Calhoun,[3] the former of whom told me that M. Fromentin had taken out M. Serrurier to be next him because he was a Frenchman, for the sake of the language, to which I replied, that M. Serrurier and I had settled our etiquette long ago, he having been sent before me to the United States and

[1]Julien de Lalande Poydras (1746-1824), poet, public servant, and philanthropist, was president of the Louisiana constitutional convention in 1812.

[2]Eligius Fromentin (d. 1822) was U.S. Senator 1813-1819, and Allen B. Magruder (1775-1822) U.S. Senator 1812-1813.

[3]Presumably John C. Calhoun (1782-1850).

therefore entitled to precedency, besides which, as Louisiana had been sold to the United States by France, dog-cheap, it was but a fair compliment to put the French envoy on this occasion in the post of honour. The party grew to be very noisy and I left them early.

The new state was limited by an act of Congress passed on the 8th April, to the territory included between the River Sabine, the 32d degree of latitude, and the River Ibberville; down the latter stream through Lake Pontchartrain and Mauripas to the Gulf of Mexico. It hardly could contain at this period above 50,000 inhabitants, although the country that went under the name of Louisiana and had been ceded by France, was stated to have contained a population of 200,000 inhabitants.

Lake Pontchartrain, which is situated close to New Orleans, is only navigable for very small vessels, and the bar of New Orleans has sometimes but eleven feet of water on it, though beyond the bar there is water enough to float a 74-gun ship. The city is about 100 miles from the mouth of the Mississippi, and vessels would sometimes take twenty or even thirty days to beat up to it.

New Orleans, according to a census received by the Government in the year 1806, contained 17,001 inhabitants, of which 8,378 were slaves. But M. Sauvé[4] whom I met in Washington at that period, and who had resided in lower Louisiana for twenty years, told me that he had known it when there were only 4,000 inhabitants of all colours in the place. Turkeys, he said, at that time cost but one dollar each, though afterwards they had risen to be worth two dollars and a half each. He remembered snow to have fallen twice in the streets, though the thermometer of Fahrenheit will rise as high as 102 degrees in the summer. M. Fromentin assured me that there existed no healthier place than New Orleans, if people will but live temperately, and he had been a resident there, more or less constantly, for twenty-one years. He was originally a priest and was of the Orleannois in

[4]Pierre Sauvé (d. 1822) was one of three delegates sent by the Louisiana Territory to Washington to petition that the territory be admitted as a state.

France, which he finally quitted in 1792 to escape the guillotine. He arrived in Louisiana in 1793. At about the distance of two miles from New Orleans there are extensive marshes and I own I could not altogether believe the atmosphere to be as pure as these gentlemen would have had me think it, remembering how very pertinaciously every American is disposed to defend the character of his immediate place of residence from the imputation of being subjected to ague or bilious fevers.

In the territory of New Orleans, truffles are to be found; they are of the white kind and cannot be propagated. They have the same flavour as the dark coloured ones of France.

The water of the Mississippi is said to be very wholesome, and the disease of the stone to be unknown in the countries through which it flows. For about sixty leagues there is a line of settlement along its banks formed upon a high natural dyke, up to Baton Rouge and Point Coupe, immediately behind which are the uncultivated swamps about ten or fifteen miles broad.

From the Balize which is just above the bar of the river, to the nearest firm land on which I was told troops could disembark, is sixty miles. The country on either side is so far nothing but mud and marsh. The immediate banks of the river from New Orleans as far as the Ibberville being the only parts cultivated; a natural mound dividing the running water from the swamp, which mound is at its broadest part but a mile wide, and is the surface whereon the planters raise their crops. From beyond the Ibberville the mounds or bluffs retire and leave a marsh between them and the river. The whole of the natural mound along the river is about 120 miles in length.

The Mississippi and the Missouri together are navigable for 4000-odd miles, according to Captain Lewis' calculation, being an extent of continued river navigation that I imagine is unequalled in the whole world beside. On the other hand from the Gulf of Mexico to Hudson's Bay there is a belt of land on which not a tree grows. The whole territory between the Atlantic and the Allegheny Mountains was found to have been formerly, and is indeed even now, in a great degree, covered with a forest, but from the Alleghenies to the Mississippi the land surveyors have difficulty in making out limits to their surveys from want of trees to form landmarks and boundaries.

During Colonel Burr's conspiracy the President received his dispatches from New Orleans at Washington in fifteen days, and he told me that he had hopes of being able to reduce the time even to eleven days.

The distance from New Orleans to Mexico is about 1,200 miles and Mexico is about 250 miles from Vera Cruz. The richest soil of Louisiana was supposed to be that which lies along the lower Red River that runs nearly 2,000 miles before it joins the Mississippi. Ten thousand head of cattle might there be seen in some of the prairies at one view, and the Applusian horses were very much esteemed. Tobacco, corn and cotton are the chief produce of the cultivated parts.

In the city of New Orleans about nineteen-twentieths of the inhabitants were said to be French or of French origin, and four-fifths of those of upper Louisiana, but the proportions of each have of course been much altered since the purchase of the territory by the United States, in consequence of the great emigration there is from the old states.

CHAPTER X

TENNESSEE became a state in the year 1775[1] and Andrew Jackson was its first Representative [, who seems to be highly respected by a large party both in his public and private capacity, though I wish that there had been more light thrown upon a portion of his conduct when he commanded in the south and acted with great harshness to the Indians as well as to two English subjects who were taken up from among them and shot by his orders. The affair was never sufficiently explained, tho' from the British government not having insisted upon a public inquiry into the matter we must presume that the Englishmen at least were in the wrong.]*[2]

Tennessee

One has only to cast one's eyes over the map of the United States to be convinced how beautifully situated must be Tennessee. It is in length 400 miles and in breadth above 100. The river which is a fine navigable stream for 250 miles, makes a bend to the south so sweeping as to give to its entire course from Tellico,[3] where it is navigable for boats, to its mouth on the Mississippi, where it is three miles broad, an extent of nearly 900 miles.

Tennessee sends nine Representatives to Congress under the latest census. It only sent three when I was at Washington.

*Material in brackets is from the HEH version.

[1]Actually Tennessee was admitted to the Union as the sixteenth state in 1796.

[2]Foster refers to the campaign of 1818, in which Jackson and his army on slight pretext invaded Florida in pursuit of the Seminoles. They captured a Scottish merchant, Alexander Arbuthnot, and later a lieutenant of Marines, Robert C. Armbrister. The two were sentenced and executed on various charges of inciting the Indians to war, giving aid to the enemy, and assuming command of the Indians in war against the U. S. Though Jackson's conduct of the war was investigated and a House Committee on Military Affairs reported against the two executions, the bill was voted down and Jackson cleared on grounds of military necessity. The matter was a campaign issue in 1824. England entered a protest in 1819 but dropped it.

[3]Tellico is in southeast Tennessee, on the North Carolina border.

Nashville on the Cumberland River was then the greatest sized town but Knoxville was the seat of government. The governor was allowed a salary of $1,000 a year.

The proportion of black to white men in the western part of this state was as nine to one, but in the eastern division only as four to one.

Mr. King of Abingdon, by birth an Irishman, was described to me as having realized a very considerable property by a speculation in salt-pits in this state.[4] He had spent all he possessed in sinking a well 200 feet deep, when the water gushed up as he had calculated that it would do, and to within fifty feet of the top. Seven barrels of the water on the very first trial made one of salt, and afterwards the water became so much more impregnated with the saline particles that four barrels of it would suffice to make one of salt. And he could make as much as he pleased, selling it for $1½ per bushel. He had besides an income from £100,000 worth of stores of which he owned the half.

Tennessee was supplied with foreign goods from Philadelphia, Baltimore, and, subsequently, from Savannah in Georgia. Nothing came to it at that time by the medium of the Mississippi, the navigation of the Tennessee being too circuitous and that up the Cumberland on which Nashville is situated, not very expeditious. These countries, however, and their capabilities cannot as yet be sufficiently known, or have become sufficiently colonized for their local advantages to have been developed and understood as they will no doubt be before many years shall have elapsed.

[4]Abingdon, Virginia, near the Tennessee border, is close to Saltville, still a mining center for saline compounds. William King (1769-1808) landed in America in 1784 and was in Abingdon by 1791. In 1795 he bought property in the Preston tract in the Saltville Valley and by 1799 had erected furnaces for manufacturing salt and operated them most successfully. Lewis P. Summers, *History of Southwest Virginia, Washington County, 1777-1870* (Richmond, 1903), pp. 585-87, 793-94.

CHAPTER XI

KENTUCKY increases her population so rapidly that, although in the year 1812 she furnished but six Members to Congress, there were, according to the statement of the *National Calendar*, already double that number of Representatives in 1828, viz., twelve, while Virginia, the parent state, had still but twenty-four.

Kentucky

Frankfort was the seat of government, an unhealthy place in summer and therefore it will probably long since have ceased to be the capital, more especially as Lexington is a much larger town. The proportion of slaves to the white inhabitants was said to be as one to seven throughout this state. It was the wildest part of the Union when I was on the American continent and sent the strangest fellows to Congress. Amongst others we had two or three Irishmen of whom one had been already a Member of Assembly in the state of Vermont,[1] a very good-humoured person but who was used to clip the King's English and call a voluminous a volumnious report, and Buenos Aires Bounness Eariss. Another was the duelist[2] to whom I have already alluded and who used to insist that nobody could be a thorough gentleman who had not fought a duel and wounded his man or been wounded himself, and he was actually, while holding this language, a judge in his own state. A third pretended at Mr. Merry's table and loud enough to be heard by his hosts, that bad Kentucky cider was preferable to the hock that was handed round and of which he had just been partaking, spitting it out behind his chair to show his republican contempt for it. Mr. Pope, the Senator, on the other hand, who was no Irishman and had never crossed the sea, or the Alleghenies before the year 1807, was a

[1]Matthew Lyon (1750-1822), Member of Congress 1797-1801, 1803-1811, cast the decisive vote of Vermont for Jefferson in 1801, and the same year went to Kentucky.

[2]Probably Stephen Ormsby. See II, n. 131.

person of very good manners and much superior in every respect to all these imported patriots. He maintained in conversing about his native country that from what he could perceive, it contained many men of talents but few men of real information. On which I lamented the difficulty there must exist in Kentucky in procuring books, but he with some confidence disputed this, telling me that in Lexington alone there was an excellent circulating library of at least 1,200 volumes.

A man who goes to settle as a farmer in Kentucky finds the business but little profitable notwithstanding the cheapness of land. Tradesmen make rapid fortunes, but the only advantageous line for a land speculator is to raise cattle, and there are great drawbacks to such enterprizes from the expence attending the driving the beasts to Baltimore, Philadelphia or other large towns which are the usual marts. Pork is in vast abundance and so cheap that 300 lbs. weight was the usual price of a pair of boots, while three barrels of corn was the cost of a pair of shoes, a barrel of corn being valued on the spot at but about one-half a dollar. Hemp is a valuable produce of the soil of Kentucky especially that sort called the water-red hemp.

Mr. Pope's parents must have been amongst the earliest settlers in this state, for I was assured by the Secretary of the Treasury, Mr. Gallatin, that previously to the year 1770 nobody had emigrated into Kentucky, which, nevertheless, in 1807 already contained 300,000 souls. The oldest settler in the state was at that very time still alive and Mr. Gallatin had just received a letter from him. His name was Boon, and Boonsborough, I believe, is called so after him. He had been constantly shifting his residence and was then on the Missouri.[3] The letter was full of complaints that different parts of Kentucky had got to be too thickly peopled for him, the game having become scanty. And as he was a great spendthrift he soon got rid of the lands which he only held by right of possession, vulgarly called "squatting" and squatted

[3]Daniel Boone (1734-1820) reached the site of Boonesborough in 1775. Some time in 1798 or 1799, when his last Kentucky holding was lost, he moved to Missouri. The letter to Gallatin has not been located.

elsewhere, gradually further and further off until he reached the River Mississippi which he crossed and left far behind him.

The Anglo-Americans employed about thirty years in surmounting the Blue and Allegheny Mountains, which are nearly 130 miles broad, before they established themselves in any considerable number near Pittsburgh where they first made a settlement. The Indians, by taking advantage of the defences afforded by a mountainous country, had thus long been able to keep off the tide of emigration, though General Braddock's march in 1755 was undertaken for the purpose of subduing them.

Mr. Clay, the Speaker, who, although originally from Virginia, is a Kentucky man, told me that one of the best inns on the continent is that at Lexington[4] to which the distance from the Federal City, by one road, is 700 miles, which is travelled over in twenty-eight days, while by another road it is but 630 miles which are got over in twenty-one days.

Senator Pope gave it as his opinion to me in talking of Kentucky that it never can become a commercial country, from its possessing no ports or harbours, and being only able to use steam boats which are slow in returning and cannot convey any considerable quantity of goods. Its great emporium at present is New York.

[4]Probably Captain John Postlethwait's Tavern, built in 1797 and burned twice.

CHAPTER XII

WHEN I first was employed in the United States Ohio was represented by but one Member of the lower house of Congress, Jeremiah Morrow, who was continued for ten years in the same situation, when he became Senator for six years.[1] In the year 1828, however, I find that the number of the Ohio Representatives had increased to fourteen.

Ohio

The capital was at Chillicothe and the governor was allowed $900, about £200 per annum.

No slaves were allowed to be retained as such in this state on which New England has stamped her own Anglo-Saxon character for honesty and good faith.

The extent of navigation of Ohio is immense and it serves to facilitate boundless means of communication over all the neighbouring parts of the continent, as the river will, in the rainy season, float vessels carrying from 1,200 to 1,600 barrels of flour for a course of 1,188 miles, being the distance from Pittsburgh to the Mississippi, whence to the sea is nearly as much again. Ohio is said to contain excellent soil, and it is the most conveniently situated of all the inland states, from its lying along Lake Erie and being intersected by a number of great rivers, of which one has the very poetical sounding name of Monongahela.

I met at Washington a German Swiss who went by the name of Muller, and who had been settled for about eight years twenty-five miles below Pittsburgh in this state. He had 10,000 acres of land for which he had paid two dollars per acre. When first he went to establish himself there he lived in a tent and around him were settled about 3,000 individuals chiefly Germans. He had 100 acres in grass, of the kind called Timothy, and 500 Merino sheep of the wool of which he brought specimens to Washington which were much praised.

[1]Jeremiah Morrow (1771-1852), Member of Congress 1803-1813, U.S. Senator 1813-1819.

Flour, he told me, sold where he resided for four dollars the barrel.

When he began to live as a resident in the back country, he said he was subject to the intrusions of any country fellow who might come to occupy his fire-side and talk of freedom and American superiority over Europeans. He, Muller, not being strong enough to beat him, and not liking to shoot him, was forced to prefer being patient and at length carried his point of being let alone. His Germans were chiefly from about Tübingen; they had, however, been latterly, as he asserted, so closely watched in those parts of Germany that they met with great difficulty in emigrating. Muller, as I afterwards understood, was not this gentleman's real name, which he thought it advisable to conceal as he probably had not quite renounced all intention of returning to Europe, and therefore did not wish to be publicly known as an encourager of emigration. I wish he had employed his talents of persuasion in Ireland where we should have had no such jealousy though it must be owned that it is very difficult to get Irish labourers to embark for America from at least the midland counties, as I know from experience, having had to pay for the passage of four persons male and female who came back from Liverpool beyond which no persuasion could induce them to go, though I had taken measures for their having good treatment on board and a sum of money on their landing in America.

Mr. Muller was a great proficient on the jew's-harp of which he could play on two at the same moment. He assured me, however, that there are amateurs in Germany who can play on nine such instruments at one and the same time.

This gentleman made wine and had introduced grapes from Europe on his estates, but I could not learn that the wine was much liked.

I was acquainted with a very worthy man from Ohio, Mr. Senator Worthington, whom I had met while on my tours and afterwards saw a good deal of at Washington. I considered him as a man of great moderation of temper and of as great good sense as any person I ever met with. For although he had once been impressed himself, as he admitted to me he had, by a captain of a man-of-war and was consequently against our doctrine on the subject of impressment, saying he would rather live on a crust than be so disgraced, yet was it without the smallest rancour that he gave his opinion, and he voted against the declaration of war, as Mr. Pope did, from pure conviction that there was not sufficient ground for it, as well as from persuasion that we were really fighting for our existence and at the same time for the cause of liberty and independence all over the world against military despotism and irreligion, for Bonaparte, at this time, had almost invited divine honours to be paid to him. Mr. Worthington pressed me very much to visit him at his place in Ohio, where he could give me, he said, plenty of fine nectarines, heath peaches and the best of apples. I need not add how happy I should have been to have accepted his invitation had I ever been able to find time for such a tour, but while I was employed at Washington there were no such people in existence as attachés nor was there even a private secretary in Mr. Merry's time, so that I had all the business of copying, and in duplicate, as well as into the book of archives. Besides which as there was no consul general in those days we had all the correspondence belonging to that officer in addition to diplomatic affairs, which were no trifle during the discussions especially on impressment, right of blockade, Orders in Council, etc. And on my second visit to the United States I had only my own private secretary to assist me and was sometimes obliged to sit up nearly all night long writing and copying.

The state of Connecticut possessed reserve lands formerly in the territory of Ohio, which she sold for $1,200,000, out of the interest whereof her schools, so deservedly celebrated, are supported, having in this manner discovered a method for deriving undisputed pecuniary resources from her colonies which we, the great grandmother of all these territorial establishments, seem never to have thought of.

The state government of Ohio receives thirty cents for every

100 acres of third-rate land, sixty-five cents for every acre of second-rate quality and ninety per acre for the best.

The inhabitants are of a very social disposition and it was not unusual for a young man to ride 120 miles for the sake of having the company of a favourite young lady at a ball. He would go twenty miles to make the invitation and go back, then twenty again to fetch her, and the return to her home after the dance make out the six twenties.

Salt pork (the money of the back country some twenty years ago) was selling in Ohio by the barrel containing 210 lbs. at seven dollars generally, and never more than eight dollars the barrel. And good flour sold at the same time for from four to five dollars the barrel containing 196 lbs. The cost of freight from Ohio to New Orleans was $1½ per barrel, and I was assured by a contractor for the American navy, Mr. Wilson,[2] that dry goods were conveyed to him at a cheaper rate on the waters of the Ohio, by fifteen per cent, when purchased at Montreal and carried from thence by means of portages and the rivers, than when they were brought from Philadelphia or Baltimore through Pittsburgh. The coal mines of this state are said to be inexhaustible.

[2]Samuel Wilson (1766-1854), the original "Uncle Sam," was a meat packer who supplied the U.S. Army with meat, etc., all marked EA US (i.e., EA for Elbert Anderson [also Army contractor and Wilson's partner] for the firm, and US for the consignee).

CHAPTER XIII

I HAVE NOTHING further to add on the subject of the western and southern divisions of the United States, nor of the territories or embryo states that have been lately, or will soon be transformed into independent portions of the Federal Union, which has already seen the original numbers of stars in the national flag almost doubled, they having increased in 1828, to twenty-four from thirteen. These newly cleared countries, however interesting to the natural or speculative philosopher, offering but little worth exciting the attention of the general traveller, unless it should be thought amusing to trace the effects of emigration into the woods upon a motley set of Atlantic or transatlantic planters Irish, Scotch or German, without connection, association or plan, of whom General Dayton,[1] a Senator from New Jersey, once told me that he had met twelve to fourteen waggons full of a day, families going to settle in the back country. A tavern keeper who had been in the habit of scoring had noted down fifty-one and fifty-seven as the number which had passed on two successive days, the most of them from New England and Virginia.

The West

These emigrants as soon as they have cut out a farm from the woods and made an habitation of logs, and that they have enough to eat, begin to talk of being a young people, and of their future greatness and advantages over the old states, but it is evident that there can be nothing national about them nor any associations or attachments connected with their new places of residence. And it is more than probable, judging from human nature, that they must be sometimes very inconvenient, if not troublesome to one another. For it cannot be asserted in any district of the United States any more than in Europe that a family will take their impressions, wholly unaffected by their parents' prejudices,

[1]Jonathan Dayton (1760-1824), Senator from New Jersey, 1799-1805.

from the new situation, institutions or customs under which they go to live, unless where the parents may have emigrated when they were still children, or have died before the second generation has been able to imbibe those habits and feelings which form the character; [and which are scarcely ever found to take the colour belonging to the new country of an emigrant in its fullest shade before they have arrived at the third generation unless in cases where the parents may have emigrated when still very young.]*

These territories, however, are becoming rapidly prepared for future empire and Indiana, Illinois, Alabama, Missouri, Arkansas and Michigan have already their Representative or delegates in Congress, and claim the land as belonging to the respective settlers just as if the Ten Nations and other Indian tribes were wholly extinct or had never existed. Of the above-named territories Michigan from its situation between three immense lakes seems to be peculiarly destined for the seat of a magnificent dominion, and at the rate at which the Federal ring appears to be enlarging, I should suppose that before fifty years shall have elapsed, a delegate, if not a Representative will be sent to Washington from the banks of the River Columbia where it flows into the Pacific Ocean. This river has already been inspected by Captain Meriwether Lewis who told me that it was navigable for 125 miles for ships of 400 tons burthen. The Indian inhabitants too from his description of them do not seem likely to offer much opposition to the land being colonized, many of them being blind from the effects of their living upon fish alone while they all appear to be of inferior health and strength to the Indians of the interior.

Vegetation in those regions bordering on the Pacific must be very flourishing according to the accounts Captain Lewis gave me of it. He had caused to be felled, he said, a tree, near the mouth of the Columbia, which was in appearance like a Scotch fir, for the purpose of having planks made for sheds under which

*Material in brackets deleted in LC version.

he and his party were to lie during winter, and he found the length of the tree to measure ninety yards from the roots to the top, being fourteen feet in diameter. Another tree at some distance from the first having been reported by his hunters to be 300 feet high, he sent a party to measure, and they came back confirming the report and adding that it was seventeen feet in diameter. Both these trees therefore were full as lofty as the trees on Norfolk Island or on Prince of Wales Island off the Malabar Coast which were supposed to be the tallest hitherto known in the world.

CHAPTER XIV

I NOW turn once more to the Federal City and District on my way to the middle and northern states.

This is the only portion of the United States that is not directly represented in Congress, and therefore its little concerns become the peculiar care and concern of the national parliament which generally has to appoint a committee for the especial purpose of superintending them. I have known debates of several weeks occasioned by the question whether a bridge should or should not be built over the Potomac. On one occasion when it had been carried in favour of the bridge I have known the votes reversed the next day by the effects of a timely dinner at the hospitable table of the owner of the ferry. The bridge, however, at last prevailed, but, as I am told, was since carried away, so that the ferry again became triumphant.

District of Columbia

There already existed a bank at Washington at the time of my residence in that city, which bank was a branch of that of the United States established at Philadelphia. But for many years before the Congress moved to Washington the monied men of the District were at a loss how to dispose of their surplus cash, and Mr. Delany of Alexandria[1] used to give presents to trustworthy individuals whom he employed to find out safe persons to lend his money to at six per cent interest, one of them being Mr. Peters[2] who having gone originally from England with but a crown in his pocket died in 1806 worth $800,000, or near £180,000, all vested in land and slaves, having become rich by buying land on credit at a low rate, and retaining it until it became very valuable. This, however, he could not have done,

[1]Benjamin Delaney, of Shooter's Hill and Alexandria, whose name appears in Alexandria court records as plaintiff trying to recover debts, is probably the man referred to. He was a friend of Washington and a great horse fancier. Gay M. Moore, *Seaport in Virginia* (Richmond, Va., 1949), pp. 173-83.

[2]Robert Peter (1726-1806) came to Georgetown from Scotland and was a principal merchant of the city. He was mayor 1789-1790.

except with certain restrictions, under the King's Government, for lands, though at that time usually granted on petition and on the condition of paying only one half-penny quit-rent per acre for every year after the first ten years. Yet if they were not cleared in the proportion of three acres in fifty, during the three years after the first ten years, and if three neat cattle, at least, were not found to every fifty acres, the compact was declared null. Under the Spanish government similar conditions were imposed on grants of land to individuals, but the American states have generally sold land by millions of acres and by square miles to companies who buy merely to make a job of speculation, and it frequently has happened that the same lands are many times sold and resold without ever being settled.

Yet this cannot happen with regard to lands purchased at the land office of the general government, maps of great accuracy being there kept, and an opportunity afforded to any individual of obtaining land that is not located, on his merely asking to have his name entered for a corner next to the latest grant made. And there was a good deal to be had even in the old states which was not yet marked off when I was last at Washington. Mr. Goldsborough,[3] a Member for Maryland, having when he came of age, found even within one of the boundaries of his own state a slice of land that had never been located and that went right through his property, on which he applied for it, had it surveyed and got it for very little money. The Indians of the Catawba tribe made grants for ninety-nine years, but these lands are now considered, by the Americans in general, whatever lawyers may say, as having been granted forever. On the other hand Mr. Livingstone who had a claim to 13,000,000 of acres in the state of New York, has been opposed by the state government which stepped in, and took it all on pretext that his father could not, according to law, have bought land from the Indians from whom he held his deed of grant.[4]

[3]Charles Goldsborough (1764-1834), Member of Congress from Maryland, 1805-1817.

[4]John Livingston's project of a perpetual lease from the Indians of all central and western New York is here referred to. On November 30, 1787, and on January 8, 1788, Livingston and his associates signed a 999-year lease with various

To the state governments, however, a person having a warrant for land, generally only pays two or three cents per acre, and for this reason it is that people often prefer applying to them and taking their chance of a good lot, to asking land of the United States authorities who require two dollars per acre. For although you may find that a previous warrant has been granted to someone else of the very land the state government has assigned to you, yet in such case, your warrant still remains good and you are at liberty to go searching about for an unclaimed spot in some other part of the state dominion. The circumstance, nevertheless, of a grant under the national government, being substantial and beyond all dispute, should, I think, render it much more advisable for an emigrant to apply there. The land too of the United States being partitioned on a map by straight lines and this open to inspection, like the books of a lottery office, there can be no possibility of your being deceived in regard to it.

The grants called proprietory grants were also esteemed to be amongst the best titles, those especially which were claimed by the Penn family, which had been surveyed by order of the states of Pennsylvania and Delaware, and which were parcelled out with lots of from 200 to 500 acres each. The Penns had been unjustly deprived of these lands, and the divisions were made thus small because as there lies by law no appeal to the courts of the Union for trifling turns, and as the whole population, nearly, profited by the spoil there was no chance of a jury being found to give a decision against themselves and in favour of the foreigner. The Penns did receive some compensation in money, from the state governments, but Mr. Bayard, a Senator of Delaware, assured me that to his certain knowledge the lawyers employed by the family had for fifteen years been non-suited in trying to obtain a verdict, no case having been fairly tried.

---

chiefs. The total property of both leases amounted to 12,000,000 acres, two-fifths of the entire area of the state. Paul D. Evans, "The Frontier Pushed Westward," *History of the State of New York*, ed. Alexander C. Flick (New York, 1933-1937), V, 151-52.

CHAPTER XV

MARYLAND does not seem to have increased the number of her representatives in Congress of late years for they were nine in 1812 and still appear to be but nine. This was one of the old original aristocratic states whose names tell us of their having been founded by royalty. Queen Mary and Queen Anne were here the rivals of Queen Elizabeth, the patroness of Virginia, as King George was of King Charles further south. The chief mart for commerce took its denomination from Lord Baltimore whose descendants, the Calverts, still possess considerable property within this state, and whose livery, black and orange, is pointed out to you by any old farmer you may meet with in the plumage of a beautiful bird called after him the Baltimore Bird, something between a starling and a crow, to be found in the open fields. Lord Baltimore's legitimate heir, Mr. Harford,[1] did not, however, escape as well as others of the family, his house having been confiscated at Annapolis and made into the seat of government, for which from its size it was well adapted.

Maryland

The governor is elected by joint ballots of the two Houses and receives £1,000 per annum Maryland currency, or $3,666.

This state like its neighbour Virginia was originally a very aristocratic state but tho' the upper classes have great pretensions to family honour, the government is in the hands of Democrats and therefore, while they make helots of the Negroes, the Marylanders have enacted that every white man, of age and a citizen, shall have a right to vote, provided he have been resident for a twelvemonth within the limits of the state.

According to the registration made by order of the United States in 1791, Maryland is 134 miles long and 110 broad, con-

[1]Later Sir Henry Harford (b. 1762), natural son and heir of Frederick, sixth and last Lord Baltimore. Harford came to America in 1785 and petitioned the Maryland legislature for the estates confiscated during the Revolution to which he was legal heir. His plea was at first denied, but later he was awarded £90,000.

tains about 12,000 square miles and was at that time peopled by 319,728 inhabitants.

The elections are all decided in one day throughout this state. Treating is allowed of before the day of election but not on the day itself, though I was assured that some years previously booths were permitted to be opened on the very day.

From the election being carried on in one and the same day at different places a candidate may be calumniated with impunity on the hustings where he is not present, and it has happened to a gentleman to be wrongfully accused of being at the head of revolted Negroes at the very time of the election, when the accusation was believed in from the impossibility of his being present to defend himself. It is obvious, however, that such a manoeuvre could only succeed for once and that a reputation of it would be more likely to throw discredit on the calumniators than the calumniated.

Mr. Key gave me a description of an election for Congress in which he was the successful candidate. They were two and they were both invited to a barbecue for the purpose of being heard. The pig or shote was placed, as usual, over a hole with a fire in it, split up so as not to cut thro' the skin of the back, thro' which the animal was roasted, and kept continually basted till it was sufficiently done, when it became extremely delicate eating. Married ladies and girls were of the party and the candidates delivered their orations sometimes mounted on the stump of a tree and sometimes on a beer barrel. Magruder, Key's opponent, talked of his blood being allied nearly to the whole district and insisted that he was therefore naturally the fittest person to represent and maintain their interests,[2] but Key retorted that if the question were about a steed that argument might be good; it was not, however, in discussion which of the two, he or his rival, were of the best breed, but which would make the best Member of Congress, when the head was more worthy to be considered

[2]Patrick Magruder (1768-1819), Member of Congress 1805-1807, was Clerk of the House of Representatives and Librarian of Congress 1807-1815. He was born in Montgomery County, Maryland, near Rockville.

than the blood, and he was accordingly preferred. After this they joked and flirted and danced till one o'clock in the morning.

The state of Maryland, which at the commencement of this century was justly entitled to the credit of being governed by some of the most respectable and fittest persons in the Union, was, nevertheless, suffering some few years afterwards under perhaps the meanest and the worst, who had become notorious for shabbiness and bad faith, as instance of which I was told the following facts. Several gentlemen having subscribed together for the purpose of building a college at Annapolis, had petitioned the legislature for support of their plan, and an arrangement was agreed to, in consequence of which the expence of the building being borne by the subscribers, the funds for supporting the institution were to be supplied by the state. An act was passed to that effect, the subscribers performed their part and the college was in a flourishing condition, when by a change of parties some foreigners and low people got into power, repealed the act and, withdrawing the funds, left the owners of the building to their bricks and bare walls, alleging publicly for a pretext that the people by whom the funds were to be furnished, could not from the expensiveness of the establishment have their children educated in it.[3]

Another fact was related to me respecting those liberal Democrats still less to their credit as honest men. The British government contrary to all expectation, with that almost romantic and scrupulous love of justice which has hitherto ever distinguished it, tho' they might have fairly retaliated for the iniquity with which Lord Carteret's and Mr. Penn's heirs had been treated as well as the heirs of Lord Baltimore, yet, looking only to their own character and dignity, consented to give up a sum of £200,000 which lay in the British funds and had belonged to the old government of Maryland. Bills like treasury bills had been circulating upon this money for some time previously, dur-

[3]This seems to be a garbled reference to the failure to unite St. John's and Washington Colleges in 1790-91 into a University of Maryland due to sectional jealousy. E. F. Cordell, *The University of Maryland, 1807-1907* (New York, 1907), I, 1-38.

ing the war, and were very much depreciated. Nevertheless the holders were the persons entitled to the benefit, and were so considered in a proclamation calling upon them to send in the bills, within a reasonable period. The new government however which just then were elected were no sooner installed in their offices than they curtailed the period allowed for the operation and limited the time for presenting the bills, so that many thousands were not produced until it was too late, and the affair became a job with but little benefit to the real claimants; and on such occasions it is that nations find out the bad economy there is in employing low persons of gross and envious dispositions, many of them refugees from other parts, instead of gentlemen of property and education who have a different compass to steer by than that of some paltry jealousy or the mere love of lucre.[4]

The Church of Rome used to be the predominant church of this state, and possessed 60,000 acres of land within its boundaries, the superintending management of which was entrusted to the different priests of their respective parishes. The archbishop, who is primate of the whole continent, resided at Baltimore. The dignity was held some years back by Dr. Carrol, a very highly esteemed gentleman who was of the order of Jesuits and had been consecrated by the Pope. The clergy of the Church of England were far from being in so flourishing a state, both Roman Catholics and independents having been much more impressed with the importance of forming good endowments for their priests in the early times of the colonies than were the Anglicans. Consequently when the Revolution burst upon these and tore asunder their connection with the mother country, the incumbents had nothing to fall back upon but individual and precarious subscription—to favour which a vestry is occasionally held, and the wants of their parson are represented to his parishioners, a book is carried round, and persons in good circumstances generally put down their names for $20 or $30 each per annum.

The insufficiency, however, and the humiliation attending

[4]Foster refers to the Bank of England stock on which Maryland issued bills of credit. J. T. Scharf, *History of Maryland* (Baltimore, 1874), II, 504-505.

such a mode of payment I learnt from the Reverend Mr. Scott, a very venerable, greyheaded clergyman of the Scotch Protestant Church whom I met at the country house of Mr. Ogle, a gentleman of property in this state, [for whom I had brought a brace of English pheasants on my second visit in the United States.]* Mr. Scott told me that his salary might be called about £400 a year, Maryland currency, but that it was difficult and troublesome for him to go about in order to get paid by each individual subscriber, and if he were to dun them he should run the risk of their withdrawing their names altogether. Indeed so irksome was this operation become to him who was as mild and almost as simple as a child, and who moreover could not stand the fatigue of it, being now considerably above sixty years of age, that he soon afterwards determined to retire and go back to Scotland after thirty-five years absence from his native country to look out for a curacy or for any other resource that he could obtain there, rather than remain on in America an object of pity, if not of contempt, humbled as well as mortified in his own feelings. I felt so for him that I gave him a letter for Lady Liverpool[5] and recommended him in the strongest terms for some preferment in Great Britain, however small. I had, however, the mortification, on my return to Europe, of learning that although he had left my letter at Fife House and had called on Lady Liverpool, yet the family having unluckily been out of town, or merely out for a drive, he poor man, who was probably possessed of a morbid sensibility that made him think himself too insignificant to be noticed by the great, had quitted London without leaving his address or any clue by which to find him. This was the more to be lamented as Lord Liverpool had been moved by my representation to compassionate his situation, having actually fixed upon a small and very comfortable living which was to be conferred upon him, but he had vanished and

*Bracketed material inserted in LC version and later deleted.

[5]The former Louisa Hervey, Lady Liverpool, was the wife of Robert Banks Jenkinson, second Earl of Liverpool (1770-1828), Prime Minister after Perceval's assassination in 1812. She was Foster's mother's sister.

I never afterwards could learn what became of him. [*Note*: I since heard from Dr. Tarrot the Bishop of Edinburgh that he went to that city and was there employed as a curate.][6]

The state of Maryland had a high agricultural reputation tho' the land there is not always well managed being in many parts very much gullied as in Virginia. Land, however, in Virginia is rendered more valuable to the owners from the state laws in regard to debt and the transfer of property, as the Virginian landholder cannot be forced to part with any portion of his estate for the purpose of paying even a just debt and this makes a pretty considerable difference in the price of the lands of the same quality on the opposite sides of the River Potomac.

Maryland, as is well known, produces the best tobacco for smoking, which is called "Kitefoot." More than a hogshead, in general, is raised from one acre and it is worth at the lowest price about $65. The state has it examined by an inspecting officer who opens it with an iron ledge in three places for examination, so attentive are they to keep up the reputation of the staple commodity of the country.

I was assured by the Comptroller of the Treasury, Mr. Duval,[7] who was himself a landowner, that the expence of a slave to his master amounted annually, on a rough calculation, to but $20 (not quite £4.10s), and that one slave should be equal to the labour employed on three hogsheads of tobacco, which in some years is sold at even $90 or $100 per hogshead for the best. So that the profit may be enormous, tho' of course somewhat more than $40 may be deducted from the gross price, when one considers that at least one half the number of the slaves whom a proprietor maintains must be set down as ineffective from sickness, infancy or age. When we reflect, however, that in England a farmer is thought to do very well if, after all expences are paid,

[6]Charles Hughes Terrot (1790-1872) did not become Bishop of Edinburgh until 1841, though he had charges in Edinburgh from 1817. The HEH version of Foster's "Notes" (ca. 1839) states that he had been unable to find out what had become of the clergyman.

[7]Gabriel Duval (1752-1844) of Maryland, Comptroller of the U.S. Treasury 1802-1811, was later Associate Justice of the U.S. Supreme Court.

he nets £4 an acre, the profit of the Marylander must appear very great. And moreover when the soil is quite new I have been assured that even more than a hogshead and a half has been raised on the acre.

There were a great number of rich proprietors in the state of Maryland. In the district nearest the city of Washington, alone, of which Montgomery County forms part, I was assured that there were 500 persons possessing estates which returned them an income of £1,000 Maryland currency, and Mr. Lloyd, a Member of Congress on the eastern branch, possessed a net revenue of $30,000 or between £6,000 and £7,000 with which he had only to buy clothes for himself and family, wines, equipage, furniture and other luxuries. Mr. Ringold, too, possessed near Haggardstown property yielding him an income of $12,000 a year, and he rented his lands to tenants, whom he was at liberty to change if he pleased every year, for five dollars per acre, tho' he was to stand the expence of all repairs. Mr. Ringold kept but 600 acres in his own hands for stock. Mr. Tayloe also, whose whole income exceeded $70,000 per annum, had a great portion of it in Maryland, chiefly at Nanjimoy.

Mr. Carrol of Annapolis, grandfather to Lady Wellesley, the Duchess of Leeds, and Lady Stafford, was said to be still more wealthy having besides great accumulation in the funds, 15,000 acres of the best land in Frederick County and several other estates.[8] He let a considerable portion of his property too to tenants with an agreement that he was to receive a fine on the transfer of a lease, which arrangement is very profitable in a country where land is so often liable to change its occupants. I am induced to mention these instances of men of property and good family settled in America from having observed what great ignorance still prevails among even the higher classes of Eng-

[8]Charles Carroll of Carrollton (1737-1832), signer of the Declaration of Independence, was grandfather of Marianne, second wife of Richard, Marquis of Wellesley (1760-1842). She was one of the daughters of Robert Caton of Baltimore. Louisa Caton married the Marquis of Carmarthen, heir to the Duke of Leeds. Elizabeth Caton married the eighth Baron Stafford. E. H. Smith, *Charles Carroll of Carrollton* (Cambridge, Mass., 1942), pp. 300-301.

lishmen in regard to the state of the colonies before the revolution that separated them from the mother country, many persons supposing them to have been in a great measure peopled by convicts, whereas, whatever were the importations of such persons as are now sent to Botany Bay, they were too few in former days to affect the general character of the colonial population and more probably restricted to the state of Pennsylvania which is still an omnium gatherum for people of all countries and religions and to the state of Georgia, which only began its political existence in the last century.

No town in the world, perhaps, has had a more rapid rise than Baltimore. It contains at the present day in all probability 80,000 or 90,000 inhabitants, and Mr. Cook,[9] a most respectable inhabitant of the place told me in 1805 that he could remember when there were not more than five or six houses in it. What contributed more than any other circumstance to its extraordinary increase was that of its being a safe position as a place of deposit, out of the reach of ships of war during the War of Independence. Capital then flowed into it, commercial houses were established, and, the market once formed, such is the stability of credit and of habit, that even the foundation of Washington City, with all its advantages arising from its being seated on a great river, with every one of the back countries nearer to it than to Baltimore, has not been able to do the slightest prejudice to the prosperity of the latter, while so great has been the advance in the value of the ground for building purposes consequent upon this great demand for it that Colonel Howard[10] told me had just sold for $150,000 a piece of land that he had bought several years previously of Mr. Key for but 800 guineas and it is on a part of this land that the Roman Catholic cathedral church has been erected.

[9]William Cooke or Cook (1746-1817) is probably the man referred to. He was a prominent lawyer and banker, British-educated, who dealt with Daniel Dulaney and Charles Carroll. *Md. Hist. Mag.*, XXXVI (Sept. 1941), 282; VII (Sept. 1921), 241; XV (March 1920), 10; XL (Sept. 1945), 227.

[10]John Eager Howard (1752-1827), hero at Cowpens, was Senator from Maryland, 1796-1803.

Dry goods were carried in waggons from Baltimore to Nashville in Tennessee in a period of about six weeks, being a distance of 640 miles, and the cost of carriage amounted to but 12½ per cent.

From Baltimore to Philadelphia the distance is 148 miles which I did in twenty-nine hours, sleeping on the road at Havre de Grace on the Susquehannah. I took the stage horses and changed at every station paying for them but $56. Thus a first step was made towards travelling post which since, as I am told, has been continued.

There was a sum of $1,000,000 subscribed for forming an East India Company at Baltimore; the average passage from which town to Calcutta was calculated at 120 days.[11]

There were several flourishing manufactures in the neighbourhood, or in the town itself, among which was one peculiarly American, namely that of moss hair mattresses, the material for which is chiefly imported from Charleston and New Orleans, being the fine moss already mentioned, that grows on trees and resembles hair, which it nearly equals in quality, while it costs but 6½ cents per lb., whereas hair costs at Baltimore 37½ cents per lb. Bed ticking is also made here, and there is a cotton manufactory in the neighbourhood at a place called Ellicot's Mills under the direction of an Englishman [Mr. Waddell]* who did not seem over satisfied with his gains tho' he was paid two dollars per day, for he told me that a very little would tempt him to go back to the Old Country. He was paid from fortnight to fortnight, and the work was principally done by apprentices, boys and girls. Two hundred pounds of cotton were spun in a day, which was chiefly worked into yarn, very little being made into cloth. A few Englishmen, nevertheless, were engaged in making jean and royal rib which is used for waistcoats, and they were paid by the piece thirty-two cents and hardly made

*HEH version only.

[11]This company was organized in 1807. It was able to go through the embargo to India and proved quite profitable. T. W. Griffith, *Annals of Baltimore* (Baltimore, 1833), p. 185.

3½ yards a day, which was hard earning, being less than a common labourer is paid who gets a dollar a day and is found in food. The girls got two dollars per week, but the lodging of these people and their board is stopped out of their pay, and they worked from sunrise to sunset, having only one-half an hour for breakfast and one hour for dinner, so laborious are people obliged to be to please their masters even in this young country.

The cotton from New Orleans was very dirty and of bad quality, tho' the worse it was the better, they said, for the coarse yarn that they wanted, and it was very cheap, costing but eleven cents per pound. The manufacturer had as yet but little profit and the shares subscribed for were under par, which was to be lamented as there was a population of 300 persons, in all, kept together by this establishment.

During Mr. and Mrs. Merry's residence in the United States we made an excursion together to Annapolis, which is about forty-four miles from Washington and is on the Bay of Chesapeake.[12] I rode the whole way, which lies for the most part through very fine woods of oaks, tulip trees and hickories. I never saw, unless on the banks of the Bosphorus, so great a luxuriancy of foliage, and it was in the month of May when the country was most beautiful. The variety of the oaks was particularly striking. The red oak has leaves, when young, fully as large as cabbage leaves; another, the black oak grows like a Portugal laurel, the leaves shaped like a flattened pear and extremely coriacious. The white oak, the most valuable of all, grows best on a slashy soil and is of an excellent quality for ship and house building, provided it is not put into contact with the timber of the live oak, for I was assured by Commandant Tingey Commissioner of the Navy Yard that if the ribs of live oak were only to rest on white oak planks the latter will rot away at the point of contact although remaining sound a few inches from it on either side.

[12]The visit was made in 1805.

The willow oak has long thin leaves without a single indenture and is a very pretty tree. The hickory grows to a large size and has leaves like those of a walnut tree, pointed but not quite so smooth. The tulip tree is very lofty and has abundance of flowers half green, half red. A gentleman of Kentucky told me he had one that was twenty-nine feet in circumference and that five men could hardly embrace with arms extended. The cedars have a red blossom, in shape very much like a tarantula, so much so that I took it at first for an insect. The woods were interspersed with beautiful creepers, and in this district they seemed filled with a variety of noisy birds, of which the woodpeckers furnish a great number of different species. At Marlborough Court House we got a clean tavern kept by a very civil innkeeper, and further on five miles from Annapolis we crossed South River, which is one-half mile wide, in a flat boat.

Annapolis was formerly the greatest city of Maryland until Baltimore took away its trade; it still, however, contains the best houses in the state, tho' only a town, now, of 1,500 inhabitants. The houses are built of brick and generally three stories high, being more lofty than those of Baltimore, and every house has a garden and trees to shade it. The best society used to be found here a few years back, and there were still several agreeable families residing in the town when we visited it, amongst the rest the Ogle family and Mr. Carrol already mentioned as a great landholder, the richest perhaps in the United States, and who looked very old fashioned, wearing ruffles and a cocked hat as in the older time. Stewart the painter told a good anecdote of one of these gentlemen. Upon Mrs. Bingham's return from England he was invited to her parties,[13] and as she gave herself fashionable airs and among other innovations had introduced

[13]Anne Willing Bingham (1764-1801), Mrs. William Bingham, a beautiful and attractive hostess, was the center of the "Republican Court" in Philadelphia. The Binghams lived at 3d and Spruce Sts. Their daughter married Alexander Baring of the great English financial family. Rufus W. Griswold, *The Republican Court, or American Society in the Days of Washington* (New York, 1856), pp. 253-63, and *DAB*. Foster's anecdote here is related of James Monroe in Claude G. Bowers, *Jefferson and Hamilton: the Struggle for Democracy in America* (Boston, 1925), p. 130.

the form of announcing company on their arrival, his name was shouted out by the servant at the door to the servant on the landing place, and by him echoed up to the drawing room while he was pulling off a tight greatcoat. When hearing himself so repeatedly called for he at last got vexed at what he thought their impatient hurry, stopt tugging for a moment and gave them all a hearty curse, exclaiming, "D——n it, don't be in such a haste and I'll be with you immediately."

There was a school for little boys at Annapolis which had considerable reputation. There was no flogging allowed of which is a discipline that is scouted throughout all this part of the continent. Roman Catholic and Protestant as well as boys of all sects were promiscuously educated at this school.[14]

I again visited Annapolis in June 1811 when I landed from the *Minerva* frigate, with Sir Grenville Temple who was going to endeavour to drive away some squatters from his lands in Massachusetts,[15] Mr. Baker my private secretary and seven servants, and I had to pay for a single day's living at the inn $36 or £8. I dined the following day on my road to the Federal City at Mr. Ogle's of Bellair, and gave him an English cock pheasant which I had brought for him with the hen, but the latter had died at sea.

The law of prescription takes effect in this state after twenty years of possession.

Mr. Ogle told me that some years previously his father and other proprietors near the shore had been much plagued by visits from sailors belonging to the *Patriote* and other French ships of war lying in the Chesapeake, four of his sheep having, on one occasion, been killed and carried off from a farm belonging to him. A complaint having been made to the Commandant, he advized the gentlemen to arm their Negroes and order them

[14]This school has not been identified.

[15]Sir George Grenville Temple, Bart. (1768-1829), married Elizabeth, daughter of George Watson of the U.S. As he remarried in 1812 it seems likely that in 1811 he was concerned with the estates of his late wife. Temple's father Sir George (1730-1798) had been consul-general in the U.S. during his son's childhood.

to fire on the offenders if they attempted to do so another time. But he never offered to pay for the sheep, and the sailors must have been under very loose discipline, for the messenger saw some of them drunk and playing cards while their officers appeared to walk by without noticing them.

Soon after my return from Annapolis I made an excursion to Harper's Ferry.[16] It was on the 20th of June and I set out on horseback which was the only way for travelling with any comfort in the United States, the stage coaches being in general so crowded that whether in winter or summer one feels the greatest inconvenience in them, for tho' they ought by law to take but seven passengers, they do take twelve or thirteen, and of these many individuals are occasionally very disagreeable companions, and either from their filthiness or manners not fit to associate with gentlemen. The drivers too make themselves formidable by choosing to drive over the worst places in a dashing manner. Whereas with one's own horses one may choose one's hours for dining or stopping and go nearly as far in a day, when the roads are bad which is pretty generally the case to the south of the Susquehannah.

It is 15 miles to Montgomery Court House
16 to a tavern kept by Scholl
13 to Frederick Town
10 to a small village called Trappe[17]
and 10 to Harper's Ferry

The tavern at Montgomery Court House was kept by a Scotchman who avoided talking of his country as if he was ashamed of having left it.

There is perhaps no country in the world in which one may

[16]Foster is referring here to his first visit to Annapolis. He wrote to his mother on June 30, 1805, that he had recently made a visit to Harper's Ferry, "This sink of the Imagination." Foster, *Two Duchesses*, p. 226.

[17]Though there are or have been other "Trappes" in Maryland, geographically this one could only be the "Traptown" in Frederick County, Maryland, on Coctin Creek, 7 miles southwest of "Frederickstown." Jedediah Morse, *The American Gazetteer* (Boston, 1810).

travel over so much space and meet with less variety, or take less interest in the objects one may see as in the interior of the states, generally speaking. The whole of my tour tended but to one gratification, that of beholding the junction of two rivers at Harper's Ferry—the character of the inhabitants hereabouts, a set of people unattached to soil, descendants of German soldiers, or Germans, or Scotch, making no permanent stay anywhere, and caring little for anything but money, being too dull or insignificant to merit attention, while the language they speak is a jargon of English and German, in which the English evidently gains ground and the German is a wretchedly corrupt patois. I conversed with several and was surprized to find that I could hardly understand a single sentence, while one of the inhabitants paid me the compliment of saying that I spoke the German too grammatically for him.

Between Montgomery Court House and Scholl's Tavern one catches a view of the Monocasis Mountains, particularly that called the Sugarloaf, which is insulated from the rest, and from its conical form made one imagine that it might be an extinguished volcano. I could not, however, approach near enough to see if there were any volcanic stones about it. The tavern stands high and as there are no rivers or marshes in the vicinity, it is perhaps the only spot for miles where no ague is to be caught. One of those sudden gusts of wind, accompanied with rain, so common in the United States, came on just as I got there, and obliged me to remain for the night. Otherwise I should have rode as far as Frederick Town on the first day. I had a wretched bed there.

On the road to Frederick Town I passed the River Monocasis.[18] The country is very much cleared and the land apparently very rich, but whether cleared land or forest it is equally sultry as the trees are tall and branch out but very little. The cottages are universally made of logs and small. Land sells for $40 or $50 the acre. There is not a single bookseller's shop in

[18]The river Monocacy flows south into the Potomac just east of Frederick, or about 50 miles above Georgetown.

Frederick, as the town is familiarly called, although it is the second inland town in the state not situated upon a river, having about 1,500 inhabitants, whose trade is principally carried on in small waggons with Baltimore.

In going to Harper's Ferry one crosses the Blue Ridge, a range of lofty hills covered with woods and from about one to 2,000 feet high. The undulations of the soil at their feet give considerable richness to the view, but there is no very striking feature to be seen, until within a few miles of the ferry where the road is confined between the heights and the river, the banks being high and rocky as well as interspersed with trees. The scenery is very romantic and the river rapid and wide, tho' not very deep at the ferry which in the dry season no vessels can pass. On crossing over to a village on the other side one sees a manufactory of arms[19] of which 13,000 stand were lying ready in the armoury when I visited the place. It is a strong position as it stands against a stony mount with the River Shenandoah on the right hand and the Potomac on the left. There is a rock suspended over two others just above the village which they call Jefferson's Rock, as it is supposed that it was from thence he composed his rant about the bursting through the mountains of the two rivers.[20] Two miles, however, beyond this point, his

[19]Of course the Federal arsenal.

[20]Jefferson's *Notes on the State of Virginia*, under Query V, "A notice of its mountains," is the passage Foster refers to: "The passage of the Potomac through the Blue Ridge is, perhaps, one of the most stupendous scenes in nature. You stand on a very high point of land. On your right comes up the Shenandoah, having ranged along the foot of the mountain an hundred miles to seek a vent. On your left approaches the Potomac, in quest of a passage also. In the moment of their junction, they rush together against the mountain, rend it asunder, and pass off to the sea. The first glance of this scene hurries our senses into the opinion, that this earth has been created in time, that the mountains were formed first, that the rivers began to flow afterwards, that in this place, particularly, they have been dammed up by the Blue Ridge of mountains, and have formed an ocean which filled the whole valley; that continuing to rise they have at length broken over at this spot, and have torn the mountain down from its summit to its base. . . ." (Saul K. Padover, ed., *The Complete Jefferson* [New York, 1943]). Isaac Weld (*Travels through the States of North America and the Provinces of Upper and Lower Canada . . . 1795, 1796 and 1797 . . .* [London, 1800], pp. 239-420) refers to and quotes Jefferson's description but does not agree that at Harper's Ferry is "one of the most stupendous scenes of nature."

imagination might have been more easily worked up, for from the high grounds on the road to Sheppardstown one catches a view of the beds of the two torrents, their junction and passage to the Ridge, as well as the blue summit of the Sugarloaf Mountain which stands in the plain.

The body of water at this season of the year is scanty and the Shenandoah is not navigable at all, nor is the Potomac much deeper, and the corn traders prefer dealing over-land with Baltimore. The freshes too of these rivers are very uncertain depending upon rains which may fall sooner or later in the year. I slept at Trappe on the floor on straw, and the inn at the Ferry was very indifferent.

It is about twenty-four miles from thence to Martinsburg,[21] tho' called twenty, and one is continually liable to be deceived in these parts as to distances, everybody appearing to decide them according to a measure of his own, calculating not unfrequently from his particular home, without reflecting upon how far he may have left it behind him.

On the road to Annapolis I was told at first that it was sixteen miles to Marlborough. Four miles further on I was told the same story and four miles after that again I found people who informed me that I had still fifteen miles to go, so that it seemed like chasing a rainbow. At Sheppardstown a Frenchman from Marseilles[22] kept the inn. At Martinsburg the inn was supposed to be one of the best in the United States.[23] I slept there in the ball room. It is a great resort in summer as a healthy place, tho' of a population of about 1,000 inhabitants seventy had died the year previous of the bilious fever, but that was an extraordinary year, it was said. These *buts*, however, are frequently introduced and you must question and cross question in order to discover from an inhabitant of any place hereabouts whether his town is really unhealthy or not.

[21] Martinsburg is now in West Virginia.

[22] According to the HEH "Notes," his name was Abert.

[23] Probably Foose's Lawn, an old tavern located at Hedgesville 6 miles north of modern Martinsburg. The inn was famous when Washington stayed there in 1769.

There is a public table at the inn at Martinsburg and all decently dressed strangers are admitted to it. I met there Mr. Worthington, a Senator of the United States who was riding thro' and stopped to breakfast. I returned by Middleton[24] in Maryland in another direction across the Blue Ridge to Frederick Town. The hills I found stony and covered with wood but no fine timber in them. The breaks afforded rich and pleasing views. I met but one beggar and his family on the whole road, and but few people of any sort. Even Negroes seemed scarce. At Frederick Town I breakfasted with the lady of the house and her family as well as some strangers. They knew me and I everywhere met with some respect, nor did I find the common people boorish.

[24]Middletown, in Frederick County, lies a few miles west of the county seat.

CHAPTER XVI

THE STATE of Delaware may be crossed in going from Maryland to Philadelphia by the eastern road, which is the one most frequented. Dover is the capital but Wilmington is the most flourishing town. There was only one Representative from Delaware in 1805-6 tho' afterwards the new states in 1811-12 admitted of two.

Delaware

My friend Bayard was one of the Senators, tho' originally from Pennsylvania, to which, he told me, he could go back again with perfect indifference, being one of those philosophers who avoid being attached too much to anything. He even expressed surprize that a man should be more troubled at a daughter's elopement than at losing a sum of money.

When travelling with my own horses and before I had persuaded the stage coach proprietors to allow of my posting with their relays, I used to make three days of the journey from Philadelphia to Baltimore. On leaving the former town about noon I could get to Chester easily to dinner, and I generally chose that place for resting in because the tavern there was kept by a Member of Congress, Anderson, a Democrat and a great original, being the man that extinguished my fire at a ball given on the Queen's birthday. But I never could get him to dine with me at his own inn, tho' Dr. Park of Philadelphia[1] and the Swedish Consul M. Soderstrom[2] who were my travelling companions had got a promise from him that he would eat with us. I concluded therefore that he was either shy of presenting himself to me after his indecorous behaviour, or afraid his party might

[1]Probably Dr. Thomas Parke (1749-1835), a Quaker born in Chester County, who had studied at London and Edinburgh. He was a prominent physician. W. J. Bell, "Thomas Parke, M.D., Physician and Friend," *Wm. & Mary Quart.*, 3rd ser., VI (Oct. 1949), 569-95.

[2]Richard Soderstrom, recognized as Swedish consul-general in 1797, had served as consul much earlier. He resided in Philadelphia.

take offense and alarm lest he should be gained over to Federalism.

From Chester it was an evening's ride to Wilmington where I slept, and on the next day I could get as far as Havre de Grace on the great River Susquehannah, famous for canvass-back ducks, and mocassins, a delicious little round fish caught on the stream. Havre de Grace is on the Maryland side of the river where was a tolerable inn, the landlady of which was in the habit of making an excellent preserve of the fox grape which grows in great abundance on the hedges and on the banks of the river.

From Havre de Grace the distance to Baltimore is thirty-seven miles of very bad road. The aspect of the country is altogether different from that of Delaware or of Pennsylvania, and passing the Susquehannah which is accomplished at a ferry three-fourths of a mile broad, one crosses the great line of demarcation between the northern and southern states, into the country of democracy combined with slavery, of log houses with cleared lands; and, it must also be said, of country gentlemen without boors or at least not so many of the latter as are to be found in Pennsylvania. It took me from before eight in the morning to six o'clock in the evening to get from Havre de Grace to Gadsby's Inn at Baltimore, where one could dine at a good ordinary or if one chose it, in one's own room.[3] When I travelled post, however, I could easily go from Baltimore to Philadelphia in twenty-nine hours, which is certainly not very fast travelling considering that the distance is but 100 miles or 105, and that one had to send on the day before to engage the horses of the stage coach for the purpose. Nevertheless as the roads were very rough one lost all desire of going faster.

It is more agreeable, however, when one is not pressed for time, to go round about by Lancaster by the road which passes through Frederick Town, from whence there is no remarkable

[3]Gadsby's Inn in Baltimore, built in 1778 as the Indian Queen Tavern, was taken over by John Gadsby in 1808. It was located at the southeast corner of Hanover and Baltimore Sts.

view until you reach the Susquehannah, tho' two little towns called Petersburg and York, lie in the way conveniently enough for the purposes of refreshment, and the road is dignified with the name of turnpike. One may have the satisfaction too of knowing that one is here travelling over one of the richest tracts of country in the United States, for Mr. Ellicott who has had so much to do in surveying different parts of the country[4] declares that the limestone district, which includes Frederick Town and Lancaster, is by far the finest tract, for richness of soil, within the republic, and Lancaster County is, of that tract, said to be the best portion.

[4]Andrew Ellicott (1784-1820) made a map of the federal territory and laid out the federal city. He was employed by President John Adams, in conjunction with Spain, to set up the boundaries between the U.S. and Spanish territory.

CHAPTER XVII

THE GENTLEMAN from the southern states who is about crossing the Susquehannah or rather, I should say, the line of frontier, into Pennsylvania, must take care how he brings slaves with him, for if they be still found within the limits of the said state after six months from the period of his arrival, the owner is bound to manumit them, and once manumitted they will eventually be entitled to their freedom. He may, it is true, ensure the services of the manumitted slaves under bond for seven years, if they are twenty-one years old, or if under that age, for a longer period, as the years of boyhood do not count. But even in the case of his going back to his state, the slave who has been once manumitted thenceforth becomes only his bondsman. The Manumission Society, thro' whom the innovation was arranged, give one copy of the deed to the master and one to the man, and at the termination of another seven year's period, he will be entitled to become equally free in Carolina or Georgia as in Pennsylvania. The Abolition Society were self-constituted, but they had established the form of application being made to them for the objects which they undertook to accomplish thro' the proper authorities.

Pennsylvania

From the Susquehannah River to Lancaster is about ten miles. This city is the capital of the state and here I passed a summer with Mr. and Mrs. Merry.[1] We found it a pleasant residence and made many excursions in the neighbourhood.

One of the very first was to Turkey Hill so called from having formerly been famous for wild turkey shooting, tho' now, thanks to the boundless liberty of killing game at all seasons and the total lack of protection from game laws, these excellent birds are scarcely ever to be met with in this part of the country.

[1]Presumably the summer of 1806 was passed in Lancaster. Small notebook in HEH, dated at the beginning "Lancaster, Pennsylvania, August 29th 1806."

Turkey Hill is situated six miles to the left of Columbia and twelve from Lancaster. This road is in general very stony and it took me near two hours to reach the river. The country is pretty well settled and the houses are for the most part built of stone. Where the land is not inclosed you pass thro' noble forests without any underwood, composed of the oaks pinnatifida, oblusiloba, tinctoria, chestnut, and rubra of which the last is the finest and tallest of the oak tribe. American poplars too or tulip trees of great height and with stems that look like fluted pillars ornament these forests.

The Lancaster Country

The country to within two miles of the river is, without being undulating, striking, and appears prosperous. Where there is Indian corn it generally grows to the height of eight or nine feet, some stalks reaching even to ten, eleven, or twelve feet, while its yellow flowers falling gracefully from the top add very much to the richness of the scenery. At about two miles from the river one descries it in looking down through the trees, and suddenly you feel as if transported into a new climate, a strange and a luscious fruit all at once appearing to grow in the greatest abundance, the papaw trees spreading in profusion on every side. As they were just then quite ripe, none of us having ever seen one before, the surprize and the novelty of the discovery, besides that the fruit is really not bad, made us think it delicious and load the carriage with it.

This plant of which the botanical name is "annona tribolata" is more properly called a shrub than a tree as it does not exceed twenty feet in height. Its leaves are broad and like those of the umbrella magnolia, of the colour of a cucumber, the fruit too being like a young cucumber, in shape and size as well as colour. It is mealy and luscious to the taste and contains five or six seeds of a dark colour, shaped like beans. In the West Indies it is eaten with Madeira wine, probably to correct its too great sweetness. Seven or eight papaws grow on one stalk sometimes and they are very heavy. There are two sorts of this fruit hereabouts which seem to differ only as to the season of their maturity, the one becoming ripe early in September and the other a month later.

After passing through these papaw trees, to us so novel and pleasing a sight, we descended to the river side, where full in front we discovered an old lime tree that seemed as if it had grown there from the creation. It has three stems that instead of being round, stretch out like ledges of wood in three different directions and form a dark and solemn shade, under which the stream itself appears to repose with delight. The channel is shallow elsewhere and there are several islands covered with trees in it, while the opposite coast is high and shows some cultivation. At a short distance from this great tree is a flat rock called the Blue Rock where Penn held his talk with the Indian tribes, and there is a hollow in the middle of it which he is said to have filled with punch on that occasion and which has in consequence been denominated Penn's Punch Bowl.[2]

Turkey Hill is very steep and covered with fine woods but the view was imperfect from the difficulty of seeing over the trees. On the top of it lived a family of the name of Frey who furnished us with bread and eggs. Land hereabouts is worth as much as $200 the acre.

On another day I rode to McCall's Ferry which is eighteen miles from Lancaster.[3] It was the 5th of September when the leaves were beginning to change colour, and the whole way was beautifully diversified, the hills being pretty high, and fine vistas, of many miles in circuit, opening at frequent intervals. American views, however, have a great deal of sameness, owing to the thinness of the population. The cleared grounds form but specks in the vast forests which you descry from lofty situations, and there being no spires and no mountains of any great height within the horizon the pleasure one derives from the novelty of the scene is soon succeeded by rather a melancholy sensation. In Europe a forest is a rarity and on entering it the imagination is a little ruffled at the idea of becoming lost within it; but in fact,

[2]Penn visited the Indians at this rock twice, in 1682 and 1700.

[3]McCall's Ferry Station, but no ferry, still exists on the railroad. It is south of Lancaster on the Susquehanna.

although we do not at once own it to ourselves, we feel that there is a sufficient security in its want of extent against such an accident, and we are eager to pass through to see what is on the other side. In America, however, we shrink from such a task. The fancy takes in nothing but lifeless, measureless space, and as we feel conscious that we might in reality by going on become the prey of wolves. The approach of dusk would be fearful (I experienced this dread once and would never wish to experience it again) besides at best instead of being cheered by the hope of finding pretty villages, or castles, or snug cottages one can here only expect to light upon a log house with perhaps some surly insolent boors as its inmates.

Near McCall's Ferry the road lies under thick shade down hill to the river which has here an extremely narrow channel. Its bed being interspersed with rocks and high romantic hills on either side overhanging the torrent, the scenery is really very wild and beautiful. I spent four hours there, bathed under one of the rocks, and drank of the water which is soft and delicious and quite a luxury compared with the limestone water that one is obliged to drink elsewhere all over this part of the country. In the woods hereabouts were still to be found some wild turkeys and deer, and a boy I met with told me that he had seen a bear. Rattlesnakes are very rarely to be seen; and I went upon an island to look under the thickest bushes for them, but in vain. The channel of the river at McCall's Ferry is of immeasurable depth from being confined by rocks to such a narrow stream. Papaws grow on the hills as at the Turkey Hill, tho' being here confounded with other trees the country does not look so like the land of papaws here as it did there. The inhabitants hereabouts are for the most part Methodists.

The sect of Dunkers have an establishment at Ephrata[4] about thirteen miles distant from Lancaster from whence I rode to

[4]Ephrata, established under that name in 1738, lies 13 miles northeast of Lancaster. It was not, however, an ordinary German Baptist group like the Dunkers, but a Seventh-Day Baptist group, as Foster points out below. The term *Dunker* may have been used loosely in 1810 as it is sometimes today.

see them, returning home by Litiz[5] where there is a society of Moravians. The country in this direction was open and varied having here and there very rich views of extensive plains and uplands, the woods being without underwood and chiefly composed of the pinnatifida white oak or the chestnut oak which latter grows in stony places and bears enormous acorns as well as a beautiful foliage. The inhabitants all speak German. It took me 2½ hours to get to Grosse's [or Goose's?] Tavern where the Philadelphia and Harrisburgh roads meet crossing the Reading Road, at one-half a mile distance from Ephrata. There I breakfasted and tho' I wanted only some meat and wine the landlady made me take coffee insisting that nobody could be said to breakfast unless he took coffee. One might pass Ephrata without observing it unless told where to strike off, for it does not lie on the road. But you enter at a gate on your left, and proceed until you get to several meadows, inclosed and scattered about, in which are the wooden houses of those who live as they term it, under the order.

This order was instituted about 100 or 110 years ago by a Seventh Day Baptist[6] who bought the land that had been, as he gave out, reserved for holy purposes by the Lord who caused it to be left fallow, on account of its apparent unfruitfulness and the snakes which infested it, and to be passed over or neglected by both colonists and Indians. This land he built upon about the year 1732 and, having associated with himself several other Seventh Day Baptists, he formed a convent or community to the members of which he left the property by his will. The term Dunker is a nick-name given to the sect from their practice of dipping full-grown persons, when they join the order, into the river in order to baptize them (children they do not receive). "Tunken" being the German for "dip," thence comes the substantive "Tunkers," but they were in fact better known as the

[5]Lititz was laid out in 1757 by Moravian missionaries from Bethlehem.

[6]Conrad Beisel or Beissel (1690-1768), founder of the German Seventh-Day Baptist group at Ephrata, had until 1728 been a member of the German Baptist Brethren.

Siebentagers or Seventh Day Baptists, called so because they follow the Old Testament in observing the Sabbath on the Seventh Day (Saturday) as the Jews do.

Since the death of their founder, Beisel, who died in 1768, and of his successor Muller, who is said to have been a learned and venerable man, who gave a renown to the establishment of Ephrata, the society has dwindled away very much. There are two large wooden houses that form the principal buildings of the place, one of them being for the brotherhood, and the other, which is opposite, for the sisterhood. There is also a paper mill and a flour mill. When a sister or a brother marries, as they may do, they are obliged by rules of the order to leave the cloister, and may build for themselves a house in the meadows. No stranger, however, would be admitted unless he became a Baptist. The children of Dunkers may during their lives remain on in the houses of their parents [but then they are prohibited from marrying under penalty if they do, of being sent away].* In the cloisters are small rooms for the brothers, where, I was told, they used to lie on boards with wooden pillows. Their food was said to consist of roots and they were allowed no luxuries or amusements. At the time of my visit to Ephrata there existed but two brothers, only one of whom inhabited the great house, and he, as I learned from an old sister, was a scandalous fellow. He wore a beard which the other did not. The latter however, had been converted but eleven years previously and resided in a house in the meadow, where he followed the occupation of clockmaker. There were still eight sisters remaining of whom five lived in the cloisters and three without them. The oldest of the five was eighty years old and the youngest sixty-five.

It is a singularly striking and beautiful spot. From each house you step out into rich meadows studded with fruit trees and other plants scattered among them and I was so pleased with the place that I remained there for several hours. The clockmaker had with him a German book which gives the history of the order and its rules. He was a very odd looking singular man,

*Bracketed material marked for deletion in LC version.

sometimes speaking in a high and sometimes in a low tone, making a thousand awkward gestures. Another odd fellow, quite an original, took me about. He professed not to be under the order, but he looked like a being not of this world. I advised him to join the brotherhood. "No," he replied, "I could not in that case live as idly as I do." He lived with his mother, a sister of the order, and will be allowed to remain on in the house as long as he exists in a single state. The land will eventually become a subject of contention if no new brothers join them and when the present incumbents, male or female, shall die off.

The order of Dunkers formerly was strict and the brothers as well as sisters met every night in their separate dwellings to pray at twelve o'clock. But now there seems to be but little attention paid to the regulations, all doing as they like. And such, no doubt, is the fate of many new sects which expire for want of a continuance of busy enthusiasm in their teachers when the charms of novelty have worn away and the world at large has ceased to wonder at the singularity of their tenets. I am surprized it is not the case with more of them for I own I never could understand upon what grounds other than those of a love of singularity, or controversy, of vanity, ambition, or cupidity these sects should any of them separate, so completely as they do, from the established church. It surely matters but little whether Saturday or Sunday originally was fixed on for the Sabbath Day though it does matter that as it has been fixed so for centuries the same Sabbath should be the Sabbath of all. Nor does it much signify whether the parson wears a round or a cocked hat, this or that dress, provided it be decent and respectable, a bow be made or not at the name of Jesus, what order the prayers are read in and so forth, though it does signify that innovations should not be lightly made and that an uniform general church should exist in the land, where all may meet who use the same language in Christian charity, praying and performing their duty to God in common and at stated intervals instead of squabbling for one's own version of some unimportant rule.

We may differ as to certain interpretations of the Bible, we may be displeased at the length of the service of the Church of England, particularly in cathedrals where the nasal chaunting of every prayer by both parson and clerk renders it almost too tedious, and we may object to its repetitions and to the Creed of St. Athanasius, but there is nothing in such objections to justify the staying away from the Church altogether, thereby exhibiting the appearance of dissension and division among Christians and Protestants. There is nothing surely in the national church to prevent our belonging to it, and holding such opinions besides as we please on points which do not interfere with the offering up of our prayers to God and to Christ, as well as listening to His Word or having it expounded by persons especially educated for the purpose. Since the time too when we got rid of what was monstrous and senseless relative to the doctrine of our eating the real body of the Lord* as well as the various delusions imposed on the weak minded, including the arrogant assumption that priests may positively damn all who differ from them even upon trifling and immaterial points.

Since we have recovered too the use of our reason as well as our native tongue in praying to, and celebrating the goodness of, the Creator I really do not see that there were sufficient arguments for any further schism. I cannot but think that we are entitled to look with suspicion upon the alleged motives of those who, not satisfied with indulging in opinions of their own—as we may perhaps all of us do, upon secondary matters—have attempted, and even succeeded in the attempt, to draw crowds after them of weak people who probably without being so stimulated, would never have separated from the establishment. I do not doubt that many separatists may begin by imposing upon themselves, but I fear they practice but little of the first Christian virtue, humility, when they fancy they are called upon to settle abstruse points, preach in woods and fields, holding meetings independent of the Anglican Church, unless indeed where they

*At this point Foster inserts a long note in which he replies "logically" and as "a conscientious Protestant" to the Roman Catholic doctrine of Transubstantiation.

may be excusable for doing so from an absolute want of room in the national temples. Vanity, however, is a subtle passion and very often the individual who acts under its influence, is unconscious of its presence within his breast, while believing himself eloquent in the Lord or called on from on high. I have been led into these reflections by my visit to Ephrata, and by seeing there upon what very trifling points a man will set about forming a sect apart, and taking measures for procuring and continuing proselytes to his own opinions. The neighbourhood, nevertheless, do not seem to have been much attracted even by Mr. Beisel's present of lands and the whole establishment is likely soon to be laid hold of by the state for want of a continuation of converts to the order.

The Moravians, whom I visited at Litiz, might come in for a share in the preceding remarks but that they are rather to be considered as Protestant communities living together under regular forms for purposes rather of industry than of religion, and in that point of view their utility is obvious in so wild a country. Nor do I believe there is any objection on their part to support and frequent the orthodox church where there is one established by law.

I cannot say the same of the camping Methodists, one of whose meetings I attended in a wood when there were twelve preachers present and about 4,000 persons. There was a regular line of tents pitched for the occasion with a capacious pulpit in front. The preaching lasted several days. I saw some individuals drop down as if in a fit during the process, and carried off, as they fell, among the trees, where they were laid on the ground, and beat themselves in a frantic frightful manner against the earth, or against stumps and stones, while persons, employed for the purpose, would go among them, carrying comfort, as they said, and telling them to be of good cheer, that they were in the right path, that it was the Devil who was forced to quit their bodies, and that this was the cause of their struggle and agitation, till at last from mere fatigue and exhaustion the wretched convert would cease to kick about and begin to doze. I went to and fro several times to see all this, but I had endeavoured in vain, tho' I sat among them during the preaching, to catch any course of argument or succession of ideas in the sermon. It seemed to be all exclamations, and "The Lord," "Christ Jesus," "the Devil," or "Hell's torments," were almost the only words which reached my ears, the imagination of each individual affected by the preaching having apparently supplied every deficiency. At night I saw much merriment going on and I was told that great disorder takes place under the tents. Indeed I believe this is what in reality brings a great part of the congregation together, and the tongue of scandal would have it that many citizens are added to the state in consequence of these meetings, while the preachers and their attendants are not left empty-handed.

The distance from Ephrata to Litiz is seven miles. This place consists of but one street of stone houses with two or three large buildings for the brothers and sisters and for a school.[7] The Moravians have a bishop, but in their church is no altar, and the pulpit is on a level with the floor. At the school there were seventy-five children who are allowed to continue in it to the age of sixteen, but the education was trivial, consisting of little more than learning to read and write with arithmetic, and needlework for the girls. For this they pay, with extra expences of washing etc., about $180 or $190, or between £30 and £40 per annum.

It is twenty-five miles to Lebanon from Lancaster over a wretched stony road. I was fortunate enough to find a farmer living one-half way between the two towns, who invited me in to dinner, it being twelve o'clock as I was passing his door. I was doubly glad of the invitation as it began to rain and I did not know quite where to go for shelter. We had boiled beef, stewed apples and sour cabbage, which I was no stranger to, having resided for twelve months at Saxe Weimar. I afterwards crossed over the Conewago hills, a very craggy deserted district, in which I rode for eight miles without seeing a single living thing, hearing the sound of a voice or even the chirping of a bird. And from

[7]Linden Hall Seminary, still surviving at Lititz, is now a school for girls, one of the oldest in America.

the highest point I could see over at least sixty or seventy miles of forest. My ears were as if weary of the dead silence that seemed to have taken possession of everything round me, and I quite shrunk and felt chill at the idea of being in such a solitude, till on descending towards Lebanon I passed a neat looking house built of red stone belonging to a Mr. Grubbs.

Lebanon is a small town without trade. It possesses two churches, one Lutheran and the other Presbyterian, and is inhabited chiefly by Germans. This town is an old one for America, and the people appeared very civil and innocent, their manners forming a contrast with those of the lower classes about Lancaster, and being a consequence probably, of their out-of-the-way situation, as it is generally observable that good manners are natural to man even in a rude state, but become bad by incomplete education or contact with the vicious and affected. I found a good inn at Lebanon and an attentive landlord.

It is now time to say something of Lancaster which is the capital of the state of Pennsylvania, and rather a pleasant town, chiefly inhabited by German families. It is situated sixty-two miles to the westward of Philadelphia, the road which is a turnpike, lying through a varied country alternately cultivated and woodland. The trees are lofty and clear of underwood. You do not see black oak or the broad-leaved red oak so common in Maryland among these trees, but on the other hand you are introduced in the stony hills to the liquidambar or gum tree, a very beautiful ornament of the American forests, some of its leaves becoming of a crimson colour early in the summer, while the rest remain of a very polished and delicate green, forming contrast with the bark of the tree which is rough and greyish white. The sassafras laurus is also a most delicate looking plant when young, covered as it frequently is with the fox grape vine, which gives it a luxuriant appearance. I heard too of a new kind of oak in these parts, the quercus filamentosa called so because the peduncule projects beyond the acorn and is very long. There are also four varieties of the hickory-nut tree to be met with, the juglans alba, glabra, ovalis and cordiformis; four of the maple, the saccharinum, rubrum, negundo and striatum; and two kinds of walnut trees, the nigra and the cinerea, the latter producing long oval nuts which have a better flavour than those of the other.

To the north of the Susquehannah scarcely any mocking-birds are to be seen. I remember meeting with but one and that was near Wilmington. When I went from Philadelphia to Lancaster I halted at three different taverns on the road which were none of them very inviting,[8] though I amused myself very well while my horses were resting in shooting larks which are as large as quails. It was with some difficulty that I got a bedroom to myself at the third tavern where I had again some excellent sport in shooting larks of which there were great numbers, as it was towards the end of August when they are very fat and excellent food.

Land is very good in this neighbourhood and sells in some places for £50 the acre, though an estate of 130 acres belonging to a General Hand[9] was put up for sale while I was at Lancaster with house and stables for £35 Pennsylvania currency per acre. Three-quarters of a dollar per day was the pay of an Irish labourer, besides their food, or a dollar each without it.

The town had a great deal of trade and contained when I was living there 10,000 inhabitants of five or six different religious communities who seemed to live together in perfect harmony having their different churches, and a college common to Lutherans, Calvinists and Episcopalians.

The Pennsylvanian legislature meets here every year on the first Monday in December in a plain house suited to the inmates who consist of twenty-five Senators and eighty-six Representatives, elected annually. No qualification is necessary but that of citizenship. The members of the Senate are elected for four years,

[8]In the HEH version Foster names these as the Buck (10 miles), the Ship (17 miles), and "at Downing" (5 miles). Then he drove 18 miles farther to Slaymaker's the next morning, and then 2 miles more to Hinkle's Tavern (just 10 miles from Lancaster), and then to Hough's Inn at Lancaster. "Downing" is the modern Downingtown on U.S. Route 30.

[9]Rockford, the former home of General Edward Hand, is a 2½-story red brick building, with a stone foundation and a slate roof.

likewise without having any other qualification. They both receive three dollars a day during attendance, and twenty cents per mile for travelling expences, and I have been told that they in general consider their seats as sufficiently lucrative. Nay, I have even been assured that many of them after a season will carry home $300 cash clear profit. They usually remain in session during five months, breaking up on the 31st March, and the whole receipt being, at the rate of $21 per week, about $400. Those who ought to have known the fact, assured me that some of the Members by engaging for their board and lodging for only two dollars per week, were enabled to save even more than $300. Such persons, however, were content to have fire and candles but at their meals, and one Member in particular, a Mr. Hume,[10] during the session previous to my visit to Lancaster, had, I was told, walked with his wallet on his back, a very considerable distance to the House of Assembly in order to save his twenty cents per mile, while the most expensive were in the habit of paying for their living but six or seven dollars per week.

The governor of the state of Pennsylvania had more power, perhaps, than any other governor in the United States, or even than the President himself, relatively to their respective situations. He had £2,000 a year, Pennsylvania currency, making about £1,232 sterling per annum, and the secretary of the commonwealth had £800 per annum or near £500 sterling. The richest offices in the state were however at Philadelphia and to those the governor had the right of nomination, that of sheriff of Philadelphia having been worth about $15,000 per annum and that of collector $20,000, though probably they will have been cut down since I was in the United States.

The state revenue arose from duties on licenses for taverns, marriages and auctions amounting to $40,000 annually, from interest amounting to $100,000 on stock that the state possessed, and from fees or writs of which the prothonotary paid to the state seventy-five per cent, making a total of $142,000 a year or

[10] John Hulme represented Bucks County in the Pennsylvania House of Representatives in 1807.

between £35,000 and £36,000 which was more than sufficient to cover the expences of the government. They had besides the purchase money due for the land that was sold by the state since the establishment of the independence of America, amounting to $5,000,000 of which the interest alone would surpass the revenue as above stated, but this money was unpaid and difficult, if not impossible, to recover. Nor indeed do they deserve to recover it, as it is money that was to come principally out of the sale of the Penn property which the state took possession of and sold for $8,000,000, giving the family but a part of it amounting to $500,000, a fact which I had from Mr. Gallatin who filled the situation of Minister of Finance. It is true that the family manors, of which Little York is one, were left to them as well as some quit-rents in the state of Delaware which are considered as irrecoverable, but they were forced by necessity to agree to the compromise, after long disputing it, while the state government made use of the transaction for the purpose of gaining partisans by not calling in payment.

To be entitled to vote for a member of the state legislature a man must have resided for two years within the state, and have paid taxes to the amount of twenty-five cents (about 1s. 5d.) for six months previously to the period at which the election takes place, having certificates to prove it if called for.

Pennsylvania had eighteen and afterwards twenty-two Representatives in Congress, while I was at Washington, none of them being much distinguished for talents, though, generally, great Democrats and ill-mannered, as well from the effects of their education as from affectation, and perhaps that wanton enjoyment of freedom which German bondsmen may be supposed to indulge in when they look back to the times in which they were under the yoke of some petty baron or count of the Empire. This feeling in the lower classes often breaking out into downright brutality when I have known them, particularly waggoners coming to Philadelphia, try to overturn a lady's carriage, crossing and recrossing before it merely, as it were, to spite the gentlefolk. And I may here relate an anecdote that I heard of an Englishman [who] was travelling in the back country districts, was driving a gig, and had left his groom at a considerable distance behind him riding at a quiet pace in order to bring the other horse in cool. On coming to a log house to get some water he found several waggoners in possession of the place, who were very noisy and would not make way for him, but, on his remonstrating, winked to each other and agreed to have some fun out of the gentleman. They formed a ring, made him get down and told him to dance. It was useless to argue with them. They began smacking at him with their whips and he had to caper and jump about from one to the other till at last to his great joy he espied his groom coming up, when rushing forward he knocked down one of the fellows in his way, and hastening to the saddle horse took out two loaded pistols which were in the holsters. "Now, you rascals," he hollowed out, "it's my turn!" and cocking his pistols he ordered them all to lay down their whips, giving one to the groom which the latter was ordered to lay about him as hard as he could. When they had all got a good thrashing he ordered them off with their waggons, and took his repose after having been complimented by the landlord who had secretly rejoiced at the lesson his brutal customers had received.

On another occasion a famous boxer got the better of one of these blackguards, to the satisfaction even of his companions to whom the bully had made himself formidable. He chose to challenge the gentleman to fisti-cuffs, thinking him too delicate to stand the trial, but he had caught a tartar. The traveller happened to have been a disciple of Jackson and gave a good licking to his antagonist. Such adventures it is to be hoped are now becoming rarer—in the long settled parts, at least—or it would be unadvisable to travel about otherwise than in stage coaches.

Mr. Gregg was one of the Representatives of Pennsylvania when I was at Washington, a MisRepresentative, as a friend of mine in the Ministry [Mr. Gallatin]* used to call him.[11] He had

*Material in brackets appears in the LC version but is marked out.

[11]Andrew Gregg (1755-1835), was Member of Congress 1791-1807.

been a schoolmaster but that business not suiting him, he took to Congress as more profitable. With him sat Anderson of Chester, two German doctors, Leib and Seibert, who had studied physic at Freyburg, many Irish Democrats and Mr. Clay (not the candidate for the Presidency) who was said to draw bills on the bank payable to "Jesus Christ or Bearer."[12] But on the other side there were Mr. Morgan,[13] Mr. Milnor[14] of Philadelphia and others, descendants of British settlers, who for the most part, as I had occasion to observe, were much superior in manners to those of German blood, and for a very natural reason when the state of the mother countries is taken into consideration. Such as it was at the time I speak of.

Candidates for seats in the legislature, either of the state or of the Union, did not go about to canvass for themselves in Pennsylvania. Their friends took that trouble for them. A meeting of the citizens of any town or district would be invited by either Federalists or Democrats, equally calling themselves Friends of the People and the Constitution. The invitation is circulated by means of an advertisement in the newspapers and at the meeting conferees are named who agree upon the candidates to be supported. The two parties have their separate conferees and upon whom in fact repose all their hopes of success and whose business it is to persuade as many persons as they can to vote for their nominee, which is best done by recommendatory writings in the papers, especially by going about to talk and gain over the citizens. Tickets are handed round having the names of the different candidates for different public offices written upon them. There is one for that of

[12]All of these except Dr. Adam Seybert (1773-1825) are referred to elsewhere. Both Leib and Seybert received their medical degrees at the University of Pennsylvania. Seybert studied later at Edinburgh, Göttingen, and Paris.

[13]The only Morgan who was a Member of Congress in this period from this region was James Morgan (1756-1822) of New Jersey, a prominent Federalist who was in Congress 1811-1813. In 1794-1799 Morgan had been a member of the Pennsylvania legislature.

[14]William Milner or Milnor (1769-1848) was Member of Congress 1807-1811, 1815-1817, 1821-1822, a Federalist; James Milnor (1773-1844) was Member of Congress 1811-1813, also a Federalist. Both were Philadelphians.

sheriff, one for a Member of the House of Representatives, one for a Senator of the state legislature, as also for a Representative in Congress and for a Senator in Congress.

Each individual, who possesses a vote, has these tickets put into his hands by a conferee, ties them all up in a little bundle and puts it into the box of the receiver who is ready to receive the votes at the court-house of the district, and it may possibly be only known to the elector himself for whom he has given his voice. For as all persons of every party throw their bundles into the same box, and as their names are not subscribed to their votes, it becomes impossible to distinguish to which side they support tho' it is evident that in reality the conferees must be able to make a pretty good guess upon the subject. There are present at the elections, clerks, inspectors and a judge all chosen by the county. Where a man presents himself for the purpose of giving his vote, his name is required and given, on which the inspector looks into the tax-book to see if it be there, when his vote is received, unless there be good reason for suspecting some foul play, in which case he is liable to be called on to produce his certificate of citizenship.

[*Note*: The inspectors are sometimes so lax in regard to questioning the voters that a Senator of the United States told me he had once seen fifty sailors brought up to vote for a candidate, who but a few hours previously had been taken to the house of a tax gatherer in the interest of the Democratic party where they each paid a fifteen penny piece into his hands to enable them to swear that they had paid the taxes. And this puts me in mind of an old woman at Norfolk in Virginia who kept a cradle made for the purpose of rocking full grown British subjects who were to be converted in a hurry into American citizens, that when testimony should be called for to prove their birth as citizens of the United States she might with a safe conscience be enabled to swear she had known them from their cradles.

That it ever became really worth while to use bribery at the elections of Pennsylvania I have no doubt notwithstanding all the above precautions, that the system of the ballot will be no defense against it, any more than it would be in this country, but only render corruption infinitely more easy by rendering it security as well as concentrating it in the hands of a few attorneys or conferees whose reward would be made dependent on their success very much.]

The 14th October is the day of election throughout the whole state, and votes are received from early in the morning until ten at night, soon after which the result might be known. According as the conferees are Federalist or Democratic the electors vote, and they support the persons named by them or are expected to do so, and they seldom inquire after any other quality in the candidate. The well-born, (an expression introduced or applied to the rich Philadelphian families by the Germans) appeared to have but little chance. Mr. Schneider, a tanner, was then governor of the state[15] and there was even a question of removing the seat of government from Lancaster to Harrisburgh, quite a new place, above forty miles further west, its chief recommendation being that the legislature would there be less exposed to the influence of the rich and well educated, than it is in a city so little removed from the great world as even Lancaster is,[16] so jealous are these land-owners of all kinds of aristocracy, which will never be able to raise its head until the inland towns become more populous than they are.

The persons we were best acquainted with at Lancaster were Mr. Barton, the Prothonotary,[17] and Mr. Matlack, Master of the Rolls, who were extremely civil and obliging. The Prothonotary had an income of about £360 a year for his office, besides some little property of his own. The Master of the Rolls seemed also to be in easy circumstances. The latter was at the time I made his acquaintance, eighty-three years old, and took great delight in gardening.[18] He had carried the cultivation of peach

[15]Simon Snyder (1759-1819) was first elected governor in 1808.

[16]Though apparently Foster did not know it, the capital had been moved to Harrisburg in 1812.

[17]William Barton was Prothonotary of Lancaster County, 1800-1809.

[18]Foster's saying that Matlack was 83 (in 1806), would make his birth date 1733 or 1734, though usually estimated as 1736 or 1738. 1806-1807 "Notes" in H.E.H.

trees to great perfection, having twenty-eight different sorts in his orchard, some of which were quite pictures. Among them was the lemon peach, called so from its colour and shape, as also a little peach, from Carolina originally, of exquisite flavour, green and smaller than a plum. Mr. Matlack was in the habit of using the horns and hoofs of cattle as manure, preferring the horns entire, or when he could not obtain them in that state, using comb makers' shavings. The horns, he said, when laid under the earth at the depth of 2½ feet from the surface become receptacles for air, and give health to the roots, making the plant thrive more vigorously. The frost, he observed, which in England penetrates to but 2 or 2½ feet deep in the earth, will in Pennsylvania pierce thro' a depth of 4 or 4½ feet, which occasions the death of numbers of plants and is particularly unfavourable to the vine, the cold taking so much time in leaving the soil when once it has taken hold of it.

The climate of the United States will in fact long be an obstacle to the acquisition of accurate notions as to the true method of treating exotic plants, of which many that are introduced into it flourish but for one year and degenerate or die in the second season. The winters are at times very severe and sometimes very sultry, no other climate perhaps, unless it be that of the north of Italy, having the same heat as this during summer, with such excess of cold as is often experienced during winter, subject also to such sudden variability in both the different seasons.

Mr. Barton took me to see some paintings at Lancaster which had been executed by West before he left America for Great Britain. They were done by him when at the age of eighteen, and were in possession of a Mr. Henry, a gunsmith of this town.[19] West was born in Chester County not far from Phila-

[19]Foster refers of course to the painter Benjamin West (1738-1820), president of the Royal Academy in Foster's time and one of its founders. Colonel William Henry (d. April 18, 1809) invited the boy West to his home and named his 13th child Benjamin West. George Steinman, "Benjamin West Henry, a Lancaster Artist," *Hist. Papers & Addresses Lancaster County Hist. Soc.*, XVI (1912), 270-72.

delphia. His father was a cooper of Lancaster and very often sent his son to drive his waggons, full of empty barrels, from one place to another when the youth would as often leave waggon and horses standing in the road, while he would be occupying himself with taking a sketch from under some tree, or, which was his favourite study, designing the figure of a country blacksmith, and endeavouring to perfect himself in the outline of the human form by drawing the man's sinewy arms and naked chest over and over again. His father would be angry on such occasions at finding that his business was not attended to by young West and his waggons brought home late, but was at length persuaded by some gentlemen of the place, who raised a small subscription for the purpose, to let the young man follow the bent of his genius and send him to study at Philadelphia where he soon procured friends and protectors and was enabled to embark for Europe.

He painted a portrait of himself and gave it, on his leaving America as a memento to Mr. Henry, observing that he felt as if he should one day become a distinguished artist, and requested the picture might be carefully preserved. It had, however, become totally ruined by the damp, the colouring being completely peeled off.[20] The other pictures which he still possessed of this master were a landscape that appeared to be a copy from some Italian painting and represented a confused tumble of an Italian town and mountain with Dutch or German figures, Chinese rocks and English ships;[21] an historical picture of the death of Socrates in which Socrates looks like a Dunker, and is sitting down drinking poison while his friends stand round him with very, very rueful faces;[22] a portrait of Mr. Henry's

[20]No record of this picture has been discovered.

[21]This is the "Landscape Composition" now owned by the Pennsylvania Hospital. For a reproduction, see William Sawitzky, "The American Work of Benjamin West," *Pennsylvania Mag. Hist. & Biog.*, LXII (Oct. 1938), 445.

[22]Colonel William Henry is said to have suggested the "Death of Socrates" as a subject to the boy. Samuel Isham, *The History of American Painting* (New York, 1942), p. 46. Sawitzky ("American Work of West," p. 461) lists this under "Unlocated Paintings."

father and of his mother and another lady.[23] The colouring and drawing in all is very bad and hard, tho' the two cows which are in the landscape have something natural about them that is pleasing.

I was told by this gentleman that the sign posts of the Hat and the Sorrel Horse near Philadelphia were painted by West. His name is annexed to all that I saw and the year 1756 faintly traced along side of it. Mr. Barton told me that when he went to England, which he did not many years ago, before West's death, he was questioned by him with regard to the above sign posts and asked if they were still in existence. At Mr. Parr's in Lancaster there is a picture of a gentleman done by him after he had been in England.[24]

I was sorry not to be able to see the houses of legislature in session while I was at Lancaster, though I fancy the loss was not great as respects the eloquence of state Members, or the nature of their discussions which would of course chiefly relate to parish business. One day the question in debate was about the means of putting a stop to the depredations committed by animals and especially by hogs in breaking down people's fences. A committee was formed to consider of it and a German Member, who was greatly dissatisfied at not having been nominated as one of this committee, complained of it to the Speaker as a hard case. "For," said he, "I have been porn mid pigs, pred mid pigs, and all my life long lived mid pigs and I ought sure to know their ways petter than any other person." This same fellow, however, was, as I learnt, not more respected in his own house where his wife used to box his ears, and when he roared out that

[23]The portraits of Colonel and Mrs. William Henry are now in the Historical Society of Pennsylvania. Steinman, "Benjamin West Henry," pp. 270-72; Sawitzky, "American Work of West," p. 448 (who dates the two ca. 1755). Incidentally, Foster's reference below to the exact date of these pictures is probably the first documentary evidence which may aid in dating them. "Another lady" may be any of several paintings, though probably it is "Catherine Ross," ca. 1755, painted at Lancaster.

[24]A William Parr (d. 1786) was prominent in Lancaster. This was probably his son. *Lancaster County Hist. Papers*, X, 204; XI, 406, 419. The picture has not been identified.

flesh and blood could not bear it, she gave it to him again squeaking out, "Eh then, skin and bone must," for he was thin as a lath and she was much the stronger of the two.

Opossums are to be found about here and I let myself be persuaded for once to go out opossum hunting, but fully determined, on my return, never to do it again. It is dreadful work among rocks and trees and by moonlight and one is not sure of distinguishing the animal from the branch he sits on, or whether one has, or not, hit him after having fired. If the "pole cat," or skunk, too, comes across you the smell is almost intolerable.

The Yellow Fever

Lancaster has been preferred for a summer residency by Mr. Merry because of his dread of the yellow fever coming to Philadelphia again, as it had done the year previous, when he was under the necessity of hiring an hotel outside the town, where we passed the sultry season. This hotel was exactly in front of one of the burial grounds for those who died of the disorder, and when we looked out of the window we never failed seeing the cart, drawn by a single white horse, which conveyed the dead, passing to and fro at a short distance from the house.[25] I cannot say that I ever felt any fear of catching infection either from yellow fever, cholera morbus, or the plague, and I attribute this to my having suddenly been informed of the plague being at the Dardanelles, the first place where I landed when on a voyage to Turkey and Asia with Baron Foster.[26] Lord Aberdeen[27] was to have joined us there and we

[25]There was no yellow fever epidemic in Lancaster, but there was a cholera epidemic in Columbia borough, along the Susquehanna River, about that time. Many who died were buried in Mt. Bethel cemetery.

[26]John Leslie Foster (d. 1842) was Baron of the Court of Exchequer in Ireland, and afterwards of the Court of Common Pleas. Foster saw much of him in Paris in 1802 and took this journey to the Near East with him in 1803. Foster, *Two Duchesses*, passim.

[27]Lord Aberdeen (George Hamilton Gordon, 1784-1860), Foster's correspondent and friend over many years, became a well-known diplomat and statesman. He spent some time in Greece and founded the Athenian Society on his return.

were to go together to Troad, but a letter came from him to express his regret he could not come, and to inform us that, should we have gone into the town, we were not even to be received by the Ambassador, nor on board the frigate he had sailed in. We were, however, then actually in Dardanelles, and had gone through all the dirtiest streets of the town in search of our consul, who was a Jew. When I read this letter I felt as if I had received a shot, and the paper dropped from my hands. But the hopelessness of the case revived us. The danger, whatever it was, had actually been incurred. We were in the very atmosphere or element of plague, and it was as well to pursue our way as if no plague existed. So we did and afterwards got to be so hardened as to go and live at an inn at Constantinople itself, taking every precaution to avoid touching the Turks, which was rather difficult to do, as they considered it, in those days, a good joke to brush past a Christian and alarm his nerves. But we had at least the satisfaction of seeing what we had gone to see, while our friends were shut up by Sir W. Drummond,[28] perfumed and fumigated every day, till, at last, they also broke loose and came to join us in order not to have to go home "re-infectû" without having seen anything.

Having despised the plague I was not in the humour to dread yellow fever which I deemed a less dangerous disorder. And I rode backwards and forwards nearly every day visiting my friends and inquiring the news.

The first time this fever was known and got its name at Philadelphia was in 1763,[29] after which it did not again make its appearance until the year 1793 when it was supposed to have been introduced by a box of clothes that had belonged to a man who died on board ship in coming from the West Indies, yet none of the crew had it when the vessel arrived in the Delaware. In that year 5,000 persons were calculated to have died

[28]Sir William Drummond (1770-1802), scholar and diplomat, was ambassador at the Ottoman Porte 1803-1806. Foster mentions him unfavorably below.

[29]Yellow fever actually appeared in Philadelphia as early as 1699. W. P. Hazard, *Annals of Philadelphia in the Olden Time . . .*, (Philadelphia, 1879), III, 65.

of it at Philadelphia. All the rich citizens fled to country houses, many of the poor formed encampments and the streets were so deserted that grass grew in them, and the noise made by the steps of some solitary individuals, echoed to great distances, was all the sound to be heard for two or three months in the greater part of the town, except when corpses were carried along in carts to be buried. In the year 1798 the yellow fever revisited Philadelphia but not so destructively. In the year 1805, however, it was pronounced to be of fully as malignant a nature as that of 1793, few having survived its attacks, and the militia was called out at the instigation of the Board of Health, in order to encompass with a cordon the infected part of the south liberties, and that end of the city, but the colonel refused to be put on such a service, on which the Board of Health insisted that he ought to be arrested. He on the other hand insisted that they had no right to have him arrested for not undertaking a service of such a nature. Nevertheless they gave the order to the constables to do their duty, when the gallant colonel scampered off in face of his men.

There was an interesting case that occurred where a very different feeling was displayed. A Miss Hozey was to be married in a short time to Mr. Bicknall, when the latter caught the fever. She insisted on going to nurse him, caught the fever and died in three days, nor did he survive her. This case was famous for having given rise to a violent dispute at the Board of Health where the non-importation or domestic-origin doctors came to blows with the advocates for contagion, Dr. Reynolds[30] an Irish physician maintaining that the disorder was contagious and that Mr. Bicknall should in consequence be removed to the hospital, while one of the others as stoutly preached the opposite doctrine and they actually fought about it. But, though Reynolds came off triumphant as a pugilist, he lost his situation at the Board on account of his indecent violence.

The first victim to the disorder was supposed to be one of

[30]James Reynolds, M.D., 33 Sansom St. Robinson's *Philadelphia Directory for 1807*.

three men who, three weeks before it made its appearance, had been unluckily employed in unloading wood at the lazaretto. He had the black vomit and died in four hours after he had been sent to the hospital. This was on the 5th September and soon afterwards the existence of the fever was publicly admitted, when there were already above forty cases in the liberties, ten in the city and twenty in the hospital. The symptoms of the malady are, a pain in the head, a languid heavy feeling, pain in the back and, above all, a pain in the chest. A Mrs. Reed had all these symptoms except the last and therefore it was decided that hers was a case of bilious fever. One could go nowhere without hearing warm disputes as to whether the disorder was or was not imported, and I was present when a gentleman was called upon by a particular friend with whom he broke off all intercourse because the latter on being asked, "What news of the Fever?" replied that he had had a servant who was just dead of it. "How," said the others, "and could you come here and run the risk of giving us the infection?" "Oh! my dear sir," answered the friend, "remember it is not contagious." "Contagious, sir," resumed the gentleman, "I say it is contagious and you have behaved like a scoundrel or a fool in coming here." He got up and flew out of the room in a tremendous passion. Such scenes were often occurring and mixed up a little ridicule with those of a tragical nature which were daily taking place.

It was a remarkable fact that scarcely any case of the disorder occurred among those who lived in the country unless it was where the person infected had left the town with the disease already in his blood. And I really believe that tho' it may be introduced, in the first instance, by a ship, yet that this fever requires a particular atmosphere for its development.

I went to Bethlehem during the continuance of this pestilence for the sake of a change of scene. Bethlehem is the seat of the first Moravian establishment founded in the United States. Individuals of the order flocked here from different quarters about the year 1742 to protect each other from the savages. Towards the close of the century they were possessed of 4,000 acres of land and built the college that exists there for boys as well [as] the schoolhouse for girls, where both are taken care of till they reach the age of sixteen.[31] The whole number belonging to the establishment in 1805 amounted to 500, of which 140 were sisters and eighty-eight girls at school. The cost of education for each amounts to about $150 or $180, and they were taught music as well as knitting and ciphering besides the rudiments of language.

It is a very pretty country about Bethlehem, and watered by the River Lehigh, but the road to it is dreadfully stony.

Owing to the interruption of nearly all intercourse occasioned by the yellow fever I saw but little of the society of Philadelphia on my first visit to that city. I returned there, however, in the following year with Mr. Erskine who succeeded Mr. Merry,[32] and I afterward passed an entire summer in the neighbourhood in 1811, having hired Solitude with a pretty tho' small garden, beautifully situated on the banks of the Schuylkill,[33] where I was visited by all the chief people of the town who introduced me to their families, and rendered my cook's place nearly a sinecure. I never met with greater hospitality anywhere, and as there exists a great deal less of that nervous susceptibility as to the opinion foreigners,

Philadelphia

[31]The Moravian College and Seminary now existing at Bethlehem was established in 1807 at Nazareth and did not move to Bethlehem until 1858. The Moravian Seminary and College for Women, the oldest boarding school for girls in America, was founded in 1742 and still survives. It now confers degrees. What Foster calls the colleges for men and women were the Brethren's House and the Sisters' House, suggests Dr. Raymond S. Haupert, President of the Moravian College and Seminary, Bethlehem (letter to the editor of June 21, 1951).

[32]Merry received about June 1, 1806, the announcement that he would be succeeded by David Montague Erskine (1776-1855). Erskine appeared on November 4, 1806.

[33]Solitude, now the grounds of the Zoological Garden at Philadelphia, was built in 1783 by John Penn of Stoke, who bought 15 acres on the west bank of the Schuylkill for the purpose. The builder, a great spender, died in debt in 1824. Evidently Foster leased from him. Arthur Pound, *The Penns of Pennsylvania and England* (New York, 1932), p. 306, and J. Thomas Scharf and Thompson Westcott, *History of Philadelphia, 1609-1884* (Philadelphia, 1884), I, 705n.

or rather, Englishmen, entertain of America, at Philadelphia than is to be found further south or even at New York, the dinner parties were more without restraint and very agreeable, though I was told that on one occasion when I was there as a young man, I was very near having a duel on my hands because in the warmth of conversation after dinner, I had ventured to deplore the effect of the climate in rendering the freshness of the Pennsylvanian belles so very ephemeral as it sometimes is. A young man present, who was just married to a very beautiful girl, conceiving my observation to be almost personal, and that he was bound to maintain "vi et armis" that female charms in America were more lasting than they are in Europe. Fortunately however he had a relation by his side who was more reasonable.

Mr. Ingersoll, author of some amusing satirical letters about the city of Washington,[34] Judge Peters, who passed for a great wit, and was a worthy man and pleasant companion,[35] Mr. Dennie, editor of a literary gazette,[36] Mr. Walsh the well-known author of a celebrated volume of letters on France of the *American Review* and other works,[37] Mr. Chew,[38] Mr. Rawle,[39] Mr.

[34]Charles Jared Ingersoll (1782-1862), Philadelphia lawyer of prominence, wrote *Inchiquin, the Jesuit's Letters*... (New York, 1810), an anonymous volume of essays purportedly by a Jesuit traveler in America who admired the native scene. Since it was indirectly an attack on the sharp criticisms of British travelers, it drew scathing comments from the *Quarterly Review* and was defended in Timothy Dwight's *Remarks on the Review of Inchiquin's Letters* (Boston, 1815) and in J. K. Paulding's *The United States and England* (Philadelphia, 1815).

[35]Richard Peters (1774-1828), brilliant conversationalist and wit, was a prominent lawyer, Revolutionary patriot, farmer, and judge. His country seat was Belmont, where Foster probably visited.

[36]Joseph Dennie (1768-1812), Federalist, edited the *Port Folio*, 1801-1812.

[37]Robert Walsh, Jr. (1784-1859), in Foster's time a Federalist, had published in 1810 *A Letter on the Genius and Dispositions of the French Government* (Baltimore). For Walsh's other writings, see Sister M. Frederick Lochemes, *Robert Walsh: His Story* (New York, 1941).

[38]Benjamin Chew (1722-1811), Chief Justice of Pennsylvania, friend of Washington and father of a famous bevy of daughters, entertained frequently at Cliveden, his Germantown country place.

[39]William Rawle (1759-1836), prominent lawyer, and like most of the others mentioned here by Foster, a member of the famous Wistar parties in Philadelphia. He wrote for Walsh's *American Quarterly Review*.

Cadwallader,[40] Bishop White, head of the Anglican Church, Mr. Pinkney of S. Carolina,[41] and others, travellers of distinction, passing through, or residents in the town, were of these parties and might have made one forget one was not in England if it had not been for the occasional pronunciation of some common word that was not uttered according to English prosody. For instance, "inquiry," which Mr. Hopkinson, a lawyer of considerable eminence,[42] would render a dactile (ínquiry) as often as he had occasion to make use of it. It is in such society too and among similar sets of individuals, whose names are too numerous to mention, that one learns the esteem in which the English are still held by their transatlantic relations of the good old stock.

I must again repeat that any hatred entertained for us, as far as my knowledge of facts can go, was in a great measure confined, independent of party subjects, to individuals, refugees, or discontented emigrants from the British Islands and their connections, although I could state instances where the sons of American loyalists or British partisans have become our very bitter foes even after having had an English education, as in the case of Mr. Irving, a gentleman formerly chargé d'affaires at Madrid,[43] the son of an American loyalist, a rich and respectable landholder in Massachusetts who had also a commercial house at Boston. He had been put to school at Winchester, went to college at Oxford, and studied at the Temple. Yet [in] spite of all this, he hated us exceedingly, as I was told, and when he

[40]Thomas Cadwallader (1779-1814), friend of Dennie and Walsh, was to entertain Lafayette in 1824. He contributed to the *Port Folio*.

[41]This may be a reference to Charles Cotesworth Pinckney (above) or another prominent South Carolina Pinckney, perhaps Charles or Thomas F.

[42]Joseph Hopkinson (1770-1842), judge and author of "Hail! Columbia!," was known as a brilliant conversationalist. Shakespearean critic, poet, and congressman, he was the son of the better-known Francis (1737-1791).

[43]George William Erving (1769-1850), educated at Oriel, Oxford, was the son of a moderate Loyalist. At 21 the son followed his father's injunction and returned to the U.S. He became an ardent supporter of Jefferson. He was American agent in London from ca. 1801, and from 1804-1809 a member of the legation in Spain. He was Minister to Spain, 1814-1819.

became American consul in London he gave a great festival on the anniversary of American independence at which he got a cannon to fire off in order to force the people of the city of London to hear of it. When the vessel, too, in which he went to France was hailed by a British 74, a person whom he had taken with him, told me he would not get up from his backgammon table to look at her, using contemptuous expressions about our naval doctrines and pretensions. It has, however, been observed that in all times and countries after a revolution there have been many loyal persons who have had reason to complain of a want of sufficient gratitude on the part of the government or prince they had served, and of course the sons of such persons may have good reason to be disappointed at the station they hold, or the reception they have met with being inferior to their deserts.

The grandsons, however, it must be hoped will take a different view of the matter and I doubt if any description of hatred can ever pass to the third generation even although it be fomented and excited by imported editors of newspapers who live upon doling out abuse of the country they had been obliged to abandon, and of whom there was no small number scattered thro' the states, though at Philadelphia there were but two in my time, Duane[44] and Binns.[45] Cobbett it is true had been also employed there in editing a paper, but Cobbett, when he lived at Philadelphia, was a warm royalist;[46] so much so, indeed, that he was the only printseller in the town who dared to have the portraits of the King and Queen for sale at his

[44]William Duane (1760-1835), born in New York state of Irish parentage, for some years edited the *Indian World* in Calcutta before he was arrested and deported. After a stay in England he came to Philadelphia and was associated with Benjamin Franklin Bache in the editing of the *Aurora*, making it after 1798 the most powerful weapon of the Jeffersonians.

[45]John Binns (1773-1860), Irish-born editor of the *Democratic Press* of Philadelphia from 1807, came to America in 1801.

[46]William Cobbett (1763-1835), better known as "Peter Porcupine," English-born and self-educated, came to Philadelphia in 1792. In 1797 he began the publication of a pro-British paper, *Porcupine's Gazette and United States Daily Register*. In 3 years he carried freedom of the press to scandalous extremes in bold and often untruthful attacks on many people.

windows. He was, however, known to be a bold man and to have pistols at hand to resent any violence. He was at the same time so outrageous a party writer that he was arrested on a suit for defamation by Dr. Rush, for having published a weekly paper which he called "The Rushlight" for the express purpose of holding up the doctor to public notice, and as the latter belonged to the then ruling party, poor Cobbett was visited with the whole rigour of the law and condemned by the jury, which was composed, as I was informed, of unmixed Democrats, to pay $9,000 damages (being about £2,000).[47] Cobbett, it is true, by the ridiculous light in which he placed the doctor, had diminished, perhaps somewhat considerably, the number of his patients, but the fine which was unreasonably heavy was more vindictive than just. Cobbett, not having been able to pay it, was forced to go back to England, where in consequence of the loyal principle he had exhibited at Philadelphia, the sum for which he was indebted to government for fines or taxes, and on account of which he had had to fly the kingdom, was remitted to him at the instance of Mr. Hammond[48] or Sir Robert Liston.

Binns, editor of the *Democratic Press*, was of a very different species of public writer from Cobbett. He was one of the original disturbers of the public peace in London at the commencement of the French Revolution and made it his boast that he had been in seven or eight British jails. As to Duane, I understood that he had been drummed out of Calcutta, so that their writing in order to depreciate the land of their birth was quite to be expected as a matter of course. The best newspaper, however, which was printed at Philadelphia was the *Register*, which was edited by Major Jackson, a gentleman of the country,

[47]Cobbett's scurrilous attack was on Dr. Benjamin Rush's practice of bleeding. Dr. Rush was accused of thus having caused George Washington's death. Rush sued and Cobbett was fined $5,000. His property was seized for payment and he left Philadelphia. In New York, on the way to England, he delivered a parting attack on Rush and Judge McKean, who had tried the case, in the *Rush-Light*. He sailed for England in June 1800.

[48]George Hammond (1763-1853) was British Minister in Washington, 1791-1795.

highly esteemed and whom I frequently met with in the best society.

I often made excursions to dine in the country, either at the Woodlands, a beautifully situated villa belonging to the Hamilton family,[49] or to Mr. Chew's at Germantown, a place founded by some German regiments, which, after serving His Majesty during the war, were persuaded, on the peace taking place, to settle down and colonize the district where they had been so often encamped that they took an affection to it.[50] Bristol, a town on the Delaware at the distance of about twenty miles, where the Spanish envoy, Don Luis de Onis, resided, was also one of my excursions, and there I heard the "viva Fernando," "l'infernal Napoleon," and other Spanish national songs chaunted with great fervour. I also visited General Moreau and Doctor Logan. The latter had been Senator of the United States, and being one of those philanthropic men whose eyes overflow at the quarrelling of the human race, and who really think that a conciliatory go-between is all that is wanting to bring the bitterest enemies to a good understanding, he had been to Paris for the purpose of bringing Napoleon to reason, but only got laughed at for his pains and much blamed by his countrymen.[51] President Jefferson, nevertheless used to employ him occasionally in conveying messages to the British or French ministers at Washington; as when he was dispatched to persuade Mr. Merry to throw off the envoy and dine without ceremony at the government house.

I was told of a very spare dinner that the Doctor once gave to General Washington. It consisted of beef, potatoes and small beer. He was well-known for being over-economical, but on this

[49]The Woodlands, built by William Hamilton shortly before the Revolution, is one of America's finest houses based upon the designs of the brothers Adam. It stands now at the corner of 39th St. and Woodland Ave.

[50]Actually Germantown was founded in 1683 by 13 families from Crefeld, Germany, under the leadership of Francis Daniel Pastorius. It was incorporated as a borough in 1691.

[51]George Logan dealt with Talleyrand and the members of the Directory, not Napoleon, on his self-instigated peace mission of 1798. Foster visited Logan at Stenton, his family estate, just outside Philadelphia.

occasion he chose to dignify the scanty meal with the appellation of republican fare. Mrs. Logan a very sensible, respectable lady, had more spirit and the dessert being her department, she had provided a very good one. The Doctor, however, when he saw it, got up in a passion and roaring out that he never suffered "them things, such trumpery on his table," to her great mortification, ordered it all away. The dress of this humble host was of a piece with his dinner. Yet he had 400 acres within five miles of the city with a comfortable large house, and he was, spite of his parsimony, a very worthy and estimable person.

General and Madame Moreau passed their summers at Morrisville and the winters at New York, and he had in his family an aide-de-camp, M. Rapatel, and a secretary, M. Frenier. The General smoked his cigar and loved talk of his campaigns. He seldom went on horseback but enjoyed shooting and fishing. She, tho' her daughter occupied a good deal of her time, seemed to be more ennuyée than the General, and was then going to France, as was reported, to endeavour to get leave to go back altogether. The Americans used to say that she was a wife merely for show. She practised dancing for two hours every day and music for as long. While at dinner she seldom or never eat a single morsel, but carved every dish in spite of all one's endeavours to take that trouble off her hands, but it was at that time the fashion for French ladies to do so, and to eat before the dinner hour, so as not to be seen at so ungraceful an operation.[52]

One of the best men whom I was acquainted with at Philadelphia, and the most active in all charitable undertakings, was Mr. Vaughan who was a native of England, and brother to a quondam Member of Parliament for the borough of East Calne,

[52]Another contemporary describes the charming Madame Moreau as she arrived in Philadelphia in 1806: "*Tout le monde* thinks and talks of Madame Moreau, parties of splendor and balls are consequently given for her. Indeed she plays on the piano, harp, guitar, and tambourine infinitely better than anyone in our own country, and is the most perfectly graceful little fairy on the floor my eyes ever beheld. I am just getting steady from a ball in the neighborhood where she danced a waltz to the admiration of about two hundred people. . . ." Anne H. Wharton, *Salons, Colonial and Republican* (Philadelphia & London, 1900), pp. 160-61.

but settled for many years in the United States.[53] He had known Volney and told me that his book on America had been got up in a great hurry by order of Bonaparte, for the purpose of reconciling the French to the loss of Louisiana and the disappointment it had occasioned to many.[54] When the First Consul wanted to get rid of 40,000 revolutionary troops all the archives relating to Law's speculations were hunted out in search of arguments to induce settlers to emigrate there, but when he found it expedient to sell the country, it was to be written against and cried down at Paris.

Having been requested by a near relation of mine to make inquiries as to the use of gypsum for manure in the United States, I procured a good deal of information on the subject from Judge Peters, who told me that he had been the first to introduce it, and that by a series of experiments he had satisfied himself that the operating quality in it arises from the ingredients it contains of sulphuric acid, without which he thought it would produce no effect. Sea air, he said, would turn it into Glauber Salts and therefore neutralize its power as manure. When, however, Mr. Short, the American Consul General at Paris,[55] was in London he spoke with Sir H. Davey on the subject who maintained that it was not the sulphuric acid, but its calcareous particles which made it operate.[56] "Nevertheless," continued the Judge, "I trust to my own experiments and to facts." He spoke to me of a Mr.

[53]John Vaughan (1756-1841), wine merchant, librarian of the American Philosophical Society, Federalist but warm personal friend of Jefferson, was an intimate of many of the eminent Americans of the day. He was a brother of Benjamin Vaughan (1751-1835), M.D., LL.D., political economist, Member of Parliament 1792-1794, and finally a resident of Hallowell, Maine. John Vaughan's breakfasts were almost as famous as the Wistar evening parties.

[54]Foster seems to refer to John rather than Benjamin here, though Benjamin Vaughan was the brother who had lived for some years in Paris.

[55]William Short (1759-1849), Jefferson's protégé, had been in Europe in various diplomatic capacities until 1810. At this date he returned to America and settled at Philadelphia, where he amassed a large fortune. He probably at one time held the title Foster assigns him here.

[56]Sir Humphry Davy (1778-1829), famous English chemist, devoted much time to agricultural chemistry, 1802-1813. Later he published *Elements of Agricultural Chemistry.*

Smith, a gentleman of Kent,[57] as he believed, who used and approved of this manure, which is found to agree best in the United States with dry gravelly soils, tho' Mr. Binns, a Virginian land proprietor, in a book on the subject published by him,[58] asserts that its effects are great also on wet clayey grounds. Its presence is best shown by the production of clover, and I have even heard it asserted by a gentleman of Connecticut that after the powder has been scattered over a field of dry soil, without any clover seed having been sown with it, a very fine field of clover will nevertheless appear. But then this must not be tried in the neighbourhood of the sea, for the saline particles, arising therefrom, being adverse to the development of its qualities.

Two bushels and a half are considered to be the proportion adapted for an acre of ground in Pennsylvania, where it costs about three shillings Pennsylvania currency per bushel. In Connecticut, at Weathersfield, which is about the very finest district of that state, plaster of Paris or gypsum is highly prized, and from several inquiries which I made on the spot it appears that those parts of the uplands which are gravelly, and which, without the gypsum powder, produced but fifteen or fourteen bushels of wheat to the acre, or even less, will, with it, produce twenty or even twenty-two or twenty-three bushels. The gypsum should be scattered on the earth in the month of April when the clover will soon show itself, and in the autumn the farmer sows his wheat. They complained that the price of the gypsum was rising very rapidly, as from having been sold at about seven dollars per ton it had increased to nine dollars—being a proof, as the rise was not imputable to any failure in the produce of the quarries, that the consumption of the article had become greater than the supply. Mr. Plater of George Town,[59] who was a very intelligent farmer and had been much in the habit of using the gypsum for

[57]William Smith (1769-1839), "father of English geology," may be the gentleman referred to.

[58]John Alexander Binns (ca. 1761-1813) published a *Treatise on Practical Farming*... (Frederickstown, Md., 1803).

[59]Perhaps George or Thomas Plater, sons of Governor George Plater of Maryland, and brothers-in-law of Philip Barton Key (q.v.).

red-clover, told me that he had remarked in buying the stone, that if it be purchased in wet weather there is a loss to the purchaser of at least one-fourth on the quantity, from the weight being that much greater in the damp state than when it is dry. I have heard that if a person were to scatter upon a virgin soil the gypsum powder in the shape of the letters which form his name, clover would in consequence grow up corresponding with the characters so drawn.

The best, if not the only good gypsum to be procured on the North American continent comes from the Gut of Canso in Nova Scotia and from the head of the Bay of Fundy, but principally from the latter place, from whence it is sent down to Passamaquoddy and there shipped for Boston or New York. The quality it has of attracting moisture is that which is believed by many to be its principal virtue.

Bartram, who published a pleasing volume of rambles in Florida,[60] was alive when I was in Philadelphia, and had a charming botanical garden which he turned to good account, carrying on a regular trade, in seeds and plants with Europe. I employed him to send some to Lords Liverpool and Aberdeen and to Mr. Foster's (since Lord Oriel's)[61] beautiful place at Collon in the County of Louth. All the acorns and other seeds which he sent to the latter came up, and I saw the trees many years afterwards flourishing extremely well.

He packed his acorns in moss and leaves. When they arrive in Europe they are found to be growing, and they should be put in the earth early in the spring. The white oak, according to Bartram, is the most useful for building purposes, and the black oak for tanning. I sent out fifteen different species of the thirty-two

[60]William Bartram, the most distinguished of the scientific observers and travelers of the middle states, published in 1791 his *Travels through North and South Carolina, Georgia, East and West Florida.* The work is remembered for its influence on European romanticists as well as for its own sake as an authentic masterpiece of early American romanticism. This scientist with the soul of a poet described regions that Foster knew only second-hand, and the latter may be indebted to Bartram's *Travels* for some of his own summaries of the southeastern states' characteristics.

[61]John Foster (1740-1828) was created Lord Oriel in 1821.

kinds of oak which exist in North America, the whole set of seeds of the North American plants, in a box three feet long and eighteen inches broad, costing from 2½ guineas to five of which the acorns alone came to £1. It was delightful to walk about at Bartram's and listen to the buzzing of the humming birds which were busy sucking the honey and darting their tongues into the flowers of the Franklinia and other beautiful, tall trees loaded with blossoms, including the jessamine that is nearly a tree in these latitudes. There were twenty kinds of humming birds displayed in the Museum of Natural History of Philadelphia but most of them belonged to the southern continent.[62] Those I saw flying from tree to tree were about the size of the Italian sphinx,[63] and as these animals employ their tongues in a similar manner, there is a great resemblance between them at a distance, but the sphinx does not hum, nor rise apparently to the height of flowering trees. Besides it is totally distinct as being an insect, and appears only towards night when the moth tribe begin to show themselves.

Having alluded to the museum I cannot say much for it, all that I remember of its contents being the bones of a large mammoth that had been found in the back country and put into shape at Philadelphia, as well as raised on a frame, so as to appear thirteen feet high.[64] I was also struck with the circumstance of their being seven different species of snipe preserved there, belonging to the American continent.

The statue gallery had very good casts in it which was all that

[62]Charles Willson Peale (1741-1827), painter, naturalist, and showman, had in 1802 founded the Philadelphia Museum ("Peale's Museum") of natural history and curiosities, the most famous American institution of the kind in this period. It occupied the lower halls of the American Philosophical Society and the upper rooms and a hall of the State House. The "Long Room" in 1808 contained 760 birds in 140 cases. For a description of this institution in 1808-1810, with a diagram, see Charles C. Sellers, *Charles Willson Peale* (Philadelphia, 1947), II, 227-46.

[63]Evidently Foster refers to the *sfingide* (English, hawk moths. Lat. *sci. Sphingidiae*), or sphinx moth.

[64]In 1801 Peale had undertaken, largely at his own expense, the excavation of two mastodons in Ulster and Orange Counties, New York. The skeleton of one of them appeared in the Mammoth Room and was the principal attraction of the Museum. Sellers, *Peale*, II, 127-48; Janson, *Stranger in America*, pp. 197-200.

it could be expected to have. The collection was exhibited to ladies and to gentlemen separately, which I thought a very stupid kind of regulation by way of a delicate one, all restraint being thereby removed from the remarks and observations of either party, and that it is so proved by some lines written with a pencil which I spied here and there in a female hand upon the legs of statues of the gods Cupid and Mercury which the keeper of the rooms assured me must have been done during a late visit of some young women, the latter being generally educated at boarding schools and consequently not so much under the influence of that timidity and reserve characteristic of young ladies in Europe.[65] And when they get together they are said to be extremely plain-spoken.

At the Academy of Fine Arts I saw a picture by West of King Lear.[66] There was too much vigour in the old monarch, as it appeared to me, but the countenances of Edgar, and of Kent supporting his aged master were fine, and the Fool is also well done. A picture that is hung opposite to this and of which the subject was taken from "Hamlet" was extravagant and disgusting. The King and Queen appear as if they each had a crick in the neck. They told me it was also by West, but I could not believe it.

Strickland of Philadelphia painted town-views, not very correctly, it is true, but with spirit and a good effect of light and shade.[67] Guy of Baltimore had done some pretty landscapes, and storms at sea.[68]

Groombridge was too crisp and hard in his colouring, else his

[65]Mrs. Trollope (*Domestic Manners*, II, 85-86) makes the same comment Foster does here regarding the defacement of statuary. She was referring to statues in the Pennsylvania Academy of Fine Arts. Foster is alluding to the collection of casts of classic sculpture, the property of Joseph Allen Smith of South Carolina, on display in the Antique Room of "Peale's Museum" until they could form part of an American academy of fine arts. Sellers, *Peale*, II, 242.

[66]According to the librarian of the Pennsylvania Academy of Fine Arts, this picture was once on loan to the Academy by its owner, Robert Fulton. It was returned to Mrs. Fulton in 1816 and has since disappeared.

[67]Probably William Strickland (1787-1854), first known as an artist but subsequently distinguished as an architect and engineer.

[68]Francis Guy (1760-1820).

tints of foliage would be faithful representations of reality.[69] Of portrait painters, when I was in the country last, Sully was reckoned good,[70] but Stewart the painter of General Washington's portraits was decidedly at the head of this branch of the art, as Trumbull of Connecticut excelled them all in historical painting.[71]

The city of Philadelphia is built too much in the shape of a chess board to be beautiful, and New York has greatly the advantage over it for striking views. There is nothing surely so unfavourable to architectural ornament as long lines of broad streets cutting each other at right angles, and yet this is the plan on which most modern towns are constructed in this part of the world, arising, I conclude, in a great degree from the circumstance that the architects employed were generally in point of fact merely masons, who had emigrated to seek their fortunes in the colonies, like him of Washington in later times who built the President's House after that of the Duke of Leinster in Dublin, and forgot the cellars. Mere workmen, of no genius, being of course fond of what is easiest to do, as well as of imitating as much as possible, or if they have some appearance of originating, it is by omitting a part of what they copy from, and spoiling its proportions, as those who build upon the plan of the Pantheon at Rome generally take but six of its eight columns tho' they cannot prevent the eye from being offended at the change, which makes the building appear wire-drawn and discordant with itself, as anyone will admit who has seen the new church of La Madre de Dio on the banks of the Po at Turin. Such streets as those of Philadelphia might in fact be built on ad infinitum, and the architect never have to get out of his bed but simply to order the next house or the next street to be finished like the preceding one. For so similar are the streets of Philadelphia that I have often fancied myself in Eighth or Ninth Street when I was in Tenth or Elev-

[69] William Groombridge, fl. 1770-1790.

[70] Thomas Sully (1783-1872), pupil of West and Stuart, made his home in Philadelphia after 1810.

[71] John Trumbull (1756-1843), another pupil of West, and Washington's aide-de-camp, painted large historical scenes such as "The Battle of Bunker Hill," "The Signing of the Declaration of Independence," and "The Surrender of Cornwallis."

enth Street, and I had to retrace my steps for a great way to find the number out.

How much more beautiful is a city where no such regularity prevails! but where each man builds according to his own fancy! as no proportion of height can exist where length is extended in long perspective, and without proportion what is architecture? In London every step you take gives you new outlines, and in St. James Street or Pall Mall the club houses may be viewed, each of them as an individual work of art independent of shops or low houses on either side. So in regard to Genoa, who would not prefer the Strada Nuova with its curved line of palaces to the regular architecture of the Dora Grossa in the Sardinian capital? Long lines of houses in fact weary one physically as well as morally, in the same manner that a long straight road wearies when one is eager to get to the end of a journey. There are some handsome buildings, nevertheless, at Philadelphia, and if Mr. Latrobe, who is a real good architect, and was employed by the nation, could not alter the original sin of the plan on which that city was built, he has, at least, done something to adorn it.[72] The Bank, tho' the columns stand on plinths and are rather too long,[73] is a handsome piece of architecture, and is faced with white marble, an expence which the establishment could well afford, although even at the time when I was last in the country, now about twenty-eight years ago, they were trembling for their charter, which Mr. Eppes, son-in-law of Mr. Jefferson, declared in Congress to have begun in party, continued in party and should end in party.

Yet with all their Federal or aristocratical tendencies, what great influence had the Bank company in the election of Jefferson, Madison or Monroe or Jackson? But the Democrats, par-

[72]Benjamin Latrobe (II, n. 13 above) designed the Philadelphia Bank of Pennsylvania (1799-1801) and in part the Bank of the United States (1819-1824), both Greek revival buildings which influenced American architecture generally.

[73]Unless Foster has confused his bank buildings, he is not a good observer here. The Bank of Pennsylvania has individual columns which do not stand upon plinths at all, but on a general pedestal or podium for all. The only plinths are at the base ends of the porch. See the beautiful drawings by Latrobe in the Historical Society of Pennsylvania, and Fiske Kimball's article in *Architectural Record*, XLIV (August 1918), 133-39.

ticularly those of the back parts of the country can suffer no opposition, and are blind to the consideration that the states have not too many ties to connect them with one another. They see an aristocrat in a well-dressed banker who, used to order, naturally dislikes their rowing, noisy, bullying ways, and reckless of the consequences they pursue the institution with an inveteracy unworthy of the chiefs of the party but which these latter submit to, where they don't provoke it themselves, for their own especial ends. This policy was first introduced by Jefferson, the enemy of commerce. He saw where the elements of power would be found when the great Washington should have departed, and paid his court accordingly, as I have sufficiently shown in the account of my residence at the Federal City, where it was amusing to see the game going on, while Jefferson had still so much respect for European opinion as to take occasion to tell me how often he washed his feet, no doubt, lest I should suppose from his dress that he was really an unclean animal. But alongside of him was a rough, sour-looking, ci-devant Federalist who had ratted from his party and who would purposely dirty his boots in snow or mud, and leave his locks uncombed when he attended Mrs. Merry's parties, in order to let it be inferred what a liberal he was and how unspoiled by his residence at European courts. He gained his end tho' it was but for a season that he gained it.

The celebrated Hamilton, an acknowledged able statesman, born and brought up I believe in Jamaica[74] but who was one of the founders of the American constitution as well as independence, and who fell in sacrifice to the hatred or envy of Colonel Aaron Burr, was the Minister on whose report a charter was first granted to the United States Bank in the year 1791, for twenty years.[75] Its capital at that period consisted of $10,000,000, divided

[74]Alexander Hamilton was born on the island of Nevis in the West Indies. Harold Larson, "Alexander Hamilton: The Fact and Fiction of His Early Years," *Wm. & Mary Quart.*, 3rd ser., IX (April 1952), 139-51.

[75]Foster's figures and his summary of the history of the first bank of the United States are substantially correct. The few corrections noted below are from John T. Holdsworth, *The First Bank of the United States*, 61st Congress, 2d Session, Senate Documents, Vol. 26, Doc. 571 (Washington, D.C., 1910), pp. 7-144.

into 25,000 shares of $400 each. Two millions were subscribed by the United States government and the remainder by individuals of whom the greater number were foreigners. The dividends were then, on an average, at the rate of 8⅜ per cent per annum. But the market price of the stock was not more than about 150, in the year 1811, because for five years there had existed very serious doubts as to a renewal of the charter being granted by Congress, which doubts were only put an end to by the quarrel with Great Britain and the necessity there was for having recourse to a new loan. Mr. Gallatin had already sold out the government shares at 145 to Messrs. Baring[76] in order to be ready for any event. But he was too much of a man of business to give way to party prejudice, and not to favour a renewal of the charter. He even, as he himself informed me, wished the capital to be extended to $30,000,000.

The hatred, however, of the institution among the Democrats was so strong that the company began to despair of obtaining the desired favour, and had actually offered $600,000 to the state legislature of Pennsylvania, and a similar sum to that of New York for a charter from each, which both these states, being governed by the same party that rules in Congress, insultingly refused.[77] The Bank company then collected about five millions of specie dollars and called in several millions of paper money in the autumn of 1811, in order to prepare for paying off the stock. They persuaded most of the owners, nevertheless, to let it still remain on for twelve or fifteen months in the hopes of being at length able to prevail on Congress to grant the renewal, and half of this time or even more had elapsed when they at length succeeded; but it was at the cost of a war with England that Congress was brought to the decision. And now they seem again to

[76]The famous English financial family. Actually Stephen Girard (1750-1831) of Philadelphia, to whom the Barings were about $1,000,000 in debt, became the principal stockholder of the Bank before it closed in 1811. His own bank (1812-1831) succeeded in location and many general features.

[77]The trustees offered Pennsylvania $500,000 for a 21-year charter for a bank with $5,000,000 capital. This was refused. But an offer of $400,000 to New York was, after some delay, accepted, and the Bank of America was the result.

be where they were though all the influence of the whole monied interest had failed in producing any effectual opposition to the election of General Jackson, and although a generous enemy might have smiled at their "imbelle telum."[78] But they had offended him and therefore must be extinguished. In England tho' we love to subdue opposition yet we like it to subsist and be respectable. The Americans on the contrary must trample it under foot and break the elements of which it is composed. It is to be hoped the time may never come when they will do worse and take the bloody democracies of the middle ages for a model.

The bank called Bank of Philadelphia, having a charter from the state, was founded chiefly in the view of favouring landed operations in the interior.[79] It was a losing concern, but popular, and each of the directors had the privilege of being discounted to in the value of $30,000 which privilege, being generally needy persons, they scarcely ever failed to use, though they had to give good security like other borrowers. Mr. David Parish, whom I frequently met, seemed to me to have but a poor opinion of the whole banking system of the country.[80]

Philadelphia was, I suppose, the richest city in the United States twenty-eight years ago. What it is now I know not, but there were then individuals living in it whose incomes amounted each to nearly £20,000 a year, such as Mr. Stephen Girard originally a French merchant, and Mr. Sims who was said to possess in land alone to the value of $1,500,000,[81] while there were perhaps more individuals in easy circumstances to be found there than in any other town of the Union.

The number of her lawyers too would argue a great extent of property to be wrangled for. They amounted to 110, none of whom, if of any eminence, would accept a fee, as I was assured,

[78] I.e., "unwarlike weapon."

[79] The Bank of Philadelphia, founded in 1803 with a capital of $1,000,000, was incorporated in 1804.

[80] David Parish, called a "notable figure in American finance," was a Scotsman. He entertained Foster and Moreau.

[81] Joseph Sims was one of the great merchants of the period.

under ten dollars, though 200 are not unusually given where the cause is of very great consequence. It was not unusual too for a lawyer to fix his own fee, in observing good-humouredly that he must have it as he found it necessary to give him spirit and activity. And it would not be a bad thing if the practice were more general as it would save both parties a great deal of trouble, needless hesitation and delicate embarrassment. [*Note*: London/It is I believe only in England that all physicians are paid the same fee, and the consequence is that ten or twelve doctors who are at the head of their profession got to be enormously rich while they have more people on their hands than they can attend to. Everybody who has a guinea to pay, naturally preferring to consult a Halford or a Chambers[82] since the fee to a young or an old practitioner is the same. Were the juniors therefore to understand their interests they would, as is done in remote parts or abroad, only take five or ten shillings a visit till they become famous, and the effect would soon be felt by the apothecaries, who are now consulted and can pay themselves but by ordering drugs by the patients who would escape many nauseous doses, and best of all by the doctors who in trifling maladies at least would have to share profits with the less generally known of their profession.] The physicians of Philadelphia have also this good habit of sending in bills but they do not become so rich as the lawyers of whom I was assured that Mr. Rawle, Mr. Hopkinson, Mr. Dallas[83] who were at the head of the bar, were supposed to pocket at least $15,000 per annum each.

Of literary men Mr. Walsh was, I think the most conspicuous. He had just begun to publish the *American Review* which brought 4,000 species M. into his pockets in the first year of its appearance, and he was to get still more in the succeeding years, provided the sale admitted it. There were already 3,000 sub-

[82]Sir Henry Halford (1766-1844), physician to British sovereigns from George III through Victoria, and William Frederick Chambers (1786-1855), physician to Queen Adelaide and to William IV and Victoria.

[83]Alexander James Dallas (1759-1817), Jamaica-born Philadelphia lawyer and financier, was U. S. attorney for the eastern district of Pennsylvania, 1801-1814.

scribers to the work[84] at $6 each,[85] tho' there was a great drawback to the profits of authors English, or American, in the circumstance that no copyright could be obtained in either country by the citizens of the other. And the only method by which they could secure a mutual advantage was by sending early copies to the printers on either side. Mr. Walsh's pamphlet on France had gone through ten editions in England, as I was assured by Mr. Hopkins his printer at Philadelphia,[86] and as he had made no agreement with the London publisher, the latter sent him a present of Chalmers' edition of the English poets[87] bound in red morocco which Walsh thought might be worth about fifty guineas. He assured me that he was in the habit of working every quarter of a year for five weeks for eight hours each day, giving up the rest of his time to reading and amusement. He had no assistance in writing for his *Review* excepting the article on Fisher Ames' life which was written by a gentleman of Baltimore.[88] He was, when I saw him, preparing a work on England which he expected would have great success.[89] But I must say that from all I heard and saw, literature appeared to me to be but a very sickly plant as yet in this part of the world, though the citizens feel hurt if you say you think so, and would no doubt subscribe very largely to endeavour to prove the contrary. They are much too anxious likewise to impress upon strangers that their great towns are on a par with those of Europe in every other respect, and even Mr. Walsh dwelt with some complacency upon the circum-

[84]Walsh published the 8 numbers of the *American Review of History and Politics* from January 1811 through October 1812.

[85]Cf. the financial statistics given in Lochemes, *Walsh*, p. 72. Actually the publisher lost heavily on the venture.

[86]XVII, n. 37, above, for the title of the pamphlet. The firm of Hopkins and Earle published it. Lochemes, *Walsh*, p. 58.

[87]Alexander Chalmers (1759-1834), ed., *The Works of the English Poets from Chaucer to Cowper . . .* (London, 1810), 21 vols.

[88]"The Character of Fisher Ames," *American Review of History and Politics*, I, No. 1 (Jan. 1811), 89-94. The author is unidentified. Walsh certainly did most of the articles. Lochemes, *Walsh*, p. 230.

[89]This work on England remains obscure. In 1819 Walsh did publish *An Appeal from the Judgments of Great Britain respecting the United States*. The materials of the *American Review* would hardly fit this description.

stance, which he related to me, of there being an eating and betting club at Philadelphia. A good house there will let for $1,000 per annum (or about £200) and pay forty or fifty in municipal taxes which is a great deal more than one should have to pay for the same description of dwelling at Baltimore.

The city gaol was too celebrated an establishment to omit making it a visit,[90] and accordingly I went there, very obligingly attended by Mr. Morris and another of the inspectors of whom there are fourteen, who, together with the president, secretary and treasurer, serve gratis and are annually elected. Dr. Leib was president in 1811, and such was the degree of party spirit then prevalent in Pennsylvania, that it even reached their institution, eight out of the fourteen being Democrats, while the president had just managed to displace the treasurer, for no other reason, as I was assured, than because he was a Federalist.[91] He himself was a tobacconist as well as physician, and was known to have a share in an atheistical paper set up by Mr. Clay, the individual who drew bills on the Bank of Pennsylvania of which he was one of the proprietors, payable to "J. Christ or Bearer."

Thirty cents per day were allowed for the labour of each prisoner, out of which sum sixteen cents were retained to pay for the expence of his maintenance, and half of the remainder was reserved as his property, the other half going to a fund for expences of the establishment.

The building was capable of containing 500 individuals, and there were in it at the time of my visit 400 prisoners for trial, of both sexes.[92] The men were employed to pull hair, and the women to spin, but chiefly as an occupation, for they cannot be kept in such good order, nor do they properly come under the rules of

[90]This model establishment, which attracted many visitors, was located on Walnut St. behind the State House, or Independence Hall.

[91]John Bacon was treasurer of the prison board in 1811, and William Peirsol in 1813. *Census Directory* [*Philadelphia*], 1811, and Paxton's [*Philadelphia*] *Directory*, 1813. Foster's figures on the prison board, etc., are borne out by James Mease, *A Picture of Philadelphia* ... (Philadelphia, 1811), pp. 169-70.

[92]For a description of the building of this Walnut St. Jail, see Janson, *Stranger in America*, pp. 190-91, and Negley K. Teeters, *They Were in Prison* (Philadelphia, 1937), pp. 17-18.

the gaol until they are convicted. Those waiting for trial lived separate from the convicts at meals, though they were allowed to go among them in the yard. This regulation however, which was admitted to be liable to great objection, was intended to be abolished on the completion of a new gaol that was then being erected in Market Street, the old one that had existed for about thirty years having been founded by Jacob Lowndes, a Quaker.[93]

Murder in the first degree was punished with death by the laws of the state, and in the second degree by imprisonment which was not at the utmost to exceed twenty-five years. And I was surprized to see several men who had been guilty of the latter crime allowed to be at work alongside of the other prisoners, one of them having been pointed out to me who was whistling while making shoes and seemingly as merry as possible. Stone cutting, weaving, spinning, knitting, tailoring and shoemaking appeared to be their principal employments. There was a man who had been confined for sixteen years there for forgery and who had been convicted on eight different indictments. Solitary confinement was only inflicted upon those who were refractory to the rules of the gaol, and it seldom lasted for many days, it being considered to be intolerable for a longer time. The gaoler had his spies in every bed room who inform the keepers if there be any movements among the prisoners or any plans for making their escape. They once did attempt to force their way out during the existence of the yellow fever at Philadelphia, but a single keeper held them at bay with his blunderbuss until succour arrived.

In a solitary cell in a brick building that stood in the prison yard, apart from the prison itself, I saw a black man who had been shut up there for having attempted to poison another by putting copperas into his mush or Indian corn in order to be revenged on him for being a tell-tale, and two others who were implicated in the transaction had been thus confined for twelve

[93]Probably Caleb Lownes, who was given credit in many quarters (e.g., by La Rochefoucauld-Liancourt) for "the creation of the penitentiary idea." In 1793 Caleb Lownes collaborated with William Bradford in writing an account of the prison. Lownes had not founded the old Walnut St. jail, which was partially finished by 1776. Teeters, *They Were in Prison*, pp. 17, 103-104.

days. The inspector told me that there had been numerous instances of prisoners who were liberated after a term of even eight years, being again taken up and confined and that this had been the case with some of them even four or five times. But those who are reformed in their habits go quite away to other districts where they are not known.

He said he thought that fewer murders were committed, in consequence of the distinctions made here in regard to the degree of punishment awarded to different crimes, and to burglary being subjected to a less penalty than murder. He admitted, however, that but few were reclaimed from vice and that the principal advantage arising from the establishment was the effect which was produced by it on the community at large. The death of a criminal being, he observed, a punishment that was soon forgotten by the guilty man's companions, whereas his imprisonment kept him present in their memory, and served to keep alive their dread of sharing his fate. The guardians of the prison are perpetually on the alert to prevent too much intercourse taking place between the convicts, and to frustrate any plans or attempts to escape. Yet I was told of a man that a short time previously had contrived to get away by burying himself in the ground with a tube in his mouth through which he contrived to breathe for three or four days, until the pursuit having slackened he managed to climb over the wall in the night time. The dinner hour of the prison was twelve o'clock when rice and mush, water and molasses are served up to them. They got meat but once a week. The work of the prisoners, as the inspector assured me, paid all the expences of the establishment and produced even a surplus.

I cannot dismiss the subject of this prison without expressing some surprize at a publicly professed atheist having ever been elected to preside over an establishment of which the main object was described to be that of reforming the morals of those who act in defiance of the commands of God as well as Man. I would certainly not persecute an individual who disbelieves in God. It is his own affair if he chooses to throw away his chance of living happily in another world, and a real sincere atheist, endowed with common sense, if such a character do indeed exist, would naturally confine his tenets to himself, and be harmless to others, unless he aim at the acquisition of power and influence by forming a sect, when I am fully of opinion that he ought to be met by at least an exclusion from every confidential situation in the state. For in such case he may be looked upon not only with disgust, but as an interested disturber of the public peace, both by the encouragement he would probably give to any scoundrel that will agree with him in his impious tenets, and by the court he would naturally be ready to pay to the worst passions of the mob, especially in troublesome times when those passions are easily excited and the people lavish their favours on persons who shout loudest about liberty and equality, without much attending to character or conduct.

Those therefore who had to elect a president of this gaol establishment showed, I think, but little consideration for public opinion when they made choice of the Doctor. I am, I own, ignorant if he gave them satisfaction or not, and I only speak on general principles, for I never knew the gentleman, as he was not one of those Members of Congress who sought admittance into general society at Washington, nor did I ever meet him at Mrs. Harrison's[94] agreeable parties or anywhere else at Philadelphia. This, however, was not extraordinary, for at the time I speak of what is called in other countries the upper class, was in Pennsylvania completely put down, politically speaking, while from her Representatives you might judge of what quality must have been composed the rest of the social world and how pleasant for a gentleman to live among them.

Some demagogues of this state could, nevertheless, be consequential enough, and I was told of one, a Member of Congress, who wishing to give his vote with peculiar weight on a particular occasion, began a preface with, "Mr. Speaker, I have the honour to represent one of the first states of the Union, I have the honour to be the first in the nomination of that state, I have the hon-

[94]Perhaps the wife of John Harrison (1773-1833), prominent manufacturing chemist. He married Lydia Leib.

our of having filled the situation of Attorney-General in that state," and some other honour that I don't remember, which a Rhode Island Member answered with, "Mr. Speaker I have not the honour of representing the first state in the Union, being from the smallest and poorest; I am the last in the nomination of that state; I never was Attorney-General for that state, but a simple attorney, and yet I hope, Mr. Speaker, that you will give me as much of your attention as the Honourable Gentleman with his four by honours." And this Rhode Islander was also a Democrat!

But it was only when democracy was imported from Europe or affected that I quarrelled with it in the United States, and even that of old Smilie an Irish settler of half a century previous I did not find fault with, considering that the time had not then come for gradually abolishing the quarantine laws enacted in Ireland against the Pretender and his creed, and that we might in consequence be looked upon by him as enemies. Much less could I quarrel with friend Sloan, the butcher, who at his own stall laid down his knife to give me a hearty shake, and an invitation to his table. What I quarrel with was the sour ill-tempered High Dutch disposition to mortify and annoy, unfortunately too common in Pennsylvania, mixed with that of a motley set of imported grumblers from Dublin, which was disgusting and made this state appear the most ungainly of any in the Union. Though at Philadelphia where life was cheerful, the markets excellent and society on a good footing one might pass the time very agreeably, the insolence of the boors being there restrained by the justices of the peace who never spared them when they were to be fined for some act of brutality, and who luckily possessed great authority in and about the city.

Nothing in general is so dull as detailed accounts of churches, hospitals and manufactures. Yet of these latter the shot manufacture of Philadelphia may merit exception. It had been established but about four years before I visited the place and it already supplied the demands of nearly the whole of the United States, which had previously been furnished with shot from Great

Britain.[95] The principal shot tower was owned by Mr. Beck of Philadelphia and the whole demand of the town was about 600 tons weight, of which he furnished half. There was another tower in the city and the superintendent spoke to me of one made out of a rock fifty miles above Natchez on the Mississippi, and which is 150 feet high. The lead used in these towers came from Louisiana, and from having been at eight to nine dollars the 100 lbs. had fallen to $7½. Beck's tower was 164 feet high. The lead is boiled in a cauldron placed with arsenic in it at the top of the tower, where two men stand with ladles to pour it into a copper basin pierced with holes of different sizes, the smallest being produced by scattering the stream into the air where all are rounded and cooled so far as not to be flattened by falling into the cistern below. The swandrops were the largest thus formed, the buckshot being too bulky to lose their heat sufficiently to escape flattening unless at a much greater height. The superintendent informed me it was for the invention of giving greater height to shot towers that the patent was taken out, and related how it originated in the accident of a kettle being overturned by a man who was covering a steeple with lead. The molten lead having fallen through a vast space in the air was found in round globules at the bottom. This he said gave the first idea of using such a tower, which was seized on by an intelligent by-stander and it made his fortune.

When the shot is taken out of the cistern, it is given to girls to be gently rolled by them over a board, and those globules which roll slowly are put aside, the round ones alone being taken up and put into a large cylinder which is turned by a horse. When polished by the rotation they are handed to others who pass the shot thro' drawers, having holes of different sizes. There were eleven persons employed in the manufacture of Mr. Beck at a dollar a day, for the men, and two dollars per week, the women. A great difference in the pay of the sexes, certainly, but the su-

[95]Both Paul Beck, and Bishop and Sparks completed shot towers in Philadelphia about 1807-1808. Beck's was located between Arch and Race Sts. and Schuylkill Front and 2d Sts. Scharf and Westcott, *History of Philadelphia*, I, 531n.

perintendent affirmed that a girl could get her board, such as it was, for one dollar per week, and the men, perhaps, had families to feed. They only have work for their people during summer when enough shot is produced for the demand upon them. Arsenic was mixed up with the lead for a long time before they ascertained the fit proportions to be used and the proprietor for some months sent shot to Baltimore in return for an equal quantity in weight of lead.

Coarse woollen cloths were also beginning to be manufactured at Philadelphia and were only limited by a deficiency of wool in proportion to the demand, and thus by degrees was Great Britain beginning to be deprived, one by one, of her inventions and former commercial advantages over the rest of the world by the descendants from her own flesh and blood; but it was found impracticable to prevent it, manufacturers arriving every month from England. And I was told of one who had recently come out from near Manchester with eighteen workmen, who had been called upon at Liverpool to take an oath that they were not manufacturers, and the master did so along with all the others. But he added in saying this to my informant, that he had not kissed the Bible in swearing, and they went on board only just before the ship sailed, when there was no time to make much inquiry. There would, however, be some check if a regulation were made at Liverpool and other ports that passengers should announce their intention of embarking a week or a fortnight beforehand and be obliged to refer to somebody who would answer for their not being manufacturers.

Perhaps, however, it is better to let matters take their course and some such checks may be needed to prevent that worst description of population, which is engendered by over-manufacturing, from swelling beyond all proportion to the rest, as it was in parts of Belgium after the peace, and rendering us in reality a nation of shopkeepers dependent on all the world for our daily bread as well as subject to periodical fears of famine from the failure of foreign supplies which might be refused when we should most want them. I own, I, for one, am of opinion we manufacture nearly enough, and I am not jealous of the Americans. Besides they increase so fast that the European workmen they have cannot work fast enough to supply their demands and therefore they will long have to rely on our assistance, more especially as they can have very little hold upon persons who are always exposed to the temptation of moving onwards in search of independence, as we should find in regard to our operatives of Manchester or Leeds if a rich tract of uninhabited land were suddenly to rise up out of the neighbouring sea offering employment and wealth to volunteer settlers. For it is this consideration that renders America different from all other nations and all calculation idle with respect to her political experiments as applicable either to her future self or to Europe.

Such men as Lafayette who see the same elements in every people, could alone be such dupes to their own fancies as to suppose that the principles which in a vast and thinly settled continent can be introduced with utility or, at least, without harm, where everyone is or may be in easy circumstances, would be equally innocuous among the needy, famishing or dependent mobs of European capitals. And I never hear a person argue from the effects of the institutions of the United States as a recommendation for copying them in old established countries, without thinking him an Old Boy, like Lafayette whose mind seemed to have stuck where Washington had left it, or something worse. Indeed I believe there is no extravagance in religion or law which might not be tried there without doing much injury except to the unfortunate individuals concerned, who would probably be looked at with pity or patience by their more enlightened fellow citizens. Accordingly it is a fine field to send our democrats to, who generally come back, as I was assured that a Norfolk baronet did a few years ago, disgusted and disappointed.[96] He made no effect and his rank gave him no precedence. They were all as good as he, and he found his old aristocratical feelings returning fast upon him, while he got no amusement in railing at church or state.

[96]The HEH version of the "Notes," at the bottom of the page, names the baronet as "Sir Thos Beavor." This was Sir Thomas Beevor (1726-1814).

Even our most liberal travellers are said to have found the people too democratic. And yet they are as they were known to be and necessarily must be for ages to come. For the fact is that the well educated and well informed in the United States are few compared to the mass, and do not throw themselves into the arms of every grumbling emigrant even when he comes with his pockets full of money from England, so that the latter perhaps gets in among a set of pseudo-Americans who are greater brawlers than himself. This may easily happen, when one considers that at least four or five millions of the whole population must be new to the country they call theirs, emigrants from other states, Europeans or sons of Europeans, and that one settler being as strange as another in the back districts there is nothing to prevent an Irishman or a German, a fiery red-hot zealot, from taking the lead in all discussions, browbeating, and giving the tone to the rest. To this even the state of Pennsylvania, tho' one of the oldest, was for a great while and is still from its vast extent peculiarly exposed, having long been the rendezvous, on account of its rich soil and the proprietary lots it had to sell, of all European emigrants, more especially Germans, who were attracted by the relations of the Hessian soldiers that remained after the war and flocked there from the countries on the Rhine as well as Hesse-Cassel. A German who has just arrived fresh and set free from serving barons or counts is like a great cart horse turned loose upon a plain, kicking and snorting in all directions. They revel in their new state and appear to be delighted with rolling about in the mire of democracy.

Having alluded to the American pronunciation of many English words so contrary to the rules of our prosody, it may be added that they often use words in a different sense or position from that which they have with us. As, for instance, when President Jefferson in a Message to Congress alluded to *mines* which he said, had been "detected,"[97] and Gov. Claiborne in a procla-

[97]Jefferson's phraseology has not been located. In a letter to his mother of November 1, 1807, Foster remarks that the President's Message (of October 27?) was remarkable for its incorrect grammar. Foster Papers, LC.

mation at New Orleans talked of "availing the country" of somebody's services.[98] I must not omit too what Mr. Monroe told me of his own saying in London when the Whigs had just gone out of office in 1806. He happened to meet Lord Holland, who had been confined to the house by a severe fit of the gout, just as he was turning into the park for a drive, and wishing to make a civil speech he put his head out of the carriage hollowing to him, in a hurried manner, "I'm glad you're out, I'm glad you're out."[99] Lord Holland stared and poor Monroe suddenly recollecting himself and what a blunder he had made, was forced to seek an opportunity to explain his Americanism to his good-humoured friend who laughed heartily at the mistake. Another instance of the misuse of words I remember in Mr. Thatcher, a New England Member of Congress,[100] who in offering his bow to me asked me if I snuffed. I could quote many such but after all, are not the inhabitants of the mother country guilty of the same tendency to kick against authority in the use and application of terms long known under one signification or pronunciation and capriciously altered for another? Not to mention "Dover," all of a sudden, one never knew wherefore, called "Dovor," or "insurance" now called "assurance"? Do not most people now-a-days instead of the manly old word "insulate" from the Latin, use the emasculated word "isolate" from the Italian, altho' they still say "insular" not "isolar"? Is not "disembark" also altered to "debark," although we do not, as yet, at least, say "debody" for

[98]The phraseology of Governor W. C. C. Claiborne does appear. In a letter to James Pitot, February 28, 1805, Claiborne begins: "Sir Desirous of availing the Public of your services as Mayor of the City . . ." (Clarence E. Carter, ed., *Territorial Papers of the United States*, XIII, "The Territory of Louisiana-Missouri," [Washington, 1948], p. 404). Claiborne probably used the expression elsewhere, as did James Madison some years before in a letter to Claiborne, when the Secretary of State (July 10, 1801) spoke of "availing the public of your services as Governor of the Mississippi." Dunbar Rowland, ed., *Official Letter Books of W. C. C. Claiborne, 1801-1806* (Jackson, Miss., 1917), I, 1.

[99]Henry Richard Vassall Fox, third Baron Holland (1773-1840), retired from office with a group of colleagues (he was Lord Privy Seal) in March 1807, while Monroe and William Pinkney were American Ministers in London.

[100]Samuel Thatcher (1776-1872), Harvard graduate, was Member of Congress from Massachusetts, 1802-1805.

"disembody," and an "egoist" is he not called "egotist" tho' why the "t" should be inserted in this word is as unaccountable as that the "n" should be abstracted from "insular."

Then, Miss Kemble herself, who has written the best account perhaps of the society of America,[101] does she not say "heart ach" instead of "heart-ache" which her uncle, John Kemble, would, no doubt, have spelt "heart-aitch"? He used too to say "cassél" in the play of *The Stranger*, for "cassel."[102] And I remember during the Spanish War that no one could venture at the opera to tell of a victory in Spain, but he was sure to be corrected as to the proper way of pronouncing "Andujar," or "Cadiz," often called "Cales"—or any other name of a place that the hearer was by chance acquainted with, while every new traveller, almost, lays down a new rule for writing "Cairo" or "Mahomet," "Tatars or Tartars," "Khans," etc., etc. Shoals of new coined words too are every day introduced into novels and poems (among the rest "shimmering," a very good word from Göthe by Miss Kemble).[103] It would really seem as if there no longer existed any "norma loquendi" for the English tongue while we still pertinaciously adhere to our insular pronunciation of Latin, introduced no one knows when or whence (the expulsion of the Romans having been more complete in Britain than any other province of the Empire), unless it be from Sweden where they assign three vocal sounds to the first letter of the alphabet, though they treat it with more punctilio than we do, since they dot it once when

[101]Frances Anne (Fanny) Kemble (1809-1893), famous English-born actress, published her *Journal of Frances Anne Kemble Butler* in 1835, tracing her theatrical career and freely criticizing American customs. Her *Journal of a Residence on a Georgia Plantation*, written in 1838-1839, was not published until 1863 and therefore was not available to Foster.

[102]John Philip Kemble (1757-1823), the great English actor. Actually Foster's two versions of the "Notes," those of HEH and LC, seem to have the accent on "Cassel" in reverse positions. Kotzebue's play, in an English translation by B. Thompson under the title of "The Stranger," was a considerable success with Kemble in the title role. Herschel Baker, *John Philip Kemble* (Cambridge, Mass., 1942), pp. 230-31. The Stranger must pronounce "castle" most emphatically in Act I, Sc. 1, and in Act V, Sc. 2, in other words, near the beginning and end of the play.

[103]"Shimmering" is unlocated in Fanny Kemble's *Journal*, though the forms she used for moonlight, etc., are frequently close to it.

they wish to make it pass for O as in Åland—and twice when they desire it should pass for E. It can hardly be supposed that our pronunciation of it should have been the same as that of Sir Thomas More's or Milton's time or they never could have conversed so freely with their literary friends of the Continent. But however difficult to account for so inconvenient and wanton a deviation from the practice of the other nations which composed the Latin world, it is certain that if there were but the will to do away with it, nothing would be more easy. To get the seniors of Oxford and Eton however to consent to such a radical change would no doubt be impracticable, tho' I wish at least that it were given for a theme to ascertain at what period such an affectation was first introduced.

I gave up my pretty villa, Solitude, on the 30th September without having experienced any inconvenience from the damp. But before I left it I went to visit a school that had been established on Pestalozzi's system, about two years previously, near the Falls of the Schuylkill by a Mr. Neef, a German and pupil of Pestalozzi.[104] I never saw a more ill-looking person. He was described to me as a deist, and the boys appeared to be very ill brought up, being allowed to give the lie to their master. They were taught little else than arithmetic and English and French, tho' he told me he intended to teach the dead languages also, "since fashion exacted it." For himself, however, he evidently had no perception of the beauties of Homer or Horace or of any advantage whatever in a classical education, having apparently never imbibed the beautiful precept:

> "Si non intendes animum studies et rebus honestis
> Invidia vel amore vigil torquebere ——"[105]

[104]Francis Joseph Nicholas Neef (1770-1854), Napoleonic veteran, was employed by Pestalozzi in the famous school at Berne, Switzerland. In 1806 Neef was persuaded by William Maclure to come to Philadelphia. In 1808-1809 he established his school.

[105]The HEH version locates the quotation as "Horace *Ep* 1, 2, 3." Actually it is from *Ep.*, 1, 2, 37. The HEH version also has *studio* instead of *studies*. Loeb transl.: "so . . . if you don't devote your mind to honourable studies and pursuits, envy or passion will keep you awake in torment."

CHAPTER XVIII

THE ROAD to New York as far as Elizabeth Town, which is fifteen miles from the River Hudson, is very good and the country rich and varied tho' nowhere presenting any very striking scenery unless it be at Trenton, about thirty miles distant from Philadelphia, where the view of the Delaware is wild, from the multitude of rocks in the channel of the river and its sloping banks. At New Brunswick too, thirty miles further on, there is a fine extensive view of a long level plain, across which the road is carried to the Bay of Amboy, where there is one of the finest harbours on the continent and hills show themselves in the background.

New Jersey

Elizabeth Town is a small but gay-looking place and a very ancient settlement, having been founded in 1664. Lord Bolingbroke known in America by the name of Mr. Bellasyse was living near it when I was there.[1]

In the neighbourhood lies Newark an equally ancient place, where I stopped for three days, having had to return from Paulus Hook on account of the yellow fever being at New York, which city I was on this occasion obliged to content myself with seeing at a distance. The situation however I could see was very fine, the entrance into the North River being particularly striking. Long Island, too, which is high and wooded, with the numerous spires of the town, such unusual ornaments in American cities (there being but one even in Philadelphia)[2] gives a great animation and variety to the scene. On the road near Paulus Hook I was hailed by a plain-looking man on horseback who invited me to go out

[1]Foster mentions Mr. Bellasyse, or Lord Bolingbroke (1761-1824), his ugly German baroness wife, and several children in a letter to his mother of September 22, 1805. Foster, *Two Duchesses*, p. 239.

[2]Though Foster apparently noted only the tallest spire in Philadelphia, that of Christ Church, he should also have been able to see that of St. Michael's and Zion's Lutheran Church. These show in a painting of the city in 1810 by Thomas Birch, now in the Historical Society of Pennsylvania.

foxhunting with him the next day when he should have collected his hounds. He could, he said, find five foxes in a day. Between the river and Newark there is a large swamp and a road like that over the Pontine Marshes, and in the middle of it a circular hill called Rattlesnake Hill but where the said snakes have long ceased to exist. There is a delightful ride from Newark to the Falls of the Passaic and along the River Passaic, the banks of which are sloping and varied.

The distance is sixteen miles and the Falls are well worth going to see. A Major Godwin kept a tolerably good tavern there[3] and I walked from his house about a mile to the cascade, the ground all about being delightfully wooded, and in the midst of the woods there is a great cleft in the rock of about 100 yards in extent which looks as if it was a rent in the ground torn open by an earthquake. The river comes along two shores covered with magnificent trees and dashes down into the very middle of the cleft which turns it at right angles from its former course. When there has been much rain the effect must be prodigiously striking. It was even beautiful when I saw it, tho' in an uncommonly dry season, but the whole scenery is so wild that one can pardon there being no great mass of water. There are three clefts, two of which had none at all in them. The rock is as hard as flint and there are numerous bold projections of it into the air, with rents on either side from top to bottom to the depth of at least seventy feet. At the foot of the rocks the river forms a noble basin. I forded it at about half a mile above the fall, and on the other side I found another torrent, a little cascatelle tumbling down some very wild crags. It seemed to be so fit a haunt for serpents that I looked about anxiously for one, but tho' I rambled in the neighbourhood for two hours I saw no living thing but some sand snipes and a pretty little squirrel that was jumping from rock to rock. From the bottom there is a very fine view of these falls,

[3]The Falls of the Passaic is now Paterson, New Jersey, an industrial center. Abraham Godwin, of Totawa (also now Paterson), kept a well-known tavern there. It fronted on the river. William Nelson, *History of the City of Paterson and County of Passaic* (Paterson, 1901), pp. 274-75, 278n.

but the upper scenery pleased me more. There were several manufactories lower down the river as well as saw-mills. I was three hours on my return to Newark, the road I took being very stony. And when I got to a tavern kept by Colonel Gifford[4] I found it full of fugitives from the fever. The Colonel, however, got me rooms for the night at a lodging house kept by a major-general so that I had the honour of breakfasting at a major's tavern, dining at a colonel's and supping at a general's, the innkeeping business being monopolized by the military in this part of the country.

Trenton is the seat of government of New Jersey, and the state sent six Representatives to Congress, who had the peculiar distinction of being the elect of the ladies as well as gentlemen, when I first visited the United States, tho' I afterwards heard that there had been a bill brought into the State Assembly which was likely to pass into a law, for depriving the fair sex of their right of voting at elections. Perhaps the men they chose were thought to be too aristocratical, for ladies have the reputation of hating democracy as well as demagogues, and I well remember, that one of their favourites, General Dayton, a Senator in the United States who had had 150 ladies' votes, was a prodigious fine gentleman, and must have been very handsome. He was, I believe, a great rake too, for he appeared "blasé" (to use a very untranslatable French word) with everything, and told me he thought a reward should be offered for the discovery of a new pleasure, a suggestion that not a little startled my ears which were then unused to these republicans. The same man was afterwards strongly suspected of having engaged in Colonel Burr's Plot, with which the Colonel had and by proclamation, invited all those to join who were tired of the dull pursuits of civil life.

With regard to this plot, I must say in passing, that it appeared to be inconceivably crude and impracticable, and showed Burr to be only an ambitious vain intriguer who had calculated noth-

[4]Gifford's Tavern, also called "Hounds and Horn," actually in Newark, was famous from 1790 for 20 years. Frank J. Urquhart, *History of Newark* (New York, 1913), I, 423.

ing but the unruly passions of back-woodsmen, or of desperate adventurers who are still too thinly scattered over the vast North American continent to be brought to act with sufficient force in any such enterprize. Burr, I believe, had never got more than 200 men together at any one time or place, and yet the Government was not very vigilant, the first account that reached it of his proceedings being supposed to have been conveyed in a letter to Mr. Henderson of the Marine Department[5] from his brother who stated that he was about sending his family into Virginia for safety from impending confusion in the state of Kentucky. The Government, in fact, long remained in a state of ignorance or perhaps, rather, of disregard of the conspiracy and the western mail did not bring us for a great while any article of intelligence in the papers respecting it, nor even a private letter, some agents of the Post Office having, in all likelihood, been gained over. What makes me, nevertheless, suspect that the Government were conscious rather than ignorant of the matter, was the conduct of General Wilkinson the Commander-in-Chief of the U. S. Army,[6] at Washington in the winter preceding the outbreak of the plot.

Burr, then Vice-President of the United States, flattered himself he should be, privately at least, supported in his attempt at forming a separate dominion in the western states, if not by the Spanish, by the British government. And (I may now admit it as he is since dead) he actually called on Mr. Merry, having requested a private interview with him, for the purpose of sounding him with regard to the probability of such support

[5]No Mr. Henderson has been identified in the Records of the Navy Department, National Archives. There was an Archibald Henderson commissioned as a second lieutenant of Marines in 1806, but no information appears in the Navy records which relates him to the Burr trial.

[6]General James Wilkinson (1757-1825), governor and military chief in 1805 of the upper portion of the Louisiana Purchase, had long had the ambition of conquering the Mexican provinces of Spain. In 1805 he entered into an agreement with Burr near the beginning of the conspiracy and then betrayed his accomplice's plans to Jefferson. Whether this was his original intention in joining the conspiracy is still a moot question.

being attainable.[7] Mr. Merry was of course bound to secrecy, but though he listened to the plot, he gave no encouragement to the hero of it, but rather tried to convince him of its impracticability.[8] General Wilkinson had also private interviews with Mr. Merry, but although he was or affected to be a disappointed, dissatisfied man, and insinuated that he was in an understanding with Burr, he over-acted his part. He left the impression on Mr. Merry that he was only seeking to arrive at some knowledge of how far he, Merry, might have listened to Burr's intrigues in order to communicate the fact to the President, who would probably have desired nothing better than an opportunity for sending off Merry or asking for his recall, not having been able to bear him ever since the affair of the dinner.

Having said so much of Colonel Burr's conspiracy, and as he was a native of New Jersey, tho' a practising lawyer of New York, I may here add that on the failure of his plot he became an outlaw and fled to England, from whence having been ordered away for the satisfaction of the American Minister, he proceeded to Sweden where I saw him in the year 1809.[9] Here his love of intrigues led him, under the pretext of curiosity, to visit the Castle of Gripsholm, in which the deposed King Gustavus and his family were then confined and closely guarded. Burr asked to see the young Prince, and being suspected from his manner, of a design to communicate some plan of the royalists for his escape, was rudely marched away, and soon afterwards ordered out of the kingdom.

Having known him in high station at Washington and wishing to be civil to all Americans, but particularly to an old acquaintance in a strange land and in misfortune, I went up to him at the Casino of the Nobles on his first arrival there and offered him my services, when I must do him the justice to say, that he

[7]Beveridge calls Burr's deception of the stupid British minister Merry the most shameful lying and deception Burr ever engaged in. *Life of John Marshall* (Boston, 1918), III, 288-90.

[8]That Merry tried to convince Burr that the plot was impracticable is unlikely. Foster may be covering up here for Merry and himself.

[9]It will be recalled that Foster was chargé d'affaires at Stockholm, 1808-1810.

showed some delicacy, for seeing that I was a young diplomatist, he told me he thought it right to put me on my guard, that I might not commit myself in any quality of chargé d'affaires by being seen with him, for that he must inform me he had been ordered out of England by my Government at the request of that of America. I mentioned this long afterwards to Lord Holland who observed that it was the only good trait he had ever heard of Burr, and then spoke to me with reprobation of his conduct to Hamilton, whose son, he informed me, by a singular fatality had perished in a duel, in the following year, if I recollect right, on the very day and on the same spot on which Burr had deliberately shot his father.[10] Burr had a daughter[11] whom he was said to have brought up under the care of his mistress and whom he allowed to correspond together, as he had no idea he said of making mysteries of his amours. Colonel Burr was a little man, well mannered and rather agreeable but looked mysterious and unquiet, his dark eyes glancing perpetually and rapidly from right and left. He was I believe ready for any enterprize that might better his fortunes. The having had the presidency of the United States so near his grasp as to have missed it but by a vote or two seemed to have been his ruin and "per fas aut nefas"[12] to have thenceforward been his motto. I think his attempt in some degree justifies the apprehension expressed in another part of this work, that ambition will or may someday successfully be excited rather than restrained by the numerous barriers placed against public men who have served the state among which the reducing them to penury seems a very dangerous policy.

[10]This refers to the death of Alexander Hamilton's favorite and eldest son Philip, who was killed in a duel at Weehawken, across the river from the Hamilton home, in 1801, 3 years *before* his father. Alexander Hamilton died in July 1804, shot on the same spot, as Foster says.

[11]Theodosia Burr (1783-1813), Aaron's brilliant and accomplished daughter, was her father's hostess after her mother's death. In 1801 she married Joseph Alston of South Carolina. She died at sea, or was wrecked, on the way to meet her father on his return from his European exile.

[12]Roughly, "by good or bad," or "by hook or crook."

But to return to the ladies of New Jersey. I was told that their right of voting at elections was confined to spinsters above twenty-one years of age and to widows, married women being, of course supposed to be ready to vote for their husbands.

In New Jersey were to be found the best coach horses in the United States, and accordingly I provided myself while there with two pair of them which cost me $650 or about $145 each. I also bought a black saddle horse for $200 which was thought cheap.

Before I left the state I made a visit to Princeton which was then considered as one of the very best universities on the American continent and was particularly frequented by young men from the southern parts.

The college is situated at a distance of about fifty-three miles from New York and forty-two from Philadelphia. It consists of two large buildings of stone in one of which all the students reside and a room with a closet is assigned in it to every two individuals. The town contains but a single street. The situation is very elevated and there is a view from it over an extensive plain entirely covered with woods. No garden or pleasure ground is attached to this house which is removed from the street by a grass plot. Next to the lodging house stands the second building where dinner is served up for all in a long plain room of which the roof is supported by arcades, the whole being white-washed without any painting or portraits or ornaments whatever. Six tables were laid out every day at one o'clock with plates for twenty persons at each. A professor always presided and the discipline was said to be very strict, for the young men were not permitted to enter a tavern nor even to walk two miles out of the town without leave. There had, however, lately been a meeting to remonstrate against the severity of the discipline, and several students had been expelled for riotous proceedings, or had, of themselves, taken their departure. There were about 120 still remaining and the riot had I understood been occasioned by the violent expulsion of a young man who in a frolic had with some others been amusing himself with blowing up a certain small building [privy]* adjacent to the lodging house.

John Randolph had been of this university and told me that hard drinking in his time was as much the fashion there as it was at Oxford, but instead of bad wines they used to drink peach brandy, toddy, punch and other mixtures. Nevertheless, notwithstanding these excesses, he spoke favourably of the classical education to be acquired at Princeton and assured me that it was not the fashion as it is at Oxford for young patricians to make it a boast that they never open a book, and that they avoid as much as possible to make the acquaintance of reading men, which I was obliged to confess I heard had sometimes been the case at least at Christ Church College. The examinations for degrees were described to me as severe at this university though I understood them to be chiefly a trial of the understanding and the reasoning faculties as well as of the student's proficiency in the classics and general history; mathematics and divinity were not so much attended to as with us, nor was it necessary as at Oxford for candidates for honours to know nearly every passage in the Old Testament.

The riotous proceedings of the Princeton youths above alluded to were not more puerile than those of Cambridge a few years ago when the staircases of the tutors were daubed with paint and a bridge blown up at Trinity College. It is, however, to be said in favour of English and American universities that their inmates do not maim each other with broadswords as those of the German universities do; neither do the professors pander to the easily excited passions of youth, for fear of losing their pupils, in the petty rivalry of one little state with another, where their chief salary is made to depend not on payments from the colleges but from the students themselves, [whereas in the English places of education the salaries of tutors are regulated by law or custom and their incomes are not so entirely made up of what they receive from their pupils.]**

*Foster uses this word in the HEH version.
**Material in brackets is deleted in LC version.

CHAPTER XIX

NOT HAVING been able to enter New York, on account of the yellow fever which was raging there, and which I let myself be persuaded by the consul not to brave a second time, I hired a periogger boat[1] and made a tour up the North River. This great stream is about two miles wide at its mouth, three-fourths of a mile wide at the distance of forty miles, and at its entrance among the highlands, five miles further on, it is but half a mile wide. It runs a straight course between lofty and well wooded banks—that nearest the city being interspersed with numerous villas which are highly ornamental—for an extent of thirty miles, reaching to the first bend in the channel, from whence Staten Island is still visible.

New York State

I stopped at Haverstraw and lodged at a private house where I could find no sort of provisions, but had coffee and rye-bread. On the next day I dined at Peekskill where there was nothing to eat but smoked beef and eggs, and I slept at the Buttermilk Falls which are situated about sixty miles up the river.[2] The innkeeper wanted to put me into the same bed with a Swedish merchant whom I fell in with on the way, but I succeeded in getting a single blanket to lie on on the floor. These falls take their name from their colour. The quantity of water which forms the cascade is small but the rocks over which it flows are very massive and the scenery is truly wild and romantic. There are not above a dozen houses at this spot and these are so divided from one another by great rocks that one must be very careful to pick one's steps not to slip down in going about the place.

[1]Piragua, or periagua. Though this word in America often referred to a canoe hollowed from the trunk of a single tree, Foster probably uses it to refer to the open flat-bottomed schooner-rigged vessel.

[2]Buttermilk Falls is 2 miles below West Point in Orange County. J. H. French, *Gazetteer of the State of New York* . . . (Syracuse, N. Y., 1860), p. 505.

The inhabitants were natives, all of them of the soil, which it was a treat to me to ascertain. It was so seldom that I found this to be the case among the vagrant or newly established proprietors of villages in the midland states. Our hostess was the daughter too of an old inhabitant who had also been born at Buttermilk. They seemed, however, to have but a poor subsistence, scarcely ever getting any meat.

The Buttermilk Falls are situated over what is called the Horse-Race, which is the strongest part of the current of the North River running through the highlands. The mountains in that neighbourhood are about 1,500 feet high covered with forests and stupendous rocks which every now [and] then present superb points of view. The wind being strong I took a row-boat and went round West-Point, the fort that General Arnold[3] had undertaken to betray into the hands of the British army, in the Revolutionary War. The old fortifications had been nearly all destroyed. There was, however, one remaining, called Fort Put,[4] which still preserved its shape and formed a picturesque object on the top of the hill. Below it at a short distance were some buildings containing a garrison of about sixty men.

The pass underneath is the most formidable on the banks of the North River and it was there that Major André was executed, whose heroic conduct seems to have caused his fate to be equally regretted by both friends and enemies, however authorized it may have been by the laws of war.[5] He was the son of a hatter in Bond Street and his death produced as much sensation as if he had been the heir of one of our noblest families.

The view of the bend of the river at this place is very striking and extends as far as Newberry,[6] a town situated beyond the

[3]Benedict Arnold (1741-1801).

[4]Three forts, Clinton, Putnam (to which Foster evidently refers), and Constitution were built at West Point during the Revolution. The military academy was established in 1802, but was not an effective institution until 1817.

[5]Major John André (1751-1780), born in London of Genevese parents, was involved against his will in Arnold's plot to turn West Point over to the British. Arnold escaped, but André was captured and sentenced to be hanged as a spy.

[6]Newburgh, formed in 1788. For a description of the early village, see French, *Gazetteer of New York*, p. 508.

highlands, terminating with one of the Allegheny mountains. The rocks are some places quite perpendicular and the water is so deep that ships of any size can lay alongside of them. I slept on my return down the Hudson at Sing Sing, about thirty miles from New York, and a very pretty Italian looking village divided in the centre by a hill. In the evening the mountains showed the pure blue tinge of the south and the water reflected it. I slept again here on the floor in a great hall of the inn which was the Free-Masons' lodge room, being the only one that I could have to myself.[7]

In conformity with the pettyfogging jealousy towards the real capital that exists in many other parts of the United States, New York like Pennsylvania, is forced to fix the seat of government in a small town, Albany, where the rustic legislators may not be subject to have their feelings wounded by seeing fine horses, equipages or dress, or any other outward and visible mark of superiority of their own. One would have supposed that such great politicians might have preferred to live in the centre of arts and sciences, trade and commerce, where minds of every description meet and improve one another, by the mutual interchange of ideas, and the polish of social life which "emollit mores nec sinit esse feros."[8] But the dreams of philanthropists are destined to be deceived in this respect as in many others and the poor commonplace passions of envy, jealousy and parsimony, as well as a certain want of concern for the dignity of government, lead the other way, while the paltry argument about a central spot being necessary, as if the whole state were a wheel, is opposed by the majority to any advantage of humanization or instruction to be derived from the chief members of the state residing in a large city. Thus men of office are to be found in one place where from having no other occupation, being gen-

[7]There were several taverns at Sing Sing in Foster's time, the best known being "Ward's Hotel" and the "Union Hotel." J. T. Scharf, *History of Westchester County, New York* ... (Philadelphia, 1886), II, 361-62.

[8]Ovid, *Ex Ponto*, II, 9, 48. The Loeb transl. of this and the preceding lines: "Note too that a faithful study of the liberal arts humanizes character and permits it not to be cruel."

erally without their families, they over-dose themselves with politics from morning till night and the men of business or pleasure live at the opposite extremity with little or no influence upon the counsels of the government. No wonder foreigners feel the effect of such a schism, and according as they are clever malcontents, or merely bilious travellers, rule the social world at New York or rail against it.

It is the intermixture of all classes that renders the great cities of Europe generally the centres of civilization, but here in this new world a preference seems to be given to two penny half-penny considerations of personal or local importance. Albany will, no doubt, have to yield to some upstart place, like Harrisburg in Pennsylvania, which was said to be about to carry the twenty cents per mile legislators away from Lancaster.

I know of but one country in Europe where the principle has been acted upon of fixing the seat of government arbitrarily in the centre of the land, and that has certainly not held out a fortunate example, Madrid being notoriously a forced fruit, even at the present day, which would soon be reduced to its original insignificance without the presence of the court. Had Charles V or Philip II established his capital at Seville or at Lisbon when one or the other might have done so, what a different degree of interest would not Spain have taken in questions of trade and commerce, and what a magnificent city her metropolis might ere now have become! But it is as well for England, perhaps, that her fanatical and vindictive passions were arrested and that she remained so long the inert mass of ignorance and wealth which, before she lost her colonies, largely contributed to feed our naval superiority and that she is now become so incapable of harm out of her own limits that her alliance would be only a dead weight to any of her neighbours.

The number of Representatives in Congress from New York State which amounted in 1806 to seventeen had already, according to the ratio established in 1811, increased to twenty-seven.

The population of the city which in 1801 was estimated at 60,489, amounted in 1806 to 75,770 and at this rate may at the present day, have doubled the latter of these two numbers. Yet there is hardly in the place a single private house above mediocrity, so completely have all old family mansions Dutch or English disappeared from the town, which seems to have suffered more from fire than any in the whole Union. Some dwelling houses, however, there are in good situations which will produce a rent of $1,200 or even $1,500 per annum.

Aristocracy nevertheless did still flourish in New York State and there was one immensely rich proprietor belonging to it in the early part of the present century, namely, Mr. Van Rensselaer, called the Patroon.[9] As late as the year 1811 he held two counties, of which he was at least the nominal owner,[10] and Mr. Glen,[11] a Member of Congress, was returned by his sole influence. One of the Ministers, from whom I derived this information, told me that Mr. Glen avowed that he never thought of giving himself any trouble to canvass his constituents, provided his Patroon was satisfied with him that was enough, as they were every one of them the Patroon's tenants. The Van Rensselaer property was in extent forty miles square and had been let according to an old Dutch mode of tenure by agreement to pay a fine to the landlord on each successive alienation by sale of the land. But there had arisen a doubt as to whether the land, under the new Constitution of 1789, would warrant the continuance of such a tenure, and as the Patroon had not exacted any fines for several years, it began to be suggested that perhaps the tenants might be able to liberate themselves altogether from the payment of them by right of prescription. Meanwhile, however, Mr. Van Rensselaer naturally possessed great influence from being able to alarm the electors from time to time with the fear

[9]Stephen Van Rensselaer (1764-1839), "the last of the patroons," was a member of his state legislature 1789-1790, 1808-1810, 1818, of the state senate 1791-1795, and Member of Congress 1822-1829. He was a major-general in the War of 1812.

[10]The counties of Albany and Rensselaer were the original tract granted Kilian Van Rensselaer in 1629. The feudal tenure was abolished in 1787. French, *Gazetteer*, p. 157.

[11]Henry Glenn (1739-1814) was Member of the Provincial Congress 1774-1776, Member of Congress 1793-1801, and clerk of Schenectady County 1767-1809.

of his demanding from them the sums due on account of alienation, and rather than run any risk they actually judged it to be more advisable to abstain from offering any objections to the individuals recommended by the Patroon for a seat in Congress or in the State Assembly. It seems, nevertheless, to be surprizing that Mr. Van Rensselaer should content himself with this advantage, when one considers that his forty miles square are equivalent to a possession of above 150,000 acres, and that the principal part of the property subject to fines lay along the River Hudson and is consequently most convenient for commerce.

There were other aristocratic families in New York State but not upon such a scale in respect to extent of possessions. The Livingstones,[12] tho' formerly very rich and owning great landed property between Hudson and Albany, having had to divide it, according to the constitutional law which will not allow of an elder son's share, the jealousy against the English system of inheritance being even stronger in the American states than it is in France. And yet do what they will, either of them, they cannot prevent there being classes in society and the existence of very rich as well as very poor persons, and even if we could arrive at establishing infinite divisions of property among scores of children, how would the inhabitants of towns be supported, how could watchmakers, cabinet makers, coachmakers, etc., etc., and all those who are settled, not on a rich soil, but on granite pavements, contrive to exist?

It is the selfish vanity of paltry little purseholders, without taste or talents, which is at the bottom of it all. They would, if they could, all of them, be lords, and yet what else is the English system but the attempt to regulate this love of distinction natural to man, by urging us to acquire it through honest or honourable deeds of every kind and description? We have a class, of which the main part, it must be owned, has been elevated by accident of birth but it is necessary to have a nucleus somewhere and human imperfection does not admit of a better. Our aristocratic

[12]Prominent Livingstons included Edward (1764-1826), Robert R., Sr. (1718-1775) and Robert R., Jr. (1746-1813).

body, too, requires frequent additions, as well as renewals, and is not encircled with such impassable barriers, as that of France was formerly, or that of Italy and Germany still is, the portals of distinction being thrown wide open in Great Britain where merit of every description or class may find its place and be received within them. While as to the argument that money might be better employed than in pampering rich drones, what will your citizens who live on rich men's orders, say to it?

Besides, setting the individual possessor out of view for a moment, just let us look upon the distribution and effect of wealth as if it were water. There is a certain quantity of this as well as of the other collected and produced out of the same country every year, and in Italy, for instance, an old settled country, under a similar latitude with New York, if they trusted to chance alone for the distribution of that water the soil would soon become dry as I am told it has already become in parts of Maryland and Virginia, and the harvests scant. But the natives of Italy employ reservoirs, aqueducts and sluices where the element is for a while retained to be afterwards by degrees distributed and sold to those who have need of it and will give the necessary quid pro quo. The same quantity would have been produced as well as mined upon the ground without the help of such reservoirs and yet will not every one agree as to the advantage of the arrangement. If that then be good with respect to water which irrigates and fertilizes the plains, why should it not be good in regard to the element which fertilizes or animates the industry of towns as well as their immediate neighbourhood? The same quantity of money is annually produced by the soil, including all its employments, whether in the shape of produce or manufacture and the retention of a part of that money for a while in rich men's hands is like the retention of the water in reservoirs. It is arrested for a season, but flows only the more plentifully, afterwards, through the shops of Bond Street or Cheapside, as well as into the millers', bakers' or butchers' pockets, and from thence to the lowest of the poor, while even the wildest extravagance in the original possessor, such is the beauty of the operation, can be injurious only to himself and the spendthrift. To others who are the first to receive it, the effect must be as of a deluge of gold.

But considerations such as these will long be strangers to the mass of society in the United States, whose artificial irrigation is not yet at least so absolutely required as in the Old World, and it would be very unfair to blame them if they do not possess the same feeling on the subject of aristocracy that we do. We may thank Providence we have had the example, not in England, but among our neighbours, of what democracy of every shade and degree from the Girondists to the Sans-culottes can produce, and we have seen that although the Restoration has not thought proper to revive old laws which ensured the succession of estates to an elder son, yet are all the other distinctions of social order restored, while the concourse of foreign lords to the capital of arts and fashions on the continent of Europe in some degree stands in lieu of and compensates to the Parisian shopkeepers for paucity of wealth in their own grandees.

I visited New York on my way to Boston just before the affair of the *Chesapeake*,[13] which event induced me to take the precaution of sending my curricle on my return care of the groom and to travel myself incognito. Fortunate it was that I did so, for the indignation of some people at New York at the rash act of Admiral Berkeley, was so great they wanted to throw both curricle and horses into the North River and were only prevented from doing so by the mere accident of a reasonable prudent person having happily been a passenger in the ferry boat with them. The ringleader on this occasion was, as might be expected, an Irish emigrant.

I cannot conceive a finer situation for a commercial town than that of New York, a broad river lying on either side of it to the

[13]The American frigate *Chesapeake* was attacked with a minimum of warning and reduced to a wreck by the *Leopard*, acting under orders from Vice-Admiral George Cranfield Berkeley. This was in June 1807. No other act of British arrogance in the relations between the two countries ever brought such a unanimity of national opinion and desire for revenge.

west and south, the latter being an arm of the sea with two islands between it and the great ocean, the other coming in direct course from the north after leaving the neighbourhood of some of the largest lakes in the world and opening a vast internal communication having plenty of rich soil in the immediate neighbourhood. No wonder that the Dutch laid hold of such a position to build on, but though they have good ideas they rarely improve them much. It is not the sole part of the world where we have reaped from what they planted, and raised that which was but a convenient port in their hands to be a great emporium in ours.

Constantinople is the only harbour in the universe that I know of which can be compared with New York. It is likewise situated at the confluence of two great channels, on a point of land easily defended and with even some advantages over its rival from such extensive internal seas as the Euxine and the Sea of Marmora existing in its immediate neighbourhood. But the prosperity of Constantinople belongs to past ages and that of New York to the present. What the latter is now the former may have been. Both cities started from being colonies to become emporiums of mighty empires, but one was nursed by freedom the other by despotism, and while the riches of Constantinople were wasted in barbaric show, her dominions gradually shrunk to the suburbs of the capital. The tide of her prosperity too having once ebbed, has never flowed again. New York on the other hand peaceably pursues her industrious course. Instead of seeing in depopulation a barrier against her enemies, as the Greeks or Turks had learnt to consider it, she has no enemy to contend with but the forests, which still cover nine-tenths of her territory but which are rapidly yielding to the efforts of agriculture stimulated by the immense trade of a vast continent, of which she is the port, the most advantageously placed, in every point of view.

The entrance to the harbour at the Narrows is 1¾ miles wide, but from Long Island shore a bank or reef that runs out in a slanting direction for about one-half a mile and at low water there is but a depth of three to six or eight feet over the reef, so that a battery might be raised upon it that, with a corresponding one on the opposite shore, would leave but the width of 1¼ miles for ships-of-war to pass through.

The Narrows are eleven miles from the town and fifteen from Sandy Hook in New Jersey. But the intention of the government was to place the principal defence of the port at Governor's Island within little more than a mile from the Battery Walk.

I was told that the ground behind this walk on which New York is built was formerly very hilly and uneven, but that the municipality issued a decree by which the inhabitants were directed to cut down the hills for the purpose of filling up the hollows and making all level. When, such was the passion of the Dutch for a flat surface, they over-did the thing, forming marshes in several places where elevations had previously existed.

Two steam vessels were being built under the direction of Mr. Fulton and at the expence of Mr. Livingstone of Clermont at the time of my first visit to New York but they had not yet been launched.[14] The first of them, however, started soon afterwards and went with Mr. Fulton up to Albany at the rate of five miles an hour. They used to stop for a couple of hours at Clermont which is situated sixty miles from the mouth of the river, being an attention to the promoter of the enterprizes that, nevertheless, had to be given up soon afterwards from the effects of competition. In 1811 they already went 170 miles in 23½ hours, there having by that time arisen a strong opposition which interfered a good deal with the profits of the original undertakers. There were then four steamboats on the Hudson and one on the Delaware.

Fortunes were rapidly made by mercantile speculations from this great port. In 1806 Mr. Ogden had just pocketed $18,000

[14]Fulton, in association with Robert T. Livingston, Jr., constructed the *Clermont*, the first American steamship commercially successful, which began in 1807 to ply between New York and Albany. Clermont was the Livingston estate on the Hudson.

net on a small expedition to St. Domingo.[15] He bought flour, at eight dollars per barrel at New York, and sold it there for forty dollars, then bought coffee which he resold at New York at a similarly enormous profit, and if he went on at that rate must now be one of the wealthiest persons in the place. But if the gain was enormous the risk during the war was also immense, although the trade carried on with the West India islands does not appear to have been that which was attended with the most danger, to judge at least from the rate of insurance that even from Martinique to North America amounted to no more than 3½ per cent. While the insurance on a cargo from the East Indies amounted to ten per cent; and yet on a capital of $60,000 employed in an adventure to Calcutta $12,000 of profit was the regular gain to be expected. The rate of insurance for vessels bound to France was at the same period effected for five per cent, where sailing direct from an American port, but if from the Leeward Islands it was nine per cent. And when war was expected between Great Britain and the United States fifty per cent would hardly have procured insurance on a cargo to and from a French port.

It is not necessary to enter into any general statements or speculations in regard to the present or the future extent of the trade of the United States, so many documents and statistical papers having been printed on the subject by Congress or by individuals. I only allude to the matter as one that invites meditation while I own that it presents itself to my mind with a slight tinge of melancholy when I think how much prosperity was ours and how stupidly we lost it. Had we from the first confined the colonists to the pursuits of agriculture or had we treated them with a generous policy and opened Parliament to their deputies on calling upon them to share our expences, or finally had we employed more active generals in the commencement of

[15]The only Ogden listed as importing coffee in 1806 in *Ming's New-York Price-Current* is Samuel G. Ogden. That newspaper, August 9, 1806, notes 3,032 bags of coffee from St. Thomas consigned to Ogden, though there are several larger accounts listed.

the war, the union of the two countries probably would still exist and the French might have made a revolution, if they were to have one, of a different sort. But it was otherwise decreed, and while France sunk into an abyss of misery and vice from whence she will probably never be able entirely to extricate herself—unless she becomes more imbued with religious feelings and that she also abandons the impoverishing laws of property left her by Napoleon—the Anglo-Saxon and Norman race divided into two fractions, apparently favored by Providence beyond all other men, have a double chance of preserving and extending their Christian virtues over at least one half the globe.

New York, before the War of Independence, was in possession of but two-eighths of its own trade, the rest having been chiefly carried on in British vessels. Whereas in Pennsylvania three-eighths of the trade was in the hands of the natives, one-eighth was the proportion in Maryland, Virginia and further south. In New England the inhabitants owned six-eighths of it.

The Report of the Lords of the Committee of Privy Council for Trade, on American Commerce, which was presented on the 28th January 1791, contains statements on the subject that are highly interesting, and from it is seen that by an ancient law, "Goods were forbidden to be imported into, or exported from, any of the colonies belonging to His Majesty in Asia or America except in British ships."[16] Had this regulation been rigidly attended to, and the term "British ships" been limited to those owned by the mother country, maritime rivalry would not in all probability have been mixed up with the political questions or the question of taxation on which we quarrelled. But colonists who navigate have other interests besides those of mere planters and landed proprietors, of whom Jefferson would have wished to see the nation composed in at least its early states. And is it

[16]The source for Foster's figures in the pages following was *A Report of the Lords of the Committee of Privy Council, appointed for all matters relating to Trade and Foreign Plantations, on The Commerce and Navigation between His Majesty's Dominions, and the Territories belonging to the United States of America, 28th January 1791* (London, 1791).

not to be feared that the development of a commercial spirit among our New Hollanders may one day lead to an unripe, for them, and unhappy separation from the parent state, forming perhaps a nation of pirates rather than a wholesome agricultural colony. Although, being even more entirely our own flesh and blood than were the Americans it is to be expected that, however remote from check, they will still be guided by the dictates of common sense and English feelings. For I hold that men are as distinct in race as horses, and that as no doctrines nor constitutions, nothing but crossing the breed can take from an Indian his wild nature, a Spaniard his love of vengeance, from an Italian his need of consideration, a Frenchman his "legereté" (an untranslatable word), an Irishman his rashness, or a Scotchman his habits of calculation, so no combination of circumstances can deprive the true Englishman of his habits of reasoning and his love of justice as well as of seeing justice done wherever he goes. He is fond, it is true, of a grievance and if he has not a row he will sometimes take out his knife to make one, and meddles rather too officiously in his neighbours' politics, but this comes of his hatred of oppression. Give him matter to work on, and he is not bilious, but set him to do nothing and he becomes unruly or commits suicide. He cannot translate the word "ennui" and yet he feels the thing and dies of it, while the Frenchman is no sooner aware of its having laid hold on him than he contrives to shake it off by calling in the aid of his animal spirits for the purpose.

It is interesting to observe in the document above referred to the effect of the loss of America upon the average value of our exports of British manufacture to the United States territories, which on a calculation of six years, was lessened after the close of the war, to £97,133–tho' the same averages, as applied to the remaining colonies in North America gave an annual increase amounting to £293,012. But it was in the shipping interest that our loss must have been chiefly felt, as it appears that for the years 1770, 1771, and 1772 the medium number of vessels, and the tonnage of those vessels entering inwards and clearing outwards in the trade between Great Britain and the United States, was as follows[17]

	Ships	Tons
	663	84,745
while that of the years 1787, 88, 89 was		
of British Ships	261	52,595
Ships of the U. States	163	26,564
	424	79,159

while the difference gradually got to be wider and wider with every successive year. Our remaining colonies however, became more flourishing than ever by the change and the effects of peace, and prevented the loss from being so felt as it otherwise would have been. The quantity of tonnage employed in the trade with them having increased in the proportion of four to one from what it had been before the war, the actual amount in 1789 being stated at 367 ships or 46,106 tons. While the trade with the West Indies was also augmented in the proportion of five-eighths.

There is valuable information on these topics to be also found in a memorial of the Chamber of Commerce of New York presented in the year 1803 to the Senate and House of Representatives of the United States against the abolition of the discriminating duties between English and American ships, in the proposed arrangements of that year between Great Britain and the United States.[18] In this memorial it is stated among other arguments to prove the American trade would suffer from such abolition, that foreigners build their vessels cheaper than Americans can do, and that it appears from actual calculation that a vessel built of European oak will have cost when equipped for sea at the rate of $36.50 per ton, and if built in Finland of fir which is equal in goodness to American oak she will cost when fitted for sea at

[17]Foster's figures on this page are substantially correct, but his figure should have been 86,745 tons of shipping, 1770-1772, instead of his 84,745. He corrects the printed reports addition of figures in number of ships, 1787-1789, given as 425, to the correct 424.

[18]Foster here used *Memorial of the Chamber of Commerce of New York. 24th January 1803 . . . Washington City: Printed by William Duane & Son. 1803* (copy in New York Historical Society).

the rate of $19 per ton. While an American vessel of similar size built of common American oak and by no means so well equipped will cost at the rate of from $40 to $45 per ton and if it be constructed of live oak or cedarwood, the average cost will be from $50 to $55 per ton. The materials composing the ships' equipment were likewise stated in the above memorial to be much cheaper in Europe, where the price of labour is, it is affirmed, fifty per cent less than in the United States in which a ship carpenter could get nine shillings sterling per day. It should be observed also that from $25 to $30 a month was the rate of wages given to American seamen, during the war between France and Great Britain.

To be entitled to vote in the state of New York for Members of Congress, electors of a president or of a governor of the state, a man should be a citizen, possess $100 New York currency, or about £60, and pay taxes. But to be entitled to vote for Members of the State Assembly it was only necessary to be a citizen and to pay the taxes.

It is a singular regulation adopted by this state that a judge, when he has attained the age of sixty years, must resign his office, lest the public should suffer through his infirmities. And I was assured that there actually had occurred an instance of a poor and respected individual being dismissed who was still in full vigour of health, for no other reason than because he was three score years old—and he had been obliged, in quitting the bench, to have recourse to the bar once more for his livelihood.

The regulation in question made a part of the state constitution, and was, I was assured, thought very absurd and disapproved of by every respectable person. But it would be requisite, in order to procure its abolition, that a convention should be called together, and it was feared that this would give rise to great excitement as well as agitation and petitions for changes in other matters.

I was three times at New York, but at a season when many of the best families of the place were at their country houses. I was each time in a great hurry, my first visit having been shortened in the hopes of being able to stay a little longer on my return from New England, but the *Chesapeake* affair made it necessary I should use all speed in hastening back to the Federal City. When I visited it for the third time, it was for the purpose of embarking for Halifax, on war being declared against us, on which occasion I had to wait eleven or twelve days[19] for the sloop-of-war that was sent by Admiral Sawyer[20] for the purpose of conveying me to Nova Scotia. But the moment was then not propitious for social intercourse, and therefore I do not pretend to be able to say much about the manners or habits of the natives. My only resources at that time were the British consul[21] and General Moreau whom I again fell in with here and who invited me to dine with him two or three times. Madame Moreau had sailed for Europe a short time previously, and he had in consequence removed his establishment from Morrisville to New York having a very good cook with him. He talked again a good deal about Bonaparte and the plot for sabreing him on the Parade, as well as of the Russian War, which he fully expected would be his ruin. But he gave me no hint of his intention, if he had formed it at that time, of joining the Allies, though I have no doubt that Rapatel, his aide-de-camp, must have borne his instructions and had full powers to treat for him, when he set out as he did in the spring of this very year, for the purpose of entering into the Russian service.

One feels surprized to find a man of Moreau's rank and illustration using the very improper word, by way of oath or exclamation, which was common to all the lower orders of France civil or military, but I conclude that he had acquired the bad

[19]"Diary," June 30, to July 11, 1812, LC. Foster stayed in New York at Mrs. Welsh's boarding house and saw a good deal of several old acquaintances, including the Abbé Corrêa, General Moreau, Soderstrom, and Siberg. He went on board the *Colibri* on July 11.

[20]Probably Sir Herbert Sawyer (d. 1833), admiral and son of Admiral H. Sawyer (1731?-1798).

[21]Colonel Thomas Barclay, British consul-general from 1799, lived in Haarlem. He entertained Foster twice. "Diary," July 1, 4, 10, 1812. For Foster-Barclay correspondence, see George L. Rives, *Selections from the Correspondence of Thomas Barclay, Formerly Consul-General at New York* (New York, 1894), pp. 300-312.

habit during his campaigns and afterwards found himself unable to get rid of it. However that may be, I never knew a foreigner gentle or simple who used it more repeatedly. Every three or four sentences out it would come. But I must observe that I have many years ago heard even colonels' wives use it in France, and that no sense being apparently attached to the sound, it must be classed with so many other dirty things that one has to shut one's eyes as well as one's ears to in travelling, as if they were neither heard nor seen, and the calling one's attention to which would be of itself an impropriety as great, if not greater than the original sin. . . . *

Moreau had been at New Orleans where he had lodged at Mr. Desforgues' the French consul's. This Desforgues had held a high office in the Department for Foreign Affairs in Robespierre's time, but wisely preferred the humbler but more tranquil station of consul in America.

When I put Moreau on the subject of the campaign just then about to commence in Russia, on which hung the question of liberty or slavery for perhaps the whole civilized world, he said that if the French were to march on Moscow and that he had the command of the Russian army he would let them go on as far as they liked, and then turn and harrass them and waste them down by cutting off their supplies. And in saying so he coincided in opinion with the Prussian General Gneisenau,[22] who gave me his ideas on the subject in writing in 1810 when I left him at Stockholm, where I had the pleasure of being in his company every day until I was myself ordered out of that kingdom at the desire of Napoleon. General Armfeld too was of the same opinion and likewise gave it to me at my desire in writing on the margin of Gneisenau's memorial of which I have the original, having sent a copy of both home to Mr. Canning who was then at the head of the Foreign Office.

*At this point Foster spends above five pages in recording the not very significant comments of Moreau on various Russian and French generals and the handling of troops.

[22]August Wilhelm Anton, Count Neithardt von Gneisenau (1760-1831), Prussian field-marshal.

When I made my first visit to the state of New York Tom Paine was still alive and resided somewhere near Poughkepsie on the North River.[23] He had but a bad character for sobriety, considering his pretensions to be a great reformer of the social world. Before he emigrated to France and became conspicuous in the National Convention he had lodged at Philadelphia in the house of a baker whose daughter he seduced and who was brought to bed in due time of a son, the only one Paine left. After this she married a Quaker who was unacquainted with the above circumstance, and the boy was totally neglected by Paine, to whom frequent application was made by his mother for the purpose of prevailing on him to contribute to his maintenance but it was all in vain. She at length confessed her weakness and appealed to the charitable feelings of the Quaker, who from mere motives of humanity had the youth taken care of and educated, and finally got him employment on board a ship, after which he in good time got to be captain of a merchantman.

Now which was the greatest friend to the Rights of Man and Common Sense, the Quaker or Tom Paine? Cobbett would be the man to decide, who bore away Paine's old bones as relics to Great Britain. For my part, I am persuaded that such is the light in which most demagogues would appear if one went to visit them in their dens to see how they practice what they preached. When the harvest's scant they appeal eloquently to the stomach and would have the nation rush to dependence on foreign lands for its daily food. When the king errs they would cart off monarchy. Not that they care for either theme but as it brings the profits of notoriety for themselves for some newspaper or book, or from mere biliousness and envy like the gentle Robespierre, yet when they are lucky or unlucky enough to outlive the storm, who cares or inquires what becomes of such beings as Wilkes,[24]

[23]Thomas Paine (1737-1809), Anglo-American-French liberal of Revolutionary fame, returned to America in 1802. Foster repeats here some of the usual Federalist gossip about Paine.

[24]John Wilkes (1727-1797), English agitator and reformer, had during the American Revolution supported the colonial cause.

Sieyés,[25] Barrère[26] or this man Paine? Let their days be ever so long, on they go rolling in their own dirt, too contemptible to be observed till some Cobbett comes like an alchemist to grub up their bones for the uses of popularity. Though Cobbett, with all his faults was far too able a writer and too downright a John Bull to need such quackery and probably threw away the ridiculous bundle of which he became ashamed into some public sewer.[27]

A very different character from that of Tom Paine was maintained by the unfortunate Thomas Addis Emmett who was living very respectably at New York, and, as I was assured by Mr. Gallatin who was likely to know all about him (Mrs. Gallatin being a New York lady), never sought to embitter matters with England or tried to irritate the Americans against us during our long discussions and disputes with the United States government.[28] He had been a college friend of Sir Grenville Temple who sailed with me to the Chesapeake in the year 1811, and from whom I heard several particulars relative to his early life. The physician, his father, was a violent republican, as many doctors and dentists are, who love to sport their political theories under shelter of the pulse or in holding your jaw, and at moments when even a Turk must acquiesce. But, not satisfied with talk, Dr. Emmett chose to bring up his children in republican principles, though the eldest broke loose from his trammels and became a lawyer in very good practice, being in the receipt, when he died, of £2,000 a year. Thomas was to have followed his father's profession which is seldom endangered by political storms [and

[25]Emmanuel Joseph Sieyés (1748-1836), French abbé and theorist of the Revolutionary and Napoleonic eras, was apparently as unscrupulous as Foster indicates.

[26]Bertrand Barère de Vieuzac (1755-1841), French revolutionist, had said "the tree of liberty could not grow were it not watered with the blood of kings."

[27]William Cobbett brought Paine's body back to England in 1819. Paine's bones were last heard of in 1854. His gravestone in America had been recovered and a monument erected to him. William M. Van der Weyde, *Life and Works of Thomas Paine* (New Rochelle, N.Y., 1925), I, 456-57.

[28]Thomas Addis Emmett (1764-1827), Irish lawyer and patriot and elder brother of the rebel Robert Emmett, was after 1803 one of New York's leading attorneys. He took a degree in medicine before he decided to study law.

may be said to give a free course to every kind of doctrine by right of prescription]* but he was tempted by the success of his elder brother to try to get into business. It may, however, be conjectured that like Theobald Wolfe Tone, who was candid enough to own in his *Memoirs* that it was from being a briefless lawyer he was driven into rebellion,[29] Emmett also had not sufficient employment at the bar to keep him steady.

Sir Grenville Temple told me that he had been a constant inmate of their house when he was a member of the University of Dublin,[30] and used to have frequent disputes with both Thomas and Robert[31] about Brutus and Caesar when they continually took the part of Brutus. Thomas, Sir Grenville added, had always had a good moral character and was when he knew him true to his principles, however erroneous. One of his tenets was that when a man had applied sufficiently of his fortune to procure a maintenance for himself and his family, the remainder should *not* be considered by him as his own, but should be applied to a common stock for his poorer countrymen. I know not if he still maintains the same argument, now that he has acquired wealth, but perhaps he would rather avoid singularity and say that circumstances are altered, and truly so they are in a great degree as respects paupers who go to America where so much land lies awaiting to be tilled. Emmett, Sir Grenville told me, had been confined a long time at Fort George before he got permission to go out to the United States, because the President had directed Mr. King, then the American Minister in London,[32] to object to the Irish rebel's being sent into exile to any part of the republic.

*Bracketed material deleted from LC version.

[29]Theobald Wolfe Tone (1763-1798), Irish patriot who fought against England in France and visited America in 1795. *The Life of Theobald Wolfe Tone by himself, continued by his son, with his political writings* was published in Washington in 1826.

[30]Presumably Trinity College, Dublin.

[31]Robert Emmett (1778-1803), patriot and friend of Thomas Moore, was captured and executed.

[32]Rufus King (1755-1827) was American Minister in England 1796-1803, 1825-1826.

CHAPTER XX

AFTER a drive of about eight miles through rich landscapes interspersed with rocks and slopes and numerous villas the road leads you over a bridge that connects New York Island at a place called Haerlem with the mainland. Twenty-two miles further on begins New England, and never did land answer better to its name or better bear the comparison of being a scion from its parent tree. If many of our bilious travellers, who, though they come to America to get rid of tyranny, they say, but really of bile, of which they go back with a double portion to Europe, were but half as fond as they pretend to be of honest, simple manners, rural felicity and plain independent good sense, without any mixture of brawling ostentation or the utopian nonsense of ultra-political ranters and constitution-hunters, they might here find ample satisfaction and the accomplishment of all that the march of intelligence can effect with the aid of morality and sound religious zeal. The soil of Connecticut certainly is not the most fertile, but it is perhaps the best cultivated of any in the Union. The inhabitants are a hardy race, very thickly located for America, and the country, which is full of hills and valleys and granite rocks, abounds in beautiful villages with neat little churches, while there is a cleanliness and an English air about everything, even to the labourers who take off their hats in passing you, which one meets with nowhere else on the American side of the Atlantic.

Connecticut

What will surprize our grievance seekers, too, is that this state, though its constitution be perhaps the most democratic in theory of any in the world, is in its relations with the federal government, looked upon as the mainstay of aristocracy, and its deputies were, I believe, to a man the most [un-]compromising opponents of Mr. Jefferson's policy. But order, good breeding and a strict attention to religious duties, which are all qualities universally to be found in this small district, would necessarily pass for aristocratic habits among the "Liberty Boys" of the west, while towards the south the ways acquired by a life spent among slaves, or a boisterous white population—tyrants at home, for the most part, and democrats abroad—are just the very reverse of those which render the people of these parts democrats at home and aristocrats abroad.

Such is the strange contrast to be observed in comparing the politicians of Connecticut with those of Virginia. The latter with Jefferson and Madison at their head were notorious for their democratic tendencies, and even Thomas Moore, the poet, could not endure it, styling it "a Gallic garbage of philosophy."[1] Yet in their own houses were they surrounded with slaves, and John Randolph, who began life by being a demagogue,[2] a course that vanity generally takes as the speediest step to notoriety, since it dispenses with the necessity of having a previous character, John Randolph, I say, assured me that possession of slaves was necessary to the formation of a perfect gentleman, which he held himself to be, and in fact was, in most things, not only as respects the world at large, but also his own slaves whom he treated not merely with the kindness of a gentleman but, as the Irish would say, of a *real* gentleman. Owners of slaves, however, among themselves, are all for keeping down every kind of superiority; and, from being rivals in their own states for the voice of the people, whom they court by dressing and looking like them as much as they can, they frequently acquired tastes and habits more suited to a tavern than a House of Representatives. I am only speaking however of the major part, for there were still many Virginia planters in my time distinguished by their aristocratic air and manners.

But generally speaking one could almost at a glance discern,

[1]This line, as it appears in the 1806 edition of Moore's *Epistles, Odes, and Other Poems* in the poem to Hume, was altered in later versions to "The poisonous drug of French Philosophy."

[2]Of course Foster means that Randolph was originally a strong supporter of Jefferson.

from his superior personal appearance, the Federal Member of the most democratic from the Democratic Member of the most aristocratic state in the Union. The climate and the non-existence of slavery may no doubt account in part for this, but we may likewise trace the difference to a purer descent from English ancestry, unmixed and uncontaminated with French, German, Dutch or any other foreign blood. It is no doubt the good sense which the New Englanders inherited from them that tempers and renders harmless a silly constitution, which given to any other people would probably have long ago set them together by the ears. Of this good sense I need no stronger example than this fact, that although the Members of the State Assembly are elected but for six months, the governor (whose chief power consists in the faculty of giving a double vote) for a year, the judges for a year, while the judges of the Superior Court hold office at the pleasure of the General Assembly, and although even the Secretary of State is elected annually, yet no inconvenience had ever resulted from such absurd provisions, these officers being all regularly re-elected unless in case of resignation or for some very flagrant offence. Nay even the office of Secretary of State may almost be said to have become hereditary since the year 1662, in the family of Mr. Willes whose father and grandfather held it before him and always by annual re-election.[3] The last Secretary was only twenty-one years old when his father died, after having filled the situation for a period of sixty-seven years. But having been brought up to business in his father's office he was unanimously chosen to succeed him, and continued to be re-elected every year for sixty years, when he was succeeded by his son, the gentleman with whom I became acquainted.

The governorship was continued to Governor Griswold, father of the late governor of that name, until he resigned the

[3]Hezekiah Wyllys (1672-1741), Secretary of the Colony, 1712-1730; George Wyllys (1710-1796), Secretary Pro Tem 1730-1734, Secretary 1734-1796; Samuel Wyllys (1738/9-1823), Secretary 1796-1809.

office at the age of eighty.[4] The official income which he received was $1,000, or about £250 per annum.

The Chief Justice had a salary of but $950 per annum.

The Members of the House of Assembly are elected but for six months and have a dollar and a quarter per day during sessions, of which there are two every year, one in May and the other in October, though these sessions do not usually last longer than for three weeks each.

The persons usually elected are lawyers, the law being in this state the high-road to popular favour and there is a sort of rotation observed in the mode of nominating the candidates. The first step of a man who seeks office is to be chosen Member of the state legislature. Then, if he have shown himself to be an orderly respectable person, he is elected Speaker, after which he becomes either a Member of the State Senate, or of the House of Representatives of the United States. When he has gone through the gradations of a Member of both Houses at Washington, he may be considered capable of becoming governor of the state. Some persons of extraordinary talents, as Mr. Griswold was held to be, are allowed to over-step the ordinary rules, and from the state legislature are sent at once to the general Congress.

The seat of government is alternately at Hartford and New Haven.[5] The Constitution like that of Rhode Island had remained the same without alteration from the year 1662, when the charter of Charles II was granted to the colony. Therefore those reformers who maintain that destruction should accompany revolution could never be brought to agree that Connecticut was possessed of a suitable constitution, since she had not assumed one on the Declaration of Independence, but slavishly continued to exist by virtue of a royal charter.

The number of acres of land in the state of Connecticut is 3,000,000, and the number of its inhabitants, when I visited the

[4]Roger Griswold (1762-1812) and Matthew Griswold (1714-1799) were governors of Connecticut 1810-1812 and 1784-1786 respectively.

[5]The original charter of the colony made Hartford the capital, but the honor was shared with New Haven from 1701 to 1875.

country, was said to amount to 250,000. There were seven hundred schools to which all persons had to contribute, and education was given gratis to every individual in the state. [*Note*: There is, I have been assured, an especial arrangement at these schools for bringing up young men to be tutors, in consequence of which no state in the Union is found to supply a greater number than this does of persons qualified to act as such in private families where from any particular reason the parents may wish to keep all or one of their sons at home. It is much to be desired that some young men should be similarly trained to be tutors in our own country, where it is so difficult to meet with a really good one and everybody almost is ready to recommend any worthy person for this most responsible of situations who has been their college acquaintance, let him be fitted or not for imbuing his pupils with the love of study, cultivating their powers of reasoning and reflection. It is no doubt to this system of Connecticut and which is also I believe the system of Massachusetts that New England is indebted for being able to send out so many missionaries to every part of the world.] Every situation of a public nature, by custom, continued to be occupied by the individual who had been in the first instance elected to fill it, until he was found guilty of misbehaviour, resigned it or died. The office even of governor having been so continued, with one exception, that of Governor Griswold (father to the late governor), who became superannuated at eighty years of age.

In this manner Connecticut, in her interior arrangements, and in theory, as before observed, was indisputably the most democratic of states, though practically and exteriorly the most aristocratic, alias federal, of the whole Union.

The sum of $80,000 per annum was allotted by the state government for colleges and schools, and this sum no doubt has been very much augmented, since I visited the American continent, to be in proportion to the increase of the population. For the purpose of levying taxes, it is obligatory on every individual to give in a statement of his income to officers in each township, who are called listers. These officers are supposed to be in general pretty accurately acquainted with the amount of fortune of every person in their neighbourhood. Should he not have given a true account of what he is worth, they are authorized to fix the rate of his income for him, which they commonly do very highly when they have any reason to believe that there was a wish to deceive. This rating is called "dooming," a word apparently derived from the Danes[6] to the natives of Connecticut, who to judge from many names of places and persons in the state originally emigrated here in a great degree from Norfolk and the new northeastern parts of England where once lay the principal Danish strength. So many cents per dollar are levied from each income for the state or church, and the former has besides this a revenue from public stock or land sold in the back countries.

Of all the different sections of the United States, Connecticut is I believe that of which the inhabitants are the most orderly, and in which the laws are most easily enforced. Even duelling is hardly ever heard of here, and it is in fact more strictly forbidden by the laws of Connecticut than by those of any other state, or even I may say of any other country in the world. For any man whatever who is known to have fought a duel becomes from that moment disfranchised, and incapable of filling any office in the land, is fined besides $1,000, and is liable to imprisonment. Such too is the certainty and effect of this severity that for many years a duel had not been heard of within the boundaries of the state, and Dr. Dwight of New Haven[7] even assured me that ever since the first settlement of New England but four duels had occurred within its limits, asserting moreover that he had never been witness at a blow being given by one man to another in any part of the country. While of the four duels alluded to, he said, one had taken place at Plymouth, on the first

[6] The *Shorter Oxford Dictionary* gives only Old English and Old Teuton origins for *doom* in this sense.

[7] Timothy Dwight (1752-1817), poet and theologian, was president of Yale 1795-1817.

arrival of the colony, one in Massachusetts that was fatal, and the survivor of which, a Mr. Millar, was obliged to exile himself. A third was between two gentlemen of New York who had come over the frontier for the purpose of fighting, and a fourth took place between two gentlemen of Connecticut who both of them in consequence had to quit their country to which they neither of them ever afterwards returned.

Quiet and peaceable behaviour as well as civil language, together with a qualification to the value of seven dollars of real property or $150 personal, and an oath of fidelity to the state were in fact all equally necessary to constitute a freeman according to the regulations as well as the practice of this government. Such was the habitual good temper maintained by these rules among all classes of citizens that the innkeepers of Hartford and of Lichfield, who from their situation in life would probably be more in the way of seeing affrays than any other individuals in their respective towns, and of whom I inquired how the people of these parts contrived to settle their quarrels, assured me that they did not know. All they could say was that although one of them had kept house for thirty years, and the other for twelve years, they never in all that time had seen above one drunken man, and he had been to ask for more liquor but was sent away. This I could the more readily believe as I had myself traversed the state in several directions without ever having heard an oath used or seen any fighting. It was even stated to me as a positive fact that during the War of Independence when Whig and Tory feelings ran high in Connecticut, not a single man was slain on either side from vindictive or merely party motives.

The emigration from Connecticut to the westward annually was estimated to consist of ten thousand persons of both sexes, and the district is generally considered as by far the most populous, relative to its surface, of all the United States. The emigrants direct their course chiefly to Ohio or the northwestern parts of the state of New York.

Notwithstanding the reputation of the inhabitants of New

England generally, it would be vain to deny that there are occasionally crimes committed within the limits even of this state and particularly as one of the most rigorous prisons on the continent is situated at a place called Newgate, but about twelve miles from Hartford.[8] This prison was described to me by Mr. Davenport, a Member of Congress,[9] as built over a mine, the prisoners sleeping in cots suspended in the air while the walls are dripping with moisture, and being in the daytime brought up to work at the forges, the hammers chained to their arms. Three crimes alone were punished with death here: murder, arson, and rape. Burglary for a second offence being only punished with perpetual imprisonment. I was assured that the prisoners though so suddenly transferred from the hot air to caves and back again are more healthy than the others above ground.

Whitney was established near New Haven at the time when I was there, and was very busy in executing some simple but useful improvements in the manufacture of muskets, such as making all the locks alike, so that in case of need they might be taken off from bad or decayed stocks and fitted on immediately with ease to those muskets which might want them, though otherwise un-injured.[10] The muskets were formed on the French model and made lighter than ours are, tho' not so long which may be a disadvantage.

This Whitney, being a man of considerable ingenuity, while tutor in a gentleman's family in Georgia, happening to hear it suggested what a useful invention for that state would be a machine for separating upland cotton from its seeds, an operation that had hitherto been a very slow one effected by manual labour, lay awake all the following night thinking upon the subject and in the morning exclaimed to those gentlemen who

[8]The caverns and harrowing relics of the grim Newgate prison are still to be seen near Granby, Connecticut.

[9]John (1752-1839) and James (1758-1797) Davenport were both Members of Congress, the former in Foster's time, 1799-1817.

[10]Discouraged by infringements on his patents on the cotton gin, Eli Whitney began the manufacture of firearms in 1798, introducing the system of interchangeable parts.

had been wishing for such an improvement, that he had found it. One of the persons present, on this, offered him men, money or whatever other assistance he might need to make the experiment, stipulating to receive half the profits in case of success, which it has had in the fullest degree. An estate in North Carolina that, previously to this discovery, was worth but $6,000 by reason of the great manual labour requisite in separating the cotton, having been raised in value by this invention to $20,000. The machine consists of a wooden cylinder with hooks of iron surmounted with teeth moving in contrary directions, with several small brushes to sweep off the seeds, which are large and very adhesive. The machine is a very simple one being turned by the hand, while the cotton is forced through slits in the iron through which the seeds cannot pass.

The appearance of the country all over Connecticut is very picturesque. Rich green turf with large flat or pointed crags of red granite scattered over it, are contrasted in various ways by the sea side with the hills or slopes on which hangs that most graceful of the fir tribe, the hemlock spruce or pinus canadensis, whose branches tipped in the spring of the year with delicate green bunches of young leaves, and bending downwards, form a beautiful drapery that I never saw surpassed. The leaves of this tree too unlike any other of the same species are not prickly, which occasions their being used for bedding by the Indians and by hunters, preferably even to fern. The highroad runs for a considerable distance within sight of Long Island Sound which is nine or ten miles wide, having both its shores equally well wooded.

I stopped early, the first evening, after entering Connecticut at Greenwich, which is thirty-four miles from New York, and I slept at a small wooden tavern kept by a man of the name of McKay.[11] The situation of the place was high and the country pleasing, and I was not at all ill off either for dinner or for a

[11]The McKay Tavern is difficult to identify. There were at least two John McKays in Greenwich at the end of the 18th century, but no evidence that either was a tavern keeper has been discovered.

night's rest. It was delightful to me to feel myself among real Anglo-American descendants of the old English race instead of a motley set of people of whom a great number are generally refugees without care or interest for the country they have left or the country they have come to, and ever ready to strike their tents and proceed further. Here on the contrary there is that look of conservation about everything so peculiar to the English and an appearance of wealth at the farms, numerous broods of poultry straying about, with sheep and cattle grazing in great numbers in the fields, no logs or stumps of trees to offend the eye, and the roads the objects evidently of great attention and labour. Turnpikes it is true are numerous but who would not rather pay than be martyrized as one is to the south and northward?

Companies in Connecticut are formed for the especial purpose of keeping the roads in order, and the operation gives work to numbers of labourers every spring. The roads, however, are in general pretty durable, owing to the rocky foundation of the soil, particularly about Greenwich, which lies but at the distance of a mile from the Sound, the interval being a landscape of grass fields with enormous ledges of rock and here and there a few bushy trees among which I sauntered with delight for two or three hours, enjoying every now and then a view of the ocean which appeared close at my feet from the top of some huge red cliff. The stone is for the most part granite that, being too hard to use for building purposes, appears as it were, left for ornament, while the houses are almost all constructed of wood. The fences, nevertheless, are usually of stone to the exclusion of the zig zag or even straight palisade of the middle and southern states. The villages are composed of houses having gardens, and every village possesses a neat white church with a steeple, the parson belonging to which is maintained by an assessment laid on each individual of the same church according to his means, one or two cents in the one hundred. The parson of Greenwich village in this way obtains between $500 and $600 per annum.

From Greenwich I went to breakfast at Moorhauses[12] in a little village called Saugatuck, on a small river ten miles distant, where I got delicious onions, of the kind which bears its fruits on the stock, dressed in cream. And I afterwards proceeded to New Haven where I stayed for the night, this being a charmingly situated little town, although in appearance more like a village, from the houses being all surrounded with gardens or having large pieces of open ground between them. The view from the Milford road is very fine indeed, several abrupt masses of rock rising immediately behind the town to which they form a magnificent background. The houses are all painted white and the style of architecture is by no means bad, while their being insulated and surrounded with many large trees gives them the appearance of villas in the midst of gardens.

I found too a good inn at this place, Butler's Tavern,[13] which was the first on a large scale that I had occasion to enter in Connecticut, and although the Governor and Council were holding a Supreme Court of Errors while I was at New Haven, and consequently the inn was much crowded, I nevertheless had my bedroom to myself, which indeed I have always contrived to manage since my arrival in the United States. We had a table d'hote, or ordinary, at this tavern which was very well conducted, and in Connecticut one may be always certain of not meeting with vulgar company at such tables—or at least that the majority of the persons present will be well behaved people.

Yale College, called so from its founder, and removed to New Haven in 1716, is one of the oldest colleges in the United States. It has a president and five professors, and there were from 200

[12]Moorhause's was probably either the Morehouse Tavern in Greens Farms, which as a part of Fairfield once ran to the Saugatuck River (*Connecticut Register and United States Calendar . . . 1814* [New London], p. 157), or the Old Connecticut Hotel in Norwalk, which was once under the proprietorship of Banks Morehouse (1830 print, etc., in *Bridgeport Daily Standard*, December 27, 1913). The latter stood at Main and Wall Sts.

[13]Justus Butler's tavern was on Church St., and was in high repute for the excellence of its cuisine. Edward E. Atwater, *History of the City of New Haven* (New York, 1887), p. 390.

to 240 students there who paid $16 each for the first year of their residence and $20 for the next. But I was assured that in order to be able to cover all his expences, a young man at Yale should have an allowance of $200 or even $400. They go to prayers at five a.m. in the summer, and were expected to be at their studies from eight to eleven, when they had to appear at recitation to be examined, and to attend lectures on chemistry and natural history. One o'clock was the dinner hour and at two they went to business again. At six they had to attend evening prayers after which they were left to themselves.

Mr. Hillhouse, a Senator of the United States, lived at New Haven and possessed a considerable property for Connecticut, about 500 to 600 acres. He was said to have Indian blood in his veins, but notwithstanding the disgust for manual labour peculiar to the Indians he was frequently to be seen digging, or breaking stones by the road side. His daughter was a particularly well-educated and wellbred person.

New Haven and Hartford are the two capitals of the state of Connecticut, and neither of them contained much above 7,000 inhabitants. The legislature sat in each alternately. The population of the state is scattered principally in small towns or villages which are very agreeably situated by the sides of rivers or brooks —the richest part lying along the Connecticut, and very fertile it seems to be as well as thickly inhabited, especially between Middletown and Hartford. The country is in general undulating and the heights bounded by thick woods. The public men, lawyers and literary persons are disseminated through the towns. I had a letter for Mr. Alsop of Middletown and found his a very agreeable family, Mr. Alsop himself and his daughter being perfectly well acquainted with the Italian language, and well read in all the books of any note in modern literature.[14] In fact

[14]Richard Alsop (1761-1815), was a minor member of the Hartford Wits. He never went abroad, and his daughters probably never did, but he was proficient in Greek, Latin, French, Italian, and Spanish. The daughters, Frances Marie (1787-1866) and Mary Caroline (1791-1819), were both probably proficient in Italian, though Foster is most likely to have been impressed by the elder at this time. Alsop Papers, Yale University.

I spent one of the pleasantest evenings which I had as yet passed in America, in his house.

I employed seven days in travelling at my leisure through this small state, and I may repeat that in all that time I never met with a single instance of disorderly conduct among the people nor did I hear an oath or see a man drunk. On driving to the taverns even with an equipage (I had a curricle and three horses) I uniformly found that though neither landlord nor waiter came to the door, which, to an English traveller just landed, would perhaps have appeared a sample of careless independence, it was certainly not meant to be so interpreted, for on the contrary they generally give you thanks for your custom when you are about to depart. But it seemed to be a rule of the country not to press a stranger to go in, or to take dinner in their house for fear of trespassing on his arrangements. The readiest attention, nevertheless, is paid to you if you have once knocked at the door and spoken with the master or mistress of the inn, and your dinner is very neatly served up to you, generally by a very cleanly dressed waiting-maid. The custom is to ask travellers what they will have for dinner, contrary to the practice of most other parts of the continent where you must take what is set before you and your fancy is very rarely consulted.

If you are inclined to converse with the innkeeper or with any farmer whom you may chance to overtake while riding on the road, they are sure to be ready to do so, and indeed they are accused of being rather too ready to accost strangers and to ask questions, as proved by the story of Brook Watson's leg that was bit off by a shark. Nevertheless as you will find them well informed about their own state, at least its laws, and mode of cultivation, and as a traveller is not to be supposed to travel merely to look at trees or hills, if he can put question for question he will have made no bad bargain, particularly as he on his side will acquire real information that may be of use and importance to him in more ways than one, whereas the others only satisfy their curiosity to learn from whence he comes and whither he goes or some such innocent matter. Some persons questioning me about my horses used a word, which I thought I never had heard before as an English word, viz., *span*. "Where did you get that fine span of horses?" they said, meaning a pair of horses.[15] It is a word, however, of Danish origin and perhaps came from Norwich where one sees many a Danish name over shop doors, but *span* in Danish means four pair of horses. The King of Denmark has his different breeds divided into spans of eight each.

The Connecticut people have a characteristic feature which I think is easily discernible and presents a sharp expression of countenance and a peculiar breadth of forehead.

Norwich is a very pretty romantically situated little town near the falls of the Norwich River, which are beautiful and are the subject of several of Trumbull's best landscapes. He was of this state and has been already mentioned as a good historical painter. The country round about is rocky and well wooded and in travelling along I met multitudes of children going to or coming from school, when they would stop quite short, take off the hat or curtsie, and even the grown lads make their bows and always say, Sir, in speaking to you.

The difference between the manners of the people of this state and those of its next neighbours whom you become acquainted with at about seven miles beyond Plainfield, is prodigiously striking. You soon discover that you have bid adieu to the painted house, the neat dress of the women and children, their little bows and smiling countenances.

I have heard that since my departure from the United States in 1812, clamour and the excitement caused by the war has at length triumphed over the good sense of Connecticut and that a majority had been found passionate enough to trample under foot the rude old democratic constitution of this state which however originally defective had become polished and well

[15]The *Shorter Oxford Dictionary* gives Dutch or Low German origin for *span* in this sense, and gives the U.S. origin for usage in reference to a team of horses or two matched horses. See, however, H. L. Mencken, *The American Language: Supplement I* (New York, 1945), 190.

adapted to their use, being one of those changes that are sometimes easily accomplished by even a minority at first very insignificant, when the youth of the country is roused to join in the hunt with a few demagogues who have purposes of their own to carry.[16] For as in a healthy condition of things the young men are too much under the influence of their families to render it easy for the ambitious to lead them into their private schemes, it is only in an epoch of rage and excitement that the thing becomes practicable. Therefore it is that revolution and war are ardently desired by bold designing men, who have little to lose and everything to gain by desperate lotteries. For the real majority, which is in fact at such times weak, being no longer listened to, must go to the wall until their opponents become calm once more, sated with gain or stilled by death.

The measure then of changing the constitution has no doubt been carried into effect and as no return to the former state of things is now to be looked for, we only hope that the habits of the people of Connecticut which were found to have been too strongly rooted to take injury from a bad constitution made good afterwards by friction, will be equally unaffected by useless innovation, and that, like their English prototypes, they will laugh at the occasional attempts which are made by temporary majorities to alter their habits or their morals by altering their laws.

[16]Though the Federalists dominated Connecticut for a generation, the development of manufactures, the discontent of non-conforming religious sects with the establishment, and the confusion of the executive, judicial, and legislative branches of the government in the constitution opened the way after the War of 1812 for a political revolution. In 1817 all the discontented elements united with the Democratic party and defeated the Federalists in the state election. In 1818 the existing constitution was adopted.

CHAPTER XXI

THE FARMHOUSES of the state of Rhode Island appear to great disadvantage on leaving Connecticut, being as dirty in appearance as the inmates are grossly ignorant, and there was not a church to be seen for the space of twenty-three miles from the frontier nor until within a short distance of the city of Providence.

Rhode Island

This city is beautifully situated on each side of a river bearing the same name and just at the head of Naragansett Bay. It is a flourishing commercial town and is already more populous than Newport, the capital of the state. The streets rise above each other and there are four or five lofty white steeples to as many churches, which with numerous groups of trees scattered through the place, and a variety of water prospect, give it a gay and animated appearance. The inns or taverns of Providence are upon the worst possible footing. At that which was esteemed the best I had the honour of supping tête-à-tête with my dirty host, Mr. Ammidon, who came to the table in slippers with his hair uncombed.[1] I had purposely contrived to arrive late in order to escape a mob of all descriptions that was in the habit, as I had learnt, of coming there every day to eat at table d'hote in a room the door of which opened into the kitchen. While we were still at supper the driver came in swearing and cursing, to settle his accounts with the host, and never stirred his hat from his head, nor ceased giving free vent to his stomach while he remained. This was all new to me, much as I had been used to familiarity in other districts, and to escape more of it, I set out in the packet for Newport which is about thirty miles from Providence, leaving my carriage and horses among the beasts of

[1]Ammidon's Tavern was well known in Providence history for 150 years. It included a ballroom, and was a fashionable gathering place. Sidney S. Ryder's *Book Notes*, V, xxvi, 66, in *Rhode Island Hist. Coll.*, XIX (Jan. 1926), 8, 108.

the inn, and trusting to get back in a stagecoach, by which means I should see more of the humours of the country.

I found, however, the same complete easiness of manner and practical equality in the other parts of this state. For at Bristol, where we stopped to dine, I had not only the company of my host, who was a farmer, at table, but that of the coach driver, who to my astonishment sat himself down very unceremoniously alongside of me, and the hostler of the tavern. We conversed about the markets, a subject on which I imagined they would all be at home. But the farmer, Mr. Birkely, assured me that he and the other farmers, his neighbours, cared not one straw for either the markets of Newport or of Providence, for that he and they, every one of them, carried their own produce to their own tables, which put me in mind of a shabby genteelly dressed Irish tenant, with a lease for life, whom I remember near Drogheda, that used to walk about among his turkeys in a dingy black coat with his hands in his breeches pockets and tell one that he cared not a d——n for Drogheda market, that he eat his turkeys himself and wanted nothing from nobody.

In Rhode Island, however, it must be owned that they live in great abundance and great ease, and if they would but be clean and civilized, no one would find fault with their familiarity. Freedom and vulgarity however are not good or bearable together, especially when the latter is dirty, greasy and stinking. It should at least be shamefaced and not seek display before a foreign gentleman.

The nonchalant humours nevertheless and perfect unconcern of these Rhode Islanders as to how time passes, or as to whatever they may be about, is very amusing when one is not in a hurry, as no traveller would be who likes to observe the national peculiarities of the people he is among. The packet was notified to sail at nine in the morning from Newport, being the hour when the tide would be perfectly favourable. Nevertheless the sailors with dawdling, and joking and picking their teeth contrived to delay it for a full hour and a half, when I ventured to put the question why they did not profit by the tide especially as there was no wind, and they were bound to go back to Providence that day. The captain negligently replied, "Oh! what you say is very true. It would be as well to profit by the tide which is in our favour, but it is too early for us," and again he used his toothpick. Perhaps in despair at the idleness of his men tho' he did not employ the Norfolk pilot's exclamation, "For the love of Jesus boys let out the mainsail." The mail stage in consequence of these fellows loitering, became my only resource, but it took me nine hours to go by it from Newport to Providence, a distance of not more than thirty-one miles, one of the drivers choosing to repose at every separate tavern, while he complained a good deal of the fatigue and of cold although he only drove for eighteen miles and it was the 20th of June in about the fortieth degree of latitude. He always left his horses standing before the door while he would come into the inn to the best room in it to sit along with the passengers. Before I left Newport I wanted to get a boat to sail about the harbour, and the owner of one, a young active-looking fellow, after keeping me waiting for a considerable time at length came to the room of the inn where I was sitting, and yawning in my face told me he believed he had got the rheumatism complaint and that his wife wished him not to go; that, however, I might have his boat but I must go and request somebody to manage the sails for me.

The mail stage was to start in the morning, but the driver was an hour past his time owing as he told me to his having waited so long in order to get his watch mended.

Nobody hereabouts seemed to care about news or having early intelligence of any occurrence, notwithstanding I was assured that there was a good deal of trade at Newport. But the people appear naturally careless and lazy, as well as inattentive to their interests, or from having an abundance of everything absolutely necessary, not to think it worth while to give themselves trouble to please other persons. While as to the vulgar familiarity of manner observable both at Newport and Providence I do not think that even Mr. Ammidon in his hat and slippers or Mrs. Ammidon, who was used to bring down the new caps, in which she said she looked so cute and smart, to show them to the lady travellers' table, meant anything intrusive by such annoyances, both having the appearance of being quite unconscious of any deficiency of good breeding in themselves, which was in fact to be attributed to ignorance or want of a good example rather than to affectation, and was evidently not the offspring of a desire to be rude. I even thought the drivers and hostlers more objects of laughter than disgust, and their humours much more easy to be put up with than those of the same class of people in Pennsylvania or the states further south where it is perhaps some whining Scotch refugee, or red-faced Hibernian emigrant who stretches out his paw to you with an air of protection. They too often give the tone to the manners of the natives themselves, in many parts of the country, as the Germans do in others.

Rhode Island at the period I speak of had but two Representatives in Congress and the constitution of this state which was every way democratic, except as regarded the Senators at Washington who were Federalists, had not been altered from what it was prior to the Declaration of Independence—being still governed under its charter.[2]

The House of Assembly consisted of seventy members and met four times a year at Newport, the capital, which although inferior in commercial importance to Providence, is of very great consequence as a naval station and is capable of being strongly fortified. Fort Adams is situated on an island in front of the town and is about one mile distant from it. Within the island or between it and Newport, tho' not quite up to the wharf, ships of one thousand or twelve hundred tons can lie very safely, while on the other side without it, there is depth of water for any size ships and a safe anchorage. The port is easy of access too for foreigners even without a pilot, as they have only to keep at about

[2]Rhode Island did not get a new constitution until 1842, and there was no general enfranchisement of all non-freeholders until 1888. Despite Foster's assertion that the old constitution was "every way democratic," it had so established proportionate representation between towns and cities that the artisan class of the larger cities was virtually disfranchised.

one-quarter of a mile from every shore and they may be sure of not touching either rock or shoals. Providence at the head of the bay, and which has been already described as being thirty miles distant from Newport, cannot be approached nearer than the mouth of the River Seekonk, which is about a mile below the town, nor by ships of above five or six hundred tons. The bay is like a little archipelago, containing twelve or thirteen islands large and small, almost all of them fertile and well cultivated.

The judges of the Supreme Court, from whom an appeal lies open to the Legislature, are elected annually by the people. The Chief Justice in former times was allowed a salary of $600 (about £134) per annum, but this has been since cut down to $400, and he was not allowed to take fees. It must be owned, however, that he has been led by such bad pay into the temptation of not refusing them.

The inferior judges enjoyed salaries of $200 each. Any contract that might be made between a clergyman and his parish in any part of this state, for the support of the former, was by law declared null and void. Voluntary support of a parson was however, permitted, tho' like that which existed in Maryland, the amount raised thereby was precarious while it was, even when paid, much less considerable than is given in the latter state.

As an instance of how justice was administered under such excessive economy, it may be mentioned as a notorious fact, that when Mr. Greenleaf[3] obtained a divorce in this state in order that he might be enabled to marry Miss Allen, the only pleas advanced as a ground for its being granted were his wife's absence in Holland, and that she deceived him in telling him on their marriage that she was but thirty years old when she was in reality thirty-five. No evidence nor any pleading in her interest was either heard or waited for by the judges, so that if this

[3]Probably James Greenleaf, who divorced his first wife to marry Ann Penn Allen. Not himself a resident of Rhode Island, Greenleaf probably stayed with his brother Robert in East Greenwich, R.I., while obtaining his divorce. Jonathan Greenleaf, *Genealogy of the Greenleaf Family* (New York, 1854), p. 75, and James Edward Greenleaf, *Genealogy of the Greenleaf Family* (Boston, 1898), p. 101.

be considered as a sample of Rhode Island justice the saving of a few hundred dollars a year in the judges' salaries may after all be a dear bargain to the community. Tho' out of a court of justice the French proverb might perhaps be quoted as applicable to the above case, "que les absens ont toujours tort."

CHAPTER XXII

THE MANNERS and habitations of the people of Massachusetts resemble in a great degree those of Connecticut. The state is laid out in townships and the regulations for schools are similar; but villages and single farmhouses are not so frequent here as they are in Connecticut, nor are the turnpike cross-roads as numerous. There is more too, I think, of the bluntness of republicanism rather than its urbanity to be observed in the men of Massachusetts.

Massachusetts

The country along both sides of the way from Providence to Boston, which is a distance of about forty miles, is very woody and rocky, but the road, although a turnpike road, was not kept in very good order.

Boston is situated on a promontory in the shape of a long pear that has had two pieces near the stalk bit out of it, and the neck of land which connects it with the main land bears about the same proportion to the site of the town that the stalk does to the pear. This is perhaps the most romantically situated town in the United States, and presents a great variety of points of view from the irregularity of its buildings as well as of its shape. There are hills within its boundaries of from 400 to 500 feet in height and on one of them is the State House, a large brick building with a raised portico and crowned with a cupola. It is not an elegant piece of architecture but yet from its prominent situation and general appearance at a distance, it is a great ornament to the scenery, while from the cupola there is a superb view of the town, the harbour, with its numerous islands, and the adjacent country to a very considerable distance. Along the shore and the wharfs warehouses have been built upon regular plans, but like all masses of mere brickwork, long, and low in proportion, they are very uninteresting sights. Towards the neck of the promontory there is a considerable open space in grass called the Park, along which is a public walk under two rows of trees.

On the opposite side is the State House and the hilly part of the town where the rich merchants and lawyers have built houses for themselves which from the steepness of the hills stand in general apart from one another, and being of a good size with gardens to almost all of them, give a very favourable idea of the opulence of Boston as contrasted with that of either Philadelphia or New York, where in general the dwelling houses are narrow and confined.

Boston contained in 1806 from about 50,000 to 60,000 inhabitants. There is sufficient depth of water in the harbour for frigates and the entrance lies between two islands that are but one mile and a quarter from each other, of which distance one half is shallow water, so that all ships of any size must pass within little more than one-half a mile of the batteries on Castle Island.

These batteries are extremely well attended to and in perfect order and I was told by General Dearborn, then Minister of War, that there was no spot where a ship could lie at anchor completely out of cannon shot.

There are twenty or thirty islands large or small in front of Boston, but unfortunately for the view they are all bare of trees, otherwise they would be a great ornament to the city.

The hospitality of Boston is proverbial, and the dinner-giving Bostonians are commemorated in some of the national dramas. From its remote situation and the not being so much the resort of strangers as other cities of the Union, arises, probably, in some degree this amiable and social disposition. Even in the middle of summer, when nearly all who can afford it are in the country, I received invitations on invitations to their houses, and a sincere welcome. Nowhere on the continent were the ladies better educated or better looking. Mr. Gore,[1] who had been employed as commissioner in London with Mr. Pinkney,[2] lived nine miles

[1]Foster refers to Christopher Gore (1758-1827), chargé d'affaires in London 1803-1804 and governor of Massachusetts 1809, as well as U.S. Senator 1813-1816.

[2]William Pinkney (1764-1822) was in London, 1796-1804, as commissioner to determine claims of American merchants under the Jay Treaty of 1794, and in 1806 and 1807-1811 as commissioner with Monroe on the capture of neutral ships and as U.S. Minister.

from Boston during summer, and had a very handsome comfortable house,[3] besides possessing a spacious town residence for winter. He was a lawyer of first-rate eminence. Mr. Mason,[4] Mr. Quincy, a Member of Congress, distinguished for his eloquence, in whose family I passed many an agreeable evening at Washington, and who has since become president of the University of Cambridge, lived in very good style. The latter introduced me to his cousin the old President of the United States, J. Quincy Adams,[5] then seventy years old, and who was living at Braintree, about nine miles from the town, where I went to visit him. But his voice was enfeebled by age and he appeared much broken so that I had but a short tête-à-tête with him. He told me that he considered the King (George III) the greatest statesman in his kingdom, and that he thought the Prince of Wales, if he did not imitate and follow in the track of his father when he should succeed to the throne would be made a cypher of by the aristocracy which he appeared to consider as almost entirely composed of the Whig party. He believed, he said, that England had a great deal more to fear from a combination of such aristocratic influence than from democracy or from royalty.

In conversing with him on the avidity for office to be found in general amongst all men, but particularly amongst canting philanthropists and pretenders to superior religious purity, he cited Dr. Priestley[6] as an instance, the doctor having had the assurance to ask him, when he was President, to appoint him one of the Commissioners for treating with the French government, at the time when Chief Justice Marshall and Mr. Gerry were

[3]Gore's mansion at Waltham was rebuilt between 1794-1804, probably by Charles Bulfinch.

[4]Jonathan Mason (1756-1831), U.S. Senator 1800-1803 and later State Senator was one of a syndicate which in 1795 bought and developed the southwest slope of Beacon Hill and turned it into a fashionable residential section.

[5]Foster of course refers to John Adams (1735-1826), not to his son John Quincy Adams (1767-1848).

[6]Joseph Priestley (1733-1804), English chemist and non-conformist minister who emigrated to the U.S. in 1794.

named for the purpose.[7] He told Mr. Adams as a reason for his making this request that his son's affairs had gotten into disorder, and that as he was not able to afford the expence of going to Paris at his own cost, it would be a great kindness on the President's part to send him there in a diplomatic situation. Dr. Priestley was of course refused as what government would employ a foreigner in such a confidential office? But Mr. Adams added that he was so offended at his non-success on this occasion he very soon afterwards took a warm part against the President personally, and probably contributed not a little to prevent his re-election.

The university of the state of Massachusetts is at Cambridge three miles from Boston and has a very great reputation. It stands in a very pretty village and consists of three ancient looking brick buildings with a small chapel annexed to them. It is the oldest establishment of the kind in the United States. The young men have no particular costume. One of the professors told me that it required $500 or about £112 per annum to cover all the expences of a student, and I even understood from Mr. Norris of Salem that his son without being at all extravagant, had cost him $1,100 or $1,200 a year while at this college, which is nearly as much as a commoner can be well maintained for at Oxford. Two dollars a week however, was the common price of boarding at Cambridge which does not seem much, and leaves one to suppose that the extras were very numerous. A history of this university from its foundation is expected from the pen of Mr. J. Quincy its actual president and cannot but be very interesting to the literary world of Great Britain as well as America.

Land about Boston appeared to be of very high value as I could not hear of any in its neighbourhood to be bought for less than $200 the acre, while as much as $500 was frequently given for some of particularly good quality.

I was told that about £30,000 a year was the sum raised in

[7] John Marshall (1755-1835), later Chief Justice of the U.S. Supreme Court, was in 1797-1798 in France, with Charles Cotesworth Pinckney and Elbridge Gerry (1744-1814), as commissioner to adjust differences between the U.S. and the Directory. This was the "XYZ Affair," which resulted in the prompt return of Marshall and Pinckney to America.

taxes throughout the state of Massachusetts. Every individual was bound to inform the collector of the amount of his income. Otherwise he was to be assessed at the rate which that officer might think fit to impose, which operation was called "dooming." Nor could the tax payer complain whatever might be his "doom," unless he chose to lay open his account books, for the purpose of proving that he was overcharged. A certain per centage is then imposed as a tax upon each dollar of income, but the assessor was understood to be bound to secrecy. Besides the amount of the sum produced by taxation, Massachusetts possessed funded property.

Clergymen in this state had salaries of from $200 to $300 a year on an average. Many were said to have incomes of as much as $1,000 a year, each, and there was even one of the Episcopal Church in Boston, who was in the receipt of not less than $2,000, or £475 per annum.

There were seventeen Representatives in Congress from Massachusetts in 1806; and in the State Assembly there were three hundred Members of the lower house, while the upper house consisted of from sixty to seventy Senators—one Representative per 150 families being considered as a fair proportion.

The constituents were under the obligation of paying the travelling expences of their deputies, while the state paid for their lodging and maintenance, the daily cost of which was estimated to be about five shillings. The governor was elected directly by the people, but when a majority of votes could not be obtained for any one individual the election was referred to the Legislature. The Democratic party at the time when I visited Boston had a majority of sixty in the lower house and of one in the Senate.

I heard a great deal of the speculation of the commercial house of Tudor and Co. of Boston, just then undertaken for the purpose of supplying the West Indies with ice, and by which they expected to realize a large fortune.[8] One of the brothers had even

[8]Frederic Tudor (1783-1864), "the ice king," with his brother William began business with the West Indies in 1806.

hopes of getting an exclusive privilege from the Spanish government for the supply of the Spanish colonies with that article, while the other brother had just gone to England to endeavour to get a patent to secure their interests in the British colonies. A cargo of ice had meanwhile actually arrived at Jamaica and with very little loss from the hot weather, having been buried under heaps of chips and lumber and charcoal. Mr. Tudor sold it at a high price and for several days he was followed in the streets of Kingston by crowds of men and boys pointing to him as the man who had brought the cold lumps of water to the island.

Mr. Braidwood, son of Mr. Braidwood, principal of the deaf and dumb school at Edinburgh, came to Boston while I was there for the purpose of establishing a similar school in Massachusetts.[9] He told me that he already knew of above 160 deaf and dumb individuals in that single state, which he stated to me in the presence of an American citizen who had been boasting of the exemption of America from such ills and of the superior nature in that respect of the native of the United States.

The people of Massachusetts have been too wise to remove the seat of government from Boston for the sake of propitiating the Democratic party. It is probably to the circumstance of this city uniting all the qualities of a real capital, which enables the opinions of respectable persons to act less indirectly than elsewhere upon representatives of this state, that we may in a great degree ascribe the superior intelligence with which public business is here conducted and the superior credit enjoyed by the state in its pecuniary transactions, the five per cents being here at par while at New York they are much lower.

[9]Presumably Mr. Braidwood was the son of Thomas Braidwood (1715-1806), founder of the first school in Great Britain for the deaf and dumb, at Edinburgh, in 1760. Foster certainly visited Boston in 1807. Foster Letter Books, LC.

CHAPTER XXIII

I KNOW too little of the states of Vermont and New Hampshire to make my observations in regard to them the subject of two different chapters.

Vermont had but four Representatives in Congress and New Hampshire but five, tho' I conceive that since I was in New England the number of their Members in the national parliament may have been very considerably augmented.

Vermont and New Hampshire

The legislature of New Hampshire is an itinerant assembly. It meets twice a year and at each period in a different town, for the benefit of the innkeepers and tradespeople to whom the expence of the Members is an object. The archives, however, are stationary, being kept at Exeter, which is nearly fifteen miles distant from Portsmouth, a town of about 7,000 inhabitants, and which is generally regarded as the capital of the state. The governor lived there, but that was from choice, and because he had a house in the town. Otherwise he might choose his residence where he liked within the state. Portsmouth has a noble harbour, that from the rapidity of the stream on which it is built, is open at all seasons to navigation, and is one of the nine principal ports of the United States.

In the state of New Hampshire the whole number of the citizens vote for each individual representative of the state in the Congress of the United States.

The Chief Justice has $1,500, or not quite £300 per annum, and the judges have each $1,000 a year.

I was assured by Mr. Latrobe, the architect, that there exist in the state of Vermont some white marble quarries which for quality equal the Pentelic and are superior to the Carrara marbles. They lie near the Lake Champlain, and the marble might be conveyed to Washington by water for the whole distance, with the exception of one single portage of not more than ten miles width.

CHAPTER XXIV

MAINE was at this time a province of the state of Massachusetts, though it has since become a state itself, and an important one, from its frontier position as well as the possession of one of the nine capital harbours of the United States, viz., Portland. The limits of the republic in this direction were, unluckily, not defined before Maine became independent, and every succeeding year has more distinctly shown the bad policy of such procrastination from the increase of hatred and ill will which it produces between the borderers both British and American. Nor is it perhaps, to be expected from human nature that such feelings, founded on self interest, should subside without a quarrel, although I think, with proper management, that a mode might be found of satisfying all parties if they are really disposed from the love of peace as well as motives of humanity, to be satisfied. That would be an agreement on the part of both governments to buy up all the individual interests involved in the question at issue. Parliament and the Congress may perhaps be still able to do this cheaply, and then, from having proprietary possession of the lands, they might mutually concede portions of them to suit each other's consciences—a few miles more or a few miles less of territorial possessions being a trifle to great nations tho' of immense importance to private individuals. This expedient will not, however, be adopted, in all probability, from the dread of responsibility on the part, more especially, of the federal government, while official men on both sides have already shown themselves but too happy to shove off from their own shoulders every embarrassing business in order to transfer it to the shoulders of their successors.

Maine

I have been told that when after the establishment of the independence of the United States it became necessary to run the boundary line (which was so incompletely done), directly north to meet the River St. Croix at its source, the commissioners who were first employed on this business, to their great surprize came suddenly upon a settlement of about thirty families which were evidently thrown into the greatest consternation by their approach, the women and children running and screaming, while men who from their wild attire might have been taken for Indians, had not their colour betrayed their European origin, were seen arming themselves with sticks for defence. Luckily one of the youths fell down and was laid hold of by the commissioners' party, and on being interrogated by signs, or in English, to their great astonishment, exclaimed in excellent French that he did not understand their meaning, on which an interpreter was immediately procured and the mystery was explained.

The settlement was French and had been cut off from all communication with the civilized world for about forty years. From the time when the British having taken Acadie from the French in the Seven Years War, determined to remove the inhabitants to Falkland Islands, at that period and on this decision becoming known, several families of poor fishermen–unwilling to quit the continent, or desiring to remain in the neighbourhood, at least, of the country of their birth–resolved to emigrate in secret to the opposite coast. After getting together a number of boats for the purpose, they stole away in the night time across the Bay of Fundy, steering for the river facing their own shores. They then rowed up that stream as far as they could go, till they at last landed in a sequestered valley where they built cottages for themselves, and lived unknown to any but the Indians who kept their secret and supplied them with tools, as well as all they needed of European articles which they were able to procure from traders whom they visited from time to time. These colonists had no regular government, but appeared perfectly simple, mild and innocent and to have a great respect for their old men. A generation had thus almost entirely passed away and when the commissioners at length broke in upon their solitude, their first impression, founded upon old recollections, was that their enemies had at length found them out and they became dreadfully alarmed from thinking they were all to be transposed to Falkland Island.[1]

I shall in referring to Maine again only repeat my earnest hopes that the unreasonable pretensions of this state, joined to the rowing bullying humour of its neighbors on the northern line of frontiers, may not lead to a fresh quarrel with us. But if it does do so, I am convinced such quarrels will have bad consequences for the whole Union, inasmuch as, by giving a temporary triumph to the noisy turbulent portion of the people, it will at length fully expose the weakness of the central government, and rouse up the old English good sense of the eastern states to act at length for itself. Then the Congress must either listen to its dictates, or its authority will fall to the ground altogether and a new and powerful government, royalist or republican, will be raised into existence on its ruins that all the remaining force of the United States would fail of being able to over-awe much less to subdue, and which if joined by New York and New Jersey might impose laws on the whole continent.

[1]Fort Kent in Aroostock County, the northernmost in Maine, was settled in 1784 by Acadian French refugees from Nova Scotia in 1755, as described in Longfellow's *Evangeline*. These were probably the people encountered by the commissioners. Maine Writers Research Club, *Maine Past and Present* (New York, 1929), 214-15.

CHAPTER XXV

I EMBARKED from New York for Halifax in Nova Scotia on board the sloop-of-war *Colibri* carrying eighteen 24-pounders, and commanded by Mr. Thomson, master and commander, who had served for twenty-three years as his father, he told me, had done before him for fifty-seven years. He was with Sir Home Popham on the expedition against Buenos Aires and commanded the gunboats when the Spanish force attacked General Beresford.[1] He was taken prisoner along with Beresford and was carried 1,000 miles into the interior of the country towards Potosi, having been as far as Cordova, over immense plains and prairies without a tree, but covered with droves of cattle, whose throats the soldiers cut with their swords, skinning the prostrate animals on the spot and carving dinners out of them. There were seventy or eighty British officers carried up the country on this occasion, who were kept to be exchanged and to enable the Spanish authorities to negotiate good terms with General Whitelocke, of the possibility of whose failure they never dreamed—and they were released when that General withdrew.[2]

Return to England

The *Colibri* having landed me in Halifax, I then embarked on board the sloop-of-war, *Atalanta*, of which Mr. Hickey was captain, for England on the 23d July. This ship was built of cedar at Bermuda—being a species of timber that is the most liable to splinter in action. This we heard for our comfort just as it was expected we should have a fight with the largest of the American frigates, the *President*, which was in reality a 64-gun ship, tho'

[1]Sir Home Riggs Popham (1762-1820), British admiral, was especially useful in cooperating with military forces in what we call "joint operations." In 1805-1806 his forces and those of General William Carr Beresford, Viscount Beresford (1768-1854), captured Buenos Aires but were unable to hold it.

[2]General John Whitelocke (1757-1833) commanded the expedition sent to recover Buenos Aires, which Beresford had been compelled to surrender. He proved incompetent and was later court-martialed, but much can be said in his defense.

called a frigate.[3] It was towards sunset that we observed in the mist and upon the horizon what we took to be our formidable foe, commanded by Commodore Rodgers,[4] who was known to have sailed so soon as war was declared, with a considerable squadron, for the purpose of intercepting the homeward bound West Indian trade that usually makes the latitude of Newfoundland at this season. So persuaded was Captain Hickey of the frigate we saw being an enemy that he summoned all his men upon deck, and being determined, with true British spirit, to measure his twenty-eight guns against the other's sixty-four, as well as not to be outdone by Captain Bingham of the *Little Belt*,[5] he made a speech to the crew which ended with a proposal that they should leave their hammocks on deck, for the night, in order to be ready for action with the dawn of day. He urged them to consider whom they had on board to bear witness to their conduct, and that they should behave with even more than their usual spirit in the presence of so many distinguished passengers, including the governor of Bermuda, (Sir James Cockburn),[6] General Bayley,[7] the Consul General (Colonel Barclay) and myself.

Sir James drew forth an Andrew Ferrara[8] on the occasion, and we all put on as bold a front as we could, but were delighted beyond expression when the suspected frigate was early on the following morning announced to be His Majesty's ship *Pomona*. Our bulkheads had actually been taken down, the boxes stowed away, and it had been coolly discussed whether it was more ad-

[3]The "frigate" *President*, of 44 guns, like her famous sister ships, was a raider, lighter and faster than the British frigate-class vessels.

[4]John Rodgers (1771-1838) had as recently as 1811 cut to pieces the British *Little Belt* with what the British called deliberate aggression. At this beginning of the War of 1812 he was placed in command of a squadron. He might well have made the British sailors nervous.

[5]The *Little Belt* was a mere corvette, commanded by A. B. Bingham.

[6]Sir James Cockburn (1771-1852), was governor of Bermuda 1811-1819.

[7]There were two generals named Bayley in the army at this time. Of them only Thomas, deputy assistant commissary general, could have been in America at this time. Actually Foster's Notebook (LC) for this period refers to *Captain* Bayley.

[8]The HEH version of the "Notes" reads "an old Ferrara."

visable for gentlemen passengers to stay in the poop or to go on deck during the action with risk of being mitraillés.

An officer too had a few days before been relating the adventures of Sir William Drummond[9] on board H.M.S. *Minorca*, which was conveying him to Sicily in quality of British Minister at the Neapolitan court when the *Minorca* was attacked by twelve gun boats from Tangiers and Sir William and his butler hid in the hold. The gun boats continued their fire during five hours. Sir William, having judged the quarter deck to be too dangerous a station, went and buried himself, with his butler Fuschini, in the captain's wine cellar, having put on his winter uniform with star and ribband, in the idea that he would, if the ship were captured, obtain more respect by exhibiting these proofs of his rank and quality. But, when, on a breeze springing up, the *Minorca* moved out of shot, and he appeared on deck in his fine dress with powdered hair, Fuschini behind him trembling and perspiring thro' fear, the tars stared and hollowed out, "What D—–d are these and where the Devil did they come from?" Till seeing the crew giggling and whispering he went down again, and got into a larger ship at Gibraltar which he reached on the following day.

As this story had been much laughed at, and we had all joined in the laugh, it was impossible to talk of anything but fighting. I must confess however I have seldom enjoyed a greater relief than in hearing that we were delivered from the necessity of putting our courage to the test, as I doubt if an American captain would have agreed to consider us under the protection of the law of nations had we claimed, as some of us suggested, to be allowed to pass with a flag of truce. I know not if the case has ever occurred of such exemption from the laws of war in favour of a foreign minister, or even if the enemy were to agree to it on condition the sloop should consider herself as prize to superior force and bound to give herself up on landing her passengers, whether her commander could consent to such arrangement.

Near Newfoundland we fell in with a British brig, a prize to

[9] Drummond was envoy to Naples in 1801.

the United States frigate, *Essex*, that had captured her the day before. She was bound, with a cargo of salt, for New Brunswick. Two American midshipmen and five seamen belonging to the *Essex* were taken on board of her, and some Bermudians were released who had been made prisoners on board a Bermudian schooner. The two American officers were Mr. Higgins and Mr. Pearce of Philadelphia, both young and very well behaved. When first they were hailed they said they came from Liverpool, and were near passing free, but a boat was sent to board them, and on looking into their log-book, there was found entered that they had been spoken with by H.M.S. *Atalanta* which had impressed two men out of her. This of course excited suspicion. They appeared agitated and the truth being discovered they were all taken out of the brig and she was sent to Bermuda.

These young officers were excessively surprized at witnessing the indulgence granted to the crew of the *Atalanta*, who were allowed to have dances on board with drum tambourine and fife, while occasionally they acted Gilpin and Norval.[10] The youngest especially could not have believed it, he said, and he did not think the officers on board the *Essex* would believe it possible, English officers being supposed by the Americans only to maintain discipline among their men by dint of flogging and severity. The eldest of these youths, a tall thin young man, always went below deck when there was music above, as afterwards did the other, who had the complexion of a Portugueze, with large black eyes. The former seemed particularly vexed at being a prisoner, he having had a promise of immediate promotion should he succeed in bringing his prize safely into port. A few days after they had been taken we fell in with H.M.S. *Pomona*, the same which we took for an enemy. When these young officers were sent for on deck and put on board of her, the elder shook hands with us all round and the younger was casting anxious looks about him

[10]By "Gilpin" Foster probably refers to the comic recitation of William Cowper's "The Diverting History of John Gilpin" (1785), which was often presented along with regular plays. The "Norval" is certainly a reference to the principal character of Home's *Douglas*. For both parts on the stage about 1809, see John Bernard, *Retrospections of America, 1797-1811*, pp. 339-40.

for a case of pistols which had belonged to him but which seemed destined to be left on board the *Atalanta*. He had seen them produced and appeared quite melancholy at the idea of having viewed them for the last time, but he said not a word. His countenance cleared up, however, when Captain Hickey and the other officers, on our seeming to wish it, very handsomely gave up their rights and the case was put in the youth's hands at parting.

We made 235 miles of our course on one day and 240 on another day. We had a pleasant society and all had plenty of anecdotes to relate. Hickey had been to China with Lord Macartney[11] and told me the latter kept the officers of the *Lion* in a continual roar of laughter with his good humour and good stories. Sir James told us how he had been once charged by a shoemaker £20 when he only owed him £16, and how he endeavoured to procure redress by going to law, and though it cost him £75 he gained his cause, while the shoemaker taking the £16, admitted he was in the wrong. Yet the costs were paid by Sir James.

Sir James told us that he was the last person Mr. Windham[12] spoke to, and it was for the purpose of asking for some buttermilk the evening before he died. He had just had a sweet and long repose, which, although he had been given over, afforded a chance of saving his life, but on the following day he went off breathing his last without an effort. He had fallen on a log of wood in saving some of Frederick North's[13] books, when the latter lost his house by fire. A small hard lump of the size of a pin's head ensued. In ten or eleven months, afterwards, he complained of its sudden increase and it grew in one day to the size of an egg, when it was declared to be cancerous, and an operation was judged necessary. But the malady had then reached an artery and was getting into the thigh bone.

[11]George Macartney, Earl Macartney (1737-1806), was governor-general of Madras 1780-1786.

[12]William Windham (1750-1810), commanding figure in Parliament and cabinet minister.

[13]Frederick North (1766-1827), later fifth Earl of Guilford.

On the 17th August we neared Scilly Islands and on the 18th, a gentleman (Mr. Hamilton)[14] was landed with my dispatches at Falmouth.

The *Atalanta* proceeded on with her passengers to Portsmouth, having been in some danger from a fog which produced the effect of making us mistake St. Albans Head for the Isle of Wight. We distinctly heard the breakers which the sloop-of-war was nearing very fast, and were only just saved by the captain himself taking the helm.

When I waited on Lord Castlereagh,[15] he received me very well but let drop a few words from which I gathered that he or some of the cabinet had expected I should have remained on at Halifax for the arrival of Admiral Sir J. Warren, to accompany him to the Chesapeake with proposals of peace founded on the partial change in our ministry and the disposition that they showed to revoke entirely the Orders in Council which gave occasion to the declaration of war. I convinced him, nevertheless, that such a step would have led to no result, as Congress had separated, and President Madison was much too fearful of compromising himself with his party to do more than take our proposals ad referendum, while it would have been humiliating to the feelings of a British envoy to be knocking at their doors for admittance, after having been sent away, or even to remain waiting for letters in the Chesapeake or Potomac, not to mention the risk of being perhaps drawn into a vain discussion with a view on their side to gain time. I had the satisfaction subsequently, when Lord Liverpool took me to Carlton House, of having His Majesty express the same sentiments and almost in the same words telling Lord Liverpool more than once that he thought I had done perfectly right.[16]

[14]Of the several Hamiltons mentioned above in the notes, this may have been John W., the British consul at Norfolk.

[15]Robert Stewart (1769-1822), later second Marquis of Londonderry and from 1796 by courtesy Viscount Castlereagh, returned to office as Foreign Secretary in March 1812.

[16]The later George IV (1762-1830) became Prince Regent in 1811. His residence was Carlton House. He did not become king until 1820.

The King on this occasion received me, being in his dressing gown and Lord Liverpool in plain clothes, while I was in uniform, which His Majesty observed was not necessary asking Lord Liverpool why he had not told me to come in plain dress. He then desired us to sit down and began questioning me about the American Government, saying jokingly that he had heard not only the Minister of War but the Minister for Foreign Affairs, were become soldiers and commanded corps. When I told him it was very true,[17] he laughed and turning round exclaimed, "By G. Liverpool you should copy their example, and then by G. you know you might execute your favorite plan of a march upon Paris." Liverpool said he had been a private and so he was with Lord Castlereagh, in the ranks of the London Volunteers, in the year 1805 when an invasion was expected and all took up arms to the amount including army and navy of 750,000 men. The King little expected at the time he held the above conversation with Lord Liverpool that in the course of the very next year, the march on Paris would have become very feasible and that in each of the two succeeding years the predication of his celebrated speech when he was Lord Hawkesbury would twice be accomplished.

[As Lord Liverpool wished me to go into Parliament, in order that I might be able to defend the measures of the Government which had led to the American War, and as I was myself very desirous of doing so, I was proposed for the representative of Cockermouth, tho' I took care to stipulate with my uncle on his asking for Lord Londsdale's[18] interest in my behalf, that I should be at liberty to vote in favour of Roman Catholic Emancipation which I thought then as I do now should be gradual but complete. Gradual, because of the respect due to the rooted feelings

[17]Foster probably refers here to General John Armstrong, brigadier-general 1812-1813, Secretary of War 1813-1814, or possibly to General Henry Dearborn, Secretary of War 1801-1809, major-general in the War of 1812. Foster probably also refers to James Monroe, who became Secretary of State in 1811 and always hoped for military command himself.

[18]William Lowther, first Earl of Lonsdale (1757-1844) by a new creation of 1807. The second Earl represented Cockermouth in 1808.

of a Protestant population that had rendered great services as well to the interests of civilization in Ireland as to the general government at all times, and complete because in the view I took of the question, when the plague against which you have established a quarantine has ceased the quarantine itself should not be kept up to the trying of innocent traders. The Pretender and his violence and that of his party was the cause that led to the exclusion of Roman Catholics from office and trust and there being no longer even the shadow of a Pretender, the precaution he gave rise to I thought should also cease. Besides in no other part of the world perhaps does there exist such an anomaly as that of a government without an organ of communication between themselves and the religious feelings of six millions of their subjects.

I had to answer Mr. A. Baring's questions on the causes of the war,[19] but after doing so and speaking for about twenty minutes, finding my mouth quite parched with dryness [not having taken the precaution of carrying an orange in my hand]* and besides being nervous from the novelty of the [situation],* I took the opportunity of having come to the end of my replies to sit down. I gave up a long tirade that I had prepared against the ambition and greediness for land exhibited by such an overgrown republic which has enough to do to keep in due cultivation one ten thousandth part of the soil that lawfully belongs to it, and yet which had been recently disgracing itself by using the tricks of common swindlers in order to drive the Spaniards from Amelia Island and E. Florida as it had assisted Bonaparte to do in regard to Louisiana, and as too many of its citizens have been lately trying to do in regard to a province of Mexico.

I never afterwards had sufficient confidence to rise in my place in Parliament, nor was there any chance of my being again forced to do so as it were in my own defence.]**

*Marked through.

**Material of several final paragraphs in brackets in the HEH version only.

[19]Alexander Baring (1774-1848), later Lord Ashburton, married Miss Bingham of Philadelphia, was Member of Parliament for many years, and firmly opposed the Orders in Council.

INDEX

Italicized numbers indicate that the person referred to is mentioned on these particular pages by title rather than by name.